PEACE, WAR, AND POLITICS

PEACE, WAR, AND POLITICS

AN EYEWITNESS ACCOUNT

Jack Anderson

with DARYL GIBSON

FORGE

A TOM DOHERTY ASSOCIATES BOOK *New York*

PEACE, WAR, AND POLITICS: AN EYEWITNESS ACCOUNT

Copyright © 1999 by Jack Anderson and Daryl Gibson

All rights reserved, including the right to reproduce this book, or
portions thereof, in any form.

This book is printed on acid-free paper.

A Forge Book
Published by Tom Doherty Associates, LLC.
175 Fifth Avenue
New York, NY 10010

Forge® is a registered trademark of Tom Doherty Associates, LLC.

Library of Congress Cataloging-in-Publication Data

Anderson, Jack.
    Peace, war, and politics : an eyewitness account / Jack Anderson,
with Daryl Gibson.—1st ed.
        p.   cm.
    "A Tom Doherty Associates book."
    ISBN 0-312-85602-4
    1. United States—Politics and government—1945–1989.   2. United
States—Politics and government—1989–   3. United States—Foreign
relations—1945–1989.   4. United States—Foreign relations—1989–
5. Anderson, Jack, 1922–   .   6. Investigative reporting—United
States.   I. Gibson, Daryl.   II. Title.
E839.5.A68   1999
973.92—dc21   99-26647
                                                                CIP

First Edition: October 1999

Printed in the United States of America

1   2   3   4   5   6   7   8   9   10

To Joe Spear
1941–1998

who deliberately left his fingerprints on
secret government documents that had
been classified to hide embarrassments,
not protect national security. He sought
martyrdom for the cause of a free press.

ACKNOWLEDGMENTS

MY NEWS OPERATION HAS ALWAYS BEEN a rare bird—a collection of reporters who combine their efforts to make a single product under my name. I think of them as fellow travelers whom I met by the roadside carrying signs saying, WILL WORK FOR THE SHEER LOVE OF IT. For decades, they made me look good while receiving little recognition themselves, because they believed in our mission as guardians of a free press and open government. I am proud and humbled as I review the accomplishments of those who joined my ride on the Washington Merry-Go-Round.

Six men have shared the column byline with me as I did with Drew Pearson. Here they are, along with their years on the byline:

LES WHITTEN (1969–1978) is part Renaissance man, part incomparable reporter. He is the author of sixteen books, including poetry, a children's book, a biography of lawyer F. Lee Bailey, and novels—notably the best-selling *Conflict of Interest* (1976), *Sometimes a Hero* (1977), and *The Lost Disciple* (1989).

JOSEPH SPEAR (1969–1988) was a sworn enemy of arrogance and a passionate defender of the helpless. His death in 1998 deprived me of a friend, and deprived the First Amendment of one of its most ardent protectors. A crusader, a teacher, a reporter, an editor, a freelancer, and a syndicated columnist in his own right, Joe was the author of *Presidents and the Press: The Nixon Legacy* (1984).

DALE VAN ATTA (1979–1982) continues to write columns for me while he is an active freelancer, contributing editor with *Reader's Digest,* and book author, most recently of *Trust Betrayed: Inside the AARP*; and co-author with me of the Gulf War bestseller *Stormin' Norman*. Nominated seven times for the Pulitzer Prize for investigative reporting, Dale has reported from all seven continents and is a prominent lecturer.

MICHAEL BINSTEIN (1992–1996) exemplifies the best of his generation of reporters and entrepreneurs, carving a niche for himself in both worlds. While working with me, he co-authored with Charles Bowden *Trust Betrayed: Charles Keating and the Missing Billions* (1993). He is now chief executive officer of Binny's Beverage Depot. This sixteen-store Chicago chain, which he built from a business started by his late father Harold, was voted America's No. I superstore for wine, spirits, beer, and cigars. Since I coined the nickname "Binny," I guess that would make me the first Mormon who every named an alcoholic beverage chain.

JAN MOLLER (1991–1999) came to me as an intern fresh out of college and now continues the tradition of the Washington Merry-Go-Round, assisted by staffers Ashley Baker and Kathryn Wallace. Far from learning everything he knows at my feet, Jan is the product of his own hunger for excellence with a healthy dose of influence from mentors who went before him on the staff.

DOUGLAS A. COHN (1999–) is the publisher of a half a dozen national magazines, and he is first and foremost a journalist.

In a category by herself is the late irrepressible OPAL GINN, who served as my right hand for more than thirty years, making me look polished and putting in their place those in Washington who fancied themselves to be better than the Fifth Estate. Rapier-tongued, generous to a fault, as quick to comfort as to afflict, Opal was the quintessential sidekick, gatekeeper, torch-bearer, and conscience for me.

WALTER ANDERSON, *Parade's* wise editor, has been my rock. If no man is a hero to his valet, the same holds true for a watchdog and his libel attorney. Our libel attorney for nearly twenty years has been MICHAEL SULLIVAN, who is currently a partner with Levine, Sullivan & Koch. We owe Sullivan, along with LEE LEVINE, BETSY KOCH, and JAY BROWN, a debt of gratitude that is impossible to repay or reciprocate. Their friendship, fidelity to the First Amendment, and fearless litigation has made our journalistic journey possible. They have been the greatest unsung heroes of the Washington Merry-Go-Round.

One of my most ardent supporters and cheerleaders over the years has been a treasured friend, JIM KEPPLER, whose agency booked literally hundreds of speeches for me over the years, and gave me a chance to spread the Freedom of the Press gospel all over this country.

Everyone should have a Rock of Gibralter to lean on.

Last are the many reporters who have provided the daily meat and potatoes for my column. I wrestled with how to thank them adequately, given the varied service they offered from internships to years of prominent assistance. I settled on an alphabetical list giving their years with me and the highlights of their careers. (I apologize for anyone inadvertently left out because of inadequate records and faulty memory.)

JON LEE ANDERSON (no relation), 1981–1986; now living in Spain, and author most recently of *Che Guevara: A Revolutionary Life* (1997), a three-year effort during which he located the handless remains of the revolutionary; previously, *Time* correspondent; co-author with his brother, Scott, of *Guerrillas: The Men and Women Fighting Today's Wars* (1993), *War Zones: Voices from the World's Killing Grounds* (1988), and *Inside the League* (1986), about the World Anti-Communist League.

INDY BADHWAR, 1980–1985; living in New Delhi, India, where he was managing editor of *India Today*.

CHARLES (CHARLIE) BERMANT, 1980–1984; freelance writer, *Oregonian* columnist and manager, Technology News Forum, MSN Computing Central; previously, columnist, *Washington Post,* and staffer for several computing magazines; author or co-author of three books about Windows, including *101 Windows Tips and Tricks.*

HAL BERNTON, 1976–1979; reporter, *Oregonian* (Portland); previously, reporter, Anchorage *Daily News,* where he was part of the team that won the 1989 Pulitzer Prize for Public Service with a series on the plight of native people in Alaska; author, *Forbidden Fuel: Power Alcohol in the 20th Century* (1982).

DEAN BOYD, 1990–1993; spokesperson, Office of Public Affairs, U.S. Customs Service; previously, editor, *Drug Enforcement Report* and Washington correspondent, *El Panama America.*

DAVID BRAATEN, 1978–1987; retired; previously, assistant National Desk editor, Washington *Times,* feature writer, Washington *Star.*

TONY CAPACCIO, 1977–1986; defense reporter, *Bloomberg News;* previously, reporter and editor, *Defense Week.*

GEORGE CLIFFORD, 1969–1970; deceased, 1985; previously, author and assistant national editor, Washington *Star.*

GEORGE CLIFFORD III, 1996–1997; policy and politics analyst, NBC News.

JACK CLOHERTY, 1972–1976; senior Washington producer, NBC *Dateline;* previously, investigative reporter for NBC Washington D.C. affiliate, WRC (Channel 4), also co-columnist for investigative column with Bob Owens, *Los Angeles Times* syndicate.

GARY COHN, 1975–1980; investigative reporter, Baltimore *Sun*, and 1998 Pulitzer Prize winner for a co-authored series exposing abuses of workers and the environment in the United States and South Asian ports during the dismantling of U.S. ships; previously, Lexington *Herald-Leader*, *Wall Street Journal*, and Philadelphia *Inquirer*.

ANDY CONTE, 1992–1994; reporter, *Cincinnati Post*; previously, Stuart (Florida) *News*.

SALLY DENTON, 1979–1980; freelance author; previously, managing partner with four different Washington D.C. private investigation firms, chief of a United Press International investigative team, and reporter for Lexington (Kentucky) CBS affiliate, WKYT TV; author, bestselling *The Bluegrass Conspiracy: An Inside Story of Power, Greed, Drugs and Murder* (1989).

JOHN DILLON, 1981–1984; Sunday writer, Rutland (Vermont) *Herald* and Barre-Montpelier *Times Argus*; previously, reporter, UPI; Knight Science Journalism Fellow (1995).

MARK FELDSTEIN, 1973, 1976; producer, *Dateline*; previously, correspondent, CNN and ABC networks, as well as Washington DC's CBS affiliate, where he logged scoops on Mayor Marion Barry's drug use.

SAM FOGG, 1978–1982; deceased, 1987.

DARYL GIBSON, 1987–1992; freelance writer, co-author of this book and collaborator with me on *Washington Money-Go-Round* and *Inside the NRA*; previously, reporter for *Las Vegas Review-Journal* and *Boulder Daily Camera*.

DON GOLDBERG, 1981–1987; vice president, Weber McGinn, crisis management firm; previously, (Clinton) White House adviser and longtime Congressional (House of Representatives) staff investigator.

JAMES GRADY, 1975–1980; novelist and screenwriter; thirteen published novels, including *Six Days of the Condor* (1974), which became the Robert Redford movie, *Three Days of the Condor*.

PETER GRANT, 1978–1983; business reporter, New York *Daily News*; previously, New York *Observer* and Buffalo *News*.

STEWART HARRIS, 1986–1990; producer, ABC *20/20*; previously, Fox Television, and Washington Bureau Chief, *Inside Edition*.

JOCK HATFIELD, 1983–1994; deceased, 1984.

ED HENRY, 1991–1996; managing editor, *Roll Call*.

BRIT HUME, 1970–1972; managing editor and Chief Washington correspondent, Fox News; *Washington Post* co-columnist (with T. R. Reid) of computer column; previously, chief White House Correspondent and Capitol Hill Correspondent, ABC News; Emmy (1991 Gulf War coverage); author, *Inside Story* (1974) and *Death and the Mines* (1971).

HUGH ("CORKY") JOHNSON, 1981–1987; freelance journalist;

previously, investigative producer/reporter for both the NBC affiliate (WLWT-TV) and CBS affiliate (WCPO-TV) in Cincinnati, Ohio, also founded Cincinnati's *EastSide Weekend Newsmagazine*; author, *Paths to Pedal* (1991).

AARON KARP, 1994–1996; freelance writer and collaborator with me on *Washington Money-Go-Round*.

JULIE KOSTERLITZ, 1980–1991; staff correspondent, *National Journal*.

DR. LARRY KRAFTOWITZ, 1976–1979; internist, Montefiore Medical Center, New York City; previously, Media General News Service, States News Service.

MICHAEL KRANISH, 1978; political reporter and former White House reporter, Boston *Globe*; previously, Miami *Herald*, Lakeland (Florida) *Ledger*.

LISA M. KRIEGER, 1982–1983; medical writer, San Jose *Mercury News*; previously, *San Francisco Examiner*, also *Journal of American Medical Association*.

HOWARD ("HOWIE") Kurtz, 1977–1978; *Washington Post* media reporter, co-host, CNN's "Reliable Sources"; previously, Washington *Star*; author of three books, best-selling *Spin Cycle: Inside the Clinton Propaganda Machine* (1998), *Hot Air: All Talk, All the Time* (1996), and *Media Circus: The Trouble with America's Newspapers* (1993).

LUCETTE LAGNADO, 1980–1987; reporter, *Wall Street Journal*; author, *Children of the Flames: Dr. Mengele and the Untold Story of the Twins of Auschwitz* (1992).

ALLAN LENGEL, 1982; staff writer, *Washington Post*; previously, reporter, *Detroit News*, and reporter, *Monthly Detroit*.

JIM LYNCH, 1988–1992; statehouse reporter, *Seattle Times*; previously, Portland *Oregonian*; winner, Polk Award (1995).

MELINDA MAAS-GAFFNEY, 1989–1995; freelance producer, public relations consultant; previously, story developer/field producer, ABC *Primetime*, associate producer, Fox's *A Current Affair*.

JAMES MINTZ, 1975, 1976; president, James Mintz Group Inc., private investigation firm in New York City, Washington D.C., and Miami.

JACK MITCHELL, 1975–1982; special assistant to the Commissioner for Investigations, Food & Drug Administration; previously, CNN correspondent, longtime U.S. Senate staff investigator.

EILEEN O'CONNOR, 1981; medical correspondent, CNN; previously, White House correspondent, Tokyo correspondent and Moscow Bureau Chief for CNN, and producer (Moscow, London) for ABC.

BOB OWENS, 1973–1977; president, Owens Group (insurance), New York City; previously, co-columnist for investigative column with Jack Cloherty, *Los Angeles Times* syndicate.

ROBIN REYNOLDS, 1974–1987; office manager, Fairchild Publications.

IRA ROSEN, 1974; senior producer, investigative unit, ABC *20/20*; previously, senior producer, CBS *60 Minutes.*

HOWARD ROSENBERG, 1976–1981; producer, ABC *20/20*; previously, producer, CBS *60 Minutes,* investigative producer, CBS Evening News; author, *Atomic Soldiers: American Victims of Nuclear Experiments* (1980).

TOM ROSENSTIEL, 1978–1979; director, Project for Excellence in Journalism, Pew Foundation; previously, chief Congressional correspondent, *Newsweek*; national correspondent, *Los Angeles Times*; author, *Strange Bedfellows: How Television and the Presidential Candidates Changed American Politics, 1992* (1994).

DAVID M. SALTZ, 1980–1981; press secretary to Secretary of Labor Alexis M. Herman; previously, press spokesman, AFL-CIO, managing editor, United Mine Workers of America *Journal.*

MICHAEL SATCHELL, 1977–1986 *(Parade)*; senior writer, *U.S. News & World Report.*

BOB SHERMAN, 1978–1983; partner, Kimbell, Sherman & Ellis, Montpelier (Vermont) lobbying/law firm; previously, executive assistant, Governor Madeleine Kunin.

SCOTT SLEEK, 1988–1991; senior editor, *EurekAlert!* (American Association for the Advancement of Science); previously, reporter/editor, the *APA Monitor* (American Psychological Association).

KEITH SINZINGER, 1979; editor, national desk, *Washington Post*; previously, managing editor, *Federal Times.*

MARC SMOLONSKY, 1975–1978; senior policy adviser, Department of Health and Human Services; previously, Congressional investigator, including House Government Operations Committee, Senate Environment and Public Works Committee, Senate Small Business Committee, and Senate Judiciary Committee.

RICHARD SOKOLOW, 1976–1977; Chairman, InterSource International, investigative consultant company in New York, Washington D.C., and Zurich, Switzerland.

MATT SPEISER, 1978–1979; producer, ABC News, Washington D.C.

VICKI WARREN, 1978–1986; independent documentary film producer.

TIM WARNER, 1990–1991; manager, corporate communications,

Immunex, a Seattle-based bio-pharmaceutical company; previously, Communications Director for Senator Max Baucus, D-Mont., and deputy press secretary for Senator Brock Adams, D-Wash.

JANE WINEBRENNER, 1977–1979, 1983–1987; copy editor, *International Trade Reporter,* Bureau of National Affairs.

PEACE, WAR, AND POLITICS

PROLOGUE

I LOOKED UP FROM MY DESK one day in December 1971 and was confronted by the ashen face of Jeb Stuart Magruder, special assistant to President Nixon. It wasn't often that any of this president's men darkened my doorway. Magruder fidgeted a moment and then, in measured words, explained his mission. He had come about a possible misunderstanding at the White House: Gordon Liddy, one of the notorious White House "Plumbers," might be under the mistaken impression that Richard Nixon wanted me dead.

Magruder explained that he had complained at a staff meeting about some columns I had written that were embarrassing to the president. Unappreciative White House reviews were common enough in those days, but following this particular review session, Magruder had added, "The president would sure like to get rid of that guy." Liddy, at that point, had abruptly stood up and walked out of the meeting.

Magruder had thought nothing of the characteristic Liddy exit—no explanations, no good-byes—but moments later his assistant Bob Reisner rushed breathlessly into the office with a look of horror on his face. "Did you tell Liddy to kill Jack Anderson?" Reisner blurted out. "Liddy just walked past my desk and said you'd told him to rub out Jack Anderson."

"My God!" Magruder gasped. "Get him back in here."

Liddy was stopped before he got out of the building and Magruder told him that "get rid of" had just been a figure of speech. Liddy sniffed with contempt, "Where I come from," he said, "that means a rubout." With Liddy, it was best to be specific.

There are few experiences more invigorating than being on someone's hit list, however briefly.

Of all the people who would have wished ill of me over the years, J.

Edgar Hoover was undeniably the most eloquent in his character assassinations: "Jack Anderson is lower than the regurgitated filth of vultures"; "a flea-ridden dog"; "the lowest form of human being to walk the earth." Louisiana's Senator Russell Long compared me to the snake in the Garden of Eden. Jimmy Carter was perhaps the most direct. He said I was "the one columnist in this nation who habitually lies."

Many monikers have been attached to me during the five decades of investigative reporting in Washington, but muckraker is the one I like the best. Theodore Roosevelt was the first to apply the name to crusading journalists, and he didn't mean to flatter. The term refers to the character in John Bunyan's *Pilgrim's Progress* who chose to keep his eyes on the filthy ground rather than lift his sights to heaven. The auspicious occasion during which Roosevelt excoriated crusading reporters was the laying of the cornerstone of the House of Representatives building on April 14, 1906. In a speech that day, Roosevelt berated the man who "refuses to see aught that is lofty, and fixes his eyes with solemn intentness only on that which is vile and debasing."

Shortly thereafter, pioneering muckraker Lincoln Steffens demurred when he was identified as the first of the muckrakers about whom Roosevelt spoke. Instead, Steffens suggested that the prophets of the Old Testament were really the first muckrakers, and that the title could be worn proudly.

My mentor and partner Drew Pearson wore the label with pride, raking up things as they were in the constant hope that it would bring reform. Lest anyone think he wasn't proud of his calling, Drew entered into a side business selling manure generated by the cows at his gentleman's farm along the Potomac River. His mail-order advertisement hailed the manure as "better than the column."

It was inevitable, despite the best laid plans of my parents, that I would ultimately work for such a man in such a profession. I wasn't raised to meddle in other people's business and came by that proclivity neither through genetics nor environment. But on numerous occasions I have thanked my pragmatic parents, who taught me not to put too much stock in the accolades of men. I would have folded fifty years ago had I worried about winning popularity contests.

PART I

BEGINNINGS

1 9 2 2 – 1 9 4 7

WHEN THE LAST BIT OF DIRT is tossed on the graves of my generation, I fear that the stories of the America we knew and treasured will be buried with us. No succeeding generation will be able to say with as much conviction, "When I was your age..."

When I was your age we started the school day with prayer and never gave a thought to offending nonbelievers. There were a few among us who were beginning to suspect we were descendants of apes and not Adam and Eve. I was only four when attorney Clarence Darrow took on as a client science teacher John T. Scopes, who was accused of teaching evolution to his rural Tennessee high school students. The brilliant orator William Jennings Bryan won the case for fundamentalist creationism and Scopes was found guilty, but anyone who heard Darrow speak or who read accounts of the trial could never quite look at an ape again with the same disdain. The "Scopes Monkey Trial" was what passed for a "trial of the century" in those days.

When I was your age we could not have wasted hours following the saga of O. J. Simpson on television. We had no television and, in fact, were just getting used to the idea of a radio. It was the equivalent of today's big-screen TV, filling a corner of the parlor and luring the whole family to listen to its crackling reception. The first of the "talking movies" debuted when I was still in short pants.

When I was your age, Ernest Hemingway was living in Paris cranking out novels about disaffected Americans; John Steinbeck stayed home to write novels about the desperate plight of those who couldn't afford the luxury of expatriotism.

When I was your age, "Negro" leader Marcus Garvey was shaking up integrationists by calling for blacks to go "Back to Africa" and work out their salvation in their "motherland."

When I was your age our heroes were the intrepid pilot Charles "Lucky Lindy" Lindbergh, home-run king Babe Ruth, Olympian Jim Thorpe, and heavyweight champ Jack Dempsey.

When I was your age we were lucky if we got an orange in our Christmas stocking. The event that turned ordinary items into luxuries was the crash of the stock market in the autumn of 1929. It was an event so catastrophic as to cause men to leap from high buildings to their deaths. The unlucky President Herbert Hoover had been in office only a few months and thought he had inherited a relatively prosperous nation. But it was a house built on sand. Within a year of the market's collapse, millions of Americans were unemployed. It took four years before the nation reached its economic nadir, just as Franklin Roosevelt moved into the White House. Roosevelt struggled mightily with his "New Deal" reform measures to put money back in the hands of the men and women at the bottom of the economic heap through jobs programs. But it wasn't until World War II that the nation finally dug itself out of the Great Depression.

In my corner of the world, isolated and insulated by the Rocky Mountains, it was a grand time to be "your age." We expected little in the way of creature comforts and were not disappointed. We had not yet been introduced to the awesome evil of the atomic bomb. We respected our mothers and feared our fathers. We didn't buy things that we couldn't pay for. And we believed that a boy with only a high school education could grow up to become whatever he wanted to be.

CHAPTER 1

MY FATHER, ORLANDO ANDERSON, NEVER CONSIDERED what I did for a living to be work. In that belief he was probably not alone. If I wasn't sifting soil and generating sweat, Dad figured it wasn't honest labor. Which is why, in the summer of 1934, while I entertained visions of a reporter's life, he arranged a job for me thinning beet plants. Atop the rock-hard Utah soil, on hands and knees, I swatted at beet greens with a sawed-off hoe. I lasted an inglorious two weeks—long enough for me to conclude, at twelve years of age, that my future was at the typewriter. I abruptly quit, pedaled my bike over to the nearest newspaper, the *Murray Eagle*, and talked my way into a reporting job. Four decades later, after I had syndicated my work in hundreds of newspapers, seen my face on the cover of *Time* magazine, and won the Pulitzer Prize, my father still did not approve of my chosen career.

The experience I brought to the *Murray Eagle* at age twelve was short on substance but long on ambition. At the time, I was president of the Boy Scout press club and presided over a weekly scouting page in the big-city paper, the *Deseret News*, in nearby Salt Lake City. I wrote in the simple style of a twelve-year-old. When it came time to cover the town budget, Murray's comptroller explained it to me painstakingly in the language a twelve-year-old could understand. I passed it along to my readers unadorned. It was years before I realized that professional journalists were supposed to do the same thing—lowball their language to the industry standard of a reader with an eighth-grade education.

My photographer at the *Eagle* was a ten-year-old kid whose name I have forgotten; I called him simply Gooch. We made an odd news team, furiously pedaling our bicycles to the scenes of fires, traffic accidents, and other small-town events. Gooch was shorter than me, so I often hoisted him up on my shoulders for a better picture. The publisher didn't care how old we were or how we covered the town. Advertising was his prime interest, and if, for seven dollars a week, two boys on fat-tire bikes could fill the spaces between the ads with local news, he was satisfied.

I took the *Eagle's* cash and the experience that came along with it, and also edited the gratis Boy Scout page in the *Deseret News* until the rival Salt Lake City newspaper, the *Tribune*, offered to pay me to write Boy Scout stories for them. Thinking I was worthy of a bidding war, I notified the *Deseret News* of the offer. They disabused me of my indispensability and released me to go to the *Tribune*.

I stayed there through high school, working my way up to the real estate page and, one great day, the city desk. Younger than most of the copy boys, I was paid fifteen cents an inch. But my output was so prolific, or perhaps so verbose, that the *Tribune* switched me over to an hourly wage lest my income outpace that of the grown-ups. I needed no more encouragement; I had chosen my life's work.

My parents were living in Long Beach, California, when I was born in 1922. They named me Jack because they reasoned if they named me John, people would call me Jack anyway. When I was two, we moved to Salt Lake City where my father worked as a postal clerk.

I made an early career of avoiding my father. He worked the night shift and spent his days composing a long list of chores for me and my brothers, Gordon and Warren, to perform. Since it was impossible to do everything he wanted, we devoted our best efforts to doing nothing. By contrast, my mother asked very little of us, but what she asked, we did.

My mother, Agnes Mortensen, was a Danish-born convert to the Mormon Church who immigrated with her mother, Judith Northman, to Brigham City, Utah. Northman, my middle name, was Grandma's maiden name. Two of her three children went back to it after Grandma weathered two grueling marriages to men whose names she preferred to forget.

My mother was a patient and persevering woman with a steely side, nonetheless, that was more sensed than seen. She could be sweetly unyielding. One day, chauffeuring my son Rodney on a two-lane highway, Mother crossed the center line to pass another car. "Grandma, there's a car coming!" Rodney shouted in alarm. "That's what the shoulders are for," she said amiably. After much honking, the oncoming car swerved out of Mother's way and onto the shoulder, thus confirming her rules of the road.

Danish was the language of choice between my parents when they retreated to confidential conversation in the presence of the children. They didn't know I understood them until one day I shot back an indignant retort in English, betraying the fact that I had been following their Danish discussion about my shortcomings.

My parents died within four months of each other at ages ninety and ninety-three. After they were gone, I learned that they had kept a meticulous record of my life's work in clippings, photos, letters, and other mementos of my career. This gave me some comfort that my father had followed my work more closely than he had ever deigned to admit.

My old man was a smoldering volcano, ever threatening to blow his top. Yet the exploding lava would quickly turn to soft ashes. He must have been born a curmudgeon, given his fearsome nature. But I learned early in life that he was really quite mellow beneath the crust.

His face showed the wreckage of a thousand disappointments. It was furrowed and anguished. Still, no disappointment got him down for long. Until the day he died, he lived his life in the future. He dreamed big dreams; he made big plans. And he wrote it all down—what he'd like to do, where he'd like to go, what he expected of life.

Then the unforeseen would invariably shatter his dreams and leave his precious paperwork null and void. He would smolder and rumble and erupt. Then he would sit down at his rolltop desk, put pen to paper, and produce a new blueprint. In his old age, he did many things he had always wanted to do and traveled to many places he had always wanted to see. But he never stayed long in the present; his mind moved on to the future.

My father's father was converted by missionaries in Sweden to the Church of Jesus Christ of Latter-day Saints, the "Mormons." Grandpa moved to Brigham City, Utah, where he molded clay bricks until he earned enough money to bring his siblings and his mother across the ocean, one by one. He outlived four wives who produced so many children that even my father lost count of the siblings who died in infancy. A dozen lived to adulthood. In time, Grandpa opened a store in Brigham City but went broke extending credit to the neighbors. He moved in with us in his old age—a Santa Claus figure with a great belly, a flowing white beard, and a derby hat.

We were never really poor, not even during the Depression. But my family's spartan lifestyle would have convinced many otherwise. When I was eleven, Dad bought a spacious house in an affluent suburb of Salt Lake City and then decided that we did not need to live in such luxury. He rented out the upstairs to a family with no similar disdain for creature comforts. They had all the indoor plumbing; our family lived in the basement and used an outdoor privy. Years later, after I had moved to Washington, the chaplain of the Senate looked me up and told me that he had once lived in the house that I had not been allowed to enjoy.

During the Depression, my father would round up derelicts and invite them to live with us. In those days, "bums" were college students and unemployed laborers. One of them, whom I remember only as Gary, stayed for a year and helped earn his keep by peddling my mother's incomparable Danish cookies door-to-door.

Perhaps it was Scandinavian penury or the Mormon work ethic, but my father never missed an opportunity to save a few pennies. From our suburban home, he rode his bicycle ten miles into Salt Lake City each day to save the bus fare. He once put the family on a train from Salt Lake City to Los Angeles to visit relatives and then rode his bicycle across the desert to join us, all in the name of frugality. To my young mind, his sacrifices were an embarrassing show of austerity and stubbornness.

By my teens, I had concluded that he secretly enjoyed playing the martyr, yet I knew my father was a decent and good man, completely without guile. Long after I had moved East, a friend of mine bumped into my father on the street one snowy night. Dad was toting a Christmas tree on his shoulder and had stopped to rest. He counted his change from the tree vendor. "That fool gave me twenty-five cents too much," my father sputtered angrily. "Now I've got to go all the way back."

THERE CAME A TIME IN MY youth when I needed Dad's car to nail down a scoop, the first story of an underground polygamist cult headquartered in Utah. I resorted to subterfuge, first to get the car and then to get the story.

At age eighteen I gleaned from the family rumor mill that I had a distant cousin, not many years off the boat from Sweden, who had acquired a second wife without dismissing the first. My fledgling reporter's instinct told me there was a story here. I tracked down the cousin—an open-faced, good-hearted fellow who was willing to confide to a kinsman that he had found the true religion. He told me that his church was led by a holy man, Joseph Musser, and he gave me Musser's address. With my father's car to get me there, I decided to go underground.

It had been three generations since America had outlawed the Mormon practice of polygamy, forcing the church to give up a peculiar custom it had adopted from ancient Old Testament law. In 1890 the church hierarchy instructed the members to obey the law of the land; anyone who failed to do so would be subject to excommunication. Yet the doctrine of plural marriage never quite died. Occasional visionaries popped up, proclaimed superior reception from heaven, and founded their own splinter churches.

By the third generation after the repeal of polygamy, it existed only behind the closed doors of the secret disciples of such renegade prophets as Joseph Musser. Mainstream Mormons, by then proud of their reputation for

THE PROPHET

THE HOUSE IN SALT LAKE CITY was a distinguished red brick of nineteenth-century vintage that at one time must have been owned by a family of status. Now it was occupied by a spooky family that didn't open the door to just anyone. I rapped on that door with as much authority as an eighteen-year-old could muster. I heard muffled sounds of movement from within and thought I glimpsed a female form at the front window. The door opened a crack, revealing a middle-aged woman who said nothing. I asked to see Joseph Musser, the holy man. Without a word, she shut the door, and I waited for several minutes. At length, the woman reappeared and silently ushered me inside. Mrs. Musser, I presumed.

She led me through a living room, then a dining room, and into a den at the rear of the house. As I passed through, I spied another woman peeking at me from around the corner. Mrs. Musser, I presumed. A third woman retreated silently through a darkened doorway. Mrs. Musser, I presumed. The omnipresence of multiple and mysterious females quickened my pulse as I was delivered into the den of their husband, Joseph Musser, spiritual leader for a few thousand outlaw polygamists.

Musser sat in an old swivel chair behind a rolltop desk. To see him in that musty, silent room with its antique furniture, its austere order, its shelves of worn books of theological bent, was to be transported back to the days of Brigham Young. Musser had a rather saintly face, creased with wrinkles and crowned with a patriarch's white hair. He projected a benevolence that seemed at odds with a craftiness of eye.

I told him cautiously that I wanted to learn more about his church, as he rocked warily in his chair, taking my measure and listening for a false note. Apparently my youth disarmed him, because Musser gradually warmed to my questioning and we slid into a discussion of his religious precepts. Outlining a "fundamentalist" faith that stressed old-fashioned virtues, he inched toward his main theme. He delivered a review of the moral shambles of modern life, tracing the downfall of Western civilization to one problem—monogamy, with its spawn of divorces and mistresses, unwed mothers and bachelor fathers, cast-off wives and abandoned children.

He became more animated as he led me to the mountaintop. In place of the sewage of modern relationships, we must go back to the sacred institution of plural marriage practiced by the Old Testament prophets. Like Abraham, modern men should aspire to stand at the head of a family, with children as numerous as the sands on the seashore. And, like Abraham, it would require a great many wives to achieve this.

Musser's prescription for replenishing the earth had a Strangelovian agreeability to it. God would provide women in abundance who were prepared to do their duty. But because the male members of the "true church" were so few, the task before them was vast. The bearers of the seed must buck up and do their duty also. Thus, our first meeting ended on a note of high purpose.

So well had I played the role of prospective proselyte that Musser gave me the addresses of his lay leaders and a letter of introduction. Thanking him, I left the wan but dedicated old gentleman to duties that apparently lay behind every door. Outside, I unfolded and read the note he had given to me: "This will introduce Jack Anderson, who is seeking the fullness of the gospel. Joseph Musser." This would be my pass to the polygamist underground.

wholesomeness, avoided any mention of polygamy in their ancestry—like Italian Americans shy away from the word "mafia." Few were aware in 1940 that a polygamist underground flourished right in the heart of Salt Lake City.

This was the underground I was about to enter. I went to Musser's home, where I played the role of prospective proselyte, and wangled the addresses of Musser's lay leaders and a letter of introduction signed by Musser himself. With this letter, I was allowed to attend their underground discussion groups, join their religious services, and dance at their parties. In time, I gained their confidence and was welcomed into their homes.

As a rule, each of the sister wives, as they called themselves, had her own section of the house where she received her husband and raised her children. I was never invited to see the sleeping quarters, a matter of considerable curiosity to me since these modest houses seemed too small to afford privacy. One man confided to me that he was short of bedrooms so his wives had to double up. He left the rest to my imagination.

An outsider might say that the polygamists had institutionalized adultery, but such an accusation would fall on scandalized ears. Among the men, there was no locker-room lip-smacking about sex. Procreation—filling the earth with believers like themselves—was seen as the central duty of their lives. They forbade their teenagers kissing before marriage. Young people were to keep each other at arm's length. At that distance, most of the dance steps of the 1940s were awkward, so it was just as well that only folk dancing was permitted at their socials. To this day, if required, I can stomp up a small storm, thanks to the parties I infiltrated in the line of duty.

On Sundays, I blended in at services, interminable ones, as I recall. Tuesday evenings were set aside for group discussions with men at one home and women at another. We men would meet in the front parlor of the host home, which was lined with rows of folding chairs. The invisibility of the polygamist colony was brought home to me when, at the meetings, I encountered occasional teenagers I had known throughout my school days without ever imagining their secret. My surprise was no greater than their own at seeing me there.

At these meetings, discussion would flow freely, with each contributor rising from his chair to make his point. These folks had a varied and complex theology ranging far beyond mere marital arrangements. But the favorite topics were always the justifications for polygamy and denigrations of monogamy.

There was a curious astigmatism about our bull sessions. The duty to procreate was always before us, yet the acquisition and impregnation of wives was never spoken of. I could not dispel the sense that polygamy troubled the women who subscribed to it. A kindly, work-worn matron, one of two wives, told me, "Don't think for a minute that it is easy to live in polygamy. It is sometimes very hard. But I believe it is the true way of life."

Eventually, I found the fault line where one might suspect it to be—in the distribution of wives. According to the cult, God told the leaders who should marry whom. This had the effect of placing in the hands of the spiritual leaders an absolute corner on the most valuable of all markets. For our group, the holder of this awesome writ was Joseph Musser. After spying on the homes of the more prominent polygamists and interviewing some who were unhappy with their allotment, I came to suspect Musser was making liberal interpretations of God's messages. Either that, or God has a partiality for old codgers. The choicest young girls were going to the leaders themselves or to wealthy laymen who were big contributors to the cause. Young girls just out of high school were being pawned off on old psalm singers in their sixties and seventies. My notebooks were filling up with quotes, and the ranks of my informants were growing.

Unbeknownst to me, I was not the only investigator on the beat. The mainstream Mormon Church was also keeping the cult under quiet surveillance, determined to protect itself from reidentification with polygamy. The task of containing the heresy and keeping the church's skirts clear, without causing a scandal, was a delicate one—but not beyond the subtlety of church elders. They hired private investigators to keep an eye on the polygamists and identify any mainstream Mormons who might be attracted to the sect. If any such backsliders were found, the church would encourage them to come back to the fold. Those who couldn't be reclaimed would be excommunicated.

Over the years, the private investigators had located the key homes of the polygamists. They would slip among parked cars during meetings and copy license plate numbers. If the same car appeared at several meetings, they would trace the license plate number and determine whether the owner was on the church records as a baptized Mormon. Thus it was that my father's old Plymouth, the only wheels I had, kept appearing in the investigators' reports. In due course, my father was summoned by his church superiors for a confrontation that utterly confounded him.

My father's intolerance for backsliding made him the most unlikely polygamist in the Salt Lake Valley. Aside from his draconian adherence to the laws of the church, he had never had an interest in any woman other than my mother. One day I came home to find my father in a towering rage. The unspeakable had been spoken. He had been accused of an undercover flirtation with polygamists and convicted by his Plymouth. His suspicion had not yet lighted on me and his wrath groped for an object, alternating between the perversity of fate and the stupidity of man. I finally confessed and spent a long time in the doghouse. I was able to clear his name, but I could not repair the affront to his dignity nor rehabilitate my own credibility around the house.

Worse, my cover was blown with the polygamists because snickers travel fast. The variety of dodges I had used to hide my investigation from my family, friends, and church lay in a ludicrous heap. So ended my early adventures with the polygamists and my dream of freelancing the big story to the *Saturday Evening Post*.

I enrolled at the University of Utah, but didn't give much thought to pursing a college degree, since I was already working in my chosen profession. My journalism courses consisted of a professor lecturing from a textbook and then turning to me for an exposition on the real world. Looking back, I didn't know much, but I was sure I knew more about reporting than any college course could teach me. A review of some of my English papers saved by my parents betrays a writing style that could have used a little less smugness and a little more instruction. ("The full moon was a pool of pale light overflowing the muddy banks of night with silvery radiance....")

I sorely needed the seasoning and humility that comes only through experience. My opportunity came in the form of a church mission. By Mormon custom, I was called at age nineteen to serve a two-year mission that my family and myself were obliged to finance. My assignment was to the Southern States Mission headquartered in Atlanta. I accepted the call in large part to make my parents happy, but like others who have begun with more compulsion than commitment, I came to view my mission as a seminal experience. With my mother back home driving a taxi to help pay my way, I couldn't do otherwise.

My two-year mission began on a day with other distractions—December 7, 1941. Like all missionaries, I was exempt from the draft and frequently had to defend my choice as I went door-to-door in the conservative

DUELING POLYGAMISTS

I HAD BECOME A WASHINGTON COLUMNIST with a receding hairline and expanding waistline before I returned to the first big story of my investigative career: polygamy. At the time of my youthful infiltration, all but a few renegade polygamists had belonged to the same gentle sect. But over the years, the polygamist movement had splintered in pieces and rotted in character. The cults seemed to demand more from their members and give less. I heard stories about disciples disappearing, their leaders getting rich, girls being intimidated, and wives being auctioned off. So, I came back to the story in earnest in 1976.

I crossed paths and shared information with a young St. George, Utah, investigator, Tim Anderson, who visited the polygamist colonies, and Salt Lake City investigative reporter Dale Van Atta, who was researching a book. Anderson later went on to law school and participated in a landmark case, testing whether polygamists had the right to adopt children into their ranks. Van Atta finished his book and came to work for me in Washington.

The polygamist movement was haunted by the ghost of Alma Dayer Le-Baron, who had preached and practiced plural marriage in Utah in the early 1900s until his peculiar beliefs forced him to flee over the Mexican border and found his own colony, Colonia LeBaron. Obsessed with the idea that the Mormon Church had gone astray, LeBaron claimed he was the true prophet of God on earth. He promised to pass that authority on to the most righteous of his seven sons. This was to spark a bloodbath that lasted more than two decades.

The first son to claim the birthright, Benjamin, wound up his ministry in a succession of mental hospitals. The second, Joel, was murdered by his brother Ervil—a charismatic, darkly handsome man with blazing black eyes and a mind that was in turn brilliant and deranged. Ervil fashioned himself to be God's executioner and was allegedly responsible for more than twenty murders. He collected at least fourteen wives and moved back and forth between the United States and Mexico, eluding the lawmen of two nations.

LeBaron added a startling refinement to polygamy: He trained his women to kill for him. On December 26, 1974, under cover of darkness, a caravan of Ervil's devotees cruised into the little Mexican town of Los Molinos, the bastion of another brother, Verlan LeBaron. While men, women, and children leaped from their beds and rushed to hide behind tumbleweeds, Ervil's vigilantes tossed firebombs into the houses and then picked off the panicked Los Molinos residents with rifle shots. The attack lasted about twenty minutes, and the toll was one dead and thirteen wounded. Brother Verlan was out of town and escaped injury.

Before Ervil could eliminate his four surviving brothers, all pretenders to the throne, he was imprisoned for dispatching an assassin to Salt Lake City to murder Rulon Allred, the leader of a rival cult. Ervil had hoped to lure his brother Verlan to Allred's funeral, where Verlan could also be gunned down. But the TV cameras that crowded into Allred's funeral made a second murder too risky.

Ervil died of a heart attack in a cell at the Utah State Prison on August 16, 1981. Two days later, his brother Verlan was killed in a car accident when an oncoming car swerved into his lane and struck him head-on.

rural South. Chaffing in the southern sun under my regulation dark suit and white shirt, I decided that my peculiar talents might be better used at the mission office in Atlanta. So I proposed a public relations program, using radio spots written by me. My orthodox mission president reluctantly agreed to my experiment, and before long we had missionaries doing guest spots on radio stations across the South. The mission president never caught the mass-media vision. Even as I rode high on my success, I was dispatched to do door-to-door tracting in the backwoods of Florida while the media experiment went on without me.

Shortly, the campaign was called off. When the word reached me in Florida, I wrote an insubordinate letter to the mission president reminding him that I had touched more people with one fifteen-minute radio broadcast than all his missionaries could talk to in person in two years. He ignored my impertinence, so I knuckled under and resumed the face-to-face preaching I had been assigned to do. In letters home, I recorded the hardships I suffered, like the time I sampled oysters as a sporting gesture to please a man I was teaching: "I figured that he might be baptized some day and the least I could do would be to eat one of his oysters. I knew it would be a sacrifice before I ever clamped my jaws on the thing. But I looked it straight in the protoplasm, offered a silent tribute to the pioneers who sacrificed everything for their religion, and gulped it down. It has been trying to get back up ever since."

Southern diet aside, I came to enjoy relating to these people individually as they let me share the faith that had shaped my life to that point. But, I continued to stew over the potential of mass media. While attending a church conference later, in Augusta, Georgia, I was invited to dinner at the home of a Mormon businessman named Heber Meeks. Over the table, I told him of my aborted mass media campaign and he was intrigued. As luck would have it, a month later Meeks was summoned by the church to Atlanta to take his turn as president of the Southern States Mission, and soon thereafter he assigned me to his office staff and put me in charge of public relations.

My first step was to syndicate news about the church to southern papers. I called our little distribution network the Gulf News Service because I figured no one would accept our news if we called it the Mormon News Service. It wasn't long before a syndicated column by Heber Meeks was cropping up in papers all over the South.

When it came time for me to go home, President Meeks called me into his office with two other homeward-bound missionaries. Frank Gibbons and I were headed for Salt Lake City, and Earl Updike was returning home to Arizona where his mother was seriously ill. Her doctor had warned Meeks that if young Earl was snapped up by the draft as he would likely be when his mission ended, the shock would kill his mother. "You three have got to take a very slow route home," Meeks told us.

That launched a peculiar pilgrimage that we dragged out for two months. The straight-arrow Frank dawdled only because he had been ordered to do so, and only reluctantly surrendered his missionary suit for casual clothes. But Earl and I threw on some loud duds as soon as we saw Atlanta in the rearview mirror.

We stopped in Washington, D.C., where I wangled my first invitation to meet a president, Franklin Roosevelt. It was FDR's custom to hold intimate press conferences in his office, with him seated behind his desk and a gaggle of reporters clustered around. The Washington bureau chief for the *Salt Lake Tribune* arranged the credentials so I could join the small cluster. I was told to keep my mouth shut. My first visit to the Oval Office turned out to be the last time that I had to sit there in silence.

While I breathed in the heady air at the White House, Earl Updike did some research on how he could serve his country during wartime without traumatizing his mother. The Merchant Marine officer training program looked perfect, although the chances of getting one of the coveted officer slots were slim. The more Earl talked about putting out to sea, the more he stimulated my wanderlust. On a lark, I applied along with him, but I needed some credible references. An old Boy Scout buddy of mine worked for Utah Senator Elbert Thomas, so I imposed on him to ask the senator to write me a letter of recommendation. What I didn't know was that Thomas was chairman of the Armed Services Committee. His recommendation was tantamount to an entry ticket for the Merchant Marine.

My draft notice nearly beat me home to Salt Lake City. The suburban draft board in Murray was notoriously anti-Mormon and had a reputation for collaring returning missionaries as soon as they stepped off the bus. But while the draft board was hastily processing my paperwork, the assignment to the Merchant Marine training program came through. Earl turned out to be 4-F when he got home, but thanks to him, I was headed for the high seas, about as far as I could get from the desk they had saved for me at the *Salt Lake Tribune*.

CHAPTER 2

I JOINED THE MERCHANT MARINE TO sail the high seas, not to march around a drill field under the hot sun. So I began officer's training in San Mateo, California, in the summer of 1944 by seeking ways to escape the parade ground.

During peacetime, all Merchant Marine cadets attend the academy at Kings Point, New York. But during World War II, satellite schools were set up in Louisiana and California. The peacetime routine required cadets to train for a year at Kings Point, ship out for a year, and then return for three more years of academy study. But during the war, our preparation was compressed into three months of basic training followed by six months at sea. We were expected to learn trigonometry, for example, in a few hours instead of a few months, and hustle from one physical challenge to the next—scaling ropes, diving from a board the height of a boat deck into a pool of burning water, vaulting high hurdles and landing on the backs of our necks.

The program was known in Washington as a haven for the sons of influential people who could pull strings with the right politicians and get an appointment. But clout couldn't keep a cadet from washing out if he didn't make the grade in basic training. I was older and more mature than most of the cadets who were arriving straight out of high school, thus my missionary years gave me an edge. At lights-out, in the barracks, I knelt self-consciously beside my bed for my nightly prayers. The first night, I heard a few derogatory cracks, and a stray shoe narrowly missed my head. The second night, the conversation was subdued. The third night, there was total quiet, and three or four other cadets dropped to their knees.

In answer to an unspoken prayer, my newspaper training rescued me from the daily drills. The school's commanding officer had one eye on

Washington and wanted to impress his superiors. Having heard of my newspaper background, he summoned me to his office.

"Can you get out a base newspaper?" he asked.

"Sure," I said, "given time and staff." My mind was already calculating the possibilities—long hours working on a quality product, no time to march, staff jobs for my new friends in the cadet corps who would rather not march either. The strategy worked, until a sharp lieutenant looked over our operation and recognized it as the boondoggle it was. He ordered us back to the field and told us to do our newspapering after hours.

We marched, but I wasn't beaten. I produced no newspaper that week. As I anticipated, the commander summoned me to his house on the academy grounds.

"Why wasn't there a newspaper this week?"

"Because the lieutenant said it was more important for us to march."

Stern frown. Stern orders. And my staff and I returned to our typewriters.

COME SEPTEMBER, I RECEIVED MY SHIP assignment to the *Cape Elizabeth* under the command of one of the most noble men I have ever met. Since his genealogy was Norwegian, we called Captain Petersen a "squarehead," our veteran term for Scandinavian seagoers. Luckily for me, he had a son elsewhere in the cadet program who was about my age, so this captain took a fatherly interest in me. When the junior third mate nearly rammed us into another ship, Petersen gave me the watch.

Our first mission was to carry a load of candy, Coke, and beer to New Guinea for delivery to American GIs who had been living on tasteless rations for two years. The temptation of the cargo was too much for some crew members to resist. The captain found out that the goodies had been pilfered so he called us all out on the deck. He delivered the most stirring, patriotic address I had ever heard. I have listened since to some of the great political orations of our times; none has matched it. In simple, humble terms, Petersen told us how wrong it was for us—who were "still pissing Coca-Cola"—to take the first treats out of the mouths of American soldiers fighting far away from home. There was no more stealing after that.

I lost my twenty-second birthday on October 19 when we crossed the international dateline. It was November before we reached New Guinea where we anchored off shore for a couple of months because of the backlog of ships in the harbor. I joined the local Mormon congregation to pass the time on Sundays. On weeknights there were movies, but the sound track raced ahead of the pictures, and inevitably a two-and-a-half-ton truck would

WHILE THE *CAPE ELIZABETH* WAS ANCHORED off the New Guinea coast, I came down with a severe case of boredom. According to local legend, there were renegade Japanese lurking in the jungle, not to mention hostile natives and even cannibals. Despite warnings to keep inside the military compound, I ventured along a trail leading into the jungle. I didn't intend to leave this exotic country without a hike through some primitive territory.

The air was thick with droning insects that penetrated my insect repellent. I beat some and inhaled not a few. Midway through my hike, I rounded a bend. There, thirty feet ahead and stalking toward me was a painted-faced native who fit all my movie stereotypes, right down to the bone through his nose. He carried a spear and wore only a loin cloth, his powerful muscles on full display. I was convinced there was a cannibals' cauldron boiling somewhere with my name on it.

Realizing this Utah boy couldn't outrun the adversary, I opted to stride straight toward him in a show of fearlessness. He did the same. As we came within striking distance of each other, he broke the silence. "Hot, isn't it?" he said, in a pure British accent.

I gratefully agreed about the weather, and we paused to chat. He had been educated in a British missionary school, and, like me, was out for a walk.

choose the tense moments during which to stage maneuvers outside the theater. The local nightspot was the Red Herring, a place where entertainment was limited to playing Ping-Pong.

By the time the *Cape Elizabeth* weighed anchor, I had exhausted all the diversions New Guinea could offer. We returned to California for a load of high explosives and then headed for India. On this leg, we had our only brush with the enemy. On watch one twilight, my eyes sweeping the horizon, I spotted a submarine just as it began a crash dive. I slammed my hand on the alarm. Captain Petersen was beside me in an instant.

"What do you see?" he asked me calmly, belying the fact that he had just vaulted from his cabin to the deck.

"Sir, there's a submarine crash-diving off the starboard side." I handed him the glasses.

"Hard right," he quietly ordered the helmsman. Then, "Hard left."

Some crew members began throwing on life jackets and scurrying in panic, but the skipper's calm demeanor brought quick order on the ship. We zigzagged into the night. As we steamed around the Australian bight into the Indian Ocean, we picked up emergency radio reports of unusual Japanese submarine activity. Approaching Calcutta harbor, Captain Petersen turned to me and said, "Take us in." It was the greatest honor he could have bestowed on a young salt.

I took star sights, carefully charted our entrance, and told the captain that we should see a flashing light off the starboard bow exactly at midnight. At the stroke of the hour, we both looked up from the charts and saw only blackness where the lighthouse beam should have been winking at us. I virtually held my breath for the next five minutes, which is how long it took for the light to appear. Close enough. I brought us in.

Shore leave in Calcutta gave me the chance to look up the war correspondents based there. I spent a week with them and learned that all an aspiring reporter needed to claim the romantic title of war correspondent was a newspaper to back him. I loved the sea, but I loved newspapering more.

Waiting for me back in the States was an assignment to Kings Point for more training, followed by more sea duty. I arranged shore leave in April 1945 and headed for Utah where I made my pitch to Mark Petersen, editor of the *Deseret News*. If he would give me credentials as a bonafide war correspondent for the newspaper, I would send him feature stories about Utah boys in the war—for free. He agreed, probably with the expectation that he would get exactly what he had paid for. By the time the Murray draft board knew I was available again, I was already in Chongqing, China, with the naive expectation that the draft board wouldn't bother a war correspondent.

I'VE TRIED NEVER TO ATTEND PRESS conferences. They usually attract enough reporters to tell the story without me. It was no different in Chongqing in 1945. I left the press hostel to fly on some raids with the pilots of the Chinese-American Composite Wing. Then I talked my way onto a cargo plane that was sent on a secret mission to a place called "The Valley," behind Japanese lines. The OSS plane flew supplies to the guerrillas who had managed to build an invisible airstrip under Japanese noses.

From one thousand feet in the air, I got my first peek at this airfield, which looked like a grassy pasture. Somehow the guerrillas had coaxed grass to grow on a hardened dirt airstrip. Day after day, Japanese pilots flew over the field and never noticed what was below them. As we circled the field, a small band of guerrillas hurried out onto the grass, rolling barrels in front of them. They lined the hardened strip with their barrels to indicate the runway. Almost before we touched down, the markers were rolled back into the underbrush and our plane was covered with camouflage netting. This routine had barely been accomplished when three Japanese Zeros appeared overhead. After the Zeros had gone and the cargo had been unloaded, the pilot signaled to me. "Okay, it's time to go back."

"I'm not going."

He didn't realize that as a war correspondent, I was obliged to follow his orders. "It's your funeral," he told me, and took off, leaving me in the unwelcome arms of an OSS guerrilla unit that had been toughened in the Burma campaign and had better things to do than baby-sit a green reporter.

"What the blankety-blank is a war correspondent doing here?" demanded the commander, Captain William Drummond, who headed a supersecret guerrilla operation that I later learned was known only by the code name GZ6.

"I'm here to make you famous," I announced. That was the last thing he wanted; he was annoyed that I was aware of his existence at all. "We don't want to become famous," he growled. "You can't stay with us."

He had enough compassion not to abandon me, and tolerated my presence in the guerrilla compound for about a week while he figured out what to do with me. This was long enough for me to learn that the unit had belonged to an elite guerrilla force, identified as Detachment 101, whose unsung exploits deserved to be rendered by the Mormon tabernacle choir. They had been dropped deep into the Burmese jungle behind Japanese lines. To survive, they had to capture or scrounge supplies. Their mission: to conduct hit-and-run strikes, to blow up bridges, to train Kachin tribesmen in guerrilla tactics and, as one commando expressed it, to "raise hell." Many wouldn't come home, they were told. They volunteered anyway.

The occupying Japanese army raised some hell of their own; they conducted a ruthless campaign to root the Americans out of their hair. Any guerrilla who was unfortunate enough to be captured could expect to be beheaded and have his head paraded on the end of a bayonet through the Kachin villages, as a warning to the tribesmen not to side with the Americans. I pledged never to write down the names of the three men I bunked with for that memorable week. One of them didn't exactly lose his head, but he fled into the wilderness without his pants one night in his haste to escape a Japanese patrol that surprised them—an embarrassment that his buddies would never let him forget. "Got your pants on?" they would taunt him whenever they left the bunker.

In 1945, the survivors of Detachment 101 were hustled from the Burmese jungle to the Chinese hinterland, where they trained Chinese guerrillas and raised more hell. They were the roughest, toughest, gruffest combat troops I have ever encountered. They took pride in the reputation of their commander, Col. Carl Eifler, as the "deadliest colonel" in the U.S. Army. They described him as a huge, virile, flamboyant man who once took his Washington superior, General William Donovan, with him on a wild, treetop-level flight in a single-engine plane more than one hundred miles behind Japanese lines into the Burmese jungle.

After my week with these jungle fighters, Captain Drummond handed me off to a band of Chinese guerrillas. I had been told that American cigarettes would please my new escorts, so I presented a carton to their commander, Colonel Chang Shangchi. He received them coldly and I later saw him passing them out to his men. A hastily recruited interpreter, King Junn-shang—a sawed-off, sad-eyed little fellow with tremendous grit—explained that Colonel Chang was a newly converted Christian who eschewed tobacco and alcohol. When I told him my religion also forbade smoking and drinking, he looked upon me with new, benign favor. I had found a friend in this stocky, squared-faced man with the shaved head and eyes like flint, who sang hymns off key while he planned military strategy.

A native of Anhui province, Chang had returned home after some military training seven years earlier and since then had been waging guerilla warfare against the Japanese. His particular mission was to disrupt train traffic on a stretch of the Beijing-Hankou railroad forty to seventy-five miles north of Hankou. My interpreter King had been a first mate on a fishing junk sailing out of Shanghai until a Japanese sentry had smashed him in the face with a rifle butt. Offended, he left the sea and walked one thousand miles to join the guerrillas.

The psalm-singing colonel commanded four guerrilla groups; I asked to join the most combative. With a rousing rendition of "God Be with You 'til We Meet Again," he entrusted me to a unit commanded by another Colonel Chang. This was a Chang of a different stripe—Colonel Chang Shuatong—who could have been cast by Hollywood for the role. Of medium physical proportions and wiry build, he seemed, through some knack of carriage, to be larger and more powerful than he was. When he entered a room, he would never merely walk; he would plow into it, scowling and stalking. He was a coarse, unsmiling, bullnecked man, with a gruff voice and a brusque exterior, whose combined traits gave off an intimation of ferocity.

I spent six weeks wandering behind Japanese lines with Chang's guerrilla fighters. They were a motley lot, rugged and remorseless. They wore ragtag uniforms that had been patched together from captured Japanese garb, with bark helmets that had been covered with black tar. We marched, single file, winding over narrow mountain trails and zigzagging between rice paddies in the valleys. Advance patrols scouted the way, rushing up high rises and scanning the terrain.

I was barred, however, from beholding the military action I had come to witness. Between the fierce guerrilla chief and my protective interpreter, I was as pampered as a Ming vase. They felt a sacred responsibility to keep their American guest alive. Every time shots were fired, I was hustled to the rear. When I wandered near the perimeter of our camp, I was surrounded by half a dozen guards with bayonets who would escort me back to safety. I protested that I couldn't report action I couldn't see, but they were adamant. They would have lost face if anything had happened to their wartime guest.

My only war wound came from the swift kick of an unruly horse who had been captured from the Japanese and was still loyal to their cause. The guerrillas had two animals, this ill-mannered horse and a worse-mannered donkey. Since I was the guest of honor, Colonel Chang, with elaborate courtesy, presented me with his horse. With what dignity he could muster, he straddled the donkey.

My mount, Tojo, was determined to earn me a Purple Heart. My saddle, a warped wooden model that could have been left over from Genghis Khan, was split down the middle, with a wicked fissure that pinched my bottom with every step the horse took. One of the guerrillas, not blessed with an excess of candle power, walked behind me in our single-file procession. The ride was tedious and the hulking man behind me—assigned to play Sancho Panza to my Don Quixote—whacked the horse on the hindquarters whenever he was dissatisfied with Tojo's progress. As often as not, the horse would bolt, leaving me in a rice paddy.

My hosts took pleasure in making sure that in addition to premium transportation, I got premium lodging whenever possible. Once, with great fanfare, they announced for several days in advance that as soon as we reached a certain village, I would be given the village chief's American-style bed. I eagerly anticipated falling into a soft bed, but the chief apparently had never been consulted about the arrangements. I was shown to my prize bed, from which he had removed the mattress for himself and left me with a set of springs that were ready to do to my whole body what the saddle had already done to my derriere. After a few minutes of creaking and pinching, I rolled gratefully to the floor.

My personal hygiene was of considerable interest to the Chinese peasants who hosted us in the villages through which we passed. My every bodily function was watched by curious men and women and their chattering children who would light up with laughter when they realized that the tall, white man was equipped with the same parts as they were.

The American guerrillas had advised me to boil my water, and my Sancho Panza willingly took on the task. He understood why a pampered

American would want hot water, but not why anyone would boil it and then wait for it to cool before drinking it. He would repeatedly find my water had become tepid, and would bring it to a boil again so it would be suitably scalding. "Boil" was one of the few English words he learned.

I gamely tried to eat guerrilla fare, but soon paid the price. Chang noticed my pallor and asked what was wrong. Trying not to offend him, I explained that Chinese food was wonderful, but that my body was accustomed to an American diet. I found that I had underestimated Chang's hospitality. One night I was summoned to his quarters for dinner. I beheld a rare spectacle; Chang was smiling. Spread before me was a meal that could have been set out by my grandmother—meatballs, corn on the cob, potatoes and gravy, peas and carrots. I still remember it as the most welcome home cooking I've ever enjoyed. From his grinning accomplices, I pieced together the story of how Chang had produced this miracle meal.

On the day that I had explained my addiction to American cuisine, Chang remembered a cook in the northern reaches of the province who had once served as chef for some American missionaries. The colonel dispatched some of his guerrillas to fetch the cook, who came against his will. Chang ordered the cook to produce an American meal, but the chef protested that he needed American ingredients. So, with shopping list in hand and weapons under their clothes, the guerrillas trekked forty miles to Hankou, which was occupied by the Japanese. The intrepid guerrillas brought back more than meat and potatoes; they returned with two prisoners—a Japanese soldier and his Korean companion—whom they had encountered at an outdoor market. I talked to the Japanese soldier, who was a most unhappy POW. I don't know what happened to him after that, but I knew better than to ask. My home-cooked meal had come at a high price.

The day came in August 1945 when King rushed to my side shouting that the Japanese had "sullounded." It took several minutes for me to understand that the Japanese were not surrounded, but had surrendered. The war was not over for Chang and his men. Almost before the shooting died down, it began again—an outbreak between rival Chinese guerrillas. Our troops, loyal to Chiang Kai-shek, and a Communist force, loyal to Mao Tse-tung, maneuvered for control of the railroad. As usual, I heard more of the fighting than I saw. But Chang didn't conceal the grim evidence that as nations around the world laid down their guns, civil war was erupting in central China.

The outpost that dominated our sector, Kun Quling, was perched high on a mountaintop overlooking the tracks. Built by the Swiss before the war, it had been an Alpine-style resort, which was turned into a fortress by the Japanese. Trains moving between Hankou and Beijing had to pass beneath

Kun Quling's guns. After V.J. Day, the Japanese commander was besieged with conflicting demands from Communist and nationalist guerrillas that he surrender his mountaintop bastion to them. He chose to turn it over to our guerrillas, I was told, because he had heard they were accompanied by an American. Fortunately, he didn't know what an insignificant American I was.

To avoid a Communist ambush, we climbed the sheer backside of the mountain. I grew up in the Rockies were I'd been dragged up many a mountain by a father who loved to hike, but never have I scaled a peak as steep as the climb to Kun Quling. To my utter humiliation, the guerrillas had to help me straggle up the last one hundred yards. We were greeted as liberators by cheering Chinese villagers, and the streets were festooned with colorful pastel signs, including a few in pidgin English. One pink banner said it all: Welcome of Our Dearest American Friend. The Japanese regulars filed out as we marched in. As they passed, each solider turned his head, looking away from me, except the last in line who stared at me curiously. "They shlamed," King whispered. They had turned away their faces in shame, he explained, because America had won the war.

From Kun Quling's commanding heights, Colonel Chang and his men drove the Communists back. He spared a detachment, though, to escort me back to the hidden airstrip, hoping the Americans would take me off his hands. On the way, a messenger appeared from one of the mud-hut villages in the area. The Communists, hoping to curry U.S. favor, had stashed a downed American pilot in this remote village, and the messenger alerted us to come and get him.

Gene Doar's face lighted up when he spotted me among his rescuers. Without waiting to be introduced, he called out: "Got a cigarette?"

"Sorry," I said. "I don't smoke."

"The only American within one thousand miles, and he doesn't smoke," Doar muttered. Then he identified himself. He had been shot down, he said, the same day he was promoted to squadron commander. "I was squadron commander for a day."

He had found it necessary to bail out over a Japanese base, but had landed a quarter-mile downwind. Happily, the Communist guerrillas spotted his parachute and reached him minutes ahead of the Japanese. This was not the first plane he had lost, he confessed. During pilot training, his aircraft had malfunctioned, and he had had to abandon it five thousand feet above ground. Later he was shot down over the Pacific and spent a week on a rubber raft. "Two more times and I'll be a Jap ace," he grumbled.

Before Doar joined us, I had lost face with Chang's officers. They loved to play drinking games after evening meals. They would challenge one another to gulp down shots of Chinese moonshine—a clear liquid that Americans called "Jing Bao" or, loosely translated, "Air Raid" juice. I always declined, explaining that I didn't drink, but my refusal was beyond their comprehension. This after-meal ritual, they insisted, was not drinking; it was a matter of personal honor. Still, I held fast to my own definition of imbibing. Gratefully, Doar had no such religious taboos. He could drink any guerrilla among them under the table. They came to look upon him with unabashed awe, thus restoring the respect I had lost for America.

Our escorts delivered us to the hidden airstrip where a few rugged American commandos had already congregated from behind Japanese lines. In contrast, Chang's guerrillas were smaller men; they were poorly trained; their patchwork uniforms were ragged; their only weapons were those they had stolen from the enemy. But they had grit. As I waved good-bye, my hand slowly formed a lingering salute.

Early in my stint with the guerrillas, I had tried to use their hand-cranked radio transmitter to send out stories. OSS monitors had intercepted my first dispatch and had fired back an angry, coded message, demanding to know whether I was stupid or what! I had just sent the Japanese an open invitation to hunt me down, the message declared. That was all right with the OSS, but the Japanese search parties might stumble onto OSS agents instead. (Thereafter, the guerrillas wouldn't let me near their transmitter.)

Unhappily, the OSS men who had preceded us to the airstrip remembered me, and the war's end had mollified them but little. More for Gene Doar's sake than for mine, they radioed news of our arrival. Not long afterward, a pilot from Doar's squadron came to pick him up. Doar gave me a parting toast with an imaginary Chinese wine cup as their plane roared down the grassy runway. I was bundled aboard the next plane out.

Decades later, when I was lecturing in the Seattle area, an elderly man in the audience raised his hand during the question-and-answer period. "Didn't you travel with the Chinese guerrillas during World War II?" he asked.

"I did."

"And you rescued an American pilot?"

The man was deceptively dignified, with white hair and a trim goatee, but I responded with growing recognition. "Yes. His name was Gene Doar."

"That's me." Doar invited me to his home where we spent several hours chuckling over our youthful wartime misadventures in China.

Those misadventures did not end for me with the end of the war. When I arrived back at the press hostel in Chongqing, the mail from home included an urgent letter from a neighbor who was also an attorney. The war may have been over, but the Murray draft board still wanted me. My neighbor informed me that the board had refused, despite my glamorous status as a war correspondent, to grant me an occupational deferment. When my draft call had gone unanswered, the board had turned my name over to the FBI.

This news subjected me to the sort of harassment that reporters reserve for other reporters. My colleagues at the press hostel celebrated my predicament. They made unkind cracks; they offered obscene advice; they wrote amusing stories about the cub reporter who had emerged from behind the lines to find his draft call waiting. I duly presented myself at the American embassy, which offered me the option of beginning my military service in China or going home for basic training. I chose to stay. My fellow correspondents made sure the world knew that I had become the lowliest GI in China—with no service record, no army training, and no points toward discharge under the army's postwar point system.

I requested a reporting job on *Stars and Stripes*. Instead, I was assigned to the army haberdashery where I dispensed socks and underwear—mostly to correspondents who didn't need them but came to witness my humiliation. After a few days behind the counter, I was rescued by the master sergeant who presided over the correspondents' motor pool. Bilko should have been his name. His glorified motor pool had a population of one jeep, which the sergeant signed out each day to the correspondent who got to him first. Then he would spend the rest of the day playing poker with the stray correspondents who, like himself, preferred to wait for life's mountains to come to them.

Indeed, Sergeant Bilko made a career of avoiding work, as did five other master sergeants who shared his barracks. He mercifully plucked me from the commissary, but then installed me in the master sergeants' purgatory. I was an innocent Snow White, as it turned out, among six incorrigibles. To a young Utah lad whose mores had been formed in an austere Mormon household, residency in their private Gomorrah was something of a culture shock. Between them, they knew every trick in the military Book of Goldbricking. They goofed off by day and partied at night. They intercepted delectables intended for the general's table; they washed them down with bootleg booze; they brought in Chinese street prostitutes for entertainment.

The best thing I could do, I decided, was to sleep through it all. I sought refuge in my bunk; I pulled the covers over my head; I held the pillow over my ears. But nothing I tried could stifle the sergeants' boisterous bonhomie. They were determined to share their blessings with me—a plate of genuine, steaming Italian spaghetti thrust under my nose at 3 A.M.; a bottle of rare wine pressed with loving force to my lips; a prostitute goaded by my hosts to display her limited charms.

One night, I rolled over on my bed and feigned sleep with grim tenacity. But this merely stirred the gang of six to try all the harder to wake me so that I might partake of the spoils they had scrounged. They formed an alcoholic conspiracy, stole an air raid siren, placed it two inches from my ear, and set it off. It aroused the whole base and left me with impaired hearing in my left ear.

EMANCIPATED FROM ALL LABOR BY THE master sergeants, I quietly offered my services to the Associated Press bureau chief in Chongqing, Spencer Moosa. The AP provided him with a modest expense account, which he paid me as a salary. My beat was Chinese Communist headquarters. Our arrangement, we agreed, should not be advertised; neither the AP nor the army would be inclined to approve. Until this writing, the AP has been unaware that in late 1945, their dispatches from Chongqing on Communist activities were reported by a moonlighting GI.

In an attempt to unify the rival Chinese factions, Washington had brought pressure on Chiang Kai-shek to allow the Communists to set up a liaison office in his capital. The approach to their compound led through a maze of slime-slick alleys that gave off an overpowering stench—a blend of odors rising from open gutters and wafting from a thousand Chinese cooking pots. I found the Communists shuttered in sparse, dingy rooms, whose windows were covered with greased brown paper.

This unpretentious place was a political headquarters and an espionage center run by an enigmatic figure who was to gain world renown, Chou En-lai. For most of the twentieth century, he operated in the shadow of Mao Tze-tung, the great Buddha of Chinese communism. Chou was a sycophant who attributed all his achievements to Mao, thus craftily keeping his head an inch below the purge line. Yet, history will record that the architect of modern China was not Mao but, above all others, Chou En-lai.

For three months, we met almost every day—the future Washington columnist and the future premier of the People's Republic of China. Chou devoted hours, incredibly, educating this twenty-three-year-old reporter about the plans, aims, ways and means of the Communist revolution. Sometimes he would turn me over to his intelligence chief, Gong Peng, who would spell out the details on maps and charts. She was an articulate and alluring woman, smooth as silk, who was married to one of Chou's aides, Qiao Guanhua. She could deliver a briefing with professional aplomb, while balancing her roly-poly baby on her hip. I spent many long days with Chou, questioning and listening, and often would return in the evening to join him and his staff for dinner.

Chou had a compelling public relations policy; he told the truth. He was scrupulously factual about events and disarmingly candid about intentions.

CHOU EN-LAI

IN ANY SUMMING UP OF MY World War II recollections, Chou En-lai looms above all others as the most unforgettable figure. He had an impassive, handsome face that lingers in my memory for its black eyes and incandescent intelligence. He affected simplicity, dressing plainly and disdaining new attire. His wife, Deng Yingchao, repaired his worn collars with pieces of old shirttails. Yet he always appeared urbane, an elegant man, graceful of movement, with a quick wit and a suave manner.

Chou was accomplished in English and French as well as Chinese dialects, buttressing his arguments with historical and literary allusions. He surrounded himself with bright subordinates, mostly students who had studied abroad. But his sophistication, I noticed, seemed to make some of his comrades uneasy. They seemed suspicious of his polish and intellect; he reminded them perhaps of the mandarins whom they sought to overthrow.

Most Communist cadres came from the peasantry. They were uneducated, and their speech was sometimes crude. They knew how to blow up bridges, but many could not read. There was even a flat-earth cult within the Communist core— those who refused to accept that the world was round. This troubled Chou, whose vision of an industrialized China depended on a skilled workforce. In the technological age, he said, a great nation could not be founded upon an ignorant populace.

In the rearview mirror of my mind, I can still see the worldly and wily Chou at a diplomatic soiree in Chongqing, standing nose-to-nose with Chiang Kai-shek's information minister, K. C. Wu. For nearly an hour, they engaged in an intense dual of words. Chou cut Wu to pieces with rapierlike swipes of his tongue, but Wu refused to concede. "We disagree," Chou ended it, adding with a sly smile, "but agreeing to disagree is already some kind of agreement."

Chou also knew when to sheathe his tongue. During the birth pangs of the Communist state, he opposed the economic excesses and human atrocities, I am told, but he never spoke out against them. He endured frustration and humiliation in deathlike silence. To explain the temper of the times, a source close to Chou offered this anecdote: Chou loved to dance, which led fanatics to accuse him of bourgeois sympathies. One critic even made a political issue of Chou's tendency to turn to the right when he danced a waltz.

Chou alone survived the frenzy that Mao Tse-tung unleashed, in the name of a "cultural revolution," against the government apparatus that Chou headed. Chou's subordinates were cut out from under him by hard-line fanatics who sentenced them to labor camps where they were forced to perform humiliating chores. Intimates later told me that Chou was left with nothing but a small clerical staff to run the government, that he was reduced, in fact, to writing letters by his own hand.

The political casualties included his most powerful ally, Deng Xiaoping, who lacked Chou's slavish skills. In earthy, peasant language, an associate recited Deng's code: "If you can't shit, don't sit on the toilet." But Chou had a more servile code, this insider confided. If Mao told him to "shit," Chou would sit on the toilet, even if he didn't feel the urge.

Chou was, however, a persevering man who never quite gave up the ghost. One by one, he outsmarted, out-talked, and out-maneuvered his enemies. When at last he regained power, he set the policies that now guide China and brought back Deng to implement them.

The late Supreme Court Justice William O. Douglas, who had kept a close watch on China, tried to persuade President Harry Truman in the 1950s that Chou En-lai held the keys to peace in the Far East. Douglas had picked up Chou's friendly signals to Washington and believed they were genuine.

That wise old jurist told me many years later that Truman, and President Dwight Eisenhower after him, had failed tragically to see through the bamboo curtain. Douglas believed that a single, foolish incident had helped to kindle two wars that the United States could have avoided. Without Chinese support, he said, neither the North Koreans nor the North Vietnamese could have sustained offensives against American troops.

The unfortunate incident, he said, occurred at an international conference in Bandung, Indonesia, in 1955. According to Douglas, Chou En-lai encountered Secretary of State John Foster Dulles and cordially offered his hand, but Dulles coldly turned his back on Chou and walked away. To an Asian who places high value on his "face," this affront caused decades of bitter Chinese hostility, Douglas said.

This was a bizarre twist of history that I felt compelled to investigate. I was unable to nail down the Bandung incident; some sources said it happened; others swore it didn't. I verified, however, that Dulles had ordered a social boycott against the Chinese Communists by all Americans attending an earlier conference in Geneva in 1954. U.S. delegates received strict orders not to shake hands or socialize with Chou and company. But I also learned that Dulles's second in command, Walter Bedell Smith, avoided the forbidden handshake by holding a cup of coffee in his right hand; then with his left hand he warmly gripped Chou's arm.

Intimates of Chou told me after his death that he never wavered from his belief in Chinese-American friendship, that he chose to forget Dulles's affront, but to remember Smith's embrace.

He laid out battle plans and political strategies, in advance, with remarkable clarity. He told the truth, that is, in order to promote a lie. He recited facts that withstood the tests of time and circumstance. These truths made him so believable that a reporter would be tempted to accept his assurances, too, that the Chinese Communists weren't really Communists but agrarian reformers.

Chou's paramount mission, I heard later, was to "rope the whale." This was a direct order from Mao Tse-tung. It meant simply that Chou was supposed to use every possible stratagem to neutralize the United States. The Communist leaders not only hoped to deprive Chiang Kai-shek of vital American aid; they also realized that America alone could help them transform a future Communist China swiftly into a world power. "It takes a long rope to catch a whale," intimates quoted Mao telling Chou, "and you, En-lai, shall weave that rope."

Chou gave me a preview of China's future that turned out to be startlingly accurate—though I failed to recognize it, of course, until it had become the past. He vowed that the Communists would gain control of China; how long it would take them to defeat Chiang Kai-shek would depend on how much support the United States gave him. After Chiang's collapse, Chou predicted, Washington "would discreetly withdraw its head from the tiger's mouth."

He was so certain of the outcome that he boldly laid out the Communist strategy, explaining the military details with such candor that it would seem to violate their security.

Chou insisted intensely that the Chinese Communists did not wear Moscow's brand as Washington presumed. After the Communists seize power, he assured me, China's immediate tribulations and future danger would come not from the United States but from the USSR. He predicted that though China and Russia might have communism in common, the 5,000-mile border between them would produce more friction than comradeship. On China's other flank, the Pacific Ocean would provide a buffer zone, he said, that would make it easier to maintain friendship with the United States. He also contended that unlike oil and water, agrarian communism and industrial capitalism could mix. Under Communist rule, he promised, the Chinese economy would be compatible with the West's.

During the years that followed, I watched in fascination as Chou's scenario unfolded as he had predicted it would. Well, not exactly. The friendship he had advocated between China and America was disrupted by two wars, with a hailstorm of crises and disputes in between. Mao Tse-tung also turned out to be better at whipping up revolutions than governing the people he had subdued. In his frustration, he wound up waging a final revolution against his own bureaucracy, causing incalculable mischief and misery. Instead of a "mixed economy," he spread economic devastation.

An intimate later confided that Chou, throughout this long nightmare, kept "still as a stone." He suffered humiliation and frustration, plus a gnawing internal cancer, in stoic silence. But he never lost sight of the future as he had described it to me in 1945. He didn't live quite long enough to see it fulfilled, but before he died in 1976, he had turned China around. His chosen successor, Deng Xiaping, completed the victory over the Maoists and implemented Chou's vision.

In early 1973, Chou broke through "all the curtains," as he put it— "the iron curtain, bamboo curtain, smoke curtain"—to establish diplomatic relations with Washington. He dispatched Qai Dzemin to be his first minister to the United States. Not long after Qai's arrival, I received an invitation to dinner at his diplomatic lodgings. I assumed this was the usual introductory gala for all the media—a social ritual that I always avoided. But I was curious to renew contact with the Chinese Communists, so I made an exception. This turned out to be fortunate, since my wife and I were the only invited guests. A grinning Qai Dzemin greeted us. "You are a friend of our premier," he said. Chou En-lai had remembered a young reporter who had spent a little time with him in Chongqing at the end of World War II.

Stars and Stripes started a Shanghai edition after the war. As the armed forces downsized, the paper began to run short of reporters. The editors got wind of one with no discharge points and extricated me from Chongqing. In the editorial rooms of *Stars and Stripes,* I found an irreverent environment that stirred my own rebellious nature. We wore no symbols of rank; the top jobs went to the best qualified; officers accepted assignments from enlisted men. Thanks to forward-thinking Generals George Marshall and Dwight Eisenhower, we were completely independent of the military hierarchy. We posted a letter on our wall attesting to this, and framed it like a Declaration of Independence. It was signed by General Albert C. Wedemeyer, the armed forces commander in China, who decreed that no officer, including himself, would give *Stars and Stripes* an editorial directive.

This was all the authority we needed to behave like katzenjammer kids with no curfew. When an officer would show up in high dudgeon to complain about our stories, we would point wordlessly to the letter. I recall the time our receptionist, Mary Graham—we called her "Sunny" because of her radiant disposition—materialized in the newsroom with the breathless announcement that a two-star general waited without. She was fresh from the States where she had been taught to salute anything.

"What should I tell him? What should I do?" she asked, all aflutter.

IKE

AT *STARS AND STRIPES*, OUR DISDAIN for protocol went clear to the top. When General Dwight Eisenhower made a stopover in Shanghai on a military tour, reporter Jim Becker and I were assigned to cover the event. We pulled ourselves out of bed after oversleeping. Unshaven, we hurried to the airfield without hats or ties. Everything around us had been buffed to a sparkle for Eisenhower's inspection. As we approached the airport, an MP stopped us. "Hey, fellas," he said. "Aren't you in the army? Don't you know there's a cleanup campaign on? Where are your hats?"

Becker reached up and felt the top of his head. "That's strange. It was there three months ago."

When Eisenhower stepped out of the plane, he was surrounded by concentric circles of generals—the more the stars, the closer to the great one. A brigadier general tried to head us off. "Ike's only going to be here for fifteen minutes and he has to meet all these generals. I don't think he'll have time for *Stars and Stripes*."

But Ike, already a politician, had spotted us and beckoned us over. He spent his entire fifteen minutes in Shanghai talking to us, genially answering tough questions about the hot topic of the day, the postwar rights of GIs. Then he got back on his plane, without ever seeming to notice the spit-polish job the soldiers had done in preparation for his inspection.

City Editor John Davies, who was editing copy, didn't even look up. "If he gets in your way, throw his ass out."

In the *Stars and Stripes* spirit, I banged heads with the brass—with the top sea dog of the Seventh Fleet, no less. I had heard that the navy was preparing to smuggle an American diplomat, Angus Ward, into Russian-occupied Manchuria. When I began asking questions, Admiral Charles M. Cooke ordered me not to write the story. With the impudence of a GI who couldn't be busted any lower, I said the admiral would find my response in the morning paper. Which he did, on page one. The furious admiral wrote a scathing letter to General Wedemeyer, demanding that I be court-martialed for violating a direct order. Wedemeyer, bless his name, replied that the admiral would have to take up his complaint with the GI editors of *Stars and Stripes*.

Throughout the postwar downsizing, the editorial staff was depleted like a slab of baloney through a meat slicer until the paper folded. In the end, only Jim Becker and I were left. He had low points; I had no points.

We were assigned to put out a mimeographed "Morning Report" for the remaining U.S. contingent. Without asking anyone, we adopted the same standard of press freedom for our little newsletter that we had practiced at *Stars and Stripes.* This quickly got us in hot water with the brass, who appointed a major to censor our stories. I threatened to call a press conference and raise a stink. The army resolved the dispute by discontinuing the "Morning Report."

Despite my cantankerous conduct, the officer in charge of the armed forces radio station in Shanghai—a Hollywood-connected captain named Mel Riddle—manipulated some backstage strings to put me on the air. For several months, I delivered the only uncensored newscast in Shanghai. The content, if not the performance, attracted a huge following.

Word of my connection with Chou En-lai filtered to G-2, as Army Intelligence was cryptically known, which pressured me to gather intelligence on China's civil war. Not without some private agonizing, I put patriotism ahead of journalistic ethics. As luck would have it, my friend, Chou's intelligence chief Gong Peng, headed the Communist mission in Shanghai. Without hesitation, she briefed me on the latest developments. I was able to inform G-2 where the fighting would break out next and what the Communist military strategy would be. My reports turned out to be spectacularly accurate, causing excitement all the way to Washington.

Even though I was technically a soldier in the employ of Uncle Sam, I felt guilty about my brief career as a spy. It ended one evening as I approached Gong Peng's office. A Chinese figure slipped out of an alleyway and hissed into my ear: "Don't go to Communist headquarters tonight." The mystery man faded into the street throng before I could react. This gave me the excuse I needed to retire from the espionage business. I told G-2 that my cover had been broken. I never saw Gong Peng again, and I never wrote another intelligence report.

Meanwhile the radio station—XMHA were the call letters—was preparing to shut down, and I pictured myself back handing out underwear and socks at the army commissary. My salvation came in the person of Chiang Kai-shek's brother-in-law and prodigal bagman, H. H. K'ung, who had been installed momentarily as head of the civilian government. Though he was Chiang's strawman, he held the glorified status of president of the China that Washington recognized. If China's head of state signed a formal letter to the U.S. Army requesting the early release of Sergeant Jack Anderson (I had wangled a promotion) for a vital service, the brass could hardly claim this lowly GI was unexpendable.

How did I pull off this caper? My superior at XMHA, that man-about-Shanghai, Captain Mel Riddle, navigated in K'ung's lofty circles. Riddle had arranged to begin his civilian life as the overpaid manager of a Chinese goodwill mission. I convinced Mel that he needed a public relations man to herald the three gifted young Chinese pianists who would tour America, staying at the best hotels and living high on the hog. But it wasn't the high life that I sought; it was the discharge paper.

Diplomacy would not allow the army to turn down President H. H. K'ung. And so my short and undistinguished military career came to its conclusion with a premature, but altogether honorable, discharge in November of 1946.

PART 2

WASHINGTON MERRY-GO-ROUND

1947 – 1960

THE SUDDEN DEATH OF PRESIDENT FRANKLIN D. Roosevelt in 1945 of a massive cerebral hemorrhage put a very different kind of president in the White House. Harry Truman was perhaps our last "ordinary man" to occupy the Oval Office. His breeding was common, his style undignified, and his speech unguarded. Although I sat in as a spectator at one of Franklin Roosevelt's press conferences, Truman was the first president I knew personally.

He was no saint; few men have reached the presidency without making some compromises. But Truman would have been disgusted by the perfidy yet to come in the Nixon years, and the scandals of the 1990s—the House Post Office and House Bank fiascos. In the top drawer of the presidential desk in the Oval Office, Truman kept a roll of stamps that he had paid for himself. Whenever he wrote a letter to a friend or relative, he opened that drawer and pulled out a stamp rather than let the taxpayers fund his personal correspondence.

One of Truman's aides told me of the day that Republican Senator Robert Taft, no friend of the president's, came to the White House for an appointment and had to rush back to the Senate for a vote. Absentmindedly, Taft left behind his briefcase, which aides to the president suspected might contain some intelligence about his latest legislative battles with Truman. "Mr. President," one aide reported with glee. "Look what Bob Taft left behind."

"Don't you touch that zipper," Truman responded. "You get that briefcase back to Senator Taft as fast as a messenger can deliver it."

One afternoon during the Truman years, I observed an old man shuffling in front of the White House, leaning on a shaky cane. He arrived at the driveway of the president's house just as Truman's car pulled in. The old man recognized the president of the United States, removed his hat and held it over his heart, his head bowed in reverence for the office and the man. There was a screech of brakes and a shift into reverse. The president jumped out of the backseat, threw his arm around the old man, and they visited briefly. Today it would be unthinkable to get that close to the president without an invitation to a state dinner. But postwar Washington, D.C., was a much more neighborly place to live.

I had occasion to call Truman after he retired to his modest home in Independence, Missouri. On my mind were the endearing photos published of him the day he arrived there, driving his own car, stopping for gas, lugging his suitcase up to the attic. I knew him to be a man of the people, but there were at least two Washington journalists he detested, myself and my then-boss Drew Pearson, because of our critical coverage of him. I was surprised when he took my call and greeted me in good humor.

"Mr. President, you sound in fine fettle."

He chortled, "I just pulled a fast one on Bess. Bess has been pesterin' me to cut the lawn and I don't want to cut the lawn. Well, she kept naggin' me so I fixed her. I went out early Sunday morning. I began cuttin' the lawn with the greatest clatter I could create. She came runnin' out, grabbed me by the arm, and pulled me into the house. She said, 'You stop that noise. You're going to scandalize the neighborhood!' She hasn't bothered me about cuttin' the lawn since."

Lest I be condemned for the nostalgia that comes with blurred hindsight, I hasten to add that Washington, and all of America in that era, was deeply troubled. Almost as soon as the war ended, a new one erupted—this one a Cold War between the United States and the Soviet Union that would span more than four decades.

At home, the Cold War pitched Americans into the depths of paranoia in the 1950s. Senator Joseph McCarthy built a sorry political career on a witch-hunt for suspected Communists disguising themselves as patriotic Americans.

Communism came to personify evil, first in the USSR and Eastern Europe, and then in Asia, as China fell to the Communists in 1949. My wartime friends, the Chinese nationalists who followed Chiang Kai-shek, retreated to the island of Formosa.

Russia and China were the bogeymen that we fought either through escalation of weapons and threats, or in real combat with their surrogates. The first to be caught in the squeeze between superpowers was Korea—a Japanese holding until 1945. When Japan lost the war, Washington and Moscow agreed to divide and occupy Korea, ostensibly until the newly independent nation could form its own government. But Russia never had any intention of letting Korea become a democracy. In June of 1950, with Moscow giving the orders and bankrolling the troops, North Korea invaded South Korea and Truman had another war on his hands.

The baby boomers, whose first remembered war was fought in Vietnam, think they pioneered the notion of unpopular war. They forget that in its time, the Korean conflict was thought by many to be just as unwinnable and unwise. Truman retired at the nadir of his popularity in 1952 and left it to his successor, Dwight D. Eisenhower, to disentangle the United States from Korea.

An amiable duffer who preferred a round of golf to just about anything the presidency had to offer, Eisenhower presided with benign neglect over the space race, the espionage race, the nuclear arms race, and the birth of rock and roll. Americans bought televisions and record players—we called it the "hi-fi" then. Women who had riveted battleships during the war retreated back to the kitchen. Automation at work gave us more time for leisure at home, so we barbecued and mastered the hula hoop and read *The Catcher in the Rye.*

Eisenhower, and Truman before him, were the last of my parents' generation to lead the United States. I, the typically cocky offspring of that generation, became a eyewitness to postwar Washington. I arrived with a resumé that was more embroidery than substance, and a style that was more bluff than experience. But I was eager to learn, and I picked the master teacher.

CHAPTER 3

J. EDGAR HOOVER WAS TO BECOME my nemesis, but in 1947 he was responsible for opening up the job that launched my career. I can thank the FBI director for a telephone call that set me up as junior muckraker for the granddaddy of investigative reporters, Drew Pearson.

On nights in Chongqing, the correspondents at the press hostel would drift into the Associated Press quarters for alcoholic gab sessions. Invariably, the talk would turn to postwar hopes and plans. Given my position at the bottom of the totem pole, press protocol obligated me to wait to chime in until the rest were drowsy from drink and had given up trying to spike my soda. After listening to everyone else's career plans, I announced one night that I would head for Washington, D.C., because that was where the news was. The AP's Harold Milks offered a suggestion: "If you want to learn that town, you should try to get on with Drew Pearson. He knows where the bodies are buried."

As soon as I had fulfilled my commitment to chaperon the Chinese pianists, I went straight to Washington and dropped off a job application at Drew Pearson's office. For insurance, I also applied at the one-man Washington bureau of the *Salt Lake Tribune*, which, as it turned out, wasn't looking for a second man. But Pearson summoned me by telegram for an interview, although I was rooming at a house only a few blocks away. He had an opening on his staff, he later told me, because of a phone tip from J. Edgar Hoover telling Drew that one of his reporters, Andy Older, was a card-carrying Communist. Drew leaned to the left but not that far left. He confronted Older, who fessed up. Drew fired the reporter on the spot, putting it bluntly: "That's not compatible with my beliefs. You'll have to leave."

Drew was approaching the zenith of his fantastic career. He was an irrepressible idealist at the height of his influence, a muckraker full of happy outrage. The list of those whose dark underbellies had been exposed by him read like a "Who *Was* Who in America."

When word of the vacancy on Drew's staff got out, the list of applicants for Older's job quickly grew to about one hundred names, including a couple of former congressmen. My name was arguably the least distinguished. What piqued Drew's interest, I later learned, was my experience as a war correspondent. He was more impressed than he should have been.

I presented myself at the faded yellow brick house at 1313 Twenty-ninth Street on a quiet, tree-shaded corner of Georgetown. It served as the rambling office and gracious home of Drew and his wife, Luvie. The building was actually two side-by-side, three-story houses—one side elegantly furnished and staffed to accommodate the Pearsons, the other side a cluttered warren populated by reporters—with a narrow, white door connecting the structural Siamese twins. When it was open, tinkling glasses and sophisticated chatter from the house would mingle with clattering teletype machines, clanging telephones, and cryptic give-and-take from the offices. Out of this unlikely news center came a daily column and weekly radio broadcast that reached an audience of sixty million.

To my grateful surprise, Drew offered me a job at fifty dollars a week. He warned that his busiest day was Sunday because of his national radio broadcast that evening. A little alarm went off in the back of my head. "I can't be here on Sunday. I go to church on Sunday." He was taken aback. No one had ever told Drew Pearson they could not work on Sunday. After a pause he said, "Can you work late on Saturday?"

"I can work as late as you want me to."

"All right, you're hired."

He never once asked me to compromise my Sabbath.

The lame duck Andy Older, whom Drew had given a couple weeks' notice, was assigned to show me the ropes. Understandably, he was not eager to waste his time on a rube from the Rockies who was taking his job. He escorted me to Capitol Hill and introduced me to probably the most insignificant freshman Republican in a Congress run by Democrats. Then without further ceremony, Older abandoned me.

There was no one to warn me that certain people had been so rattled by Drew that it was best to steer clear of them. I discovered this for myself when I knocked on the door of Senator Kenneth McKellar of Tennessee, the ancient chairman of the Appropriations Committee. I didn't realize that McKellar hated Drew with such a passion that he once had devoted a full hour's speech on the Senate floor to calling Drew a liar, using every variation of the word that a thesaurus could supply. Among the epithets he chose were "ignorant liar," "peewee liar," and "pusillanimous liar"—all delivered

THE SLAP HEARD ROUND THE WORLD

IF J. EDGAR HOOVER WAS RESPONSIBLE for opening up a job for me with Drew Pearson, General George S. Patton was responsible for the partnership slot with Drew. The Washington Merry-Go-Round had begun as a partnership between Drew and Robert S. Allen after the two reporters anonymously authored a book of the same title in 1931. The exposé of behind-the-scenes Washington was such a success, that they produced a sequel, *More Merry-Go-Round,* in 1932. This time Drew was found out and fired from his job as a reporter for the *Baltimore Sun.*

That year, Drew and Allen signed on with the United Features Syndicate to produce a column about inside Washington. When World War II broke out, Allen, an officer in the reserves, answered the call to military duty. Drew, the Quaker pacifist, agreed to keep the home fires burning for both of them by producing the column and leaving the partnership open for Allen when he returned.

Under Drew the enterprise flourished. In a radio broadcast on November 21, 1943, Drew broke the story about General Patton that took the shine off his brass. Pearson announced that "Blood and Guts" Patton, while touring an army hospital in Sicily, had come upon an American soldier who was bedridden not with war wounds but with "shell shock" or "battle fatigue." Patton ordered the man out of bed, and when the soldier did not leap to his feet, the general pulled him up and then slapped him back down. A doctor intervened and reminded the general that Patton was in charge of the troops in battle, but the doctor was in charge of the troops in the hospital.

The story was a natural for Drew who, throughout the war, had made himself the champion of the GIs. He admired only a few men who wore the rank of general, and Patton was not one of them. To Drew, the slapping episode typified the oppression of the rank and file by swaggering, pompous, dangerous brass hats. Drew aired the broadcast without consulting Patton's public relations man in Europe, which was typical of Drew. But in this case, the PR man was none other than Robert Allen, who had been assigned as an aide to the general and had become an almost slavish admirer of him in the process.

Allen dashed off a handwritten note to Drew. Their partnership was over and Drew could keep the column. Drew held on to the letter and went to see Allen after the war ended. "This letter gives me ownership of the column, but I know you wrote it impetuously and I'm not going to hold you to it," Drew told him. "You're still a partner if you want to be." The friendship was mended, but Allen declined Drew's offer.

"In that case, you have a financial stake," Drew told him. They settled on a payment of $45,000 over six years from Drew to Allen for the privilege of using the Merry-Go-Round trademark that belonged to both of them. For his part, Allen agreed not to go into competition with Drew as a columnist. But, a few years later, Allen did start up a rival column. Drew wasn't going to be walked on. "I don't intend to subsidize the competition," he told Allen. But Allen refused to stop publishing.

"Fine," Drew said. "I've been using the trademark. Now you use it and pay me forty-five thousand dollars." Allen was beaten. Drew had become such a celebrity that any column he wrote would succeed on the strength of his name alone. Dropping the issue of further payment, Allen signed the Washington Merry-Go-Round logo over to Drew and continued to write his own obscure column.

Drew harbored no ill will toward Allen and occasionally invited him to take over the column when Drew went on vacation. I recall one such stint not long after I joined Drew. Allen disliked me immediately, maybe sensing that I would one day have the partnership he had forfeited. I produced several good stories while Allen was on the byline that summer, but each of them sat on his desk unused, never to see the light of print until Drew returned.

with such energy that McKellar retired to the men's room after his outburst and promptly fainted.

The old curmudgeon was at first cordial to me as a reporter of unknown origins. Then he asked whom I represented. "Drew Pearson," I said innocently. His face turned the blue hue of a man who urgently needs oxygen. He lunged awkwardly around his desk with remarkable speed for a man in his eighties, and began pummeling me with his fists and kicking the calves of my legs, which was as high as his trembling foot could reach. I beat a hasty retreat, fearing the old codger would die from the exertion of his attack. Later, when word of our set-to reached the ears of other reporters, I salvaged my own dignity by saying McKellar's flailing fists were like pillow puffs.

Going door-to-door in the halls of Congress, I decided, had its hazards. So I sought advice from another staffer, Tom McNamara, who explained the Drew Pearson peculiarities to me. The kind of stories the boss liked, Tom said, were behind-the-scenes stuff from secret meetings. He referred to "executive sessions," which were held behind closed doors. I should pump each participant for details, Tom suggested, and then try to reconstruct the discussions that had gone on in the secret meetings. I used this dubious technique for a year before I found out that verbatim transcripts were kept of the meetings.

That discovery started me on a new course of investigative reporting. No longer would I piece together dialogue based on the fallible memories of the participants. Hereafter, I would quote their exact words, taken from the classified transcripts. These were hallowed records, I should add, invested with national security. Publishing classified government documents so soon after World War II was akin to treason. "Loose lips sink ships" was still the standard, even for reporters. But I had learned enough about politicians to suspect that the ships they wanted to keep afloat were not navy battle-wagons at all but political bandwagons.

To wrest these secrets from their keepers, I would first seek a verbal account of the closed session. I learned which senators would talk, and I would ask them what was said at the meeting. Then, with such nonchalance as I could muster, I would tell them that I needed to see the transcript for accuracy's sake. "You've already told me who said what," I reasoned. "I just want to get the quotes straight. I need to copy them verbatim."

Most senators were horrified at the suggestion, but a few gave me a peek at their secret transcripts. When verbatim excerpts began appearing in the column, howls of anguish and outrage reverberated in the backrooms on Capitol Hill. To plug the leaks, congressional leaders eventually stopped entrusting members of Congress with anything classified. The members were required, thereafter, to do their classified reading in designated committee rooms under watchful eyes. Nevertheless, I managed to persuade a few risk takers to copy excerpts for me.

Though I was free to sniff out stories wherever my nose led me, I began to concentrate on the Senate and the Pentagon. I approached the generals the same way I had the senators—by developing contacts, cajoling them to tell me forbidden stories, and then twisting arms to get the classified documentation.

Increasingly, I was able to peer under the secrecy stamps where the scandals had been swept. Classified documents not only told the story but also provided official evidence. A person's words could always be questioned, but a government document was as irrefutable as the scarlet "A" on Hester Prynne's chest.

Yet even Drew was apprehensive about my forays into this subterranean world of half light, where all information bore the mark of national security. He didn't mind skewering the foe with words and witnesses, but he was skittish when I began bringing him government documents stamped Secret. Before too long, however, both of us clearly detected a pattern of secrecy that was being used to protect scoundrels in high places. For every legitimate national security document, dozens of classified labels were being affixed to paperwork that was merely embarrassing, unsavory, or downright illegal.

ON A MONDAY NIGHT, JUNE 26, 1950, President Harry Truman notified a highly selective "war cabinet," including the Joint Chiefs of Staff, that he planned to launch a limited war against North Korea. He would make the announcement, he said, at noon the following day. I arrived at the Pentagon Tuesday morning about nine o'clock. At the office of a high-ranking source, I detected a buzz of excitement.

"What's going on?" I inquired.

The source glanced around to make sure no one could overhear him. "The president is going to declare war on North Korea," he said in a low voice. "We'll intervene with air power. The president will announce it at noon."

I couldn't reach Drew who was on a plane somewhere in the friendly skies. On my own, I called our radio network, ABC, and told them to break the story.

"We can't do that on your word," said a nervous news director.

"Then attribute the story to Drew."

The network broadcast the news, attributing it emphatically to Drew just in case it should turn out to be a bum steer. That meant I had to reach Drew before anyone else did, or he might unknowingly repudiate his own scoop. I called the airline and persuaded them to deliver an urgent message to Drew in flight. "Tell him to call Jack Anderson as soon as he lands before he speaks to anyone else."

Drew obeyed the instructions. "What's up?" he asked.

"You just announced that we're going to war," I said.

"I did not!" he protested, thinking someone had grossly misquoted him.

"I did it in your name." I explained the particulars. "You have just scooped the president."

"Good. Good," he said.

Throughout the Korean War, my access to military secrets caused constant panic inside the Pentagon. I wrote stories about military screwups that caused a frenzy of investigations to find my sources. On one occasion, top brass from every branch of the service were summoned to a strategy meeting to discuss how to stop me. Someone suggested keeping a tail on me from the moment I entered the Pentagon. But an army major general spoke up. "Has anyone counted the number of doors in the Pentagon?" he asked. "Are we going to keep our entire security force waiting at the doors on the chance that Jack Anderson might come through one of them?" The assembly agreed it was unworkable, and the major general breathed a sigh of relief. He was one of my Pentagon sources, and he did not want military gumshoes following me to his office from the main entrance facing the Potomac River, the only door I ever used.

As an apprentice to Drew, I quickly learned that things were done differently in Washington from the way I was trained in Salt Lake City. I had been reared in the tradition of objective journalism, but there was nothing objective about Drew Pearson. Never satisfied with merely bombarding

WAKE ISLAND

THERE WAS BAD BLOOD BETWEEN DREW Pearson and General Douglas MacArthur going as far back as the 1930s when MacArthur sued Drew for libel. The general wisely dropped the suit when his ex-mistress gave Drew a bundle of their love letters.

Drew's mistrust of MacArthur never ebbed, and he kept up his written assaults on the general during the Korean War. I tapped my sources at the Pentagon to find out the truth behind MacArthur's image-making machine. Our big scoop came after the Wake Island Conference between MacArthur and President Truman in October of 1950, the only face-to-face encounter between the two men.

MacArthur had pressed Truman for approval to move his ground war over the 38th parallel into North Korea. That accomplished, the general began needling the president for what MacArthur saw as the next logical step—a sweep right up to the Yalu River, on the other side of which loomed China. MacArthur wanted to rattle his saber at the Chinese, but Truman feared the reaction of a nation that had infinite layers of troops and measured its wars in decades.

Truman flew to Wake Island to tell MacArthur to leave China alone, or so he claimed. Their meeting lasted half a day, and when Truman left, he gave the impression that he had set MacArthur straight. MacArthur, however, pushed on to the Yalu River, occupying a forty-mile zone on the North Korean side, which included several hydroelectric projects that supplied Manchuria. MacArthur, who fancied himself an expert on the Asian mind, miscalculated the Chinese reaction. Hundreds of thousands of Chinese troops swept across the Korean peninsula and pushed the American forces south.

I puzzled over what had happened at Wake Island that led MacArthur to make this terrible mistake. In January of 1951, I began in earnest to find out what had gone on there behind closed doors. What I learned was that the doors had not been completely shut. Truman had ordered that a stenographer be stationed behind a door left ajar so that she could take down, verbatim, everything the general and the president said. As it turned out, the general had done all the talking and the president had rolled over.

A colonel in the Pentagon slipped me a copy of the transcript. I confess that while my eyes saw a major news story of undeniable public interest, my mind was registering Pulitzer prize. The story did win the coveted prize, but not for me. Three months after Drew and I published the essence of the transcript in one short column, the New York Times did an ambitious series of stories on the same thing, and they won the Pulitzer.

the beaches, Drew had to wade ashore and plant the flag. And he expected me to do the same.

Often I found myself playing the role of reporter-advocate, one who makes the news, reports it, and then manipulates the outcome. Drew got a tip that an appointee to the Federal Communications Commission, Robert Jones, had once been a member of the Black Legion, the Ohio stepchild of the Ku Klux Klan. On the basis of that tip and a few vague intimations, Drew hurried up to Capitol Hill, got himself sworn in as a witness at the confirmation hearing, and announced to the startled assembly that Jones was a bigot, a racist, and an anti-Semite.

Jones leaped to his feet, denied everything, and called Drew an unmitigated liar—much to Drew's chagrin. He had expected Jones to make excuses for his past, perhaps even defend the Black Legion or, at the very least, issue a demure "no comment." During a recess in the hearing, Drew summoned me to the corridor with an assignment. I was to hop the next train to Jones's hometown, Lima, Ohio, and scare up somebody, anybody, who could testify to the truth of the charges Drew had already laid out.

I was back four days later with three good ol' boys from Ohio in tow. They weren't choir boys, but each of them claimed to have belonged to the Black Legion when Jones was alleged to have been an active member. In my haste to find witnesses, I had no time to check their bona fides. In that I erred grievously, especially since the opposition was much more thorough.

My first witness took the stand and, awestruck by the array of power brokers before him, instantly forgot everything except his wife's admonition before he had left home to keep his mouth shut. My second witness's memory was intact, including his admission under cross-examination that he was a convicted forger. My third witness stood his ground and gave explicit details about how he personally had inducted Jones into the Black Legion. With equal conviction under cross-examination, he admitted that he had once been confined to an Ohio hospital for the insane after shooting a man.

The next witness was me. Despite the battering our side had taken, I still sat in awe of the congressional process. After all, this was the Congress of the United States. The only testimony I was prepared to give, therefore, was "Yes, sir" and "No, sir." But that wasn't what Drew had in mind. He yanked me aside moments before I took the stand and said tersely, "You've got to raise hell with them. We can't let these hypocrites piss on us like that, Jack." In an instant, I was transformed from an awestruck Utah boy to Drew Pearson's attack dog. I remember a few of my words—"whitewash," and "bias," and something like "it takes a thief to catch a thief"—in defense of my three sorry witnesses.

I was gaveled into silence in middiatribe, and the hearing ended. Jones was confirmed unanimously by the Senate, and Drew patted me on the back for doing my best. That was my first real taste of Drew Pearson journalism. Although I became more comfortable with advocacy as the years went on, it never fit me quite as well as it did Drew.

Of all our early crusades, the most gratifying was an all-out assault on Senator Joe McCarthy. Contrary to popular theology, there is nothing that produces as much exhilaration and zest for living as an ugly, protracted, bitter-end vendetta that rages for years and comes close to ruining both sides. In the early 1950s, I was caught up in Drew's mortal feud with McCarthy. For me, this was not only a crusade but also a redemption. I must now confess that for a short while I had supported McCarthy.

For a tumultuous and ravaging decade, the fanatics of the right un-leashed a national witch-hunt for suspected Communists. McCarthy was their Witchfinder-General. This became a guerrilla war that had begun be-fore McCarthy's "ism" thundered across the land. It was fought on so many fronts and smashed so many careers that I can attempt no ambitious his-torical project here. Rather, I will merely recount some of the highlights of my own involvement.

I had helped to defrock McCarthy's most notorious predecessor, Con-gressman J. Parnell Thomas, the House UnAmerican Activities Committee chairman who conducted a political inquisition that terrorized Hollywood. It is scarcely credible today that such a figure could wield the power to dominate the news, wreck careers, and cause moviemakers to grovel in fear. But indeed he did, and they did. The motion picture industry was almost totally intimidated by Thomas's blustering, and to appease him, instituted the blacklist that would spread to broadcasting and degrade the entertain-ment world for a decade to come.

Thomas was an improbable archvillain who would never have been cast by Hollywood in that role. He was obese, ballooning over the arms of his chair like a cartoon caricature of glutted triumph. He had a bald head and a round face that glowed perpetually in a pink flush. The eyes were small, or perhaps they only seemed small, encroached upon as they were by fat cheeks.

While he was rummaging through the closets of movie moguls in a frenzied search for Communists, I got a glimpse into Thomas's own private closet. It contained some skeletons that he had taken pains to lock up. He had been putting people on his congressional payroll who had never worked there a day in their lives. What's more, he was taking a generous portion of their federal salaries in the form of kickbacks. I learned about this in 1948 through the help of a woman scorned.

Thomas, at sixty-three, fancied himself a ladies man and was lavishing his attentions on a young woman in his office, much to the dismay of his

MEETING MY MATCH

AFTER TWO YEARS IN WASHINGTON LIVING the bachelor life, I spotted Olivia Farley in church. My friend saw her first and sidled quickly over to introduce himself. I followed at a respectable but noticeable distance. When Olivia gave my friend a chilly reception, he filled the awkward silence by introducing her to me. The air became slightly warmer.

I wasted no time in telling her what I did for a living. She was not impressed, so I dropped some names of big shots that I mingled with. She was not dazzled. I soon learned that Libby, as she is called, was an unusual Washington woman, unimpressed by any show of wealth, power, or influence. She puts herself on equal footing with the mailman and the president of the United States, and each gets the same degree of attention from her.

Despite my bumbling overtures, Libby liked me. A few months later, while Libby and I were touring New York City with my mother, I popped the question. The way Libby remembers it, I said, "My mother likes you. Will you marry me?"

Our union was the cause of consternation for J. Edgar Hoover. Libby had come to Washington to escape the coal-mining region of West Virginia. Like many young women of her day, she ended up in a low-level job at the FBI. Hoover was fond of recruiting young women from the boondocks as worker bees in his massive bureaucracy.

From the moment we were married, Libby was under covert surveillance by her bosses to make sure that nothing ever fell into her hands that would be of interest to me. Since she worked in the fingerprint section, that was highly unlikely. The FBI itself was responsible for her only leak. One day Libby was asked by sheer coincidence to fetch a certain fingerprint file and deliver it to higher-ups in the agency. The file held the fingerprints of none other than Drew Pearson, and the superiors to whom she dutifully delivered it immediately regretted the messenger. The number-four man in the FBI, Stan Tracy, summoned Libby to his office. Tracy just happened to be an acquaintance of ours from the small Mormon congregation in Washington. With feigned nonchalance, he assured Libby that the review of Drew's fingerprint file was routine. Then he added, "You understand that what happens here can't be repeated outside." In other words, don't tell your husband.

When Libby got home that evening, she immediately told me everything. We were never able to determine why the FBI was interested in Drew's fingerprints. From then until the time Libby quit the FBI to stay home with our children, she was under constant surveillance on the job.

older secretary, Helen Campbell. Miss Campbell had devoted her life to waiting on Thomas and had fallen in love with him, in unreasonable expectation that her affections would one day be returned. One night when Thomas offered to drive Miss Campbell's young rival home from work, the heartsick secretary followed them. Helen watched as Thomas was invited into the young woman's apartment, and then waited in vain for him to emerge. She finally went home, despondent, but awakened before sunrise to resume her vigil. Thomas's car was still parked outside the young woman's apartment building.

Helen was willing to give her man the benefit of the doubt, hoping that perhaps Thomas had left the young woman at a decent hour and returned gallantly in the morning to give her a ride to work. If that was the case, then the car's engine would be warm. Helen stepped from her own car and touched the hood of his. It was stone cold.

Miss Campbell went to the office, where she began assembling information on the irregular payroll practices. She took her evidence to a congressional insider who eventually brought the story to me, and Thomas went to prison for eighteen months. The unemployed Miss Campbell found a new job, as a secretary to Drew Pearson, and McCarthy took up the cause of the far right that Thomas had dropped.

From the beginning, Drew had McCarthy labeled: "McCarthy's a bad man," he would say without embellishment. But I was slow to see McCarthy's dark side. From the day I began investigating scandals on Capitol Hill, McCarthy's door was always open to me.

Like others, he courted me to curry Drew's favor. Sometimes, when we were alone in his office and his secretary would announce a call from a bigger name than myself, Joe would wave the call away. "I can't take any calls. I'm talking to Jack. Tell them I've gone to China." On other occasions, he would take calls and put me on the extension while he pumped his colleagues or government officials for information that I needed. Once I asked him what had occurred in a key policy committee session behind closed doors. "I missed the meeting, but I'll find out," he said conspiratorially. Then he picked up the phone, called Senator Robert Taft, and motioned for me to pick up the extension while the two men went over the details of the meeting. As far as Taft knew, it was a senator-to-senator conversation.

Joe had all the tail-wagging appeal of a tramp dog. When he scurried down the halls of the Capitol with his white-haired and more senatorlike aide Ray Kiermas at his side, tourists would say, "Hello, Senator," to Kiermas. Far from offended, Joe took great delight in the mistake.

From time to time, Joe tried to coax me into joining him on double dates. I would beg off, secretly fearing that my meager finances and Mormon abstemiousness would keep me out of his league. Our relationship flourished nonetheless, and I became a familiar figure in the inner sanctum of his office. When I married Olivia Farley in 1949, he came to my wedding. But four years later when he wed his secretary Jean Kerr, I was not invited. Our friendship was one of the early casualties of McCarthyism.

McCarthy launched the era that came to be known by his name on February 9, 1950, at a meeting of the Ohio County Republican Women's Club in Wheeling, West Virginia. Intuition told McCarthy that Americans, spooked by the specter of communism, were looking for a standard-bearer, and he decided to nominate himself in Wheeling. Waving a closed file, McCarthy claimed to have in it the names of 205 State Department employees who were known Communists. If he weren't rushing to catch a plane, he explained, he would have taken the time to read the list aloud. In the days to follow, McCarthy repeated the charge while his message picked up steam in the press. The number was flexible, owing to the fact that there was no list in the file. He admitted as much to me upon his return from his barnstorming. He urged me to search Drew Pearson's investigative files for leads on Communists in high places.

Now I come to the part that I would like to leave out of my autobiography. But when a reporter makes a mistake, no matter how garish, he has an obligation to come clean. Unlike politicians who put a spin on the facts, reporters should honor the facts and oppose the spinning.

It is a fact, a most awkward and embarrassing fact, that I searched Drew's files for information that might help my friend Joe. I turned over to McCarthy raw files on two high officials. Oh yes, I told him the information had not been verified and needed careful investigation. But deep in my gut, I knew what I didn't want to admit to myself; I knew Drew was right about Joe McCarthy. Drew had X-ray eyes that could see right through most politicians. He reserved a simple sentence for the most contemptuous among them. From the time he first laid his eyes on McCarthy, Drew told me: "He's a bad man."

And bad he turned out to be. But I lacked Drew's X-ray vision; the McCarthy I knew was quite different from the ogre that later emerged. I also owed him, and Drew granted limited immunity to news sources. I was slow to admit that Joe had exceeded the limits. Nor did his anti-Communist crusade offend me at first. I assured myself that I was as eager as Joe to ferret out spies and traitors. If they were undermining our government from the inside, that was headline news. Yet I sensed it was the headlines, not the spies, that Joe was pursuing. The bottom line: He was an unprincipled senator but also a valuable informant who would share any confidence with me. I simply didn't want to lose him as a source.

I was also slow to recognize that Joe had become a national menace. He did not fit the image of the charismatic demagogue astride a white horse. As a speaker, he was unpolished. His Irish baritone under stress would soar up into a whine. He would plow into his text with earnest ferocity, scowling and stalking and waving his arms. He would rummage through papers as he spoke, as if his documentation was so overwhelming that he just couldn't locate the right piece of paper. He had a gift for straightforward deviousness, with deliberate stumbling and bumbling that was mistaken for sincerity.

For the first ten days of McCarthyism, I waited with growing uneasiness for him to present his case, which he promised to do on February 20, 1950. Drew didn't wait. In withering columns, he accused McCarthy of trumping up charges against innocent public servants. The red-letter day came, and I gathered with others in the Senate and listened with horror as McCarthy began to flesh out his allegations. Although he named no names during that first round, I recognized one of his subversives. Clearly, he had lifted the charges from a file I had given him. It was equally clear that McCarthy had done absolutely nothing to verify the raw tips in the file. Back at the office, I told Drew I was ready to join his battle to bring down this particular bad man.

McCarthy proved to be a formidable foe, both in and out of print. One evening McCarthy cornered Drew in the cloakroom of the exclusive Sulgrave Club. As Drew later described it, McCarthy "proceeded to use his knee in the accepted manner of the waterfront." Drew claimed McCarthy dealt him two blows to the groin, but that it didn't hurt. Richard Nixon pulled the two men apart. "If I hadn't pulled McCarthy away," Nixon said, "he might have killed Pearson." McCarthy later claimed he was deluged with congratulatory calls and letters from fellow members of Congress. Among those commenting on the fisticuffs was Harry Truman who said he "enjoyed seeing those two skunks piss on each other."

While we churned out columns discrediting McCarthy and his Red-baiting, he added Drew to his list of subversives and by December was calling my boss an outright spy for the Soviet Union. As a result, Drew lost his radio sponsor, Adam Hats, and newspapers began dropping the column, but Drew would not back down. He gave me time off to write a book about McCarthy, sealing my place at the top of Joe's hate list. When McCarthy learned I was researching the book in his home state, he confronted me. "I hear you've been going around Wisconsin posing as my friend," he said.

"Joe, I thought I was your friend," I replied.

My last encounter with him came one day as I was waiting for the Senate elevator. McCarthy strode up and pushed the call button three times, the signal to the operator that a Senator was waiting. When the elevator arrived and the door opened, McCarthy stepped in and motioned me to stay back. "You wait for the next elevator, Jack. I don't want you stinking up this one."

In the end, it took the United States Army to face down Joe McCarthy, and it took several swift kicks in the butt to move the army. I supplied the boot, and Drew furnished the foot.

IT BEGAN WITH THE MODEST DISCOVERY that two of McCarthy's aides on the Government Operations Committee had never served in the military, although both were twenty-six years old and the Korean War had been raging for three years. One of them was Roy Cohn, the committee's chief counsel who was destined to become a high-priced Manhattan lawyer and one of Washington's legendary movers and shakers. But under McCarthy, he was just a cocky young man who avoided the draft as a member of the inactive reserves. The second aide, almost always at Cohn's side, was David Schine, who had used a variety of excuses to keep one step ahead of the draft. We published the excuses and within two months, David Schine, the son of a millionaire and a habitué of trendy nightclubs, was Private Schine.

McCarthy was annoyed, but Cohn was devastated. He pulled strings trying to get Schine commissioned as an officer, but without success. Cohn did what he could to make the army easier for Schine, getting him out of much of basic training, arranging leave, and exempting him from KP. But Cohn's frenzied campaign to cushion Schine reached a climax when Cohn threatened to use McCarthy's power to have the secretary of the army fired.

For eight months we hammered McCarthy and his "katzenjammer kids," as we derisively called them. Column after column spelled out the petty details of Schine's military malingering and the complicity of superpatriot Joseph McCarthy. Finally, the army released its own report of McCarthy's improper interventions, and a cry went up for a Senate investigation. Thus were born the Army-McCarthy Hearings, which ended in December of 1954 when the Senate voted to condemn McCarthy for what he had done.

He stayed in the Senate for another four years, now and then churning the waters and spouting small geysers. But like Moby Dick, he bore deep in his vitals the mortal wounds from a dozen harpoons. The last one, fired by his colleagues, really finished him off. The repudiation of the Senate crushed his spirit. He became a hunched, shuffling man, alternately bloated from alcohol or gaunt from being on the wagon.

Those who had once feared McCarthy or collaborated with him now

ABUSE OF POWER

THE ARMY-McCARTHY HEARINGS IN 1954 RESULTED from the passion of one man, Roy Cohn, to keep another man, David Schine, out of military service with the help of Senator Joseph McCarthy. My reporting uncovered the scheming and led to the hearings that spelled the end of McCarthy's political reign of terror.

But Cohn and I reached a truce and even became cordial after the hearings. His legal career blossomed and his influence in Washington became phenomenal. Cohn's private life was none of my business because it didn't slop over into his public life, at least not until 1986 when my partner Dale Van Atta brought me a tip from a source; Cohn was dying of AIDS.

It was an unsavory story, one that I would not have done about an ordinary private citizen. But Cohn had never been ordinary. The mean-spirited Cohn was still in the public limelight for his celebrated legal career, which had ended in shame with disbarment for "dishonesty, fraud, deceit, and misrepresentation." Court testimony, for example, claimed that Cohn wronged an eighty-four-year-old multimillionaire client who was nearly blind, partly paralyzed, semi-comatose, and drugged. Cohn had allegedly gone to the man's deathbed and induced him to sign documents naming Cohn trustee of his estate. Cohn told the man the documents were related to his divorce. When caught, Cohn threw himself on the mercy of the court, claiming he had a life-threatening disease.

The rumor of Cohn's disease had already been aired by *60 Minutes,* but without the kind of evidence that Dale had brought me. Dale obtained Cohn's medical records from a friend of a friend on the medical team. They contained incontrovertible proof that Cohn had AIDS. The disease was just beginning to gain notoriety and most of its victims shunned any public acknowledgment of it because of the "homosexual" label that accompanied the illness in those early days.

I was tempted to let my old enemy Cohn die in peace until Dale told me the details. Always the manipulator, Cohn had apparently pulled strings in the Reagan administration to get on a list of only twenty-eight people to be given the experimental drug AZT that was then being tested by the National Institutes of Health. Of the 10,500 people who were then dying from AIDS and desperate for some relief, Roy Cohn had managed to get himself classed with the privileged few. The rest of the victims had to beg, borrow, or steal if they wanted AZT.

Sealing my resolve on the story was additional information from Cohn's medical file that he was balking at the notion that he should adopt a celibate lifestyle to curb spread of his disease. Publicly, Cohn was telling everyone he had liver cancer, not the highly contagious, sexually transmitted AIDS. And he was threatening to sue anyone who said otherwise.

I was criticized for revealing the truth about Cohn's virus, a virus that eventually killed him. Many readers wrote that I had wrongly violated Cohn's privacy by quoting from his medical file. NIH briefly considered prosecuting Dale and me. The *New York Times* published essentially the same story a few days after we did, attributing Cohn's favored position on the NIH list to direct White House intervention. But the staid *Times* didn't take near the criticism Dale and I did. I believed then as now that Cohn's final abuse of power was the public's business and transcended any right he had to keep his medical records private.

shunned him. At a Republican political rally in Wisconsin, he came uninvited to the dais to register his support for the man of the hour, then Vice President Richard Nixon. This was McCarthy's home ground; as senior senator from Wisconsin, he was entitled to a seat next to Nixon. But he was asked delicately to leave so as not to embarrass the vice president. A reporter who followed McCarthy outside later told me that the senator sat down on a curbstone and wept bitterly.

Drew Pearson wasn't the only newsman who fought McCarthy; others contributed to his downfall. Establishment journalists have given most credit to one of their own, Edward R. Murrow, who truly was a giant among broadcasters. But Drew battled McCarthy in the trenches more than a year before Murrow launched his first air attack. I'll leave it to McCarthy to identify by his actions the newsman he feared the most. He tried to destroy Drew, assailing him as a Soviet agent, attacking his radio sponsor, and driving him off the ABC network. McCarthy hardly roughed up Murrow. Drew also paid my salary and expenses while I researched and wrote the book that became the bible of the anti-McCarthy movement. There was one final item of evidence. Visitors reported that McCarthy kept in his bedroom a baseball bat with the name "Drew Pearson" engraved on it—a name that signified the bat's intended use.

JOE MCCARTHY, WHO HAD DOMINATED THE early 1950s, was followed in the late 1950s by a parade of lesser rascals. In 1959, Drew called me into his office to discuss one of them. "Lewis Strauss is a bad man," Drew announced.

I winced inwardly. I knew what this meant; Drew was girding up for another mortal battle. Strauss was President Dwight Eisenhower's nominee to be Commerce secretary, subject to Senate confirmation. Drew would expect me, as his legman in the Senate, to run a campaign against Strauss. I would be asked to pull backstage wires, to manipulate senators, to make news rather than report it. I sensed that I would soon be knee-deep in things that journalists should never do. I could persuade myself that we were justified in waging unconditional war against McCarthy. But Strauss? I did not consider him a national menace.

Drew got right to the point; he wanted to know whether we could block his confirmation. "Not a chance," I advised. Strauss had served five presidents of both parties. Two of his appointments had required confirmation, which the Senate had overwhelmingly granted. He had now attained elder-statesman status. His competence had never been questioned. And he was the choice of a popular president; no Cabinet nominee had been rejected by the Senate in almost half a century. "Why don't you just write a couple columns and get it off your chest?" I suggested hopefully. Even as I said it, I knew it wouldn't be enough for Drew.

"There's one slim chance," I ventured hesitantly. "If you could get Lyndon Johnson's support, you might get a shot at Strauss. But you'd have to make a deal to lay off Lyndon, and I don't think you want to do that."

Drew had been a thorn in the Senate leader's side, calling him "Landslide Lyndon" in honor of his eighty-seven-vote margin of victory in his first Senate race, then changing the nickname to "Lying Down Lyndon" because of his failure to support Drew's liberal agenda.

In the silence that followed my mention of a deal, a sly smile crept beneath Drew's mustache. "Lyndon Johnson is a fellow I like to make peace with," he paused, "frequently."

I told him I couldn't be a party to a deal he had no intention of keeping. He agonized for a few moments. "All right," he said with a heavy sigh. "It would be worth it. I'll keep the deal. Go talk to Lyndon."

I had established a good working relationship with Johnson only because I had been able to convince him that his bad press in our column was Drew's fault and not mine. He curried my favor, hoping to win over Drew.

"How would you like to get Drew Pearson off your back?" I asked Johnson when I walked into his office.

"Who do I have to kill?"

"Lewis Strauss."

Johnson's ample jowls drooped in disappointment. "Oh, no. Oh, no. That's impossible. I agree with Drew, Strauss is a terrible man. But we have a tradition that if the president wants to choose an SOB, he's entitled to choose his own SOB."

"Okay," I said, rising from my chair. "I just thought I'd try." I proceeded as slowly as decorum would allow toward the door and had my hand on the knob when I heard a sigh behind me.

"Sure would like to get Drew off my back." I waited. "Tell Drew I'll see if I can work something out."

It wasn't enough, and I knew Drew wouldn't accept it. "Senator, it's not enough to just try. I know you have the power to do this and I'm obliged to keep an eye on you for Drew."

"I'll try," Johnson said.

"And I'll watch."

Strauss was defeated, and Johnson suddenly became "Likeable Lyndon" in the Drew Pearson column.

CHAPTER 4

IN MY PRIME, THE *COLUMBIA JOURNALISM REVIEW,* the holy writ of journalism, called me the "King of the Muckrakers." I was a mere pretender. The true king—long live his memory—was the courageous, the outrageous, the oft-damned and be-damned Drew Pearson.

In my twenty-three years as Drew Pearson's employee and then partner, I watched him aggressively pursue scoundrels in high places, while remaining a gentle, compassionate man who was true to his pacifist Quaker upbringing. The Drew Pearson the world knew was the merciless enemy of thieves, perjurers, chiselers, scoundrels, and predators, a man who could step over the line of reason if he believed the cause was just. But the Drew Pearson I came to know balanced that courage with compassion. He passionately believed that public office was a public trust, and with his own brand of personal journalism, he went after the corrupt, the incompetent, and the pompous. Yet, even in the middle of his assaults on those he had found doing wrong, he felt enormous sympathy for them as human beings.

President Harry Truman in 1949 publicly referred to Drew as an "SOB," an epithet Drew liked to translate as "Servant of Brotherhood." Soon after Truman's outburst, Drew received a letter at his office addressed only to "The SOB" with no city specified. It was correctly delivered to Drew's office.

A call from Drew Pearson was a dreaded thing during his heyday. But if that call came on December 13, Drew's birthday, the recipient was in for a surprise. Drew made a practice of using his birthday to right old wrongs and heal old wounds between himself and those about whom he had written during the year. He would call to apologize if he had erred in telling some-one's story, but he would also call to offer help and support to people whom he had justifiably skewered.

I always maintained a healthy fear of and respect for Drew, who remained larger than life for me no matter how close I got to him as a friend and colleague. He had a habit of sniffing before he began a sentence. The only jump start I needed in my workday was to pick up the phone and hear that telltale sniff on the other end of the line. My co-worker Fred Blumenthal knew how the sniff affected me. Fred would call me and do nothing but sniff lightly. "Drew?" I would reply, as all the nerves in my body jumped to attention. "Is that you?"

Our partnership became a smooth-working machine over the years, in part because I was able to disregard his celebrity when necessary. At staff meetings when Drew announced which stories we should be working on, he would always call on me last for my opinion. The feedback from most of the staffers reflected the awe with which they regarded Drew. But when my turn came, I would tell him frankly whether something was a good idea, and he would listen. He knew that "yes" from a yes man didn't mean anything.

We were opposites in many ways, but our differences generally seemed to enhance our working relationship. Drew was the country squire with the gentleman's farm on the Potomac and the brownstone in Georgetown, where the capital's glitterati gathered. I lived in the suburbs with Libby and the clutter of, eventually, nine children. Drew relished his role as dinner host to Cabinet members and heads of state. My idea of a big evening was a movie and popcorn. Drew had a butler and cook. If I had brought home a senator or secretary of state for dinner, my egalitarian Libby probably would have made sandwiches for him.

Drew started his day at 8 A.M. by merely walking through the door that separated living quarters from office. I usually didn't arrive until 10 or 11 A.M. because I worked late into the night and spent the mornings at home polishing my copy. "It would help me if you could get here at eight-thirty or nine so I can get my day started," Drew told me late one morning when I dropped my copy on his desk.

"Yes, sir. You're the boss." I replied. "But if I come in at eight-thirty, I'll have to leave at five. If I have to punch the clock, then I'm going to punch it both directions."

"Okay, okay," Drew groused. "You've made your point. Come in whenever you want to."

In my early years with Drew I enjoyed the benefits of anonymity. Drew's practice was to have his byline on the top of each column, no matter which reporter had done the legwork. We never got credit in print. That was fine with me because, as a faceless legman, I could go about my business without setting off alarms on Capitol Hill. Drew could barely walk into the Capitol

WARREN WHO?

DREW PEARSON COUNTED PRESIDENTS AMONG HIS closest friends, yet I never felt comfortable hobnobbing with the prey. I'm possibly one of the only top reporters in Washington who has never been invited to a state dinner at the White House, a circumstance that gives me some satisfaction.

President George Bush once attempted to invite me to lunch. My assistant, Opal Ginn, familiar with my mistrust of reporters who socialize with their subjects, declined the invitation, relayed by Press Secretary Marlin Fitzwater, without even asking me. "I'm sorry, Mr. Fitzwater," she said with her native Georgian courtesy. "Mister Anderson will be out of the city at a speaking engagement."

My staffers never let Opal forget that she had turned down the president so as not to disappoint a group of midwestern Rotarians.

In the end, although I would have enjoyed lunching at the White House and swapping lofty ideas with the president, it did not fit the role in which I had cast myself. Drew had taught me to be the voice of the voiceless and the champion of the underdog. I knew I was in danger of forgetting my constituency if I allowed myself to breathe the heady air of the Olympian heights.

I've never been comfortable with the Hollywood crowd either. Any given soiree at the Pearson home was likely to be graced by one or more Hollywood celebrities. Knowing of my distaste for formal occasions, Drew rarely invited me to his parties. He probably saved us both the embarrassment of having me draw a blank when I was introduced to someone I should have recognized.

I bluffed my way through one such encounter on the telephone. It began when my secretary Robin Reynolds rushed breathlessly into my office. "Jack, Warren Beatty's on the phone!" I took the call and we chatted for about twenty minutes on some now-forgotten issue that the actor was championing. He invited me to lunch with him in New York the next time I was there, and I accepted. After I hung up, I turned to my still-breathless secretary. "Robin, who is Warren Beatty?" With disgust, she enlightened me.

Sometime after that, Beatty graciously invited me and my wife to the premier of one of his films. Libby avoids such occasions, so I took my teenage daughter, Tanya, in her place. After the screening, we were mingling in the lobby with other guests when Beatty spotted me across the room. "Hey, Jack!" he waved. Tanya was rendered speechless to think that her old dad knew Warren Beatty.

I once embarrassed myself in front of a friend when we passed Robert Redford on a Washington street. "Hi, Jack," the actor said as he passed. "Hi," I responded as I searched my mind for a name to attach to this vaguely familiar face. My companion recognized my blank look. "That was Robert Redford," he whispered.

Fortunately, I had a chance later to redeem myself when I invited Redford to a banquet at which the Drew Pearson Foundation was honoring *Washington Post* reporters Carl Bernstein and Bob Woodward for their work on the Watergate story. Redford had played Woodward in the movie adaptation of their book *All the President's Men*, and he graciously agreed to be a part of the event. Sitting with him at the head table, I noticed that Redford wasn't eating anything. "Is there something wrong with the food," I discreetly asked him. "I can't stand to chew with three hundred people watching me," he replied. I looked around the room, and sure enough, every eye in the place was on Redford.

without his name rebounding from office to office. But I could sit comfortably in the dining hall and listen to other reporters (oblivious to the presence of one of Drew's worker bees) gossip about my boss.

Eventually, though, all work for no credit lost its shine. My first showdown with Drew came when he took out a full-page newspaper ad to blame me for a mistake. It began when a source told me that a juvenile offender had been carelessly locked up with hardened adult criminals in the same Kentucky jail cell. I took the source's word for it and wrote a column. Then I learned that the young offender was actually being held in an adjoining cell.

For the mistake, Drew took a beating from several Kentucky newspapers and felt obliged to buy an advertisement in the *Louisville Courier-Journal*, one of his most important clients, to tell his side of the story. The ad included a reference to me by name as the underling responsible for the goof. He let me review the ad copy before he sent it to Kentucky, and I decided to lay down the law. "If you run that ad pointing out my mistake, then you'll also have to include in the ad all the major scoops I've given you that you didn't give me credit for."

He was angry, because he knew I was right. "You've got a point," he said. And he crossed my name out of the ad.

Our second showdown came in 1954 when, on a matter of principle, I quit the Washington Merry-Go-Round. Drew had taken on another columnist, Tris Coffin, as an associate. Word came to me from Fred Blumenthal that Tris was calling himself Drew's heir to the column. Fred had seen the evidence in some memos he'd read while snooping around Drew's desk. I was happy to play second fiddle to Drew, but not to Tris Coffin whom I judged to be a producer of fluff. I confronted Drew and he confirmed the news that Tris indeed had been promised the Washington Merry-Go-Round byline when Drew retired. "Fine," I said. "You have my two-week's notice."

During that two weeks while Drew stewed over the problem, I found another job, as Washington bureau chief for *Parade* magazine. With time running out, Drew came to me and said he had made a mistake. I could keep the new job with *Parade*. In time, he said, he would put my name on the byline with his, and when he retired, the operation would be mine if I wanted it. I held on to both jobs, with *Parade* paying me more than twice what Drew did, but I always considered the column my first priority.

I figured if I was going to succeed the great Drew Pearson, I should have the benefit of his accumulated wisdom. Ready to absorb all he could offer in the way of advice, I made an appointment with him, sat down in his office, and prepared for enlightenment. "Write a good column," he said. That was all.

Our differences as reporters were marked. Drew was forever meddling in affairs of state, needling congressmen to do his bidding, even writing speeches for them to deliver on the floor. He believed that to get the job done he must intrude during all phases of the battle. Not only would he expose the abuse, he would hound the tribunal until it investigated, instruct witnesses on their testimony, propagandize the galleries, help draft the remedial legislation, and write a popular history of the affair.

I developed a ready apology for my news sources who complained about how their words were twisted when they appeared in the column. Drew would take the facts that I gave him and mold them to suit his own vision. His convictions were strongly held, and if the powers of hell were to rise up against him and those convictions, he would take on hell, using whatever ammunition he could squeeze from his version of the truth. Drew did not intentionally lie, but he was capable of serious hyperbole and omissions of the truth when it suited his agenda. Those times when his critics came closest to nailing him for stretching the facts were also the times when Drew's stories grew into legitimate blockbusters and his instincts proved correct.

I slowly learned that a columnist does not work under the same set of restrictions as the so-called objective journalist. Drew had a right to express and even shout his opinions. I also learned that objectivity among the rank-and-file reporters is an elusive goal, and that those who profess it are often hiding what should be a matter of public record. Some of the purists even refuse to vote. I not only vote, but will tell anyone who asks whom I voted for and why.

No reporter is free of his or her background. Drew made no secret of the fact that he was a pacifist Quaker and mistrusted most things military.

VINTAGE NIXON

IF RICHARD NIXON HAD DRAFTED HIS "enemies list" in the 1950s, twenty years earlier than he actually did, the names Jack Anderson and Drew Pearson would have been at the top. Drew mistrusted Nixon as he did no other politician. And the more I saw of Nixon, the more I had to agree with my boss.

In 1952, when Nixon was running for vice president with Dwight Eisenhower, we found evidence that as a senator Nixon had allowed an $18,000 slush fund to be set up for him by a group of California businessmen. The money had been intended to supplement his federal salary. I was busy trying to confirm whether Nixon had returned the favor by arranging special treatment for those businessmen when I got a call from my friend Bill Rogers. He had been attorney general for Eisenhower and twenty years later he would be secretary of state in the Nixon cabinet, but in 1952 he was running Nixon's vice-presidential campaign from a railroad car in the old tradition of whistle-stop campaigns. He called me from Montana, and I could tell he was trying to keep his tone apologetic. It had come to Nixon's attention, he said, that Drew and I were about to break the story of the slush fund. "If this story is used, Dick wants Drew to know that he will regard it as an attempt to defeat him, and he will respond accordingly."

Nixon's plan was to expose Drew as a Communist. "It's one thing to have Joe McCarthy attack Drew as being a Communist," Rogers said. "It would be quite another thing to have Richard Nixon go after him."

"Bill, are you sure you want me to deliver that message?" I asked. He did, so I passed the word along to Drew, who responded exactly as I had expected he would. "All right, I'll change the story. I'll make it stronger." Unfortunately he didn't have the chance. Several newspapers broke the story simultaneously before we were ready to go with it, though Nixon managed to wiggle out of it with some fancy verbiage.

Nixon's advisor Murray Chotiner urged Nixon to go on TV and throw himself upon the mercy of the electorate, humbly defending the gifts and money he had received from his personal friends, and stubbornly refusing to return one gift, a cocker spaniel named Checkers. It was shameless pandering and it worked. The Checkers speech was one of Nixon's few shining moments on television.

I learned from him to make no secret of the Mormon philosophy that shaped my thinking and writing—that life is not just a struggle between evil and good but between coercion and freedom.

From the beginning of my service with Drew, I was schooled in the relentless Pearson style. We never conceded the field if there was a sliver of a chance that we could scoop the competition. In retrospect, some of the chases were more memorable than the stories themselves.

In one such chase, the prey was an unassuming and well-intentioned academic, Professor Bernard Schwartz. In 1957, Schwartz was hired by a House committee to investigate the state of regulatory affairs in the federal government. With a Republican, President Eisenhower, in the White House, and Republicans in the majority in Congress, the report was destined to be a whitewash of the administration, but nobody told the earnest Professor Schwartz. He dove enthusiastically into his study and began quietly amassing evidence that federal regulatory agencies were in bed with the industries they were overseeing.

Schwartz was appointed and forgotten, by everyone except me and my friend Clark Mollenhoff, the never-say-die Washington correspondent for the *Des Moines Register*. I pressed my own findings on Schwartz and tried to cajole him into sharing his findings with me exclusively. Mollenhoff did the same. Schwartz demurred at first, but it slowly began to dawn on him that his overseers in Congress were planning to bury his incriminating evidence so deep that it would never see the light of day. When our column began to shed sunshine on Schwartz's information, the meek professor was transformed into an uppity American with a cause. Predictably, the House subcommittee fired him and dispatched U.S. marshals to confiscate his files.

Clark Mollenhoff got there before the marshals and convinced Schwartz to gather up the most important file box he could carry and follow the reporter. One step behind, I was busy getting Drew to call in a favor from his ally in the Senate, Wayne Morse. Morse agreed to meet with Schwartz and accept his files before they were snatched up by the House. I called Schwartz's home and got his wife, who said he had already left for a meeting at the Mayflower Hotel with Senator John Williams. I recognized immediately the hand of Clark Mollenhoff, who had talked his own Senate ally into giving sanctuary to Schwartz and his files.

Trying to remain calm, I asked Mrs. Schwartz if she had a *Congressional Directory*. She did, although she puzzled over the relevance. "Look up John Williams," I told her. "What is his party affiliation?" She drew in her breath. Williams was a Republican, a member of the enemy camp. I didn't bother to tell her that he was also a decent man who would have done right by her husband's files. In my most somber tones, I urged her to call her husband at the Mayflower and tell him to get his files and himself out of that room. I told her Drew Pearson was waiting at his home to deliver the professor and his files into the friendly arms of a Democrat, Wayne Morse. Then I hopped into my car and drove to Drew's, just in time for the arrival of the

THE OLD SOLDIER

DREW AND I WERE NOT WELCOME at the White House during the Eisenhower years. We used the column to remind our readers that with Ike in the White House, the nation had no president of substance. The old soldier viewed the presidency as his due after a distinguished military career. Eisenhower retired to the White House and the golf course the way many generals retire to the corporate boardroom. The American people seemed content to give Ike his due, admiring him for the glories of the past and excusing the laissez-faire of the present.

No matter what we wrote about corruption around Eisenhower, he remained untouched, and almost always unruffled. Once he deigned to respond to our barrage with, "I don't read any newspaper I consider irresponsible, and I consider any newspaper that carries Pearson's column to be irresponsible."

Eisenhower was gracious in retirement on the day in 1962 when he gave me a tour of the Gettysburg battleground, which provided the backdrop to his gentleman's farm in Pennsylvania. It was a remarkable history lesson for me as the former president and consummate soldier recounted details of the Civil War battle with the familiarity of a general on a front-line inspection. The ghosts of the past in faded blues and grays seemed to take form before us as Eisenhower described their battle maneuvers. He watched then as a group of Confederate-capped teenage tourists imagined themselves in the battle. "Kids can come here, get up on a hill, and visualize these events," he said. "The fighting was to save them. This is what I would like them to understand."

As we walked back to the parking lot, I asked Eisenhower what had been the hardest thing about leaving the White House. He said his challenge was to stop worrying about affairs of state as if he were still the head of state who could actually do something about them. "Sometimes," he said, "you have the comforting thought, 'I don't have to. Somebody else does.' But there is some egotism in all of us. I say to myself, 'I can do this better. Why am I not in there fighting?' "

fugitive Schwartz with a very angry Clark Mollenhoff on his tail. I got the files, a gold mine of stories.

Sherman Adams was the biggest name I could find in the files. He was the holier-than-thou chief of staff for President Eisenhower. Some said Adams was the most powerful unelected public official in American history— the puppeteer behind the scenes, the Henry Kissinger of his day. Schwartz had turned up evidence that this previously untouchable icon was on the take, accepting gifts from textile tycoon Bernard Goldfine in exchange for favorable treatment before the Federal Trade Commission. I spent a few months confirming and fleshing out what Schwartz had discovered—a trail of influence-peddling and bribery, including the crowning touch, that both Adams and Eisenhower had been gifted by Goldfine with vicuna fur coats. Eisenhower claimed to have passed his coat along to someone else. Of Adams's conduct, the president said, "What Sherman Adams did was imprudent, but I need him."

Baron Shacklette, my friend and the chief investigator for the House subcommittee that had hired Professor Schwartz in the first place, decided to bug Goldfine's suite at the Sheraton-Carlton Hotel. When Baron invited me to eavesdrop with him, I accepted, giving only slight thought to the propriety of the invitation. I settled in with Shacklette for a long night as he assured me that the bugging device, which listened through the wall, was perfectly legal, like listening at a keyhole without trespassing into the suite.

During the night I called Libby and asked her to drop by to keep us company and bring some sandwiches. She knocked at our door, unaware that a private investigator hired by Goldfine was loitering in the hallway. I opened the door, exposing the room and all its electronic equipment to the detective. I pulled Libby in and slammed the door, but it was too late. Goldfine, wanting to make maximum hay out of this invasion of his privacy, called a press conference on the spot, assembled my colleagues outside the door, and pounded. Shacklette and I had no choice but to let them in.

I made some excuse about how I had simply been invited to someone else's bugging, and if J. Edgar Hoover wanted to invite me to a bugging, I would accept that invitation too. By morning, the press was demanding that Drew suspend me. Instead, he issued a statement: "Jack Anderson, of course, has been imprudent, but I need him."

PART 3

LOST INNOCENCE

1 9 6 0 – 1 9 6 8

WHEN JOHN F. KENNEDY WAS DUE to deliver his inaugural address, I was at the Pentagon pumping a general for information on some now-forgotten story. As the appointed time approached, the general said, "The president's about to be inaugurated. We'd better go watch it." He took me down a hallway and into a back room full of brass watching a small black-and-white TV screen. The other generals didn't see us come in, so I had the advantage of being able to stand at the back of the assembly and gauge their response to the new man in the White House.

Before the address began, I could tell by the cracks I overheard that the group didn't like this young upstart and had no confidence that he would do right by the military. But, as Kennedy moved further into his speech, the atmosphere in the room began to warm. By the time he reached his climax line—"Ask not what your country can do for you"—the electricity was palpable. When Kennedy finished, the generals rose to their feet and applauded the TV set.

Kennedy had ushered in the decade of the sixties, the decade that would make that number forever synonymous with rebellion, renewal, and finally lost innocence.

When Kennedy made his bid for the Democratic presidential nomination in 1960, he was justifiably fearful of the considerable power wielded in print and on the air by Drew Pearson, who was more interested in seeing Senator Lyndon Johnson's name on the ballot.

Drew was no fan of Johnson's in those days, but Kennedy had a big strike against him in Drew's mind. While Drew would never have admitted it to anyone, perhaps not even to himself, I sensed that he didn't want a Catholic in the White House. He harbored a distrust of the power of the Catholic clergy from his days entangled in a libel lawsuit with Father Charles

Coughlin, a notorious right-wing radio priest whom Drew had exposed as the other man in an "alienation-of-affection" divorce case. Coughlin sued and lost, but his followers instigated copycat lawsuits in seventy different jurisdictions. Drew won thirty-five trials before Coughlin's friends called it quits, but, even in victory, Drew was financially drained and distrustful of the Catholic establishment.

Today the fear seems laughable, but in 1960 millions of Americans expected serious papal meddling should the country elect its first Catholic president. JFK overcame the opposition, defeated Johnson for the nomination, and invited Johnson to be his running mate. Before confronting the Republican nominee, Richard Nixon, in the general election, Kennedy hoped to neutralize Drew, so Kennedy came to me and asked whether I could help him. I grandly promised to take care of it, because I knew something Kennedy didn't. Drew would rather put the entire College of Cardinals in the White House than let Nixon occupy the Oval Office.

Two weeks before the Nixon-Kennedy election, we broke the story that Nixon's troublesome brother Donald had "borrowed" $205,000 from billionaire Howard Hughes. Donald wanted to save the Nixon family's fast-food restaurant chain that featured a menu item called "Nixonburgers." Hughes had accepted as collateral for the loan a piece of land owned by Nixon's mother that had been assessed at only $13,000. Donald Nixon never repaid Hughes.

Nixon credited Drew and me for helping to seal his defeat, but the truth is there were plenty of other reasons Americans voted for Kennedy. Not the least of those reasons was Kennedy's youth and vigor. He was the youngest man ever elected president and he promised in his inaugural address to "get the country moving again." The comparisons to Camelot would come later as Kennedy was mythologized in death. But in 1960 it was already obvious he represented a generational change in Washington and the promise of better things to come.

Kennedy didn't live to keep that promise. His biggest blunder came only three months into his presidency in 1961 when he allowed a group of two thousand Cuban exiles trained by the CIA to attempt an overthrow of Marxist leader Fidel Castro. The botched "invasion" at Cuba's Bay of Pigs left Kennedy looking foolish and impulsive. His decision that same year to send U.S. troops into South Vietnam to fight the Communist threat there would only prove disastrous in hindsight.

Ironically, much of what Americans nostalgically credit to Kennedy was actually accomplished by his successor Lyndon Johnson, who left office a broken man. The highlights of Johnson's term—the 1964 Civil Rights Act, his "Great Society" war on poverty, the Clean Air Act, the creation of

Medicare and Medicaid—were overshadowed by his monumental mistakes and outright lies as he micro-managed and escalated the war in Vietnam.

At the time of Kennedy's assassination in 1963, there were 16,000 American troops in Vietnam. When Johnson left office in 1968, there were more than 500,000, all sent without a Congressional declaration of war. And the cost of keeping them there was running $20 billion a year. Patriotism could only carry American sentiment so far before the tide of public opinion turned against the president and, sadly, against the soldiers themselves. In the end, it would take the ubiquitous Richard Nixon to extricate America from the tangled web that Kennedy and Johnson wove.

CHAPTER 5

AFTER THE TORCH WAS PUT TO Adolf Hitler's corpse, his ghost abandoned Germany and settled in Argentina where his most fanatical followers fled. They formed a Nazi underground that spanned the South American continent and reached into its most remote areas. This subterranean network was operated by former Nazi functionaries and toadies—most of them small fry, too inconsequential to trouble the postwar world. But they took their orders, as always, from top Nazis who now congregated in Argentina—leaders who brought with them enough rank to reestablish an invisible Third Reich.

It started as a loose, mutual-protection association. But given the macabre mentality of the members, it developed into a sinister, secret society, financed with blood money that they had looted from the Jews. Millions of dollars, deposited in Swiss banks, were transferred to the accounts of strawmen in Buenos Aires who laundered the money by purchasing ranches, front companies, and complete industries.

This was the story that was bubbling beneath the surface in 1960 when Adolf Eichmann was whisked off the streets of Buenos Aires by Israeli commandos. The bold kidnapping sent shock waves reverberating to the outer reaches of the Nazi grapevine. Overnight, those who had hunted Jews for Hitler became the hunted.

Secret cables from the U.S. embassy in Buenos Aires carried fragments of the story in 1960. They cited tantalizing details—the names of notorious war criminals on the lam who had been spotted, rumors about a society of mass killers that operated under the noses of Argentine authorities, reports of gold and currency transfers from Swiss to Argentine banks. I had access to some of the cables, which intrigued me mightily. Here was a story, I told *Parade* editors, that should be investigated.

I WAS SOON HEADING SOUTH OF the border with the case histories of a dozen war criminals who were believed to be hiding out in
Argentina and Brazil. Tracking them down was no easy task. With my
telltale American appearance, I could hardly go underground. So I mingled
among the Nazis as an American journalist with questions to ask and a
story to write. I had enough background, much of it classified, to know the
places to go and the questions to ask. And I had enough ingenuity to word
my questions delicately.

One contact led to another until I gained the confidence of a former
Nazi SS officer. He was a stern, darkly handsome man who had adopted
the Brazilian name "Mario." But he still retained his German last name,
"Busche." Because he worked at the Sao Paulo airport, a major airline hub,
he was a key man in the invisible Nazi network. He could route notorious
Nazis with new identities to the far corners of the continent.

During the chaos that followed World War II, Mario began helping
fellow SS officers escape to South America. The anonymous flow was led
by those who had persecuted Jews, run concentration camps, and committed
other atrocities. Though Mario was not a war criminal himself, he knew
where the most wanted had scattered. For example, he remembered assisting
a slight, middle-aged officer with a drooping nose, flop ears, and apologetic
manner who posed as a Catholic priest and hid out in a succession of
monasteries. His name was Adolf Eichmann, lord of the gas chambers.

The Catholic trail from Germany through Italy was their favorite escape
route—the same underground passageway, ironically, that Jews before them
had used to flee the Nazi horror. Now the oppressors were granted sanctuary
in the same monasteries. Of course, the priests didn't realize that they were
aiding mass killers. The good fathers asked few questions and let God be
the judge.

All Nazi refugees received essentially the same treatment—priest's robes
as a disguise, falsified papers, and boat passage across the Atlantic. When
the phony priests arrived in Latin America, Mario confided, they were met
by friends, outfitted in civilian garb, and photographed for identification
documents under new names. Mario showed me some of the ID cards, and
I noticed that these Aryan-looking men with Italian names all wore the same
suit. Apparently there was just one jacket that new arrivals donned for the
photographs, leaving it behind for the next Nazi. Like the other short-term
priests, Eichmann faded into the Latin American population. His new name
was Ricardo Klement.

Mario started his new life not in Brazil but in Bolivia where he joined one of its recurring revolutions. As his reward, he was appointed chief of the secret police—a position that enabled him to secure fake papers for his Nazi friends. He offered to help Eichmann establish himself in Bolivia, but Eichmann preferred to settle with the top brass in Argentina.

About two dozen major war criminals had escaped to South America, Mario told me. By 1960, they had stopped watching over their shoulders; some had even started boasting about their true identities. That brief period of openness ended abruptly when Eichmann disappeared off a street in Buenos Aires and resurfaced in a jail in Israel. Not even Mario knew where they had scattered. Nevertheless, I questioned him closely about the biggest names on my list:

Martin Bormann, Hitler's private secretary and heir apparent, had stayed at Hitler's side in the Berlin bunker until his suicide. Then Bormann notified the military command that he was on his way to join them. He never arrived. Testimony before the Nuremberg war crimes tribunal claimed he was killed by a Russian bazooka as he was crossing Berlin. But Mario had heard that Bormann commandeered two submarines to smuggle his family and personal entourage to Argentina. Mario was never privy to his whereabouts.

Dr. Josef Mengele was the notorious "angel of extermination" at Auschwitz concentration camp. He decided which Jews should go to the gas chambers, which should be used for medical experiments, which should be worked to death. Mario said I had missed him by three weeks. He had operated a small chemical plant in Buenos Aires where he had lived comfortably, moving in elite Nazi society. His favorite pastime was discussing history and philosophy. One of his last discussions with a mutual friend, Mario said, was about the Soviet Communists' supposed ability to breed brilliant scientists who obeyed without thinking. After the Eichmann kidnapping, Mengele vanished into the Brazilian jungle, Mario told me.

Heinrich Mueller, the Gestapo chief, was last seen in Hitler's Berlin bunker on April 29, 1945. Mario reported that Mueller had fled to Buenos Aires but had moved south to Patagonia where he lived in the mountains. But he, too, had been scared into hiding by the Eichmann kidnapping.

IT TOOK ALL THE SKILLS DREW Pearson had taught me to keep Mario talking. Wording my approach carefully, I asked whether he could take me to any big-name Nazis. We went over the names on my list. They had all taken flight, he said, except one who sometimes provided the transportation. He operated three seaplanes, which he kept gassed and ready for any Nazis who needed to make a quick getaway. He would fly them deep into the Brazilian jungle where they would dock at secret sites on lakes and rivers. By the grisly numbers, he was a minor-league war criminal who took part in massacring 32,000 Jews. His name was Herbert Cukurs.

Because his seaplanes were in demand, he stayed at his post but appealed to the local constabulary to give him round-the-clock police protection from Jewish kidnappers. I asked whether Mario could arrange for me to meet this man. He agreed to try.

While I waited in my hotel room, I studied the Cukurs file that I had brought with me. It identified the Latvian-born Cukurs as former right-hand man to Viktor Ajars, head of the Latvian pro-Nazi Perkonkrust (Thunder Cross) Party. The German conquerors ordered Ajars and Cukurs to liquidate the Jewish population of Latvia's capital city, Riga. Classified cables, quoting eyewitnesses, charged that Cukurs barricaded and burned Jews in their own synagogues. The witnesses saw him scrounge the neighborhood for Jewish children and heave them into the funeral pyre. On slow nights, he would allegedly break down the doors of Jewish homes and rape young girls he found inside.

As an alternate method of execution, Cukurs and Ajars brought caravans of big blue buses to the Jewish ghetto in Riga and loaded them with Jews. The buses then were driven to the woods outside the city where the captives were lined up along pre-dug, mass grave pits and shot, the cables reported. Witnesses gave a chilling description of this ogre: stocky, muscular, cruel. He always wore a leather jacket and carried a pistol in his back pocket.

He was rumored to have brought a pretty young Jewish girl, Miriam, with him and his wife when they fled to Brazil. They reportedly raised her as their daughter, treated her kindly, and saw her married to a respected Jewish doctor in Rio de Janeiro. She was to be his rebuttal, the cables suggested, in case he ever had to answer for his crimes against the Jews.

My files included another curious fact: Cukurs and his wife, both in their sixties with three adult children, had suddenly produced another child. There was a strong suspicion that they had picked up a homeless boy and claimed him as their own natural Brazilian-born child—just in case they needed to curry sympathy with the locals should things get hot for them.

As a functionary of the Nazi underground and former head of Bolivia's secret police, Mario had the credentials to arrange for me to meet Cukurs. After a hot and dusty jeep ride over dirt roads, I reached his home in a fashionable lakeside resort area called the Paulista Riviera. Tied to a dock in front of his house, I noted, were three seaplanes. He lived in a blue-and-white Spanish bungalow, surrounded by a white picket fence, in a tranquil, picture-postcard setting. Two plainclothes policemen at the gate stopped me and took my White House press card into the house. Soon a stocky man in a leather jacket stepped out on the front porch, looked me over from a distance, then waved for me to come in. As I approached the porch, he greeted me in broken English. "So you came to see the great war criminal. Are you Jewish?"

"No."

He turned to open the front door. I noticed the barrel of a pistol poking out of his back pocket.

I had read all about the Holocaust. I had visited Auschwitz. I had studied the macabre case histories of mass murderers. But until I met Herbert Cukurs, I had never looked upon the face of evil. He spoke in a soft, plaintive, almost whining voice about his innocence. He walked to a large closet and pulled out tattered, yellowing documents to make his case. While the door of the closet was open, I saw a row of neatly pressed Nazi uniforms, complete with swastikas.

Cukurs waved his paperwork at me, claiming he had been a truck mechanic during the German occupation of Latvia. His only contact with Viktor Ajars, he pleaded, had been to repair three of his trucks. "I was too busy for politics and Jew killing," he said. It was the Jews who had committed the atrocities in Latvia, he claimed, not him. "I do not have the blood of any Jews on my hands." He spat out the word "Jews" contemptuously.

As final evidence, he told me proudly and in detail of the Jewish girl Miriam whom he had saved from death in Latvia and raised as his own daughter. The cables had sized up this horrible man correctly; he had planned ahead for a moment such as this, when he could produce Miriam as proof that he was not a killer of her people.

As he talked, I gave encouraging nods and verbal signals, all calculated to make him think he had found a sympathetic ear. I didn't want to blow my prospects of penetrating deeper into the Nazi underground by betraying the anger that was seething within.

Five years after I had exposed Cukurs in *Parade*, vengeance caught up with him. I read in a newspaper that his bullet-riddled body had been found in Uruguay, stuffed in the trunk of a car. Police found a note pinned to his leather jacket: "This was done by those who can never forget." The avengers had taken pains to make sure everyone would know that Cukurs had been punished.

But was it the Israelis who had settled another score? It was my story, and I wanted to know how it ended. A quiet investigation determined that there were at least two executioners: a tall, thin man in his sixties who spoke French, and a shorter, younger man who spoke Spanish. Insiders convinced me that the two were not Israeli agents but Nazi hit men who wanted it to appear to be a Mossad assassination. Apparently, Cukurs had double-crossed his Nazi associates and cheated them out of money.

I COULDN'T LEAVE SOUTH AMERICA WITHOUT trying to locate Hitler's heir, Martin Bormann. Mario was out of Bormann's circle and could be of no help. Most Nazis I met echoed the official version: that Bormann had been blown to pieces in his car when a Russian rocket hit the German tank he was following through Berlin. They repeated this story with such precision of word and detail that they began to sound rehearsed. I was led to one man who claimed to have recognized Bormann at a settlement called Xavantina in the Brazilian interior. My source was told that Bormann was posing as a German steel executive named Herman Meng, whose trail disappeared in thin air. I finally gave up on Bormann and headed for Buenos Aires where Mario had arranged for me to meet Adolf Eichmann's family.

I established a quick rapport with Eichmann's oldest son, Nicholas. (He preferred to be called "Nick" rather than the German form, "Klaus.") He seemed like a perfectly normal young man in his early twenties, with dark hair, blue eyes, jug-handle ears, and a long nose like his father's. Nick and his two brothers had seen little of their father during the war. After the war, they remained with their mother in Austria for seven years while their father slipped out of Europe and established a new identity in Buenos Aires. When at last the Eichmann family sailed for Argentina, they were met by their "Uncle Ricardo," who bore a strong resemblance to the father they only vaguely recalled. The boys never asked any questions when a fourth child, Ricardo Jr., was born.

The family lived in Buenos Aires in a house that their "uncle" had built with his own hands. It was a humble home, without plumbing or electricity—not a place where investigators would expect to find the *obersturmbannfuerhrer* of the gas chambers. When on May 12, 1960, he disappeared on his way home from work, the family searched for him, but found only his eyeglasses in a ditch near their home.

When the news was flashed around the world that Adolf Eichmann had been snatched off the streets by Nazi hunters and would be tried in Israel for war crimes, Veronika Eichmann finally admitted the truth to her sons: "Uncle Ricardo" was actually Adolf Eichmann. The accused mass killer was their dad.

I sensed a streak of rebellion in Nick Eichmann. He had married an Argentine girl and thumbed his nose at his father's strict German upbringing.

I was curious to know more about the family life of a monster, and I felt that I could get Nick to open up. But I needed more time, and Drew was insisting that I get back to Washington. "Have you ever been to the United States?" I asked Nick. He hadn't. So I invited him on the spot to spend a few weeks with Libby and me. He accepted, and we found ourselves with one of the more unique houseguests we had ever hosted.

Nick blended right in with the eclectic lifestyle of our family and, in some ways, was not unlike our own teenagers. For three weeks, I stayed close to Adolf Eichmann's oldest son, listening to his life story, studying his reactions, seeking an insight into his thoughts. I saw the legacy his father had left; the son who vaguely resembled him bore the grotesque imprint of a hideous past.

Most people liked Nick the first time they met him. He was friendly, with a boyish expression and a ready smile. He spoke fluent English that he had learned from GIs in postwar Germany-Austria. He liked to ogle girls, watch TV, and talk about cars. I took him to a movie theater to see a documentary on Hitler and the horrors of the Nazi death camps. He watched the movie, and in the darkness I watched him. He was repulsed by the same things that repulsed the rest of the audience.

But there was a bitterness in him that slowly surfaced as he became more comfortable with us. When I would mention his father, a chip would pop up on his shoulder. "My father?" he once responded, "He used to eat Jews for breakfast." One afternoon I found him watching an episode of *Have Gun, Will Travel* on television. During a commercial break, he looked up at me with a wry smile and said, "Have gas chamber, will travel."

Foolishly, I decided on the spur of the moment to take him to a Jewish event at the Mayflower Hotel in Washington. I wanted to see how he would react. When I introduced him as Eichmann's son, hands initially extended in greeting were drawn back in horror. I delivered a little lecture to the effect that Jews should be the last people to blame the son for the sins of the father. But I realized that my little experiment had been inappropriate, so I beat a hasty retreat.

After Nick returned to Argentina, we continued to correspond. He sent me the letters his father wrote to the family in the weeks leading up to his Israeli trial. They were the poignant letters any father might have written from a faraway jail cell. "Be brave and stick together," Adolf Eichmann told his boys. And he advised his wife: "Never lend money and never borrow money."

He wrote only brief references to the charges against him: "On the eve of my monster trial, I will repeat once again. I assure you by the eternal peace of my dead parents and of my late father-in-law, their fathers as well as our brother killed in the war that I: (a) never have killed; (b) never have given a command for killing. . . . I have done my duty, and I was obedient to the orders of my superior SS generals. I was always conscious of my vow which I have sworn to the flag. As an SS colonel, my honor and my loyalty was as important as the last SS man." But the case against him was compelling, and he was convicted.

Nick agreed to chronicle his own memories for an article for *Parade*. These were his sentiments, which I helped him put into words: "I bear one of the most despised names in the world today. Yet I still love the man who gave me life. My father, Adolf Eichmann, is about to stand trial in Israel for the murder of 5 million Jews in Hitler's gas chambers and concentration camps. He is reported to have boasted: 'I will leap into my grave laughing because the feeling that I have 5 million people on my conscience is a source of extraordinary satisfaction.' It is not easy for a son to believe such things of his father."

Someone told Eichmann about his son's article, and, without reading it, he wrote a letter to Nick. "You can imagine how much I enjoy this, especially today on my birthday. It is, by the way, the first and probably the only article which publishes something positive about me. Although I could not read the mentioned article yet, I cannot imagine anything else but something good in it."

Nick's last letter to me was a bitter one. He scolded me for being part of the "Jewish conspiracy." I thought then that of all the millions of people Adolph Eichmann had sent to their graves, there was one more victim: his son.

CHAPTER 6

FOR A MEMORABLE MOMENT IN TIME, Washington lost its tarnish and was transformed magically into Camelot. The politicians who populated the place acquired a brief nobility, and Americans began to ask not what the country could do for them but, rather, what they could do for their country. Truly, a special aura illuminated the White House for the three years that John Fitzgerald Kennedy occupied it. This aura captivated Americans and spread, like an intoxicating vapor, around the world.

I first detected this while watching his inaugural address with the generals in the Pentagon. Then I began to notice that Kennedy seemed to have a Pied Piper effect on people who turned out to see him. In Mexico, he attracted the largest crowds in the country's history. In Europe, people reached out to touch him as if he possessed divine power. Across Latin America, his photographs began to appear over hearths alongside paintings of Jesus Christ.

His image was enhanced by Nikita Khrushchev, who played Darth Vader to Kennedy's Luke Skywalker. The Kremlin czar pulled off a shoe and pounded it on a desk at the United Nations. He raged at Kennedy in Vienna, threatening to deploy his 175 divisions to close down Berlin. Kennedy asked him to identify a medal that hung on the breast pocket of his rumpled suit. When Khrushchev said it was the Lenin peace medal, Kennedy retorted dryly: "I hope you'll be able to keep it." Afterward Kennedy flew to Berlin and pledged to defend the besieged city. "I am a Berliner!" he declared.

Khrushchev backed down from the Berlin confrontation but created a new crisis on America's back doorstep. He planted nuclear missiles in Cuba, and Kennedy promptly invited him to remove them. The world held its breath as the two leaders maneuvered on the brink of a nuclear holocaust.

Then Soviet ships, loaded with more missiles bound for Cuba, received orders from Moscow to return home. Secretary of State Dean Rusk told subordinates: "We've been eyeball to eyeball, and I think the other fellow just blinked."

Despite the overhanging nuclear cloud, the spell of Camelot lifted spirits and added a little rose coloring to the national outlook. For a while, Americans could see the roses instead of the thorns in the White House rose garden. Then on that dreadful day in Dallas, the dream was shattered by an assassin's bullets. I spent the next twenty years trying to find out who really fired those shots.

Jack Kennedy and I had a special kinship. It was a small bond, an insignificant thing. Yet it became my personal pass to his ascending offices as he scaled the political heights. We had arrived in Washington in our unequal status in the same year—1947. He was a thirty-year-old freshman congressman and I was a twenty-four-year-old freshman muckraker. Kennedy had been born to power and bred for politics. No less than Franklin D. Roosevelt's godson, Langdon Marvin, who had been Kennedy's classmate at Harvard, served as his advance man. It was Langdon who brought us together.

Kennedy never forgot that I was the first correspondent he met in Washington. All I needed to do was call his secretary, Evelyn Lincoln, to get an audience. Then he would go straight to the heart of each question I asked with an impressive lack of fluff and jargon. He seldom indulged in the verbal foreplay that reporters count on to loosen up their sources. "Well, Jack, what stories are you working on now? What leaks do I have to plug up?" would be his only concession to small talk. If I asked a delicate question, he would never agonize over it. Sometimes he would respond; sometimes he would cut me off. In a few minutes, I would find myself out in the hall again amazed at how much ground we had covered in so short a time.

I saw unchoreographed emotion in Jack Kennedy only twice. During his Senate days, he let loose a quick flare of anger when I questioned him about a rumored father/son rift. His father, Joe, had arranged a position for brother Robert on Senator Joe McCarthy's staff. Jack Kennedy had no respect for McCarthy, but old Joe Kennedy was taken with the witch-finder. When I asked about their differences, Jack uncharacteristically lost control. "Are you trying to get me to say something against my father?" he snapped, then he quickly regained his composure and dismissed the subject.

I got my second glimpse of Kennedy's essence in his Georgetown townhouse after he had become the president-elect. As we talked, his little daughter Caroline scampered into the room. He greeted her softly, calling her

BIRTH OF A HOT LINE

PRESIDENT KENNEDY WAS NEVER DISCOURTEOUS TO me, but I knew if I wanted answers from him, I had to get quickly to the point. During the interim between the election in 1960 and Kennedy's inauguration in 1961, *Parade* magazine editor Jess Gorkin had a brainstorm; he suggested that a hot-line telephone should be installed between the White House and the Kremlin so Kennedy and Nikita Khrushchev would never be more than a phone call apart if international tempers flared.

Gorkin wanted to propose the idea in a *Parade* article, but he wanted some guarantee that the magazine wouldn't fall flat on its face. He asked me, as *Parade*'s Washington bureau chief, to get a commitment from the president-elect. I found Kennedy striding down the hall of the Senate office building, as yet unhampered by a Secret Service army. I briefly explained the concept of a hot line and asked if he would seriously consider it. He promised he would, and moved on.

The idea was bogged down in bureaucratic inertia until the Cuban Missile Crisis in 1962 when both sides agreed that the need had become urgent. Gorkin never got proper credit for his suggestion. That went instead to junior staffers in the State Department who finally gave the hot line the nod.

"Button Nose." She wanted to be scooped up in his arms, but his bad back prevented him from lifting her. Emotional pain flickered across his face as he gently brushed her outstretched arms away. I've forgotten what weighty matters we discussed that day, but I remember that look on his face.

I was attracted to Kennedy, not so much because of his charm and grace, but because he had one of the sharpest minds I had encountered. I am convinced that America would have avoided the debilitating Vietnam War, for example, if Kennedy had lived to serve out a second term. He once asked me, "Jack, have you read Khrushchev's 'Wars of Liberation' speech?" I confessed I had not. He called to his secretary. "Evelyn, bring Jack a copy of that Khrushchev speech." On my next visit to the Oval Office, he asked whether I had read the speech. I had. "That's Khrushchev's *Mein Kampf*. He tells us what he's going to do. He's going to stir up insurrections—wars of liberation."

Kennedy believed that Communist aggressors would never again crash through the front door as they did in Korea but would infiltrate through back doors as they were doing in Vietnam. It would take a crack counterinsurgency force, he said, to stop them. So his strategy was to develop the

OH, JACKIE!

AMONG JACK KENNEDY'S MOST ENDEARING QUALITIES was the sense of humor he necessarily cultivated about his wife Jackie. A friend of mine was with Kennedy on the West Coast when he learned that Jackie had been thrown from a horse, and her ungraceful sprawl had been captured by the lurking paparazzi. Kennedy called the White House and determined from Jackie's tone of voice that the only thing injured was her pride. As his wife vented her outrage about the photographer, a smile crept across Kennedy's face. When she gave him the chance to speak, he said, "Well, Jackie, when the first lady falls on her ass, it's news."

A few months before Kennedy was killed in Dallas, I began to hear rumors that Jackie was miserable in her role as first lady. I put together a story for *Parade* magazine with information gleaned from people close to her. It was scheduled to run in late November 1963 and was well along the *Parade* pipeline, already distributed to hundreds of newspapers, when the president was assassinated. We scrambled to stop the newspapers from running it and succeeded in yanking that edition of the magazine from all but one paper.

For those who saw Jackie Kennedy as the keeper of the flame, her sudden marriage in 1968 to Aristotle Onassis—the aging gnome of colossal wealth—was a shocker. I didn't normally stray from politics to dabble in other people's marital relations, but when I heard from an unimpeachable source that this marriage was no Camelot, I couldn't resist the temptation to investigate.

The source was Aristotle Onassis himself. He called my office one day in December of 1974 and asked if I would have lunch with him the next time I was in New York. I was intrigued, and, although I had no set plans to go to New York, I told Onassis that I was going to be there within a few days. He had a chauffeur meet me at the airport. We toured a building he had under construction in Manhattan and then we sat down for lunch and a bit of gossip.

He complained about Jackie's horsey-set friends and her profligate spending habits. Onassis also revealed that he had negotiated a prenuptial agreement with his wife that left him feeling as though he had just haggled over the price of a horse. I listened and discerned that Onassis was not just spilling his thoughts on the spur of the moment. He had the look of a man laying the groundwork to dump his wife. I assigned my best reporter, Les Whitten, to look into the story.

Within a few weeks of our strange meeting, Onassis was dead. He must have mentioned my name favorably to his inner circle, because after his death we had little trouble getting them to confide to Les the details of the marriage of convenience that had turned out to be terribly inconvenient for the groom.

In a series of columns in the spring of 1975, I spelled out the details of the prenuptial contract—the $20 million cash payment up front, the dickering over allowance and taxes and cost-of-living increases. Onassis's secretary recalled for me how Onassis had come back from the negotiating session with Jackie's lawyer pale and badly shaken. "Where's the bottle we keep around here?" Onassis had asked. The secretary fetched a bottle of scotch and held up her thumb and forefinger less than an inch apart by way of asking how much he wanted. Onassis, who rarely drank straight liquor, spread his own fingers two inches apart.

Les saw the original draft of the contract, complete with Onassis's changes scrawled in. Then Les tracked down the rumors about Jackie's spending and discovered, among other things, that she had been buying clothes on Onassis's account and selling them to consignment shops after wearing them only a few times or not at all.

My friend Lilly Fallah Lawrence, an Iranian oil heiress and international jet-setter, provided the most telling story. She said her father, Iran's top oilman, Reza Fallah, had invited Jackie to be his houseguest in Tehran. She arrived with an entourage so large that Fallah had to put them up in a hotel. Then Jackie charged her shopping sprees to her hotel room and left the bill for Fallah to pay. "Daddy could afford it," Lilly told me, "but it was a little tacky."

best Special Forces in the world, not to fight guerrilla wars for our allies, but to train them to fight their own insurrections. "If we give them a crutch," Kennedy said, "they'll never be able to stand on their own feet."

On the day Kennedy was shot—November 22, 1963—I was meeting in a hotel room with Jess Gorkin, then editor of *Parade* magazine, discussing story ideas. The phone rang. Jess picked up the receiver. His face turned ashen. "The president has been shot!" he said as he strode across the room and punched on the television set. For the rest of the afternoon, we were absorbed in the crushing news.

Then and there, I made a silent commitment to use my investigative skills to verify the official version of the tragedy. I found the various conspiracy theories long on melodrama and short on evidence. Then, in 1971, I met Johnny Rosselli.

JOHNNY WAS A GANGSTER—NOT A godfather but not a common hood either—who rubbed elbows with Hollywood's "B" list and ran Las Vegas operations for Chicago mob boss Sam Giancana. Johnny had taken a blood oath never to betray mob secrets, but in agonizingly slow detail, one jigsaw piece at a time over a period of five years, he unfolded an incredible tale to me: The CIA had contracted with the Mafia to assassinate Fidel Castro. But Rosselli had learned from his underworld connections that Castro had found out about the plot and had recruited the Mafia to retaliate against John F. Kennedy.

Do I believe this mobster, whose credibility would be challenged in court? I do. I believe him because I had to drag out every fact through tight lips. I believe him because I confirmed 70 percent of what he told me and never caught him in a lie. That gives me confidence in the 30 percent I couldn't confirm. I believe him because other Mafia and CIA sources verified that he had told the truth. There's one more reason that I believe what he told me. I don't think he would have been killed for telling me fibs.

Kennedy had hardly settled in the White House when he had his first skirmish with Castro, who easily repulsed the disastrous Bay of Pigs invasion on April 17, 1961. According to Johnny Rosselli, this began a chain of events that would end in national calamity on November 22, 1963.

The Bay of Pigs was a CIA fiasco that soured Kennedy on the spooks. Angrily, he told friends that he wanted to "splinter the CIA into a thousand pieces and scatter it to the winds." Instead, he entrusted it to his brother Robert, the new attorney general; Bobby's assignment was to make sure there were no more surprises.

For Robert Kennedy, every assignment became a crusade, and his crusades against criminals often became personal. He would pit the almighty powers of government against one lone prey. He once wrote a nasty, three-page letter to me about some now-forgotten issue, ending the letter with an angry summons, in effect, for me to appear in his chambers and get a dressing-down in person. I wrote back that such a meeting "would be a waste of my time."

Not long afterward, I called on JFK who greeted me with a chuckle. "I read your letter to Bobby," he explained. Then he assured me: "Don't worry about Bobby. I've got a hand on his shoulder."

But not even the president's hand could restrain Bobby, who turned the CIA upside down and inside out. He uncovered the CIA's plot to kill Castro, demanded a top-secret briefing, and then asked for the details in writing. On May 7, 1962, he received a petulant memo from Colonel Sheffield Edwards, director of security for the CIA, warning that it had never before been thought wise to put the details in writing. Edwards spelled out the facts and said knowledge of the assassination plot had been restricted to six people, whose exchanges had been strictly verbal. The memo constituted the full written record that the attorney general had requested, the CIA security chief added—one copy for Kennedy, another for the CIA. That was all.

Then the memo laid out the terrible secret: that the CIA had made a pact with the Mafia to assassinate Fidel Castro so he wouldn't be around to rally his troops when the Bay of Pigs invaders landed on the beach.

NOT UNTIL NEARLY A DECADE LATER did I begin to pry the story loose from Johnny Rosselli—as beguiling a hood as ever dealt in the rackets. He began life as Filippo Sacco on the Fourth of July, 1905, in Italy. In his teens, he changed his name to John Stewart and ran away from home to work for Al Capone. The Chicago mob boss convinced his new intern to take a more Italian name. Young Stewart chose a name that rippled off the tongue, borrowed from one of the painters of the Sistine chapel, Cosimo Rosselli.

In the late 1960s, Sam Giancana had become boss of the Chicago mob, and he sent Rosselli to protect the Chicago mob's interests in Hollywood and Las Vegas. As a Mafia don, he had one foot in the underworld, but as a dapper, mobster-about-town, he had the other foot in the world of starlets, celebrities, and high rollers. It was in the former capacity that he was approached by the CIA. As the CIA's Mafia connection, he became personally involved in the plot to knock off Castro.

Rosselli found it necessary to confide in his attorney, Edward P. Morgan, what he knew about the Kennedy assassination. Morgan was an old friend of mine, but his professional ethics prevented him from identifying his client or revealing what he had learned. Meanwhile, I had gotten a faint whiff of the story. For years I needled Morgan, until January 11, 1971, when he persuaded Rosselli that I could be trusted and arranged for me to meet this mysterious client. It was the most unusual interview of my career. Rosselli had agreed to answer my questions, yet he couldn't quite bring himself to talk directly to a reporter. He resolved the dilemma by talking to another lawyer, Thomas Wadden, a member of his legal team in Washington, behaving as if I were not in the room. I would ask Wadden a question; Wadden would repeat the question. Johnny would direct his answer to Wadden who would convey the gist of it to me.

Rosselli confirmed that in 1960 the CIA had hatched a plot to assassinate Fidel Castro as a warm-up for the Bay of Pigs invasion. I later learned from CIA sources that the idea had come from President Eisenhower's loose cannon, CIA Director Allen Dulles, though no record was kept of Dulles's chilling proposal, nor of any debate that may have followed. This was one of the dirtiest conspiracies in U.S. history—to make a pact with Mafia hit men to murder the leader of another nation.

The CIA's Sheffield Edwards was supposed to make the contact with the underworld. He approached a former FBI agent and CIA operative, Robert Maheu, who moved at the subterranean level of politics. Maheu knew his way around the shady side of Las Vegas; he had been recruited by billionaire Howard Hughes to oversee his Las Vegas casinos. Happily, Hughes was a friend who owed me a favor. Intermediaries persuaded Maheu to confide in me. He confirmed that the CIA had asked him to sound out the Mafia, strictly off the record, about a contract to hit Fidel Castro. Maheu had taken the request straight to Johnny Rosselli.

Rosselli had a reputation inside the mob as a patriot; he was quite willing to kill for his country. But as he told me, there was an etiquette to be followed in these matters. Santo Trafficante was the godfather-in-exile of Cuba after Castro chased out the mob. Rosselli couldn't even tiptoe through Trafficante's territory without permission, and he couldn't approach Trafficante without a proper introduction. So Rosselli prevailed upon his boss in Chicago, Sam "Momo" Giancana, to attend to the protocol. Since Giancana had godfather status, he could solicit Trafficante's help to eliminate Castro. The project appealed to Giancana who had commiserated with other dons over the loss of casino revenues in Havana. Killing Castro for the government would settle some old scores for the mob, and it would put Uncle Sam in the debt of the Mafia.

Maheu had been ordered to keep a tight lid on the involvement of the U.S. government. The CIA was ready with a cover story that the Castro hit had been arranged by disgruntled American businessmen who had been bounced out of their Cuban enterprises by Castro.

On September 25, 1960, Maheu brought two CIA agents to a suite at the Fountainebleau Hotel on Miami Beach. Rosselli delivered two sinister mystery men whom he introduced only as Sicilians named "Sam" and "Joe." In fact, they were two of the Mafia's most notorious godfathers, Sam Giancana and Santo Trafficante, both on the FBI's ten-most-wanted list. They discussed the terms of Castro's demise, with Giancana suggesting that the usual mob method of a quick bullet to the head be eschewed in favor of something more delicate, like poison.

The wily Giancana was less interested in bumping off Castro than in scoring points with the federal government, and he intended to call in as many chips as he could before the game was over. At one point in the bizarre negotiations between the mob and the CIA, Giancana told Maheu that he had a personal problem; he suspected that his girlfriend, singer Phyllis McGuire, was cheating on him with comedian Dan Rowan. Both were popular entertainers on the Las Vegas nightclub circuit. Implying that McGuire might say too much during pillow talk, Giancana convinced Maheu to arrange a wiretap of Rowan's hotel room. When Maheu's wiretap technician was caught red-handed by Las Vegas police, the incident was hastily covered up. Maheu called the CIA, the CIA called Robert Kennedy, and the Justice Department dropped the illegal wiretap charges.

Meanwhile, the plot against Castro, blessed by the godfathers, took a wacky twist. Rosselli recruited some anti-Castro Cubans as sidekicks and the CIA supplied a brew from its labs—guaranteed to take out its victim over the course of a few days, like a bad case of food poisoning, and leave no trace. The Cubans managed to slip the poison to a relative of Castro's chef. There was a flurry of excitement in Rosselli's coterie when a news item appeared in the Miami papers that Castro was under the weather. "Bobby's gonna be very happy," Maheu told a confidant.

When Castro refused to die, Rosselli tried a more direct approach—boats and guns. But the small band of anti-Castro assassins attempting to make a beach landing in Cuba, Rosselli among them, was intercepted by Cuban patrol boats, one of which sank Rosselli's boat with heavy gunfire. He dove overboard, swam to a backup boat, and beat a hasty retreat with his men.

There were other unsuccessful schemes in what came to be called "Operation Mongoose"—poison pens, contaminated cigars, a deadly virus, an "accident" at the bottom of the ocean while Castro was scuba diving, even depilatories to make his beard fall out so that if he wouldn't die, he would at least be inconvenienced. Some spooks at the CIA suspected Rosselli might be yanking their chain with these wild stories. But the two CIA agents who worked directly with the brassy mafioso from Las Vegas swore he was pulling out all the stops to kill Castro for Uncle Sam.

The final assassination attempt in early 1963 was arranged by Trafficante himself. As the local godfather, he had a working knowledge of Havana's hit men. He selected three of the best, a trio of marksmen, and placed them on a rooftop in Havana—rifles presumably at the ready—while Castro was delivering one of his windy speeches in a public square. The sharpshooters allegedly were spotted by Castro's security men, captured, and tortured until they talked. At least that was the story that got back to Rosselli. But he later learned that the plot had taken an ominous twist.

On September 7, 1963, the Associated Press office in Havana was alerted that Castro would have something important to say that night at the Brazilian embassy. It turned out to be a warning to President Kennedy: You try to kill me; I'll try to kill you. AP correspondent Daniel Harker quoted Castro as saying, "We are prepared to fight them and answer in kind. United States leaders should think that if they are aiding terrorist plans to eliminate Cuban leaders, they themselves will not be safe." Eleven weeks later, John Kennedy was dead, reportedly at the hands of Lee Harvey Oswald, a pro-Castro misfit who claimed he was someone else's "patsy."

———————

AS A NEUROTIC YOUNG MAN, OSWALD had defected to the Soviet Union, proclaiming that he would give the Soviets all the secrets he had learned during a brief stint with the marines. Then, inexplicably, he was allowed to return to the United States with his Soviet-born wife Marina, no questions asked. They lived variously in Dallas and New Orleans, where his uncle, Charles "Dutz" Murret, was a minor underworld gambling figure who hung out with members of Carlos Marcello's crime syndicate. Oswald passed his time as a pro-Castro agitator, carrying placards and handing out leaflets for the Fair Play for Cuba Committee.

In the fall of 1963, he bought a war-surplus Italian rifle through a mail-order firm. He allowed someone to take his picture, proudly posing with the rifle, which later was found, along with three spent shells and Oswald's thumbprint and palmprint, on the sixth floor of the Texas School Book Depository where he worked.

At our first meeting, Rosselli refused to make the connection between Operation Mongoose and the Kennedy assassination. Instead, he wanted to talk about his patriotism, his answer to the CIA's call, and his refusal to take any money for serving his country. But I knew from the hints of his attorney Ed Morgan that the story didn't stop with Castro's ultimatum that two can play the assassination game.

I found out later that the CIA had poured thousands of dollars into Operation Mongoose, although Rosselli claimed he had paid many of the bills himself. I was also aware that Rosselli needed to drape himself in the flag at that point in his life; he was probably motivated by something more than a desire to serve his country. In 1968, he was implicated with four mobsters who had rigged a gin rummy game at the celebrated men-only Friars Club in Hollywood. They had swindled several big stars, including Zeppo Marx, out of $400,000 by spying on their cards from peepholes in the ceiling. Rosselli faced deportation and needed to remind Uncle Sam that when his country called, he had answered.

Knowing that Rosselli's legal problems may have tainted his story, I needed corroboration, so I had my partner Les Whitten track down William Harvey, the cold-eyed CIA operative whom Rosselli said had run Operation Mongoose for a time. Les reached Harvey by telephone in Indianapolis, and, to our surprise, Harvey obliquely confirmed everything Rosselli had said about Operation Mongoose. Harvey expressed an odd loyalty to Rosselli. "The Friars Club indictment is phoney," he said. "Rosselli had no more to do with that than I had." Les asked him to help us flesh out Rosselli's story. "I'd like to, but I can't," he said.

FOUL PLOTS

D ID JOHN F. KENNEDY KNOW ABOUT the plot to kill Fidel Castro? Inside sources told me that one of the eight CIA officials who knew about the Castro plot, Sheffield Edwards, gave President-elect Kennedy a full briefing in December 1960.

Kennedy also confided to one of his closest friends, Sen. George Smathers, that the CIA probably had something to do with the killings of two other troublesome heads of state, Ngo Dinh Diem of Vietnam in 1963 and Rafael Trujillo of the Dominican Republic in 1961. Smathers told me that when he asked the president about plots against Castro, Kennedy just rolled his eyes, as if the idea were too crazy to discuss.

But when Kennedy made his brother the overseer of the CIA, Bobby wasn't told to stop crazy covert plots, but merely to monitor them so his brother wouldn't be caught by surprise. Insiders told me that Bobby displayed a schoolboy's excitement over the plots against Castro. Bobby was advised of the CIA-Mafia pact in writing in May of 1962, and the last hit team was sent in early 1963. Clearly, President Kennedy didn't object to the Castro assassination plots because he didn't stop them. He had inherited the plan from Dwight Eisenhower just as he had inherited the Bay of Pigs plan; he canceled neither.

I thought back on our talk about "Wars of Liberation." Fight insurrection with counterinsurrection, Kennedy had told me, and leave no fingerprints. I reached the troubling conclusion that it would not have been beneath the morals of "Camelot" to authorize a hit team to kill another head of state.

Kennedy's CIA director, John McCone, swore to me that "no plot was authorized or implemented" to assassinate Castro, Trujillo, Diem, or anyone else. In the case of Castro, McCone said, "Whenever the subject was brought up—and it was—it was rejected immediately on two grounds. First, it would not be condoned by anybody. Second, it wouldn't have achieved anything." It didn't take long for me to prove that McCone didn't know what he was talking about. A copy fell into my hands of the 1962 CIA memo to Robert Kennedy outlining the deal with the mafia.

There was also a second CIA memo from November 1970 repeating the history of Operation Mongoose in more detail, long after it had been dropped.

Here was an explosive story that I was eager to detonate. But it was peopled by CIA agents and Mafia hit men, none of whom were noted for keeping written records. I needed Rosselli to talk without his lawyers present—which is what he eventually did. He came to trust me and ventured into my office. I kept a light in the window for him, and he began dropping

SMOKESCREEN

IN APRIL 1967, THE DISTRICT ATTORNEY in New Orleans, Jim Garrison, was hot on a conspiracy trail of his own. He bore down on seedy pro-Castro elements in the Big Easy with vague ties to the CIA; he sought to pin Kennedy's assassination on two unlikely weirdos who lived on the fringes of society. Garrison's investigation seemed to me to be a convenient diversion that shifted the spotlight away from New Orleans' most notorious crime boss, Carlos Marcello.

I flew to New Orleans to see what Garrison had uncovered and was met unexpectedly at the airport by two beefy men. They were to escort me to Garrison's office, they said. I was early for my appointment, so they suggested lunch. We drove to one of the more elegant restaurants in New Orleans where the maître d' showed us to the best table in the house and fussed over my escorts. I figured they were probably plainclothes cops, and wondered why they warranted such treatment, but then I remembered that this was New Orleans where the easy relationship between the police and the locals allowed both of them to do their jobs without too many questions asked.

When we arrived at Garrison's office, he dismissed my escorts and we got down to business. Then, inexplicably, about half an hour into our conversation, Garrison blurted out: "Why did a couple of Marcello's men pick you up at the airport?"

"Marcello's men?" To this day, I don't know why they picked me up or who told them I was coming.

Garrison dismissed the incident as an unsolved mystery. Over the course of the next few hours, I badgered him into opening his files to me, but was not persuaded by anything I saw. I was not nearly as impressed as film director Oliver Stone was in 1991 when he released *JFK*, a dark and speculative movie that made a hero out of Garrison and made history out of his contorted theory.

by whenever he was in Washington. He enjoyed chatting with my assistant Opal Ginn who had a smooth Georgia sense of humor and kept a ready bottle of equally smooth scotch in her desk.

Ever so gradually, Rosselli unfolded the story to me as he saw it from his observation point inside the Mafia. He was excessively cautious at first, taking pains to preface each terse new disclosure with a disclaimer: "I don't know, but..." or, "This is what I think..." or "This is what I hear..." I understood Rosselli's cautious wording was his way of protecting himself from retribution by the mob—a precaution that failed him in the end. For he became more candid and, apparently, more careless.

I pieced Johnny's statements together, one by one, until the puzzle began to take shape: Castro, enraged by the attempts against his life, struck back at Kennedy; the Mafia, enraged by Bobby Kennedy's unrelenting war on organized crime, became Castro's willing accomplice; thus the plot against Castro was transformed into a plot against Kennedy.

As I tracked the story for two decades, I was able to verify much of Rosselli's information through other sources. He never gave me a bum steer that I was able to check. To this day, however, no hard proof exists to back up his full account. Yet I believe it to be true.

The mob's early affinity for Kennedy probably grew out of mutual friendships with the "rat pack," a clutch of Las Vegas entertainers and actors who hung out with underworld figures and were regarded by the mob as a diversion—Frank Sinatra, Joey Bishop, Dean Martin, Sammy Davis Jr., and Kennedy's brother-in-law Peter Lawford. Perhaps unknowingly, Jack Kennedy and Sam Giancana had once romanced the same girlfriend—Judith Campbell Exner, who was also a friend of Johnny Rosselli's. Patriarch Joe Kennedy also had enough business relationships with organized crime figures that the godfathers probably figured the new president owed them some slack. Instead, Kennedy appointed his brother Bobby to wage a relentless war against the crime syndicate.

In the months leading up to the assassination, godfathers around the country were spitting out invectives against the Kennedy brothers—invectives that were preserved in three hundred volumes of FBI wiretap transcripts. On the FBI wiretaps, minor mobster Willie Weisburg told Angelo Bruno, the godfather of Philadelphia, "With Kennedy, a guy should take a knife, like all them other guys, and stab and kill the [expletive]. I mean it. This is true. Honest to God. It's about time to go. But I tell you something. I hope I get a week's notice, I'll kill. Right in the [expletive] White House. Somebody's got to get rid of this [expletive]." Buffalo crime boss Stefano Magaddino ranted on the phone, "They should kill the whole family. The mother, the father, too."

The FBI was unable to wiretap the phones of the two godfathers my sources linked to the Kennedy assassination—Santo Trafficante, who ran Florida mob operations from Tampa, and Carlos Marcello, whose criminal jurisdiction stretched from New Orleans to Dallas. Marcello's and Trafficante's predictions about Kennedy's future, though unrecorded, were remembered by witnesses. Las Vegas private investigator Ed Becker would later tell the FBI and investigators for the House Assassinations Committee that Marcello threatened to kill President Kennedy. Becker recalled a meeting with Marcello near New Orleans in September 1962—a meeting the crime boss swore never took place. Their conversation reportedly turned to Bobby

FOILED PLOTS

AN IMPORTANT PIECE OF MY PUZZLE in the Kennedy assassination didn't fall into place until 1989 when Joseph Shimon, once an undercover Washington cop who hung out with the mob, finally spoke candidly to me about what he remembered. Shimon was eighty-two at the time. I had dogged his career before he retired, suspicious of which side of the law he was on, and I had written unflattering columns about him. But in 1989, we met as two old enemies who realized the battle was over, with nothing left but the tale swapping.

In the 1960s, Shimon was close to Sam Giancana, who used him as his ears in Washington. Shimon knew who was dirty, who could be bought, where the weak spots were in the system. Giancana let Shimon sit in on some of the sessions plotting the hits against Castro. Shimon couldn't believe that the best Mafia and CIA hit men working together could not pull off the simple assassination of a banana-republic dictator. Every time a hit team was deployed by the mob against Castro, the scheme was foiled, as though Castro knew they were coming. Shimon began to suspect a double cross. "It started to shape up in my mind that it had to be Trafficante," Shimon told me. "The thought went through my mind, Trafficante is working for Castro."

Shimon had once asked Giancana if the boss of the Florida and Cuba mob, Santo Trafficante, could be trusted. "Frankly, he's a rat," Giancana answered. There was nothing subtle about Trafficante. If someone got in his way, his response was, "Kill 'em," Shimon remembered.

Shimon mulled over the characters in Operation Mongoose and Trafficante kept invading his thoughts. The mobster had operated thriving casinos in Havana until Castro had overthrown Fulgencio Batista in 1959, seized control of Cuba, and shut down the gambling dens. Trafficante and his ilk had been booted into the Trescornia minimum security prison in Cuba on June 6, 1959. (There is some evidence that Trafficante was visited in Trescornia by Dallas nightclub owner and mob errand boy Jack Ruby who was making frequent quick trips to Cuba in those days.) Without explanation, Trafficante was released after just two months behind bars, and sailed grandly for Florida, none the worse for wear, with his yacht and his bank accounts intact.

Kennedy, who had deported Marcello briefly in 1961. Is Kennedy, "giving you a rough time?" Becker asked. Marcello's alleged response was to spew an old Sicilian threat against the Kennedy brothers; "Livarsi na pietra di la scarpa!" or "Take the stone out of my shoe!" Then he likened Bobby Kennedy to the tail of the dog and offered another Sicilian homily, "If you cut off a dog's tail, the dog can still bite you. But if you cut off the dog's head, the dog will die, tail and all." Becker then claimed Marcello said President Kennedy would be assassinated and a "nut" would be used to do it. The FBI dismissed Becker's account as not credible because he consorted with mobsters.

As for Trafficante, he also may have had loose lips. Jose Aleman Jr., one of the innumerable Cuban exile leaders with a minor coterie of followers and dreams of becoming the next president of Cuba, talked to House Assassinations Committee investigators. Aleman claimed he was involved in a business deal with Trafficante, and one day their conversation had turned to politics; Trafficante had muttered that President Kennedy would "get what is coming to him," that he was "going to be hit." But Aleman panicked when he was asked to repeat his story before the House committee. For the record, he said Trafficante must have meant only that Kennedy was going to get what was coming to him at the polls in 1964, that he was going to be hit "by a lot of Republican votes."

Two of my sources, Johnny Rosselli and Washington detective Joe Shimon, were tuned in to the underworld grapevine. They gleaned enough inside information to conclude that Castro instigated the Kennedy assassination, Trafficante supervised it, and Marcello allowed it to take place in his jurisdiction.

LIKE EVERY AMERICAN, ROSSELLI REMEMBERED VIV-IDLY the day John F. Kennedy died. Rosselli had been awakened from a nap to be told the news. His immediate reaction was: "The Cubans must have gotten him."

When CIA chief John McCone learned of the assassination, he rushed to Robert Kennedy's home in McLean, Virginia, and stayed with him for three hours. No one else was admitted. Even Bobby's priest was turned away. McCone told me he gave the attorney general a routine briefing on CIA business and swore that Castro's name never came up. Yet McCone's agency had been trying to kill Castro, and just two months earlier Castro had threatened to retaliate if the assassination attempts continued. Another thing: On November 22, 1963, when I could talk about nothing else, when my wife could talk about nothing else, when the entire world was riveted on Dallas, the director of the CIA claimed that he spent three hours with the brother of the slain president and that they discussed routine CIA business.

Sources would later tell me that McCone anguished with Bobby over the terrible possibility that the assassination plots sanctioned by the president's own brother may have backfired. Then the following day, McCone briefed President Lyndon Johnson and his National Security Advisor McGeorge Bundy. Afterward, McCone told subordinates—who later filled me in—what happened at that meeting. The grim McCone shared with Johnson and Bundy a dispatch from the U.S. embassy in Mexico City, strongly suggesting that Castro was behind the assassination.

The CIA chief put this together with what he knew of the mood in Moscow. Nikita Khrushchev was on the ropes inside the Kremlin, humiliated over backing down less than a year earlier during the Cuban missile crisis. If Castro were to be accused of the Kennedy assassination, Americans would demand revenge against Cuba, and Khrushchev would face another Cuban crisis. He was an impulsive man who could become dangerous if backed into a corner. McCone warned that Khrushchev was unlikely to endure another humiliation over Cuba. This time he might do something reckless and provoke a nuclear war, which would cost forty million American lives. It was a staggering figure that the new president repeated to others.

A trusted source told me that Johnson later picked up the phone and called a man who had been his neighbor in Washington for three decades— FBI Director J. Edgar Hoover. From all that I have learned about those two men, I can speculate what Johnson told Hoover. More than likely, LBJ invoked flag, country, and the fate of forty million Americans who might die. He probably asked Hoover to make sure that the FBI postmortem on the Kennedy assassination did not even hint at the name Fidel Castro.

In times of national trauma, many people fancy themselves heroes. Witnesses see things that never happened; eavesdroppers overhear things that were never said; patriots fabricate stories to protect the national well-being; bureaucrats doctor paperwork to fit the official line; statesmen hide the truth while it is too painful to tell. Lies are told and rules are broken in the name of a greater good. Hoover was a man of many motives, but above all he was a patriot and a master bureaucrat. He despised many of the presidents who were his bosses; he was loyal only to his perception of the United States and the FBI. But LBJ knew how to appeal to Hoover's patriotism. To save forty million Americans from nuclear oblivion, the J. Edgar Hoover I knew would not only have agreed to whitewash the most important murder investigation of the century; he also would have agreed to use his power and control over the FBI to impose his will.

In less than a week, Hoover notified Johnson that the FBI investigation into the assassination was almost complete. It would lay the blame on a lone gunman, Lee Harvey Oswald, who could no longer challenge the findings because by then he was dead.

I'LL LEAVE TO THE FORENSIC EXPERTS the endless debate about how many bullets were fired by how many people from how many guns that day as Kennedy's motorcade rolled past the Texas School Book Depository. My own conclusion is that Oswald, if he did fire any of those shots, did not act alone. Rosselli indicated that the mob set up Oswald to take the rap. Then once the blame was pinned on him, he had to be eliminated.

The man who eliminated Oswald, a sleazy Dallas nightclub owner named Jack Ruby, claimed he was overcome by grief for Jackie Kennedy and her children. He shot Oswald as the accused assassin was being transferred from a city jail to a county jail on November 24. It could hardly have been an impulsive act. He infiltrated the jail with a loaded pistol in his pocket at the exact time of the transfer. Then he confronted Oswald, whose front was strangely unprotected in a phalanx of seventy armed lawmen.

Ruby hardly fit the model of a patriot-turned-vigilante. By his own admission, he hadn't voted for Kennedy, nor had he bothered to watch the president's motorcade in Dallas. Witnesses had overheard him making derogatory remarks about Kennedy that indicated he shared the mob's animosity for the first family. By all accounts except his own, Ruby was a two-bit nightclub operator who had never shown passion for anything except money.

He was a refugee from Sam Giancana's Chicago domain. As a teenager, Ruby had run messages for Al Capone and had matured into a small-time hoodlum. He protected himself from police harassment by becoming cozy with the cops—too cozy for the comfort of the mob. So he was given an invitation he couldn't refuse—to leave Chicago. Ruby shoved off for Dallas in 1947, with a loan from the mob to set him up in business in territory controlled by Marcello.

Because Ruby's sidelines, gambling and prostitution, crossed the bounds of the law and community morals, he resumed the business practices he had developed in Chicago of ingratiating himself with the police. He hung around the police station jawing with officers, brought box lunches to cops on duty, served them free food and drinks in his nightclub, even arranged dates for them with his strippers and co-signed loans for officers who needed cash.

Washington cop Joe Shimon told me it was Trafficante who called in the mob's chits with Ruby and ordered him to kill Oswald. Ruby had become such a familiar face around the police station that he could stride unnoticed past officers and reach fail-safe shooting range of the prisoner. According to Shimon, Ruby had no choice. "When the mob tells you to make the hit, you're gonna make the hit," Shimon told me. "It you're part of the thing and you took that oath, they tell ya to shoot your brother, you're gonna shoot your brother or they're gonna shoot you."

J. Edgar Hoover immediately called for the FBI file on Ruby. It was full of evidence of mob ties, which should have triggered an investigation into a conspiracy. But Hoover had entered into his own private conspiracy with Lyndon Johnson. Five days after Oswald's death, when Hoover called the president to tell him the FBI investigation was almost finished, Congress was breathing down Johnson's neck, threatening to conduct its own investigation. For the record, Hoover summarized his conversation with Johnson in a memo: "The president stated he wanted to get by just with my file and my report. I told him I thought it would be very bad to have a rash of investigations. He then indicated the only way to stop it is to appoint a high-level committee to evaluate my report and tell the House and Senate not to go ahead with the investigation."

Thus was born the Warren Commission. Johnson needed a "high-level" committee, so he summoned the Chief Justice of the Supreme Court, Earl Warren. I noted the press reports of that day said Warren emerged from his meeting with the president with tears in his eyes. I thought at the time that he might have been moved by the soberness of his task, but in the intervening years, I have wondered just how much Johnson told Warren in that meeting. I knew Earl Warren; Drew Pearson used to vacation with him. Warren was a noble man who, if told he must suppress the truth to save America from a possible nuclear broadside, would have had difficulty holding back the tears. Thirty-five years later, there is scarcely an American who believes the Warren Commission's conclusion that Lee Harvey Oswald acted alone.

I had watched Lyndon Johnson long enough to learn how his mind worked. He had lined up Hoover to control the evidence that the FBI laid before the commission, but he needed an inside man to bury any conflicting evidence that might slip through the cracks. That man was Allen Dulles, the erstwhile CIA director, who had hatched the plot to kill Castro. What in the world was Dulles doing on a commission that was supposed to hush up the Castro connection? I believe the wily LBJ put Dulles there to steer the commission away from Castro. Dulles had to suspect that his plot to assassinate Castro had backfired. Yet not once did Dulles breathe a word that might implicate Castro. On the contrary, he led the commission down an opposite path. At the first meeting, behind closed doors, Dulles handed out copies of a book that claimed assassinations in America have invariably been carried out by deranged, lone killers. And throughout the investigation, Dulles stuck to that theory.

Apparently, one person belatedly wanted to tell the Warren Commission the truth. Jack Ruby, after he had been convicted of murder and languished for months in a lonely cell, offered to come clean. He petitioned the Warren Commission for a hearing, and Chief Justice Warren went personally to Dallas to interview him. I read fear between the lines when I reviewed the transcript of their June 7, 1964, meeting. Ruby began with a prepared statement under his lawyer's guidance, and then abruptly broke off his narrative. "Is there any way to get me to Washington?"

"I beg your pardon?" said Warren.

"Is there any way of you getting me to Washington?"

Warren said he would talk it over with Ruby's lawyer, and then tried to continue the interview. But Ruby asked for the police and his lawyer to be removed from the room. "I am not accomplishing anything if they are here." The police and lawyers left Ruby alone with Warren and his entourage. Ruby said he wanted to tell his story in Washington. "I want to tell the truth, and I can't tell it here.... Does that make sense to you?... Gentlemen, my life is in danger here.... I tell you, gentlemen, my whole family is in jeopardy."

Warren wouldn't move Ruby to Washington, but agreed to let him take a lie detector test, which was inconclusive. Later, Ruby encountered reporters as he was being moved to a court appearance. He made a fleeting remark about a "complete conspiracy," and added, "If you knew the facts, you would be amazed." In 1966, Ruby was granted a new trial, but he died of lung cancer in a Texas prison in 1967 without ever gaining the safe forum he wanted to tell his story.

IN THE SAME YEAR JACK RUBY died, Ed Morgan came to me with a painful dilemma. He was bound by lawyer-client privilege, but he felt he had information that belonged to history. He chose me because of our personal friendship, but also because of Drew Pearson's friendship with Earl Warren. It was common knowledge in Washington that the chief muckraker and the chief justice were best friends. With agonizing caution, Morgan told us what he felt he could—just the bare bones of the story—withholding Johnny Rosselli's name. He appealed to Drew to alert Warren.

Drew passed the message on to Warren and from there, I learned years later, it was passed around the Johnson administration as if it were a jigger of nitroglycerin. When Drew and I published our first tentative column on the Castro-Kennedy conspiracy on March 7, 1967, President Johnson asked Hoover to find out how serious the leak was. Hoover's agents went straight to Morgan, who had once been a high FBI official. Morgan dutifully told the FBI what he knew in a memo he stamped Top Secret, but he still refused to divulge his client's identity.

Through the media grapevine, I learned that Johnson made a startling statement to broadcast newsman Howard K. Smith in 1965. The respected Smith had been talking to Johnson without the cameras rolling. Their informal discussion turned to the Kennedy assassination and Johnson blurted, "Kennedy tried to get Castro, but Castro got Kennedy first." Smith was flabbergasted and tried to extract the details from Johnson, but the president tightened up, as though sorry he had let the words slip. Smith verified the story for me, but said he was never able to get Johnson to return to the subject.

Throughout the early 1970s, with Rosselli now talking to me, I continued to pepper my column with references to the Kennedy story, reporting new evidence when I found it and raising old revelations when I feared this important story was fading from public attention. Finally, in 1975, it stirred the attention of Idaho Senator Frank Church, who questioned me about it. Intrigued, he issued subpoenas to open locked CIA files and to summon tight-lipped witnesses before his Senate Select Committee to Study Governmental Operations with Respect to Intelligence Activities. Church served subpoenas on Rosselli, Giancana, and Trafficante. Trafficante disappeared.

Rosselli answered the subpoena, but told the Church Committee practically nothing. He gave a few details of Operation Mongoose, reminded them that he was a patriot who loved his country, and then clammed up on the subject of Kennedy. After the session, he showed up at my office where I was waiting to hear that my years of hard work on this story had finally born fruit in the halls of Congress before a committee that could bring the guilty to justice. I eagerly asked Rosselli, "Did you tell them?" He smiled indulgently as though I was crazy. Of course not. He was no snitch.

On June 19, 1975, five days before Sam Giancana was scheduled to testify before the Church Committee, the semi-retired mafioso was alone in his suburban Chicago home, frying a pan of sausages, when someone shot him in the back of the head. The killer then fired half a dozen bullets into his face, grouped about his mouth and jaw—the mob warning, "Don't talk." There was no sign of forced entry, leading police to believe that Giancana was shot by someone he knew. CIA Director William Colby felt compelled to announce, "We had nothing to do with it."

IF THE CHURCH COMMITTEE HAD BEEN more vigilant, it would have found the third mobster it sought, Santo Trafficante, having dinner on July 16, 1976, at the fashionable Landings Restaurant in Fort

Lauderdale, Florida. His guest was Johnny Rosselli, still under Senate subpoena, painfully aware that Sam Giancana was dead, but too easygoing to hire his own bodyguards as his lawyers had urged. Instead, he had been invited to a feast that turned out to be a last supper, in the mafia tradition. His host, Trafficante, had the most to gain by eliminating him.

Twelve days later, on July 28, Rosselli was lured aboard a private boat by friends who promised a day of fishing in Biscayne Bay. The *New York Times* later speculated on what happened next: While Rosselli, then a stooped and hawk-faced senior citizen with emphysema, sat sipping a drink, one of his companions slipped a cord around his neck and strangled him to death. A metal drum was rolled out, and a chain saw produced. It had been brought along in anticipation of the fact that the five-foot-nine-inch Rosselli would not fit into his final resting place. His killers sawed off his legs, stuffed Rosselli piece-by-piece into the drum, weighted it down with chains, and rolled it overboard.

As this drama was unfolding, I got a phone call from Plantation, Florida. "Johnny is missing," said Johnny's brother-in-law, Joe Daigle. I expressed concern, but wondered why Rosselli's kinsman was calling me to announce that a seventy-one-year-old retired mafioso had wandered away from home. In the cryptic language of one who distrusted the telephone, Daigle answered my unasked question. He suggested Rosselli might have met with foul play because he had talked to me.

Johnny's killers hadn't counted on the fact that gasses from his decomposing body would bring the drum to the surface and that it would then wash ashore to be found by fishermen. Police from Miami flew to Washington and knocked on my door. They told me that Rosselli had been given a full-dress Mafia execution, and that they had heard from their contacts inside the mob that he was executed for talking to me.

Three years later, the House Assassinations Committee, looking into the killings of John Kennedy and Martin Luther King Jr., subpoenaed Carlos Marcello. He said he knew nothing about the killing of the president and, furthermore, was not involved in organized crime. The Assassinations Committee concluded that there was indeed a conspiracy to kill JFK, but never settled on who or how. The committee report acknowledged that there may have been a plot by the Mafia, and that the most likely duo to have masterminded it would have been Marcello and Trafficante. But there wasn't enough evidence to prove the committee's suspicion.

CHAPTER 7

IT SHOULDN'T TAKE MANY WORDS TO relate an experience that lasted only two days. Yet those forty-eight hours stand out in my memory like sunlight bursting through the clouds.

In 1964, Major General Anthony McAuliffe allowed me to tag along while he revisited World War II. No one who followed him across those battlefields could doubt the influence of personality upon history. As we relived the terrible battle his men had fought, I discovered in this rugged old soldier a warming strain of kindliness. It seemed to affirm that the grounds for hope outweigh the proof of man's folly.

Twenty years earlier, in the tiny Belgian town of Bastogne, McAuliffe had made history by uttering a single word. He was the acting commander of the proud 101st Airborne Division, which was surrounded by German forces during the bitter cold of late December 1944. McAuliffe had received a courier message from the German commander: Surrender or face complete destruction of the American forces and annihilation of the townspeople.

"Nuts!" McAuliffe spat out when the message was delivered. He mulled over his options and then turned to his assistant chief of staff, Lt. Col. H. W. O. Kinnard. "What should I tell them?"

"That first crack you made would be just the ticket," Kinnard replied.

"What was that?" McAuliffe said.

"Just, 'Nuts!' "

So the reply was handed to the puzzled German courier who asked for a more specific translation from one of McAuliffe's aides.

"It means, go to hell!"

History records that McAuliffe held out just long enough. The overhanging clouds broke up the next day, and an air drop brought urgently needed ammunition. The Germans were driven back, and the people of Bastogne were saved.

Twenty years later, McAuliffe returned to Bastogne with his wife, Helen. He was a modest man, who had always been a mite embarrassed about the fuss that had been made over his four-letter response to the German ultimatum. He expected to slip quietly into town and tour the battlefield unnoticed. But within a few minutes of our arrival, the word had spread through town like electricity. "McAuLEEF est ici!"

Our small party moved slowly through the growing throng of townspeople who wanted nothing more than to embrace their hero and present him with whatever gifts they could offer on short notice. One plump grocer, Gerard-Marie Collard, shrieked, "McAuLEEF!" and waddled toward him with a cluster of grapes. A butcher presented him with sausage. Children not yet born at the time of the battle begged him for autographs.

McAuliffe inched through the crowds, his eyes moist, acknowledging the adoration of the people of Bastogne. Their demonstration was spontaneous; "adoration" is the right word to describe it. They hadn't forgotten the general who had made sure they received food and fuel during the German siege—the American commander who would not retreat, who would not abandon them.

When we were able to break away from the crush, McAuliffe showed me where the Battle of the Bulge had been fought. He pointed out where his men, hugging the frozen terrain, had stood off the German attacks. He remembered with sober clarity where many had died. He told how he had massed his artillery in the center of his forces. As the Germans tested the perimeter for weak spots, he would wheel his artillery around to bombard each assault with all his firepower.

The site of the last battle, a scene of grisly carnage in 1944, had become a peaceful, pastoral peasant farm in 1964. McAuliffe suggested self-consciously that we get the permission of the owners before we wandered over the landscape where he had stopped the Germans for the last time. He walked alone down a long path and approached a humble shack where he introduced himself to the farmer, Raymond DuMont. The humble farmer called to his wife, Juliette, who reacted with disbelief. "McAuLEEF! ImpossEEB!"

I watched from a distance as she bustled around the farmyard gathering her children to greet their historic visitor. He slowly made his way back to us, surrounded by excited, babbling children. The parents were even more animated, regarding him as if he had just descended from on high. As they pressed around him, the squat, wobbly farmer's wife suddenly remembered something and disappeared on the run into the house. She emerged carrying her thirteen-year-old daughter who was recovering from an appendectomy. Staggering under the load, Mme. DuMont lugged the heavy child up the path and deposited her at McAuliffe's feet. When at last she was satisfied that the children had had their audience with McAuliffe, she began flagging down passing cars to share their good fortune.

McAuliffe contrasted the pastoral scene before us with his memory of the frigid battlefield on Christmas Day 1944, when the dead lay where they had fallen, frozen into grotesque postures—a German stretched half out of his blackened tank, the horror of death stamped on his face; German infantrymen snared on a barbed wire fence, caught in the crossfire, frozen there like so many scarecrows; an American GI sprawled in a foxhole, his body contorted in an agony he could no longer feel.

When General George Patton finally broke through to the 101st at Bastogne, McAuliffe said he and Patton walked through the battlefield of frozen German bodies. "Patton was wearing those breeches and carrying that swagger stick, and he was exulting, 'Good. These are the kind of Germans I like to see,'" McAuliffe remembered. "I never did care for that man after that."

Few people I have encountered in my seventy-plus years have impressed me as much as Tony McAuliffe. He had the rare ability to maintain genuine humility in the face of personal celebrity. It is a quality I have occasionally glimpsed but more often found lacking in the celebrated inhabitants of my town.

CHAPTER 8

NOAH WEBSTER WOULD HAVE HAD TO invent a new word to describe the thirty-sixth president of the United States. Lyndon B. Johnson was "multi-phrenic"—a man of many personalities crowded into one complex being. He could be domineering, demanding, callous, cantankerous, impatient, vain, and shortsighted. But he could also be compassionate, sensitive, humble, thoughtful, and foresighted. Above all, he was unpredictable, a man of many moods.

He had a Caesar-sized ego that brooked no insubordination. He tended to speak to people like a Texan talking to a Rhode Islander. His voice was usually quiet, with a slight flavor of southern syrup. But he could raise it to a terrible crescendo when the volcano inside him was disturbed. Then he would berate anyone within bomb burst of his voice, letting epithets and accusations fly like shrapnel. He kept the Oval Office door closed, reversing John F. Kennedy's open-door policy, for no other reason than to provide insulation for his outbursts.

Yet this same formidable Lyndon Johnson squirmed with inferiority in the presence of Kennedy and kin. When JFK and LBJ teamed up on the 1960 Democratic ticket, they regarded one another with cold political eyes. Of all political marriages solemnized before the altar of expediency, none seemed less likely to succeed. For eight years, Johnson had been Kennedy's Senate leader; Kennedy had been a mere back-bench senator. Even more pronounced was the difference in personality. It would have been hard to find two men more opposite: the Irish Catholic intellectual, laconic, crisp, ruled by New England reserve; and the southern Protestant politician, loquacious, homespun, with outbreaks of Texas flamboyance.

Johnson's chemistry made it painful for him to sit still while another led, and as Kennedy's vice president, he brooded over his subordinate position on the totem pole. But he was awed by Kennedy's sophistication and felt as if he were wearing cowboy boots at one of Jacqueline Kennedy's exquisite, white-tie balls. Kennedy and Johnson simply could never seem to get on the same wave length. LBJ thought the Kennedys looked upon him with disdain, as if they viewed him through invisible monocles. He felt ill at ease in their presence and responded by being humble and respectful.

As an investigative reporter who had a habit of getting in Johnson's hair, I was one of those small annoyances that great men must put up with. He treated me like a hot stove. He sought the warmth but was afraid to get too close because he had already been burned by Drew. In the early years, I was the one who defended him; I thought he was an effective Senate leader. I would commiserate with the pained LBJ over Drew's frequent attacks on him. But by the time Johnson reached the White House, he and Drew had become bosom buddies. In an ironic turnabout, I became the one churning out stories that rankled Johnson, and Drew would sympathize with him, thus absolving himself of blame.

Drew became a frequent visitor to the Oval Office, where he would expound on his vision of better government, and LBJ would stroke him just enough to make Drew believe he had been elevated to the status of inner-circle policy-maker. Johnson was the only man I know who ever conned Drew Pearson by puffing him up. The big, facile Texan had to wait until Drew was aging and mellowed before LBJ could catch Drew with his guard down.

During the Johnson presidency, there were many subjects on which Drew and I agreed to disagree. As Drew grew older and came to trust me as his eventual successor, our disagreements ended with each of us allowing the other to say what he wanted in print. When I became obsessed with the deviances of Connecticut Senator Thomas Dodd, Drew was skeptical, but he cut me a wide berth.

ONE DAY IN MID-1965, A TROUBLED, idealistic young man named Jim Boyd appeared in my office and said he wanted to talk to me about Dodd. I had been sniffing around Capitol Hill asking questions about the senator, driven mostly by an instinct that told me something was not quite right. Word of my interest had reached Boyd, who offered to help. He was in a position to know what was going on in Dodd's back rooms, because he happened to be Dodd's chief of staff. He had a tale to tell, Boyd said, of Dodd's political sellout, of petty corruption piled upon petty corruption until the sum of the parts was reprehensible. I stopped Boyd and called in my assistant Opal Ginn who could type as fast as most good secretaries took shorthand. Get it all down, word for word, I told her. Then out of earshot of Boyd, I added, "Keep him as long as he'll stay. He may not come back tomorrow. In fact, we may never see him again."

So golden a source was Boyd—and so great was his personal and professional risk—that I fully expected him to have a change of heart. Politics breeds a rare form of dedication. People who work closely with a politician begin to think of him/her as an extension of themselves and find themselves blinded to his/her flaws. Boyd had helped Dodd get elected and had come close to worshiping the ground he walked on. But he became aware of some acquisitive ventures that suggested something was gravely wrong. He began sharing his disillusionment cautiously with other staff members. From intimate glimpses into Dodd's political life, they began putting together a grotesque mosaic made up of the compromises, equivocations, and sellouts they had seen.

Boyd felt that he had been betrayed and that the voters of Connecticut had been violated. He came back to my office for three days running and sat opposite Opal's typewriter, spilling his boss's secrets. After three days, I popped my standard question. "Can you back this up with documentation?" He brought in six members of Dodd's staff, first singly, then in a group. Over a twelve-month period, they covertly collected and copied documents out of the senator's files, presenting them to me on behalf of his bosses— the American people. We would meet at my home where the seven of us put the scraps of evidence together like a great jigsaw puzzle.

Senators on the make have discovered a number of shortcuts to the easy dollar, and Dodd had tried most of them. If not for the temptations and the tolerance on Capitol Hill he might have become a worthy legislator. He was a victim as much of the Senate's shortcomings as of his own, because the failings of one brought out the failings of the other. The Senate has produced statesmen of heroic mold, but more typical has been the limited politician with a narrow background and parochial interests. The corrosive power available to him or her is more often a temptation than a challenge. It is not the ennobling power to shape bold national policies or the awesome authority to make great decisions and be held accountable by the nation and by history. More characteristically, it is the petty privilege to frustrate and delay the proposals of others, to hold up appointments made by the president, to bargain selfishly for patronage or pork as the price for support for national programs.

Most senators are honorable men and women who serve the nation as best they can. Some senators are exemplary public servants, devoted to the national welfare, whose contributions will never be adequately appreciated. But others are irresponsible opportunists who slide through their careers, taking rather than giving. The collectivity and secrecy obscuring the unheralded dedication of the former also cover up the dereliction of the latter.

Only insiders can truly distinguish the doers from the drones. The rules and customs that prohibit one senator from disparaging another keep the public from recognizing who is good, who is bad, and who is ugly. If this system frustrates the best, it is ideally constructed for the senators who regard their membership as an avenue to special privilege and personal gain.

THE SYSTEM ALMOST SAVED TOM DODD. My first few columns brought an outcry not against Dodd for his corruption but against his staff for documenting it. Senators reserved their outrage for the Senate employees who copied Dodd's incriminating documents. Powerful senators protested to Drew and to our flagship paper, the *Washington Post.* Drew asked me tentatively, "Don't you think we ought to call this off?"

"I've got too much hot stuff."

Drew never raised the question again.

The informants from Dodd's office were treated worse than they had expected. I had told them that their candor would help make the case against Dodd but that they would be harassed and blackballed by the Senate. I had offered to protect their identities if they wished to remain anonymous. Four agreed to step into the spotlight. Two elected to remain in the shadows. To this day, the anonymous pair remain unidentified.

As the sordid details of Dodd's machinations were presented to the public, he denied the charges and called for a Senate investigation of his own conduct. He was confident that the Senate apparatus would protect him as it always had. The investigation, sure enough, turned into a merciless probe of his four visible staffers. The FBI, perhaps mindful that Dodd served on the Senate committee that had jurisdiction over the Bureau, also undertook an exploration into the lives of the four staffers.

Attorney General Nicholas Katzenbach invited Drew and me to his office and unctuously assured us that we were not in any trouble for printing the Dodd exposé. But the senator had filed a complaint about "stolen" documents, and Katzenbach was obliged to prosecute our informants, he said. He was sure we would understand, wouldn't we?

No, we wouldn't. "There is no corpus delicti," I shot back.

"What are you talking about?"

"No documents have been stolen. The documents in question are in the senator's office right where he has always kept them." With the cool restraint that I thought the situation called for, I told Katzenbach he apparently intended to prosecute four Capitol Hill employees for using their access to records in their own offices in file cabinets to which they legitimately held the keys. I was the one with the copies, I reminded him. "Let me make this clear. If you're going to indict them, you will have to indict me along with them." Nobody was indicted.

The behavior of the Senate was no better than it usually is. Senators, who cannot be sued for their utterances on the Senate floor and can change their spoken words before they appear in the *Congressional Record*, took advantage of their privileges to lambaste those who had dared to open the inner workings of the Senate to public scrutiny. As the case dragged on, our 120 columns laying out the evidence against Dodd began to have an effect. Letters showered down upon Capitol Hill from every section of the country, expressing dismay and outrage.

A reluctant Senate Ethics Committee, feeling the pressure, was obliged to carry out its mandate. Although the committee had full access to all the evidence, it saw fit to indict Dodd on only two minor counts: converting campaign contributions to his personal use and billing the government for travel expenses that had already been paid by private organizations. The Ethics Committee revealed its own sense of ethics by adding a withering attack on the four whistle-blowers.

Taking his cue from the committee, Dodd based his defense on the perfidy of his former employees. He swore to the Senate: "I am telling you the truth as though I had to face my Maker in a minute. I am telling the truth, and I am concealing nothing. May the vengeance of God strike me if I am doing otherwise." Some colleagues, as a safety measure, visibly backed away from him, and cynical reporters in the press gallery suggested that everyone wear rubber-heeled shoes.

The evidence, nevertheless, was too overwhelming to ignore. The Senate voted ninety-four to five to censure Dodd for misuse of his campaign funds—a toothless penalty, though it had been exercised only five previous times in history. All other charges, though painstakingly documented, were simply dropped: that he accepted cash and gifts from industries under investigation by committees he served on; that he took money and loans from people he'd backed for official appointments; that he took money and gifts from people he'd performed congressional services for; that he interceded with the federal government to help his private law clients; that he charged the government for trips that were really vacations; and that he padded the Senate payroll with people who performed no official services. But the voters had the final say; they rejected his bid for reelection.

I expected our Dodd stories to win the Pulitzer prize for national reporting that year. Drew was more sanguine; he had stopped looking for recognition from his peers. The Pulitzer jury did, in fact, vote to give us the prize in 1967, but was overruled by its own advisory board. Instead, the award for "national reporting" went to the *Wall Street Journal* for an exposé of gambling in the Bahamas. To avoid honoring Drew, the Pulitzer board temporarily annexed the Bahamas, which hadn't previously been part of the United States and thus a topic for "national reporting."

Drew's reputation as a hip-shooting, outlaw reporter probably kept him from ever seeing a Pulitzer with his name on it, although he broke a number of big stories that should have won journalism's top award. If the slight hurt him, he never mentioned it to me. But I suspect he would have found a place on his wall for the award had it been granted.

LYNDON JOHNSON SEEMED TO SENSE THAT Drew, in his golden years, was vulnerable to a pat on the back. But LBJ would never limit himself to backslapping. I can describe the "Johnson treatment" from personal experience. By his sheer size, he was an intimidating man who would loom over me. He favored the two-handed shake, a vigorous pumping action with the right hand while his left hand grasped my wrist, elbow, or shoulder. He called this "pressing the flesh." Then he would get intimate, clamping those huge Texas hands on my shoulders or throwing his great arms around me to hug me to his bosom.

Johnson's pockets were usually bulging with secret documents, which he would pull out and lay before my eyes while he studied my face closely, watching for signs of astonishment. When he had a point to stress, he would lower his head two inches from my ear and whisper conspiratorially. He would dominate the conversation, steering it in the direction he wanted it to go. More than once, I went in to see him with a list of hard questions and ended up saying, "Yes, Mr. President. No, Mr. President." The only alternative, I found, was to be rude to the president of the United States. I would listen briefly to his monologue and then interrupt him with, "Yes, but that's not what I came to talk about." He would shake his jowls in annoyance and say, "Oh, okay, okay, what do you want?"

Once he interrupted me before I could interrupt him. "Let's go see the daa-awgs," he drawled, making a two-syllable word out of "dogs." If the leader of the free world had a hankering to see his beagles, who was I to object? We stepped outside the Oval Office, and Johnson let loose a whistle suitable for the Texas range. No dogs responded. He tried again, louder; I felt sure no dog would dare disobey his second whistle. But still no dogs. Johnson hollered to a Secret Service guard, "Where are the daa-awgs?" He pronounced each word slowly, stretching "daa-awgs" to its acoustical limit. "I'll find out, Mr. President," the guard offered, scrambling to the telephone at his post.

"Let's take a walk," the president proposed. We strolled across the White House lawn, with Johnson keeping a more vigorous pace than I was accustomed to. When I commented on his energy, he invited, "Feel my muscles," flexing his biceps. We were engrossed in assessing the presidential muscle when suddenly he remembered why we were outside. He whirled around and thundered, "Where the hell are the daa-awgs?" The guard dropped his phone and fled from his outpost, calling over his shoulder, "I'll find out, sir!" He returned in a few minutes with the news that the beagles had been taken for a routine veterinarian visit. "Well, why didn't you say so in the first place?" the president drawled, and ushered me back inside.

Once when my wife, Libby, and I were vacationing in Atlantic City, we happened to be staying at the same hotel as President Johnson. We had been invited to a party—an elegant get-together that obliged Libby to wear a dress. Except in extreme emergencies, she always dressed informally in slacks.

After the party broke up, Libby suggested we take a stroll on the board-walk, and she headed for our room to change out of the dress into something comfortable. I was waiting for her in the lobby when President Johnson strode in with his entourage. He spotted me and sent an aide to invite me up to his suite for a private gathering.

From the presidential suite, I called down to our room and told Libby to come on up. Then I mingled with the high-brow crowd, including the Duke and Duchess of Windsor. Before long, a Secret Service agent ushered Libby in; she was wearing her favorite uniform—casual slacks, cheap blouse, and scuffed shoes.

I took her aside. "Libby, we're guests of the president of the United States! The Duke and Duchess of Windsor are here! Why didn't you wear your dress?"

"I thought we would go walking on the boardwalk afterward," she replied matter-of-factly, as though I was the one who had lost my senses.

Lyndon had an eye for the ladies, and even in casual clothes, Libby was the prettiest woman at the party. He kept her by his side the whole evening, apparently charmed by her complete lack of pretension.

I AM OBLIGED TO RATE JOHNSON as one of the worst presidents in history, attributable in part to the era in which he was raised. Before World War II, he watched Adolf Hitler swallow one country after another until the allies finally decided he had to be stopped. Johnson viewed Vietnam similarly, as the first domino, and he wasn't about to let it fall to the Communists.

The heroes of Johnson's generation were the great military minds— Dwight Eisenhower, George Marshall, Douglas MacArthur, George Patton.

KOREAN HOSPITALITY

MY SWING THROUGH ASIA IN 1968 included a stop in Korea that began my romance with the Korean people and their culture. Among my most precious souvenirs is a Korean screen, a room divider, that taught me something about Eastern hospitality.

One evening in Seoul, while dining at the home of my friend Park Chong Kyu, then the presidential security chief for South Korea, I admired his exquisite screen. In my eagerness to be polite in front of his other guests, a coterie of cabinet members, I praised the screen a bit too much. The next morning, it was in my hotel room. I had forgotten the oriental assumption that when a person admires an item, his host is obliged to give it to him.

I called Park's aide, Kim Um Yong and tried to undo the damage. "I only admired the screen to praise Park's taste. I would like to return it."

"Oh, no," Kim said. "That would be an insult." Kim agreed that I could give Park a comparable gift in return, so I asked him for a ballpark figure on the value of the screen. "I would say in American money, maybe ten or fifteen thousand dollars."

I was stunned. I knew Park was a collector of unusual guns, so when I got back to Washington, I found a gun that I knew he had been looking for and sent it to him. But it wasn't a $15,000 gun. After that incident, I learned to temper my compliments when I traveled in Asia.

So, Johnson developed a deep respect for military men, who conned him into escalating the Vietnam War. It was the perfect testing ground for their toys and theories, the perfect training ground for their generals. But there were no Marshalls or Eisenhowers or MacArthurs in Vietnam. There were just bureaucrats in uniform.

I visited Vietnam once during the war, arriving at the tail end of the Tet Offensive in 1968. I was a war correspondent again for a few weeks. I hitched a ride on a C-123 transport plane that was to fly ammunition to the embattled American forces at Khe Sanh. The plane was supposed to touch down, dump its load of supplies out the back end onto a pallet, and take off again without stopping.

Our steward was a grizzled sergeant with a cigar clenched between his teeth and the visor of his cap turned straight up. He looked me over disapprovingly, then directed his spiel to a couple of colonels and a major who were going to be dropped off. "Gentlemen," he rasped. "When we hit the ground, there are some thirty-millimeter cannons that will open fire on us.

The record on the ground is thirty-nine seconds. We're going to try to beat the record. When we hit the runway, we're going to let the ass end of this plane down. I'm going to pull this toggle, and this bed is going to roll out on the runway. As soon as that happens, jump out and run like hell to the nearest bunker."

I turned to the officers. "Does anyone know where the nearest bunker is?" They didn't. Fortunately, I never had to find out. The airfield was fogged in, and we turned back after circling Khe Sanh for an hour.

My next appointment was in the Mekong delta where I was checking out a story (which I later confirmed) that American oil companies were paying off the Vietcong to leave their refineries alone. I asked the Air Force to fly me over a refinery in the guerrilla-infested Mekong delta, so I could see for myself whether it had been damaged. The Air Force brass helpfully arranged a flight with Major Gene Mooney, a "bird-dog" pilot.

He led me across an airfield past all the solid, swift, safe-looking jets. He stopped next to a flimsy, single-engine prop plane covered with red patches. "Where's this bird dog?" I asked, not wanting to hear the answer.

"This is it," he said.

"What are all these colorful patches?"

"They cover the bullet holes."

Once we were in the air, I asked at what speed this low, slow-flying plane was taking me over enemy territory.

"About one hundred twenty-five."

"Isn't that a little slow?" I asked pensively.

"That's the idea," Major Mooney replied. "I'm supposed to locate the VC. We're flying over dense jungle. We can't find them unless they fire at us. If I'm going too fast, they won't shoot at us. They should start shooting soon." That's how I learned that a bird dog was a flying target.

We attracted enemy fire as he had planned. Mooney dropped smoke bombs on the area where the gun flashes had appeared and called in the jets, which swooped down on the target and blasted the whole area with firebombs. Mooney then flew me over a refinery—a huge, silvery, Rube Goldberg–looking structure that positively glittered and gleamed in the tropical sun. Yet it hadn't been touched by the Vietcong who surrounded it.

BACK IN THE UNITED STATES, THE war was unpopular and divisive. LBJ's military strategy had bubblegummed in his face. It wasn't easy for me to take sides. I hadn't seen what Jane Fonda saw. I had seen ordinary American kids who couldn't tell the enemy from the allies. I had seen kids hunkered down taking mortar fire from the Vietcong, refusing to shoot back because the enemy had set up the mortar amid innocent villagers. There were scandals, and I wrote about them, putting myself on record as an opponent of the war. But I could never see the story in black and white.

Once, speaking to an audience at the University of Nevada, Las Vegas, I took a question from an earnest young man with long hair and fire in his eyes. He referred to "aggressors," meaning the United States, and "victims," meaning the Communists. I couldn't let it pass. "Do you have a dictionary in your room?" I asked him, and he said he did. "When you get home, look up the word 'aggressor' and while you're doing it, keep this in mind: There are no South Vietnamese troops in North Vietnam. There are no Cambodian troops in North Vietnam. There are no Laotian troops in North Vietnam. But there are hundreds of thousands of North Vietnamese troops in South Vietnam. There are tens of thousands of North Vietnamese troops in Cambodia. There are thousands of North Vietnamese troops in Laos. Now, you look up that word and come back and tell me who the aggressor is." The young man didn't like it, but I think I made my point.

Vietnam haunted Lyndon Johnson through all of his waking and sleeping hours as he micro-managed the war from the White House. He didn't merely lay down military policy in Vietnam; he personally decided which targets should be hit in North Vietnam. "They don't hit an outhouse without my approval," he once boasted to me. I vividly recall the day I had an appointment with him just as dusk was falling in Washington. I was shown into the Oval Office and found him standing at the window, with his back to me, talking softly to himself. When he acknowledged my presence, he motioned me to the window. I had been an unwilling participant in enough staged dramas in that office to know when Johnson was acting a part. This was not one of those times.

"The worst part of this job," he began, "is sending young men on missions knowing some of them aren't going to return. They leave about midnight our time for North Vietnam. It takes a couple of hours to get there. Lady Bird and my doctor want me to go to bed, but I can't sleep. About three in the morning, I pick up the phone by the side of my bed and ask for the Situation Room. I ask, 'How are my boys.' If any of them are missing, I have a terrible time sleeping. Mind you, I believe that I'm doing right. I believe their sacrifice will save many lives. But I'm just not sure. I pray about it. But it's hard to know what God wants you to do."

Johnson made a tragic mistake by plunging the country into the Vietnam War. When he finally came to terms with it, he did what must have seemed unthinkable at first for his Texas-sized ego. He retired and gave up the presidency. LBJ didn't have to be dragged out, kicking and screaming. He simply quit.

When I had first arrived in Washington, both the House and Senate were run by people of Lyndon Johnson's ilk. LBJ could be outrageous, but he could also be wonderful. Like the other old tigers of his political peer group, he used the earthy language that is missing from today's media-diluted, sound-bite presidents. Johnson and his peers would be branded as eccentric by today's standards, but in fact they were rugged, practical, and forceful.

A consummate political manipulator, Johnson nevertheless understood that the president is the servant of the people, not their master. He upheld a presidential tradition that a politician could be a wheeler-dealer—in fact he had to be the best of the political wheeler-dealers to reach the White House—but when he arrived at 1600 Pennsylvania Avenue, he put the national well-being ahead of his personal gain. That tradition lasted until the arrival of Richard Nixon in the White House. Bill Clinton, in many ways, is a slick Nixon.

Drew and I deserve at least part of the blame for the current state of presidential politics. We lobbied furiously against the selection process that birthed presidential candidates in smoke-filled back rooms. In fact, Drew beat the phrase "smoke-filled back rooms" into an overworked cliché. Political professionals, meeting secretly in those legendary back rooms, would pick their party's man based on who had punched the right tickets and who could sway the right regions of the country. When the votes were counted in November, the new occupant of the White House was invariably someone who had paid his dues. Fortunately, however, the manipulators in those back rooms were usually patriotic enough to choose someone who would do his duty.

In retrospect, that was better than the current system of state primary elections that Drew and I crusaded for. We had no way of foreseeing that the silent majority would stay at home on Super Tuesday while the extremists picked the tickets. It is a system that produced Michael Dukakis as the Democratic nominee in 1988—though he hadn't a ghost of a chance of carrying much more than his home state of Massachusetts, a state the Democrats would have won no matter who their nominee was. The system also produced George McGovern in 1972, whose nomination was welcomed as much by the Republicans as the Democrats. The Democrats were too starry-eyed to admit that he had no hope of victory. They were not so much interested in winning as they were in fielding a candidate who was pure. With McGovern on the ticket, the Republicans knew their man was a winner. The GOP party machine, with one notable exception, could shift into idle.

The exception was the paranoid Republican incumbent Nixon, who, as history records, could not leave well enough alone.

CHAPTER 9

DREW PEARSON TOOK OFF THE MONTH of August 1969 for a vacation and, as had become his habit, left the office in my charge. Just a few days earlier, Senator Ted Kennedy had fallen victim to the family curse: he drove his Oldsmobile off the narrow Dyke Bridge into Poucha Pond on Chappaquiddick Island, plunging his passenger, Mary Jo Kopechne, to her death. Drew left behind a column to run under his byline predicting that the tragedy would dog Kennedy for the rest of his life.

I was busy mobilizing the staff to break through the thick net of half-truths thrown up by the Kennedy propaganda machine when I got a call from Luvie Pearson. Drew had suffered a heart attack. Luvie's voice was even and unruffled, calming the anxiety that welled up in me. Drew needed a few weeks to recuperate, Luvie said. She suggested that no one from the office stress him with phone calls or visits.

One night a few weeks later, I answered the phone to hear Drew's weakened, thin voice. Why hadn't I come to visit him? I hurried out to his farm on the Potomac the next day and found him sitting at his typewriter. He had a paragraph in the making about the state of medical care. "I thought I would help you out," he said, with a tone of sheepishness. I assured him we would muddle along without him. Two days later on September 1, 1969, he collapsed in his garden and was dead.

I was overwhelmed with grief and suffocated by the challenge of carrying on without him. My agitation crept into my sleep, where more than once I dreamed that he was still alive, and each time I was startled to see him. Drew's ghost offered even less guidance than had my living mentor when I had asked him the secret of his success. I had to assume that his advice then—"Write a good column"—was still the only credo I needed.

I signed a hasty contract with the Bell-McClure Syndicate, which had been distributing the column, that I would pick up where Drew had left off. There was a brief skirmish with Drew's stepson Tyler Abell over my right to continue using the "Washington Merry-Go-Round" trademark. It was settled in the same way that Drew and his first partner, Robert Allen, had settled a similar dispute—with the realization that the column could stand alone without the trademark. My name had become recognized alongside Drew's, as he had intended, so Bell-McClure agreed to take me on as a syndicated columnist in my own right. I told Luvie that I had promised Drew, in case of his death, to pay her a monthly stipend; Drew had enough trust in me that he hadn't bothered to tell her about our arrangement. Of course, I kept my word, and Luvie, in turn, let me continue to call the column the "Washington Merry-Go-Round."

My staff was small but strong and included two of Washington's best reporters, Les Whitten and Joe Spear. Joe had been raised on Drew Pearson in his hometown paper since the age of ten. He had joined my *Parade* staff earlier that year, but it was the column that stirred his soul. The steady and scrupulous Joe Spear would become the eye of my hurricane. Les was a hotshot reporter who had worked for the *Washington Post* and Hearst newspapers. When he heard of Drew's death, he waited a barely respectable four days before applying for a job. He turned out to be an eager, earnest news sleuth, who was incapable of telling a falsehood.

The Washington Merry-Go-Round, under my new management, could not afford to observe a period of mourning. We scrambled to hold the business together, with me struggling to fulfill all of Drew's speaking and broadcast commitments. Chappaquiddick was to be my first major story without the hand of Drew Pearson to guide me. I quickly discovered that Drew's death had not changed my status. I was still a pariah.

I got a running start on the Chappaquiddick story by studying a stack of internal memos to *Time* magazine editors from their reporters on the scene in Massachusetts. I published some quotes that *Time* had neglected to include in its cover story, causing the magazine to complain in print about how I could get my hands on all sorts of secrets, even their own.

The ace up my sleeve was a close friend of the Kennedy family whom I still cannot name today. Under my persistent persuasion, he slowly leaked details from inside the family circle. I took his meager information to other Kennedy friends and authorities who were investigating the accident. Bouncing from source to source with more facts from each encounter, I was able to patch together an independent account of what happened the night of July 18, 1969.

TEDDY, THE LAST HOPE OF THE Kennedy political dynasty, had left a barbecue on Chappaquiddick in the company of one of the pretty "boiler room girls" from Bobby Kennedy's presidential campaign. Almost no one believed Kennedy's own account of how he was innocently driving Mary Jo to the ferry, of how his car went off the bridge because the road was unfamiliar to him, of the confusion and disorientation that kept him from calling for help.

Stacked against him were the facts: that he failed to report the accident to the police; that he walked from the bridge back to the party, passing several places where he could have used a telephone to summon help; that he returned to his motel room, changed into dry clothes, and deliberately established an alibi by showing up in the motel office to complain about a loud party next door; that he got up the next morning and passed some time with friends before going to the police station. All the while, Mary Jo Kopechne, perhaps alive for a critical few minutes, was floating in his car at the bottom of the pond.

There was no mention in Kennedy's story of the truth I uncovered: that in his initial panic, he hatched a plan to claim that one of his aides was driving the car and that this plan drove his bizarre actions throughout the long night following the accident. Here's what Kennedy intimates told me:

As darkness fell on the barbecue, Kennedy invited Mary Jo for a mid-night swim on a beach that was familiar to him, accessible by a road that he had used several times. (My sources told me that his late brother John had frequently visited a secluded section of the beach, owned by New Hampshire's former governor Robert P. Bass. John could swim privately there without encountering curious stares at the heavy corset he had to wear because of a back injury. As president, he continued to use this private beach, in the company of his family, likely including brother Teddy.)

Teddy's car hit the narrow Dyke Bridge at a speed too fast for safety, shot out over the water, flipped, and landed bottom up in the cold, swift tidal water.

Kennedy wiggled out of his open window and rose to the surface. I have no reason to doubt his claim to friends that he dove repeatedly trying to find Mary Jo, but could not see her in the murky water. Kennedy walked back to the party cottage, passing four houses along the way where he could have stopped to use a telephone and summon help. At the party, he managed to draw two aides away from the others without being noticed. They put their heads together and came up with a deception. One of them would say he, not Kennedy, had been driving Mary Jo to the ferry. (The Kennedys had a standing joke among their intimates, a facetious test of loyalty: "If I committed a crime, you'd take the rap for me, wouldn't you?")

The three men went back to the pond to survey the scene. By this time

Kennedy may have been able to convince himself that if Mary Jo had escaped, she had certainly taken care of herself, found help, gone back to her motel. Perhaps the circumstances of their midnight liaison were too embarrassing for either of them to call attention to themselves or the accident. They'd had a few drinks. Neither one was thinking clearly. That is the only benefit of the doubt I am willing to give Kennedy even after the mellowing passage of the years.

Kennedy would later claim that thinking there was nothing more he could do, he swam the 150-yard channel between the islands of Chappaquiddick and Martha's Vineyard and returned to his room at the Shiretown Inn in Edgartown. My sources told me that Kennedy didn't swim that night, but that his two aides found a rowboat on the beach and rowed Kennedy over so he did not have to make an appearance on the ferry, which would have fixed the time of his return.

Whatever his mode of transit, Kennedy, in dry clothes, walked into the office at the inn at 2:25 A.M., complained to the night manager about a noisy party that was disturbing his sleep, and made a point of asking for the time, explaining that he had lost his watch. He had established his alibi.

The next morning the trio met at the inn and took the ferry back to Chappaquiddick where the ferry operator Richard Hewitt left them at the landing. Kennedy headed for a public phone when an unidentified old man with thin strands of white hair approached him. "Senator, did you know they found a body in your car?" Kennedy was visibly shaken.

Hewitt made several more round-trips with the ferry and noticed that Kennedy and his party hadn't left the landing. He figured they must not be aware of the submerged car, which by that morning was the talk of Chappaquiddick. So the ferry boat operator approached the three and asked them if they knew there had been an accident with Kennedy's car. The senator sidled away, but one of his aides answered, yes.

Kennedy's personal delusion had been shattered. He could no longer tell himself that somehow Mary Jo had managed to escape and go home, and he could not pin her death on someone else. Witnesses told me that he struggled visibly to control the emotions rising in his face. Then he got back on the ferry for the crossing to Edgartown. Kennedy hit the landing running and didn't stop until he reached the police station. An officer there put him on the phone to Police Chief Dominick Arena who took the call in a cottage near the accident scene. Kennedy refused to answer questions over the phone. Instead, he asked Arena to come back to the office. When Arena arrived still in his wet swimming suit, Kennedy's first words were, "I was driving the car."

District Attorney Edmund Dinis decided to handle the investigation as an inquest rather than turn it over to the grand jury. He had to beat back the Dukes County Grand Jury, which was eager to conduct its own investigation. I cultivated sources on the investigative team and scored my biggest coup—copies of the secret interrogation transcripts from the inquest. The documents allowed me to drop several bombshells.

Kennedy himself gave contradictory testimony, saying at one point that he believed Mary Jo to be dead after his initial dives to rescue her, and saying later that he held out hope she was still alive. The inquest also revealed that a deputy sheriff patrolling Chappaquiddick that night saw a car on Dyke Road at 12:40 A.M. and when he approached it, the car sped off. It was the same car, he said, that was later pulled from the murky water.

Most damning was the testimony of John Farrar, the diver who finally found Mary Jo's body. He said her face was pressed up into a spot in the car where an air bubble would have formed. Farrar concluded that Mary Jo may well have spent a terrifying few moments sucking the last air out of the car before she died. "Had I received a call within five to ten minutes of the accident occurring, and was able, as I was the following morning, to be at the victim's side within twenty-five minutes of receiving the call, in such event there is a strong possibility that she would have been alive upon removal from this submerged car," Farrar told investigators.

Kennedy and his lawyers parried any and all evidence that the senator had left Mary Jo to die. They saved him from official culpability, but they could not save him from a political disaster. He held on to his Senate seat, all right, but his family's hopes that Ted would some day sit in JFK's place in the Oval Office died with Mary Jo Kopechne.

Unlike some who forever after Chappaquiddick saw Kennedy as an irredeemable character, I set aside the incident as one of those terrible hands dealt by fate. The intervention of fate does not absolve Kennedy from culpability, but there comes a point where the past must be forgotten. I liked Kennedy, and I hoped the American people would let him move ahead with his life. He could still be an effective force in the Senate, even if he had, by his actions that night, removed himself from contention for the presidency.

THE SECRET INQUEST TRANSCRIPTS FROM THE Chappaquiddick investigation helped launch the Jack Anderson column into orbit. Then I had to do something—or felt I had to do it—that, to this day, I'm not proud of. As soon as I began publishing excerpts from the transcripts, I got a call from the tabloid the *National Enquirer*. The owner of the paper, Gene Pope, had been a friend of Drew's. He told me the word was out that I had a thick file on the inquest. Would I sell it?

SHOPPING WITH IMELDA

MAKING TIME FOR MY WIFE AND nine children often meant taking them along on my news-gathering trips. In 1970, I spent August hopping around the world picking up interviews with as many heads of state as I could gain access to. I took Libby and two of our daughters, Cheri and Laurie. As always, the presence of my family changed the dynamics of my encounters with the power brokers of the world. The news of the day has long since faded, but the family snapshots remain in my mind.

When we stopped in the Philippines, President Ferdinand Marcos and his flamboyant sidekick Imelda rolled out the red carpet for us. I expressed disappointment that I did not have time to travel to Bataan and Corregidor, and Marcos immediately produced his helicopter to take me there. Imelda took the ladies to lunch by presidential limousine. In the evening we went nightclubbing and ended up in a spot where Filipino dancers tried to coax me into a tricky native dance that would have required me to do a two-step while they slapped bamboo poles around my bare feet. Cheri saved my ankles by volunteering to dance instead of me. She was a practiced folk dancer and had no trouble prancing in and out around the pounding bamboo, much to the delight of the Filipinos.

Years later when the Marcoses were driven out of power and the obscenely extravagant contents of Imelda's clothes closet were exposed, Libby and the girls were not surprised. When they had expressed an interest in seeing the sights of Manila, Imelda had taken them to her favorite spot—an open-air shoe market.

Drew's death had left the office finances in limbo, and I had no money to make the payroll. Under normal circumstances, I would have said no to anyone who asked to buy my research. But when the *Enquirer* called, I paused only to draw a deep breath before I said, "How much?" The offer was $12,500—a huge sum in those days—and I took it. I had already gleaned what I wanted from the inquest files and planned to print no more excerpts. The money went immediately to pay debts, office expenses, and salaries.

As the Chappaquiddick story and the attendant gossip was easing off the front pages and into the history books, I turned my attention to another senator, the likeable, light-footed George Murphy. A veteran of forty-five motion pictures before he traded in his dancing shoes and makeup for the Senate, Murphy's flaw was that he could not completely leave his old profession behind.

I received a phone call in early March 1970 from a source who passed on an incredible tip—that Murphy had remained on the payroll of Technicolor Inc. for the five years that he had been in the Senate, collecting $20,000 a year as a consultant to a company that did business with the government. My source said not only was Murphy collecting a salary, but he carried company credit cards and Technicolor picked up the rent for his luxury apartment in Washington, an apartment with its own movie projection room.

History is crowded with senators and congressmen on the take, but few have been so bold as to moonlight as the salaried employees of big corporations. At the time, Technicolor had a $3.5 million contract to handle all the filming at Cape Kennedy. The owner, Patrick J. Frawley Jr., was a right-wing extremist who had a record of trying to use his corporate weight and money to manipulate Washington. He had made his money in ballpoint pens, then bought the Schick Razor company before acquiring Technicolor.

My source swore to me that the tip was accurate, but he did not have any proof—no check stubs, no tax records, nothing. My best approach was to confront Murphy, himself, and try to get him to admit he was on the Technicolor payroll. I left a message with his office, and he called me back promptly. With as benign a tone as I could muster, I told him I had heard of his salary and allowed as how it might be some old business arrangement from his movie career. Apparently I was not understated enough, because Murphy didn't bite. He denied outright that Technicolor was paying him.

This denial called for a different tack—the bluff. Because he was a nice guy, I said, I would ignore the lie he had just told me and begin the conversation afresh. I told him I knew that he had recently fessed up to the Senate Ethics Committee and that they had given him their stamp of approval, saying there was no conflict of interest in his side job. I knew no such thing, but I figured that anyone who had attained the senatorial heights might try to cover himself by getting the secret approval of the Ethics Committee just in case he was caught. I was right. Murphy began to spill out the truth, how he was merely a consultant to Technicolor, that he never used the credit cards for anything except company business, and that the company only paid for half of his rent in exchange for letting Technicolor executives use the apartment when they were in town.

Had Murphy given me those excuses from the get-go, I might have weakened in my resolve, but his first reaction had been the classic response of a man caught red-handed—deny everything and admit nothing. He knew his little sweetheart deal was wrong, and now I knew that he knew it. I thanked him for his candor and pulled another reportorial trick out of my hat, suggesting he not mention our conversation to anyone. I needed time to think about his response and decide what I was going to do, I said.

In reality, I already had enough information to publish a solid column, but the editing, fact checking, reviews by libel lawyers, and finally distribution through the syndicate would take at least four days. That was valuable time during which Murphy could preempt me with a press release putting his own spin on the story. By the time my column appeared, it might be old news.

It was a problem we grappled with every day. The hotter the story, the more likely the subject might attempt damage control. Equally likely was the possibility that one of our subscriber newspapers might steal our scoop, independently verify the facts, and print their own story. I didn't like leaving Murphy or anyone else with a false sense of hope, but I also knew I wouldn't last a week in my business if I couldn't buy some time.

It was unseemly for Murphy to be eating from Frawley's hand, but apparently not illegal. As I had guessed, he had taken his little problem to Senate Ethics Committee Chairman John Stennis who patted Murphy on the back and told him there was no problem, no conflict of interest. I packaged everything I knew into a column and held my breath. We made it into print without losing the scoop.

Then, I sat back with curiosity to watch the reaction in California, where the *Los Angeles Times* had stopped buying my column months before. The column ran in other California papers, and I noted with satisfaction that the *Times* had to do a follow-up story giving me credit. Murphy was standing for reelection that year, so the rest was up to the voters. Eight months later they gave him his walking papers. Murphy's opponent, John Tunney, had made loud and repeated use of the Technicolor story throughout the campaign.

In writing about the George Murphys, Ted Kennedys, and Tom Dodds of the Senate, I must repeat that most senators are leaders of proven ability, decorum, and character. That has been my observation after more than half a century watching from the ringside. Nevertheless, when people in positions of trust cheat, the public has both a right and a need to know. Thus I find myself making a living uncovering the mistakes of honorable but imperfect people. I have ruined not a few reputations, and I have never enjoyed it.

That said, I confess there are moments of pure joy when some public servant forgets who the true bosses are and I am around to remind him. Like Ed Fike, who expected to become governor of Nevada. My brush with the aforesaid Fike began on a slow news day with a tip from a source in Nevada. The tipster told me that Fike, the Republican lieutenant governor who was leading the race for the top job, had bought some land along the Colorado River from the state at a suspiciously cheap price, and his company stood to make more than $2 million by developing the land.

State politics, even hotly contested gubernatorial races, don't usually catch my fancy. They simply don't hold enough interest for a national audience. But

THE GOOD COP

I N MY BAG OF REPORTORIAL TRICKS is the tired old ruse of good cop, bad cop. I am constantly surprised that something so obvious is still so useful in eliciting information from otherwise reluctant subjects. I prefer being the good cop and have had the most success casting my younger associates in the role of bad cop.

It worked like a charm in late 1970 when a tip came my way from the Mafia. A mob courier, with an agenda that wasn't quite clear to me, came to my office with a tip: Connecticut Congressman Bob Giaimo had pulled some strings to keep the courier and a friend out of the army. At the time, I was working on a story about the burgeoning loan-shark business in Washington run by New York City mobsters who were threatening to break bones and worse if borrowers didn't make good on their loans.

I knew that the Washington grand jury looking into the loan-sharking operation had evidence that it was being fed by underworld money flooding into Washington from mob families all over the country. And some of that money was coming from New Haven mobster Paul Coppola, whom I knew to be a friend of Congressman Giaimo. Now all I needed was to confirm the tidbit about Giaimo doing favors for the mob.

Les Whitten had been working the story for me, so I took him along to Giaimo's office. I opened the conversation by stroking Giaimo with rumors that his name had been mentioned as the best prospect to fill the governor's seat in Connecticut. He beamed until my own face took on a troubled expression. "I felt obligated to bring Les Whitten with me today," I said, turning a withering look on Les, a look I hoped would convey the impression that this young pup was about to lose his job for sloppy reporting. "Les has come across some information from the Justice Department," I continued. "I understand you wrote some letters to the army to get two men of questionable reputation out of service. And I heard you had some ties with Paul Coppola. I just wanted to clear up this little misunderstanding." I looked at Les again as if to puzzle over why I had ever hired this muckraker.

Giaimo stepped into the trap. Everything was above reproach, he said. His business dealings with Coppola were minor and he had no idea the two young men he had helped had Mafia ties. "My files are open," he said. Those were the magic words.

"Then you wouldn't mind if I let Les here look at those files while you and I continue our discussion about Connecticut politics?" I asked. He was cornered. Les disappeared into another room with the files while I bought time with Giaimo, dredging up everything I knew about his home state. When Les came back forty-five minutes later, I was on the verge of asking Giaimo how he planned to redecorate the governor's mansion.

A few days later when we published the story of the loan sharks and the ties to Giaimo, the congressman had only one complaint: We could at least have noted that we read the files with his permission.

there was something special about the frontier flavor of Nevada politics, mingled in those days with the mob influence in casino operations.

Joe Spear pulled together the details about Ed Fike, and we unleashed the story about Fike and his real estate wheeling-dealing. To give it a national flavor, we added some tidbits about a campaign stop in Las Vegas by Vice President Spiro Agnew to stump for Senator Bill Raggio. In blatant violation of the state rule against corporate meddling in campaigns, signs announcing Agnew's visit and rally for Raggio had been plastered on casino marquees. The Republican governor, Paul Laxalt, sweetened the story by ordering schoolchildren out of the classrooms and onto buses for a "field trip" to swell the crowds greeting Agnew at the airport.

It was a solid story, and we had the documents to prove it. But I didn't expect much reaction. I underestimated Las Vegas. The unwelcome attention to local politics from a Washington columnist set off a nasty skirmish between the town's competing newspapers. Hank Greenspun, the publisher of the *Las Vegas Sun* was backing the Democratic candidate for governor, underdog Mike O'Callaghan, so the *Review-Journal* lined up behind Fike. Hank—the *Review-Journal* always snootily referred to him by his full name, Herman Milton Greenspun—stood up for me and my right to cover Nevada politics. The *Review-Journal*, which carried my column, smugly announced that I owned stock in the *Sun*, implying a conspiracy. (I did hold a few shares of stock in the *Sun*—a token gift from Hank in appreciation for my help in saving him from a libel judgment.)

Oblivious to what was brewing in Nevada, I flew off to Davis, California, to deliver a lecture two days after the column ran. My return flight included a stopover in Reno. When I got off the plane, I noticed that the waiting area was crowded with reporters and photographers, all of them craning their necks in the direction of the passengers from my flight. I looked around to see what celebrity had stepped off my plane. It turned out to be me. The reporters swarmed around me and began firing questions. Did I know that Governor Laxalt was calling me an outside agitator? Was it the desperate Democratic underdogs who had put me up to it? Could I prove my allegations about Ed Fike?

JAMES FORRESTAL

EARLY IN MY APPRENTICESHIP WITH DREW Pearson, I saw him go through an ordeal so traumatic as to forever impress upon me the value of the human lives about which I write.

Drew had been a relentless critic of James Forrestal, secretary of the navy under Presidents Roosevelt and Truman and secretary of defense for Truman. Drew saw him as a tool of Wall Street and the military industrial complex. In addition to castigating Forrestal for his politics, Drew let it be known that this man, who served in positions that were critical to the national defense, was also mentally unbalanced.

In the spring of 1949, Drew learned that Forrestal had been locked up in Bethesda Naval Hospital outside Washington. The reason, as Drew put it in his blunt style, was that Forrestal was "out of his mind with a nervous breakdown." The man whom Drew considered his archenemy had blown his cork, just as Drew had predicted he would.

Forrestal had been vacationing in Florida at the home of Averell Harriman when he crossed the line between tenuous stability to all-out paranoid delusion. A fire station siren went off near the home and Forrestal ran out into the night wearing only his pajamas and screaming that the Russian army was invading. He was coaxed back into the house, sedated, and flown to Bethesda where he was under constant guard for fear that he might harm himself. He had already tried to kill himself three times while in Florida.

Two things the guards carefully kept out of Forrestal's reach for more than a month while he was a mental patient at Bethesda were newspapers and a radio. Still, each Sunday evening as the time approached for Drew's weekly news broadcast, Forrestal became visibly agitated—pathetic testimony to the impact that Drew's stories had had on Forrestal's fragile psyche.

On May 22, 1949, Forrestal was inexplicably left alone in his room in the tower wing of the hospital. His windows were barred, but he wasted no time getting to an adjacent food pantry where the window was open. Forrestal jumped to his death at 1:45 A.M.—a fact that Drew reported with even tones in a news broadcast later that day. In conversation, Drew refused to take blame. He blamed the navy doctors for leaving the suicidal Forrestal alone. He blamed President Truman for allowing Forrestal to continue in a critical, high-stress job when the president knew that Forrestal was teetering on the brink of insanity. He blamed Forrestal's friends for covering up and denying the reality of his condition instead of getting help for him.

To those who blamed Drew, and there were many, he responded without apology, "If we are to withhold criticism of a man because of possible illness or danger to his life, then congressional investigations, a free press, and our entire system of government by checks and balances becomes difficult." Publicly Drew was stoic, and he was right about where the blame belonged. Knowing the conclusion of the story would not have caused him to report the earlier chapters any differently. But privately, Drew's turmoil of conscience taught me a lesson—that protection of a free press can come at a high price.

I had already forgotten about the column, which had been Joe Spear's work. Lacking knowledge of the facts, I resorted to rhetoric. "I challenge Governor Laxalt to debate me on television. I'll produce my documentation and he can produce his." If memory serves me well, I fueled the fire with some references to Laxalt making accusations from the safety of the governor's mansion. "Meet me face-to-face like a man," I taunted. Then I boarded my connecting flight, confident that I could declare victory and leave. Laxalt was unlikely to take me up on an invitation to a televised debate, which would focus the spotlight on the dark doings of the man he supported to succeed him.

But, by the time I arrived back in Washington, Laxalt had already accepted the challenge. He invited me back for a slugfest on statewide television. I had neither the time nor the appetite for a showdown with Laxalt, who was an accomplished trial lawyer and a popular governor. He would be a tough opponent. But I had thrown down the gauntlet, and he had picked it up. In less than two weeks, I was back on a plane for Las Vegas, armed only with the Fike real estate documents and some background memos from my staff.

NEVADA DEMOCRATS WERE NOT THRILLED TO see me. In fact, Senator Howard Cannon begged me to cancel the debate, fearing that I would make a poor showing against the polished Laxalt, thus sealing the election for Fike and dragging other Democratic candidates down to defeat. I politely told the feverish Democrats that the election was their problem. "I'm here because the governor accepted my challenge, and I don't intend to duck out."

I arrived at the studios of TV station KSHO at 6:30 P.M. armed only with lightweight briefcase and a fervent prayer. Once inside, I learned that the station was owned in part by a crony of Laxalt's. I blustered a bit about fairness and a loaded deck, and wondered out loud what the Federal Communications Commission would think of such a setup. It was a lame ploy, but it worked. The anxious owner pledged his objectivity and assured me the FCC would have nothing to complain about.

When Laxalt arrived, we shook hands and came out swinging even before the cameras were turned on. The governor said, "You're the challenger, you go first." I refused, hoping to upset his strategy. "You're the host. You go first," I said. I suggested that we settle the impasse, Nevada style, by a coin toss. "Of course," the moderator interjected, eager to please me and the FCC. The toss went in my favor, and I told Laxalt to lead off.

Just a few moments into his opening remarks, I realized with satisfaction that he had not done his homework. He rambled on about what a decent guy Ed Fike was, ignoring the documentary evidence I had against Fike. Then, with exaggerated courtesy, Laxalt addressed me: I was an "Eastern columnist" wandering like a naïf in a state I didn't understand. Nevadans were hospitable people, who loved visitors and welcomed me. But they resented an outsider trying to tell them how to run the state.

Laxalt obviously didn't know anything about me. Nevada was heavily populated by Mormons, and its politics were frequently dominated by Mormons. I was as good as home. Laxalt paled as I launched into my bona fides: I was a dyed-in-the-wool westerner, raised just up the road in Salt Lake City by orthodox Mormon parents; my mother drove a taxi to support me on my church mission; Nevadans were my people too and my people believed that public office was a public trust.

I wound up with a challenge. I had a room at Caesar's Palace, I said, and I would be there right after the show to share my documentary evidence against Fike with any reporter who wanted to drop by. I invited Laxalt to join me and bring any materials he might possess to defend his man. The reporters showed up to pore over Fike's real estate deals, but we saw neither hide nor hair of Laxalt.

The next day's headline in the *Las Vegas Sun* declared me the winner by an eight-to-one margin, according to their informal survey. The *Review-Journal* spent its ink making more ado about my stock in the *Sun* and accusing me of being in cahoots with Greenspun to bring down the Republicans. There was no such conspiracy, but I admit I felt some vindication two weeks later when Fike lost the election.

The victor, Mike O'Callaghan, wrote me a letter to say that he owed his victory in part to me and the publicity over the debate. He was in my debt, he said, and hoped some day to be able to properly show his gratitude. I didn't know it at the time, but later I would cash in that valuable chip when I came back to Las Vegas to investigate a mystery that transcended local politics—the disappearance of billionaire Howard Hughes.

PART 4

NIXONGATE

1 9 6 8 — 1 9 7 7

By the time Richard Nixon assumed the presidency in 1969, I had been reporting on Washington for twenty-two years under Drew Pearson's tutelage. I have pondered how my own career might have been different from that point on had there been no Nixon making a nightmare out of government, straining at the chains of the Constitution, and embroiling himself in scandals that were an investigative reporter's dream. I probably would have found trouble no matter who was in the White House during those turbulent years, but Nixon made it so much easier.

My face-to-face encounters with him were few in the five decades through which I covered his cycles of victory and defeat, success and shame. I was never allowed entry to the Oval Office for an interview with him. He had distrusted Drew and automatically distrusted me. The stories I wrote after joining Drew did nothing to gain Nixon's confidence.

Murray Chotiner, Nixon's legendary political advisor, taught Nixon early on never to leave anything to chance. Chotiner's battle cry was, "Attack, attack, attack!" But he was better suited to withstand the counterattack than the sensitive and insecure Nixon. It was the ruthless, dirty-trickster Nixon who assailed his political enemies, but it was the shy, friendless Nixon who was wounded by the retaliatory blows. Seasoned political veterans who recovered quickly and completely from their tangles with Nixon would approach him years later and discover that he had not forgotten, nor had he forgiven.

Nixon ran the country with an amateur gang of White House aides who had not lived long enough to offend him. Anyone with more political experience had necessarily deserted Nixon at one point or another through his numerous ups and downs, and those who had jumped off his losing bandwagons of the past were not welcome in the inner circle when he became president.

He confided in few people, and even when he was with his closest friend, Bebe Rebozo, he had little to say. Senator George Smathers related to me how he sometimes socialized with Nixon and Rebozo, or did what passed for socializing. The three of them would sit in silence, with Nixon and Rebozo communing wordlessly while the gregarious Smathers itched for someone to talk to. In quiet conversation with his wife and daughters, Nixon called himself "I," but when he talked politics, he frequently lapsed into the third person, talking about himself as an absent party: "Nixon should do this . . . ," or "Nixon should say that. . . ."

Other presidents looked out the windows of the White House and saw the world. Richard Nixon looked out those windows and saw his own troubled reflection staring back at him. He judged everything by the impact it had on him. Drawn in like a turtle inside the Oval Office with his close circle of coconspirators, Nixon saw the world in terms of "us" and "them." "Us" was the handful of young operatives whom he had suborned to do his bidding, and "them" was everyone else.

The year that brought the election of Richard Nixon, 1968, also saw the assassinations of Martin Luther King Jr. and Robert F. Kennedy. While Democrats met in convention in Chicago that summer to choose a candidate to run against Nixon, police brutally clubbed antiwar protestors on the streets outside. The election was close, but Nixon finally won what he had sought his entire political career.

The Nixon years will be remembered for the scandals, but for which there would be little to mark this presidency. On the domestic front, Nixon made few changes. He is remembered as a brilliant foreign policy manipulator, lifting trade embargoes to China, negotiating détente with the Soviet Union, and reluctantly withdrawing U.S. troops from Vietnam. But those accomplishments were more the doing of his ingenious, if self-serving, foreign policy advisor Henry Kissinger. With Kissinger shuttling around the world to do the president's bidding, Nixon had time for his domestic priorities—digging up dirt on his political enemies, trying to muzzle the press, and scheming to ensure his reelection in 1972.

He did win, by a landslide, but his campaign, in fact his whole presidency, left a trail of dirty tricks and outright lawlessness that reporters were only beginning to uncover when Nixon took the oath of office for his second term in 1973. The dirtiest of the tricks had a name that became synonymous with the era, Watergate.

On June 17, 1972, a team of burglars broke into the Democratic National Committee headquarters in the Watergate office building in Washington. What they expected to find is still a matter of speculation. They were caught almost immediately, but it took two more years before the trail of evidence led to the White House and forced the resignation of Nixon himself.

Nixon was a grim man looming over a grim era. Antiwar demonstrators were killed at Kent State and Jackson State universities in 1970. Arab countries squeezed oil shipments to the United States and dried up the gas pumps in 1973. The Supreme Court legalized abortion in the *Roe v. Wade* case in 1973, opening a painful gash in the American body politic.

Vice President Spiro Agnew was forced to resign in 1973 when he was accused of tax evasion and taking bribes as governor of Maryland. The Justice Department's report detailing Agnew's sins was forty thousand words long.

An antiestablishment mishmash calling itself the Symbionese Liberation Army kidnapped newspaper heiress Patty Hearst in 1974. While the nation searched for Patty, she fell into line with her captors, changed her name to Tania, and announced that she had found happiness with the SLA, calling the band of thugs and losers "an environment of love in the belly of the fascist beast."

America's idea of a good time at the movies in 1970 was the maudlin *Love Story* where the leading lady succumbs to a mysterious disease after teaching the audience that "love means never having to say you're sorry." Our idea of a hot concert ticket was to watch rocker Alice Cooper (né Vince Furnier) rip the heads off of dolls while a boa constrictor slithered around his neck.

It was the worst of times—in short, a grand time to be a chronicler of events.

CHAPTER 10

J. EDGAR HOOVER, WHOSE BULLDOG VISAGE became a national symbol of the crusade against public enemies, Communist spies, and other evildoers, was 10 percent lawman and 90 percent bureaucrat. He loomed larger than life on the American scene during the mid–twentieth century. He not only lasted on top of the bureaucracy longer than any other American, but he also became the most powerful, most feared bureaucrat in the history of the republic.

He was the revered head of the FBI, whose crime statistics became the official yardstick of just how much evil lurked in the hearts of mankind. The arithmetic did not reflect favorably on the FBI, which appeared powerless to cope with the soaring crime rate. The G-men, however, showed no embarrassment over the increase. The more crime, the more money they required to fight it.

Under Hoover's one-man tyranny, the FBI devoted an incredible proportion of its manpower, its budget, and its priorities to spying on ordinary citizens who didn't fit Hoover's profile of patriotism. In 1970, when I found out that he had been keeping a file on me for thirty years, I decided it was time for me to reciprocate. I reached this decision after a plane flight across Pennsylvania, with Congressman Hale Boggs sitting beside me. We talked politics until, as we were approaching Washington National Airport, I wondered aloud when the nation's top cop was going to retire and why no one seemed to have noticed that he had passed retirement age.

No one would dare question J. Edgar Hoover's fitness for duty, Boggs said in a low, conspiratorial voice, because the FBI had files on everybody. Hoover could open up Washington's most exalted closets, with a great rattling of skeletons. "Anyone who takes him on will be destroyed," Boggs said knowingly. He described how Hoover engaged in delicate blackmail to hold the nation's leaders in his sway. The venerable lawman would place a friendly call to a high muck-a-muck, warning that enemies had gotten wind of some deep, dark transgression but that the FBI could be counted on to make sure the secret stayed safely buried. It wouldn't be necessary to add that Hoover might occasionally need a favor in return.

What Hale Boggs told me was hardly a surprise. But here was the House majority leader confessing that the nation's elected leaders, including himself, were afraid to offend Hoover. I was suddenly struck with the realization that the FBI chief wielded far too much power. There was grave need for someone to bell the cat. I decided that I would have to be the sacrificial mouse.

I leaned back in my seat and watched the Potomac River snaking below toward the Washington skyline. As we drifted down, it all came back to me, with a rush of mental images and impressions. I remembered my shock the first time I discovered that Hoover kept a file on me. It was back in 1950 that I got my first unauthorized peek at my FBI file. Until then, I had assumed naively that the FBI's files were a repository for the black deeds of criminals—murderers, rapists, arsonists, thieves, panderers, and the like. Growing up on the other side of the Wasatch Mountains in an austere Mormon household had allowed me little opportunity for mischief. The only organization I had ever joined, besides my church, was the Boy Scouts—hardly a hotbed of subversion.

I was not then inured to being the object of a criminal investigation, and a slow burn began smoldering in my gut. The next morning, I stormed into the office of the FBI's number three man, Stan Tracy, an acquaintance who was high enough to have some answers. I accused the agency of keeping a file on me and demanded to know what right it had to dog me.

Tracy laughed, though I detected more nervousness than mirth in his voice. "We don't have a file on you," he assured me. I offered to help him find it. I provided him with the file number and began quoting excerpts from the file. He blanched. "This is over my head," he said. "I can't comment on this." At that time, there weren't too many people over Stan Tracy's head at the FBI.

The sun hadn't set that day before Hoover himself called Drew Pearson. "Tell that young man not to worry," Hoover said. "The White House ordered it. You know how Harry [Truman] is. We have to follow orders and make inquiries." Drew didn't have a clue what Hoover was talking about, but he played along. Later he called me in. "What's going on over at the FBI?"

Still steaming from my encounter with Tracy, I unloaded my outrage. FBI agents were asking questions about my military service—whether I'd been a draft dodger and whether I'd ever given away army secrets. When I confronted the FBI, I told Drew, the FBI lied. Assistant Director Stan Tracy not only denied I was under investigation but denied the existence of a file on me. Yet I had seen the file, which contained evidence of the investigation. Furthermore, I said, I doubted this was the doing of Harry Truman. No, this was the work of J. Edgar Hoover. Drew merely chuckled. His own FBI file was four thousand pages long. If the FBI had a file on me, it meant I had arrived.

An entry on March 3, 1950, in the file that wasn't supposed to exist, noted that I had complained to Tracy and that I had been told there was no investigation of me. Hoover frequently penned his own reactions to FBI reports in the margins. Scrawled on this entry was a note from the chief in response to my claim that I had proof of the investigation. "Yes, I would like to see it as I somehow doubt all of the hullabaloo Anderson has raised about this."

(Hoover's notes in the margins were often sophomoric and petty, sounding more like the doodles of a temperamental schoolboy than the executive remarks of the nation's chief law enforcement officer. But they were as good as marching orders to his lockstep agents. On one occasion, a green agent submitted a memo and didn't leave enough room in the margins for Hoover to scribble. So the chief squeezed in an order, "Watch the borders." Within days, agents were being dispatched to beef up border patrols on the Canadian frontier and along the Rio Grande. They had no idea what they were watching for, but they knew the boss had told them to watch. The stakeout continued for weeks until someone ascertained that Hoover had merely wanted more room in the margins.)

The first entry in my file dated back to 1940. As a patriotic teenager schooled by the Boy Scouts in duty to God and country, I had informed J. Edgar Hoover of possible hanky-panky in my own hometown. The FBI files reflected that "Informant 42," (they assigned me the number), by the name of Jack Anderson had visited The People's Bookstore in Salt Lake City where he spent three hours discussing Communist philosophy with the local leader of the Communist Party. In the course of the conversation the informant, me, had gotten the distinct impression that the local leader was plotting to overthrow the U.S. government. The FBI thanked me for my information, but the notes in the file indicated that the agents were skeptical that a revolution would begin in Salt Lake City.

DREW'S RELATIONSHIP WITH HOOVER had started off in the clouds but lost altitude rapidly in the 1950s. In the beginning, Drew was impressed with Hoover, who had molded a group of misfits into a formidable law enforcement agency. In 1951, Hoover continued to turn a benign face toward us, but it was illusory. What we didn't know then—but what I found out years later from FBI documents—was that the FBI chief had started to keep a hostile, watchful eye on us. Memos were routed to him on everything pertaining to us, however trivial—gossip picked up about us; comments of our relatives overheard by eavesdropping agents; rumors of dissension on our staff; summaries of massive field investigations into where we got hold of classified documents.

On April 30, 1951, Hoover found before him a report that I had called to ask why an FBI agent was chauffeuring Senator Joe McCarthy's vacationing girlfriend, Jean Kerr, around Hawaii. Hoover was stirred to scrawl this note in the margin: "This fellow Anderson and his ilk have minds that are lower than the regurgitated filth of vultures." Hereinafter, the "young man" of happier days was to be known as "a flea-ridden dog," and the Bureau was instructed to treat any person in any way associated with me as "infected."

Perhaps I would earn those epithets in the years to come, but in 1951 I was still more Boy Scout than flea-infested canine. What had I done to arouse Hoover's terrible wrath? For one thing, I had shined a bright light into a murky world that he claimed didn't exist. Undercover narcotics agents had assured me—Hoover's denials not withstanding—that there was a Mafia.

I developed a confidential relationship with the chief of the Federal Bureau of Narcotics, Harry Anslinger, who was Hoover's nemesis. Harry was the real bulldog that Hoover only pretended to be—a gruff, growling watchdog who had taken a bite out of organized crime. Anslinger's agents had infiltrated the Mafia and had compiled a rogues' gallery of Mafia godfathers, dons, and soldiers—complete with their names, nicknames, Mafia connections, criminal records, and photos. I wheedled a copy of these confidential biographies from Harry. It was a complete *Who's Who in the Mafia*, with the lowdown on hundreds of colorful characters who answered to such names as Greasy Thumb, The Enforcer, Little New York, Dandy Phil, Little Big Man, The Camel, Jimmy Blue Eyes, Trigger Mike, and Golf Bag. All of them belonged to a criminal combine that Hoover swore wasn't there.

Some critics have charged that Hoover was paid by the crime lords to lay off the Mafia. I ran down every likely lead, checked every credible rumor, nailed down every possible fact. I can report with confidence that he took no bribes; the reason he denied the Mafia's existence can be attributed, rather, to his bureaucratic mind-set. Hoover had no intention of risking his reputation on so uncertain an imbroglio as a war against the Mafia, whose shadowy Sicilian roots were beyond his ken. So he simply proclaimed that there was no Mafia. Because he had built his reputation on arrests and convictions, he preferred to engage his agents in more statistically satisfying pursuits such as tracing stolen automobiles and chasing bank robbers.

Hoover's showboat law enforcement—with glorified statistics and agents who looked as if they had been selected by a Hollywood casting office—drew Anslinger's scorn. Hoover's agents could never find their way around the real underworld, Harry scoffed. "Their idea of going under-cover," he sneered, "is to take off their ties."

With the Mafia social register for reference and Harry Anslinger to guide me, I set out to prove that J. Edgar Hoover was wrong about the Mafia. I visited Mafia haunts. I met half a dozen Mafia godfathers. I toured nightclubs in New York City and Chicago with Mafia figures.

I even called on the boss of the bosses, Charles "Lucky" Luciano, who had been banished to Italy. My sources said he was still calling the shots from a luxury apartment in Naples. Anslinger slipped me a file of details about Luciano, including his address, private phone number, and auto tag number. I flew to Naples where I dialed Luciano's unlisted number. The Mafia overlord himself answered. Impressed, perhaps, that I had his number, he agreed to meet with me that night at a fashionable restaurant that my file identified as his.

It was an evening straight out of the *Godfather*. In fact, I was amazed when the movie was produced many years later at how accurately it por-trayed the Mafia. Like the other godfathers I had already met, Luciano was soaped, manicured, pressed, and pomaded. He appeared relaxed, but I sensed a tenseness in him.

The room seemed to revolve around our table. As we talked, sinister-looking men would materialize, one or two at a time, and lurk in the background until they caught his eye. Then with quiet courtesy, Luciano would excuse himself, leave the table, and hold a whispered conversation with the petitioners, who would disappear into the night. The ritual was repeated over and over throughout a long night that produced more drama than information.

Next, I backtracked Luciano's trail to New York City, where he had ruled the underworld. After Luciano got the boot from Uncle Sam, Frank Costello stepped into his shoes. I asked enough questions that the word got back to Costello. The phone rang in my hotel room one evening, and the voice on the other end said: "I understand you're asking around about Costello. I may be able to help you. Can we meet?"

In a darkened nightclub drenched with drama, I met the caller, who turned out to be a professional public relations man. His biggest-paying client, I gathered, was the Mafia. "What do you want to know about Fran-kie? He's a respected businessman who's just trying to live down a checkered past." I said that I had a copy of the Narcotics Bureau's file on Costello that showed his business was less than savory. The PR man ticked off a list of Costello's interests—oil, real estate, ice cream, household accessories, kewpie dolls. "And gambling, prostitution, and extortion," I added.

The press agent tried in his best Madison Avenue fashion to court me—short of arranging a meeting with Costello, who was media-shy. A few days later, he called me from Miami and offered a deal. "You leave Frankie alone, and we'll deliver Joe McCarthy." He hinted that Senator McCarthy had done favors for the mob in exchange for mob money. Drew and I were engaged at the time in a mortal feud with McCarthy. "You've aroused my interest," I said.

The PR man gave me a name, a date, and an address in Milwaukee, with cryptic instructions that I show up at the appointed place at an appointed time. The first thing I did was check out the name in my Mafia mug book. I verified that I had an appointment with a notorious Mafia figure. So I flew to Milwaukee and kept the date. The mobster was expecting me. But when I asked for the evidence on McCarthy, he growled: "I don't know what you're talking about." This appointment was not my idea, I said. I told him who had sent me and what I was supposed to be given. "I don't know what you're talking about," he said again. I asked why he thought our appointment had been arranged. "I don't know what you're talking about." I flew back to Washington and wrote a column about Frankie Costello.

It occurred to me that my forays into the underworld, armed only with a pad and pencil, might be a mite dangerous. I took some comfort from the knowledge that in the past, mobsters had reaped a whirlwind of bad publicity for killing reporters.

I was threatened only once. It was delivered by a nervous messenger on behalf of Moe Dalitz, who had taken offense at some unflattering stories I had written about him. At the time, he was ensconced in Las Vegas, where the mob then had its hand in the till. I figured he was just trying to scare me. So on my next visit to Las Vegas, I confronted him at the Desert Inn, which he then owned. "I got your message," I told him. He pulled a puzzled face. "What message? What message?" he asked in manner that suggested he knew exactly what message. He invited me to be his guest. I declined. And that's the last I heard from Dalitz.

Under Drew's byline, I wrote a series of columns about the Mafia. I got a call from Tennessee Senator Estes Kefauver who asked whether I could back up my columns with enough solid evidence to sustain a congressional investigation. I pledged to cooperate and also put him in touch with Harry Anslinger. The last person who should have opposed this full-court press was the nation's top policeman. Yet J. Edgar Hoover yanked some political strings behind the scenes in a frantic attempt to block the investigation. He had good reason to fear it would destroy his credibility and make him look foolish. But Kefauver's resolution calling for hearings got stalled on the way to the Senate floor. Senate Majority Leader Scott Lucas, under pressure from Hoover, was holding it up, Kefauver reported. This might be an appropriate time, he suggested, for me to ask Lucas some pointed questions. I asked Lucas why he opposed an investigation of organized crime. Was the Chicago mob in his home state of Illinois applying pressure? And why was the FBI director, of all people, helping the mob sidetrack the investigation?

Lucas didn't like the questions, but he recognized a hot potato when he juggled one. Not long afterward, he announced grouchily that he didn't want to be held responsible for impeding a crime probe, and so he allowed the resolution to come to a vote in the Senate. Anyone who voted against it would appear to be coddling crime. Yet thirty-five senators were more afraid of Hoover than they were concerned about the public perception. The vote ended in a thirty-five to thirty-five tie, which Vice President Alben Barkley broke in Kefauver's favor.

To Hoover's dismay, the Mafia was laid bare for all to see. An estimated twenty million Americans became glued to their television sets, tracking one of the first televised congressional investigations. They heard strange talk of "bagmen" and "ice" and "the fix." They watched with morbid fascination as a long, colorful, nauseating parade of mobsters took the witness stand and pleaded the Fifth Amendment. Kefauver turned over a compost pile of gangland-business-political connections, of payments and payoffs and bribes. When it was all over, America knew that the Mafia was alive and active. Never again could Hoover deny its existence. But he couldn't bring himself to utter the word "Mafia." He insisted on identifying the criminal combine ever afterward by its nickname, "La Cosa Nostra."

WITHIN NINE MONTHS FROM THE TIME I visited Stan Tracy to protest that I was under investigation, the FBI had me under the microscope twenty-four hours a day. The impetus was a column I had written quoting from secret communications between General Douglas MacArthur's headquarters and the Pentagon. My approval rating inside the FBI having plummeted lower than a vulture's vomit, Hoover's minions had decided to find out who in the Pentagon was talking to me. The unfortunate agents who were assigned to my case dutifully followed me to my night classes at George Washington University, to movies in the middle of the afternoon (one of my vices), to the homes of friends, to the car wash.

My FBI shadows thought they were onto something when I showed up with an "unidentified" woman at Garfield Hospital on March 10, 1951, deposited her there, and returned three hours later. Thus, the FBI chronicled the birth of my first child, Cheri. Alas, the only dirt to be overturned there was the discovery that Jack Anderson hadn't paced the floor in the maternity ward with the other expectant fathers.

Seeking information on my habits and weaknesses, FBI agents pumped anyone they thought might become a snitch. They came up dry, with the exception of this description from one unnamed person: "Anderson was an energetic, conscientious young reporter, idealistic in character and temperate in all of his habits. He was somewhat talkative and indiscreet on occasions and reacted quickly to needling or criticism, and at such times he told more than he should about his sources and operations."

At one point in the surveillance, Hoover's number two man, Clyde Tolson, asked for a search of the rule books to determine whether the Justice Department had ever banned FBI surveillance in the Capitol building. I spent many hours in those days combing the corridors of the Capitol, and apparently my shadows worried that in spying on me, they might find themselves also spying on members of Congress—something Hoover disingenuously claimed he never did. No rule was found to the contrary, so Tolson and Hoover signed off on surveillance inside the Capitol wherever I wandered. But the agents were ordered to be "most discreet."

The original purpose of the tail was to find out who my Pentagon sources were. But after a few months, the FBI's bloodhounds, unable to find the leak, gave up the goose chase. Hoover stopped the surveillance, but he kept me high on his personal blacklist. My file thickened through the years, with his increasingly vehement commentary in the margins.

In 1957, Elizabeth Oldfield, a writer from the New York office of *Parade* magazine, innocently inquired as to whether Hoover would cooperate with her on an article about crime. She would do the research and writing and Hoover would get the byline in the "as-told-to" style. Aware that I was the Washington bureau chief for *Parade*, Hoover balked. With my encouragement, Elizabeth assured Hoover that I would keep my hands off the article and that it would be printed exactly as he wanted it to be. But Hoover would have nothing to do with a magazine that had a flea-infested dog as its Washington editor. Attached to the FBI report about the Oldfield request was Hoover's note: "I am opposed to giving any cooperation even indirectly to this outfit. Oldfield is a part of it and that is her hard luck. You just can't fool with a flea-ridden dog without becoming infested."

My file includes one flattering note from Hoover. I was "no friend" of the FBI, Hoover noted, but at least I was a "nice-looking fellow." The occasion for this high praise was my visit on June 11, 1969, to one of

Hoover's more talkative loyalists in the FBI hierarchy, C. D. "Deke" De-Loach. An untested source of mine had confided that H. R. Haldeman, John Ehrlichman, and Dwight Chapin (all Nixon White House aides who would become notorious during the Watergate era) were gay. The source told me they were frolicking with a naval officer who was a "notorious homosexual." Worst of all, the source said, the three aides met in the early morning hours before going to work at the White House. Those trysts were supposedly devoted to "perverted activities."

I didn't believe for a minute that the reports were true, but I bounced the rumor off DeLoach, hoping to shake loose from him something less scandalous and more newsworthy. His report notes that I claimed Drew was chomping at the bit to print the information, but that I had restrained him. We frequently used the good cop/bad cop tactic with satisfactory results, but this time it stirred up a minor panic in the White House and the FBI.

DeLoach's report reminded his superiors that former Vice President Hubert Humphrey was my personal friend and that I was no doubt smarting over the fact that Nixon was occupying the Oval Office instead of Humphrey. Haldeman, Ehrlichman, and Chapin were all interviewed, and the rumor rightfully was put to rest. They were promised that the notes from their interviews would be kept in Hoover's personal safe and not shown to anyone else.

Finally, Hoover himself wrote a long memo for his personal files, in which he called me "a rat of the worst type." He added that "Anderson is no friend of this Bureau because he knows he cannot get information from the Bureau," a fiction that Hoover passionately wished was true. Then Hoover added, "He is a rather nice looking fellow and is not like Pearson, who looks like a rat. . . . Pearson looks like a skunk and is one."

The contents of my FBI file were tame compared to the goods Hoover compiled on others. Around Washington, his archives were the equivalent of a call girl's little black book—confidential as long as the relationship was cozy, but deadly if the woman was scorned. Under the self-assumed mandate to investigate "domestic subversives," the FBI tapped the phones, peeped into the bedrooms, and rifled through the bank accounts of Americans who were minding their own business. Lobbyists' rooms were bugged so the FBI could spy on their dealings with members of Congress. Movie stars were followed so Hoover could prove his dark suspicions that they were Communists.

All the files were sacred property, supposedly hidden from the eyes of all save the FBI. But choice tidbits were sometimes bootlegged to influential politicians. Hoover ingratiated himself with presidents by sharing with them information from his files on their enemies. Yet all the while he kept files on those presidents, too, preparing to share their files with the next person who would occupy the Oval Office.

Franklin D. Roosevelt needled Hoover in public about his secret files. "You should see what they have on my wife," FDR joked in 1942. But for Hoover it was no joke. He hastened to issue a statement claiming he had no file on the saintly Eleanor Roosevelt—though, in reality, he kept a thick dossier on the first lady, even monitoring some of her most private conversations. The FBI chief took satisfaction in his suspicion that Eleanor carried on flirtations with a New York state trooper and later an army colonel.

The file on John F. Kennedy was probably the hottest in Hoover's presidential collection. I never saw this file, but those who did see it verified that it was steaming with descriptions of one-night stands, afternoon trysts, and long-term romances. Kennedy himself once mused aloud, "I'd sure like to see the file the FBI has on me." His remark reflected no surprise, no outrage, no challenge. He didn't question why such a file should exist. It was just taken for granted that Hoover watched everyone. Apparently the Kennedy file paid off for Hoover. Kennedy's first official act after he was sworn in as president was to call Hoover and ask him to stay on as head of the FBI.

Hoover's pernicious files became Lyndon Johnson's favorite bedtime reading; he often ordered them up as he might a library book. He and Hoover passed many a titillating hour swapping stories about the high and mighty. Richard Nixon occasionally checked out a file or two from Hoover's lending library in his quest for dirt on his enemies. The notorious tapes Nixon made of every word uttered in his office included his observation about Hoover, dripping with envy: "He's got files on everybody, damn it."

Hoover's secret file on Nixon before he became president included the suspicion of an FBI agent in Hong Kong that Nixon had romanced a beautiful Chinese woman there in the 1960s while on a business trip. In this case, the agent was not merely pandering to Hoover's thirst for scandal; the agent was worried that the former vice president might open himself up to blackmail by the Hong Kong locals.

The political files didn't match the criminal files in either number or volume. But their mass was substantial, and their existence was irrefutable proof that the FBI was, indeed, a political police force deeply involved in thought control. The FBI folders provided typical police blotter information. But they also contained rumors, chitchat, and vicious slander. Little of this information was generated by the FBI itself. Instead, a network of informers fed the FBI's agents, and the whispers became turgid prose that was forwarded to Washington.

Read singly, the political files might have seemed merely another dreary

FBI SECRETS

MY REPORTER JOE SPEAR DIDN'T KNOW quite how to respond the day I told him to get me some secret FBI files. I had heard rumors that they existed, but I needed to see them myself. Joe marched over to the FBI head-quarters, knocked on the door of the press office, and told the press liaison there that he wanted to see some secret documents. "Let's strike a deal," Joe offered without much hope of success. "I won't say where I got the files and I'll give you some positive press in return."

Needless to say, the direct approach didn't work. "Joe," the press aide replied, "we don't have secret documents."

A year later, Joe took great satisfaction in proving the man a liar.

It was an unusually slow day in 1972 and the rest of us had taken off for lunch, leaving Joe alone in the office. His usual pattern was to put all the phone lines on hold so he could eat his sandwich in peace, but for some reason that day he decided to answer the phone. The voice on the other end sounded like it belonged to an agitated flower child. "Man, you won't believe what I'm seeing here. Hey, man, I'm working in an FBI office and I'm seeing all these investigative reports on people who didn't do anything. Man, it's ridiculous."

"What do you mean, 'didn't do anything'?" Joe asked, while he fished for a pencil.

"They're not criminals! I'm talking about Tony Randall. I'm talking about Jane Fonda. I'm talking about Joe Namath. I'm talking about Ralph Abernathy, Martin Luther King, Coretta Scott King."

"I can't take something like this over the phone. I've got to see some-thing," Joe said. He gave the man our office address, hung up, and went back to his lunch. Within an hour, the caller was at the door with a thick lawyer's briefcase. He opened it up on Joe's desk to reveal the FBI's three-inch file on Jane Fonda—not a photocopy of the file, not a carbon of the file, but the original.

When Joe recovered from his shock, he fired up the copy machine. Once or twice a week for the next month and a half, the man spirited files out of his office and brought them over to our copy machine. We collected dossiers on twenty or thirty celebrities. From them we extracted two dozen bombs that we exploded in the column over a period of weeks. Hoover, seething with anger, scoured the FBI for the source. He never found our man.

example of bureaucratic excess. But examined in larger lots, they provided an intriguing case-by-case study of just how far the government had intruded into the lives of Americans.

The FBI followed the affairs, sexual and political, of actors and actresses, athletes and other celebrities, as avidly as did the fan magazines. But Hoover had a special hostility for black people who dared to believe in equality. In Hoover's mind, the civil rights movement of the 1960s was nothing less than a Communist conspiracy. He hounded Dr. Martin Luther King Jr. from Montgomery to Memphis. King's offices, hotel rooms, and home were bugged. For five years, the FBI listened in on the private and public life of this civil rights leader.

When King won the Nobel Peace Prize in 1964, a prize coveted by Hoover, the FBI chief reached his boiling point. He and his trusted sidekick Clyde Tolson dug up a surveillance tape of a party that King had attended at Washington's Willard Hotel. On Hoover's orders, the FBI lab doctored the tape to make it sound as if the reverend were having a more festive evening than befitted a married man of the cloth. The tape was sanitized of fingerprints, packed in a box, and addressed to King's wife, Coretta. An FBI agent flew to Florida to mail the package so it wouldn't bear a Washington postmark.

Then Hoover ordered a separate letter to be typed and sent to King suggesting that suicide was the better part of valor. The unsigned letter told King he had thirty-four days to take the "one way out." The deadline coincided with the Nobel Prize ceremonies in Oslo, Norway.

As luck would have it, the doctored tape found its way, unplayed, from Mrs. King's mailbox to the stack of tapes that workers at King's Southern Christian Leadership Conference were sorting through as they made a collection of his speeches. Neither it nor the letter was opened until after King returned from Oslo. Undaunted, Hoover placed in King's FBI file an unverified rumor from the CIA that King had commemorated his peace prize by chasing a woman through his hotel in Oslo while he was clad only in his birthday suit.

When Hoover couldn't find any real dirt on King, he manufactured it. One despicable attempt to besmirch King's reputation was all the more reprehensible because it came posthumously. Deke DeLoach invited me to his office at FBI headquarters where he passed on the details of a story he had heard from Hoover. Deke said that King's assassin, James Earl Ray, may have been hired by a jealous husband—a Los Angeles dentist enraged because his wife had borne King's child. I had never met Dr. King, but I liked what I knew of him. Drew and I had fought on the civil rights battlefield. Nevertheless, I felt compelled to check out what DeLoach had told me. I flew to Los Angeles where I conducted a quick field investigation of the dentist. I then waylaid both him and his wife in separate conversations. She was a spectacular beauty who undoubtedly could have turned King's head, and it seemed obvious to me that she was a handful for her meek husband. She acknowledged having a brief flirtation with Dr. King. But there was no child of dubious parentage and no evidence of foul play.

Nothing in Hoover's bag of tricks surprised me. I learned that the federal government kept a list of potential assassins—people who by liberal definition had a snowball's chance in hell of trying to kill the president. One of the lists was called "CP" for potential assassins who were also members of the Communist Party or simply leaned too far to the left. Another list was called "BP" for Black Panthers, although most of the black people on the list were not members of that organization.

One particularly brave source slipped me those lists on a stack of fanfold computer paper, which I toted up to Capitol Hill one day. Joe Spear and I had been summoned to testify before the Congressional Black Caucus in a hearing on investigative abuses against black Americans. As the hearing droned on, I decided it was time to liven things up. I put my hand over our microphone and whispered in Joe's ear, "Look, when they refer to this material, I'm going to grab one end of this fanfold paper and run. You stand here and hold the other end." A few minutes later, one of the congressmen said, "So, Mr. Anderson, how many names do you have there?"

"This many," I said. I stood up, took one end of the list, and, followed by scurrying TV cameramen, trotted across the hearing room and out the door as the paper unfolded dramatically behind me. Joe held on to his end, grinning.

The J. Edgar Hoover who kept tabs on the sex lives of everybody who was anybody was himself a bachelor who espoused Victorian virtues and regularly purged agents caught in sexual dalliances. His files, so replete with references to amorous encounters, were at the same time models of restraint. Never once, in the hundreds of confidential FBI files I got my hands on, did I come across a single use of indelicate language. Hoover would not have tolerated it. The agent who heard a naughty word escape the lips of someone he was assigned to follow had better find a prim way of telling the tale. Thus, the agent who followed Jane Fonda and her antiwar road show included the notation that one number in the show was a song called, "Kiss my A———." When atheist activist Madalyn Murray O'Hair wrote a nasty letter to the State Department concerning a passport mixup, the FBI file quoted from her letter, "I do not care to ——— around with you further." The author of the report felt the need to explain the deleted expletive lest the reader not be able to fill in the blank: "The above omitted word is a four-letter word which has sexual connotation and was omitted because of this."

It took almost twenty years for writers and researchers to summon up the courage to write about Hoover's own sex life. So different were the times and so powerful was the mystique of the FBI chief, that it would have been considered almost an act of treason to expose him during his lifetime. I suspected early on that Hoover might be homosexual, but it would not have occurred to me in his heyday to report on it. Despite his carefully cultivated image of priggish celibacy, despite his hypocritical treatment of homosexuals, and despite the way he accumulated proof of the sexual indiscretions of others so he could wield that information like a sword, I convinced myself that Hoover's own sexuality was not the public's business. The number two man at the FBI, Clyde Tolson, was Hoover's constant companion, a fact that I dutifully chronicled. Hoover's biographers today are not shy about pinning a label on his lifestyle and calling Tolson his paramour. But I think the outing has gone too far in the hands of those who claim that Hoover and Tolson attended gay parties dressed in drag. The Hoover I knew was too image conscious and too prim to risk being caught in such garish circumstances. I suspect that his paranoia would have kept him from cross-dressing even in the privacy of his own home for fear that someone might peek through his windows. Tolson was Hoover's only indulgence, his one risk, and he stayed close to that sole companion most of his adult life.

The FBI boss spent untold millions of tax dollars and countless man hours on nickel-and-dime investigations of people whose private lives were none of his business. My conversation with Hale Boggs on that 1970 flight sparked an idea; by the time the plane landed, I knew what I was going to do.

I checked newspaper morgue files and found decades of laudatory, often idolizing coverage of Hoover, the result of his successful carrot-and-stick approach to public relations. Back at the office, I gathered my staff together and recounted what Congressman Boggs had told me—that anyone who crossed J. Edgar Hoover would be destroyed. "I'm afraid we're going to have to find out if this is true," I said. "We're going to do an FBI-style investigation of Hoover." This would be a comic-opera caper, I explained—a burlesque that hopefully would make people chuckle. If Hoover's power lived up to the legend, then we had better begin with a burlesque.

We all knew the FBI's style—follow the subject and take note of everything, no matter how inconsequential; interview neighbors and friends; stake out homes and offices.

Our mini-FBI hit the road. Les Whitten tailed Hoover, who usually followed the same beaten paths. Precisely at 11:30 A.M. every day, he would stride into his favorite restaurant, the Rib Room at the Mayflower Hotel, where he would join Clyde Tolson always at the same table. Hoover's standing order for grapefruit and cottage cheese salad was always served as soon as he sat down. It was consumed within twenty minutes; Les carefully timed him. Tolson ate cream of chicken soup every day except on Tuesday when he ordered bean soup and spiced it with catsup. Les took copious notes.

Joe Spear sought out all Hoover's living relatives, which was easy to do because there was only one. Hoover's nephew, Fred Robinette, had made his uncle proud by joining the FBI and then had tweaked him by resigning after ten years. Robinette had nothing but praise for his famous uncle, but my dutiful agent Joe went door-to-door through the neighborhood asking questions. The neighbors reported that Robinette had asked Hoover for money to care for Robinette's dying mother, Hoover's sister, but had been turned down. Not so, Robinette insisted; he never asked Hoover for a loan.

The toughest task was assigned to our junior staffer Chuck Elliott—a short, beefy young man with a Jesse James mustache and a worn trench coat that Columbo might have given to Goodwill. Chuck was to stake out Hoover's house and, most important, go through his trash. It was no more than Hoover's own men would have done. What Chuck discovered in the garbage cans was that the seventy-six-year-old bulldog was painfully mortal. Empty Gelusil antacid packages forced us to conclude that the living legend suffered from gas pains. Crumpled Cepacol lozenge wrappers suggested he also had a sore throat. He brushed with Ultra Brite, washed with Palmolive, and shaved with Noxzema. Each day, in his distinctive longhand, he wrote out what he wanted his housekeeper, Anna Fields, to fix for meals. We found the menus on a pad impressively headed, "From the Office of the Director." The menus explained the empty Gelusil cartons. Hoover was always careful not to be seen drinking in public because of the wrong message it would send adoring young Americans, but his trash included empty Jack Daniel's and Irish Mist bottles.

Chuck was relentless, going back day after day to lurk in the alley waiting for the household help to bring out the trash. Not wishing to paw through the garbage on the scene, he would toss the bags into his little red sports car and speed away. Despite Chuck's careful tactics, however, Hoover's butler caught on and was waiting for Chuck one morning. "Young man, you're going to be in trouble if you keep taking that stuff." Chuck didn't miss a beat. "Sir, the trash was put out to be picked up and I'm picking it up."

A relentless sleuth, Chuck missed only one load of trash. The household staff had been hoarding it, hoping Chuck would go away. At one point, thinking he had finally given up, the staff set out several weeks worth of accumulated garbage all in one morning. Chuck arrived and determined there was too much for his little sports car, so he took off to borrow my station wagon. When he returned, the city trash crew had already scooped up the evidence.

When he wasn't collecting garbage, Chuck took notes on Hoover's comings and goings, following Hoover's bullet-proof Cadillac around town. The car was one of five armored limousines Hoover kept for his use around the country at a cost of $50,000 a year. At the time, the president of the United States had only two limos available to him.

Each morning Hoover departed from his jewel-box home located in a stately Washington neighborhood and was chauffeured to the back entrance of Clyde Tolson's apartment building where the tottering deputy chief would be whisked aboard. The daily drama was executed with such stealth that the doorman at the front entrance didn't even know Tolson lived there.

Despite the armored protection, Hoover was a frightened old man, hunching down in one corner of the backseat while his hat was propped up in the opposite corner. More than once, some long-haired kids in the neighborhood noticed that Hoover would crouch in his car if they were loitering on the street when he arrived home. He refused to leave the car until the "hippies" were gone.

We learned that Hoover never ate seasonal gifts of food that came from unknown admirers, fearing that someone might poison him. Yet he would donate the suspect goods to orphanages and other institutions, allowing their charges to take the risk. Hoover's fears drove him to nightmares, and his nightmares drove him to a high-society psychiatrist who, shrieking, denied to us that he had ever treated Hoover.

Chuck Elliott's Waterloo came on February 17, 1971, when he had the misfortune of pulling up to Hoover's house shortly after the arrival of Sam Donaldson and an ABC film crew. Donaldson was staking out the house unannounced, hoping to catch Hoover on the fly and get a comment on some story. While waiting, the ABC cameraman turned his camera on Chuck, who was examining Hoover's trash. The drama mounted as Hoover's chauffeur and housekeeper flew out of the house to scold Chuck. Unruffled, Chuck flashed a "V" for victory sign at the ABC camera, threw the trash into his car, and drove off.

Within minutes, Hoover's car drove off as well and ABC gave chase, only to learn that Hoover was not in the car. Donaldson returned, but soon gave up the stakeout, figuring that Hoover was holed up in the house or had escaped in another car. Back at ABC, the news executives were mortified that Hoover, the icon, might think the tacky trash collection was their doing.

THE POOP SCOOP

THOUGH OUR FBI-STYLE INVESTIGATION OF J. Edgar Hoover was reduced to the level of garbage, we didn't abandon our standards altogether. At least we spared his innocent dog, suppressing the fact that the trash contained poop.

It was clear to us that Hoover's dog was not adapting smoothly to the housebreaking routine. Yet, we decided to respect the dogs' privacy and never printed that story.

But White House aide John Dean was less discreet. In Dean's memoir of the Watergate era, *Blind Ambition,* he tells of a visit with Hoover to enlist the FBI lab to prove a letter a forgery. The letter was critical evidence in my investigation into government deal-making with International Telephone and Telegraph. Hoover was only too glad to oblige if it meant pulling the rug out from under my story (which, as it turned out, his lab was unable to do). Dean wrote that Hoover responded, "I'm delighted to be of service. Jack Anderson is the lowest form of human being to walk the earth. He's a muckraker who lies, steals, and let me tell you this, Mr. Dean, he'll go lower than dog shit for a story." Hoover explained, "Well, one day Anderson and his boys came out to my house to fish in my trash cans for a story. To look at my *trash,* can you believe that? Anyway, they fished all through that trash and all the way to the bottom, underneath the dog shit, to see what they could find. So when you're talking about Anderson I know you're talking about a man that'll go lower than dog shit to find his stories."

The thought of us going through his trash unnerved Hoover more than anything else we could have done. I suspect had we peered into his bedroom window, which we opted not to do, he would not have been as angry as he was over those trash cans. In a speech to FBI agents gathered at the Kennedy Center a few months later, he growled, "(One) of my more virulent critics—his name escapes me for the moment—has apparently fallen off his merry-go-round once too often. Last spring he spent considerable time sifting through my garbage. . . . My only reason for mentioning it is that I understand he is becoming increasingly confused between the trash he examines and the trash he writes. . . ."

I understand Hoover's minions burst into enthusiastic applause, including the ones who had leaked information to me.

One of them called the FBI to wash ABC's hands of the mess and put the blame on us. It seems that Chuck had begun to take real pride in his accomplishments. He wanted credit and had called ABC to make sure the news team knew exactly whose idea it had been to abscond with Hoover's garbage.

ABC continued its damage control, showing a deference to Hoover that years later a more seasoned Sam Donaldson would eschew. An FBI agent's memo to Hoover on the incident describes a telephone call from one ABC executive who agreed that "Donaldson and the camera crew used poor judgement in going to Mr. Hoover's residence in the first place, after Mr. Hoover had indicated that he would not grant any interviews, and that they should have at least advised the FBI in advance of their intentions to film Mr. Hoover departing his residence." Furthermore, the FBI was now satisfied that news executives "had given sufficient instructions to insure that no ABC cameramen would ever again take pictures at Mr. Hoover's residence."

Hoover's margin note indicated that he didn't believe ABC's denials of culpability. He quickly put his agents on the trail of the car caught fleeing the scene in ABC's film footage. That morning Chuck had unfortunately been driving his girlfriend's car. The license plate was traced, and FBI agents followed her to Chuck's apartment. From there it was only a matter of time before they spooked him. Two FBI agents appeared at his door, snapped his picture in a blinding flash of light, and rushed off triumphantly.

By dint of bad luck, meanwhile, Chuck's roommate happened to be the son of an FBI agent and felt it his duty to spill the beans about Chuck to his father. The father relayed the information to Hoover, and Chuck's roommate soon received a letter from Hoover: "I am grateful for your actions with respect to Charles Elliott. Your concern for my personal safety means a great deal to me personally."

When I found out about the letter and printed it, the roommate hastened to tell me that he had said nothing to his father that might make Hoover think Chuck was a danger to Hoover's "personal safety." Then he had to do damage control at the FBI; he made a quick call to assure them that he hadn't given me a copy of Hoover's note. As roommates, Chuck and the agent's son were washed up. Unnerved by the FBI surveillance, Chuck left Washington for a job in Delaware.

Our investigation had suffered its first casualty, but we weren't finished with Hoover yet. The burlesque of the garbage caper served as the launching pad from which we could begin to attack Hoover's more serious flaws. His affection for Tolson had caused him to keep the old gentleman on active duty long past his retirement age and long past the point when he had become feeble. Technically Tolson had retired and then been rehired as a

DESTROYING EVIDENCE

To ASSURE THAT NO ONE WOULD ever again snoop through his trash, Hoover passed the word to his subordinates that he wanted a garbage compactor that would smash his trash into cubes so solid no one could pry them apart. His aides took up a collection and presented him with a costly compactor at a ceremony to commemorate his forty-seventh anniversary with the FBI in May 1971.

This wish-list method of acquisition proved very successful for Hoover, whose aides could usually recognize an order in disguise. Hoover would muse aloud about how nice it would be to have something or other and the aides would scramble to raise the money so they could gift Hoover on appropriate occasions. Clyde Tolson shopped this way also, furnishing his apartment with gifts ordered from his underlings.

At least once, a gift was given to save the agents' own necks. While Hoover was off basking in the Del Mar sun, an agent who should have known better crept into Hoover's office to breathe the heady air. Overcome by the moment, he spilled his coffee on Hoover's rug and the agency was thrown into a full-scale cleaning frenzy. Even the chemists in the crime lab were pressed into service to come up with a cleanser that would rid the rug of the stain. But nothing would work, so the agents passed the fedora to purchase an identical rug.

Alas, with Hoover's return only three days away, they learned that the rug pattern they needed was no longer manufactured. Employees who worked for another boss might have given up at that point and thrown themselves on the mercy of the man. But Hoover's underlings knew better than to expect mercy from him, especially when his inner sanctum had been defiled.

The best minds at the bureau came up with a solution: Commission the factory that had made the original rug to make a duplicate, over the weekend. The weavers worked round the clock, and when Hoover arrived back at the office on Monday morning, the new rug was in place. He was none the wiser.

---

consultant. Thus, he didn't have to submit to the annual FBI physical, which would have revealed the fact that he had suffered a series of minor strokes.

Tolson and Hoover always vacationed together, usually slipping off to La Jolla, California, where Hoover would undergo his annual physical and the two would while away the rest of their stay at the Del Mar racetrack. I learned that their room tab at the luxurious Hotel Del Charro was picked up by millionaire oilman Clint Murchison. For one trip, the tab was more than $15,000, which was more than a trifle in those days. Always the gentleman, Hoover sent a thank-you note.

Once while at the track, Hoover lamented to Murchison what a shame it was that the profits from the oil business couldn't go to something worthwhile, like combating juvenile delinquency. Murchison promptly formed a nonprofit agency to reform wayward boys, and that agency bought the track. Cynics who saw the move as a tax dodge changed the motto of the seaside track from "Where the Turf Meets the Surf," to "Where the Oil Meets the Soil."

At the track, the image-conscious Hoover liked to leave the impression that he was never guilty of excess. He remained a $2 bettor, he said. But at least one racing companion told me that Hoover sent messengers to the $100 window with his bets. When at home in Washington, Hoover haunted the tracks in Baltimore and Laurel, Maryland.

The FBI publicity people, who were employed to sing Hoover's praises, developed lockjaw when I presented them with proof that Hoover had collected more than $250,000 in royalties on three books that bore his name. The books had been researched and ghostwritten by FBI employees working on government time. After stonewalling me for months on the distribution of the royalties, the FBI announced that Hoover had given the money to the FBI recreational fund and the employees who had written the books, and kept only one-fifth for himself. I dug deeper and found that Hoover had indeed pocketed only one-fifth of the royalties, but had given an equal share to Tolson, who had done no work on the books, and the same amount to Lou Nichols, his former PR man. The recreational fund got one-fifth and the rest went to a middleman.

HOOVER WAS SEVENTY YEARS OLD WHEN we did our FBI-style investigation. He was an anachronism living in a black-and-white past while the world around him had turned shades of gray. The world had changed significantly since his gangbusting days in the 1930s when his men had shot it out with the likes of John Dillinger and Baby Face Nelson and when Hoover himself arrested Public Enemy Number One, Alvin "Kreepy" Karpis, binding Karpis with a necktie for want of a pair of handcuffs. Hoover had built a formidable law enforcement agency that had broken up spy rings, nabbed Nazis, and blasted Bonnie and Clyde.

The Hoover I investigated in 1970 and 1971 reigned over sixteen thousand agents who risked being fired if they were caught by TV cameras without their suit coats on during a bust. There was no job security for an agent who made the mistake of shaking Hoover's hand with a sweaty palm. Agents who tried to follow spies could be easily spotted because they had the cleanest cars in Washington. They knew they could protect their jobs better by buffing their cars than by catching a spy.

I concluded my investigation with a public suggestion that Hoover retire. It was past time. John F. Kennedy had intended to put Hoover out to pasture when he reached seventy, but Kennedy died first. Lyndon Johnson had been Hoover's neighbor for many years in Washington and enjoyed the old man too much to get rid of him. The president who would be Hoover's last boss, Richard Nixon, understood that Hoover was hurting himself by hanging on to the job. But Nixon was too afraid of Hoover to fire him, and too fond of Hoover to make the old curmudgeon bow out.

My suggestion that Hoover retire in 1971 struck some of my readers as a sacrilege. "In this household, Jack Anderson has become and will continue to be a dirty word," one reader wrote. From another came this advice: "If your recent columns on J. Edgar Hoover constitute your best efforts toward responsible journalism, you are unnecessary."

Hoover outlived my suggestion by a year. His last weekend was true to form. On Saturday he went to the racetrack with Clyde Tolson. On Sunday he puttered in his garden. Monday morning, May 1, 1972, he spent the morning at his office, lunched with Tolson at the Mayflower, worked through the afternoon, and left for Tolson's apartment at 5 P.M. for what was his last meal with his old friend. He was home in time to watch some TV before going to bed. The next morning, housekeeper Anna Fields went to awaken Hoover and found him dead.

I had scheduled a column the next day chiding Hoover for discriminatory hiring practices at the FBI. Instead I hastily substituted a tribute to him, at least as much of a tribute as my well-documented opposition to him would allow. I said the nation should pay homage to him for his accomplishments, but that it would be hypocritical and even dangerous to forget his excesses. Hoover was beyond the judgment of his critics.

I later learned that about a month before he died, Hoover had made a remarkably un-Hoover-like decision: to stand up to Richard Nixon. The president had signed off on a plan that would have put Hoover at the head of an interagency committee that would have the power to use illegal wiretaps, mail searches, and even burglaries to catch suspected subversives. The irascible old investigator said he would not be a party to it. In the end, there were some things that even J. Edgar Hoover would not do.

CHAPTER 11

RICHARD NIXON TAUGHT ME THE ADVANTAGES of being born ugly. Ugly he was—the drooping dark jowls, the unfortunate sloping nose, the marionette hand gestures, an appearance black and gloomy. For him, the ballot box would have seemed the least likely springboard to success. Yet he had carried his unfair burden up through the House and the Senate to become vice president and then president of the United States. This had to bespeak the inner superiority that unkind fate can nurture— the compensating enlargement of brains, tenacity, guile, and fortitude. On the hard testing ground of grueling election campaigns, of numberless speaking halls, of smoke-filled back rooms, he had somehow managed to warm the chill his visage cast, to triumph over his physiognomy.

Through his personal friends, including one who had lived in the Nixon home for eight months, I got to know the deeply private Nixon. He was a warm, shy, sensitive man who would refer to Nixon, the politician, in the third person as if he were a separate being—a political performer on the public stage, whose performance he would assess and analyze objectively.

I got a rare glimpse beneath the psychological scar tissue he had accumulated as he drove himself into one bruising battle after another, slashing his way to the top, suffering inwardly from the return fire. His political war cry was "Attack! Attack! Attack!" It was always that other Nixon, the politician in the spotlight, who did the attacking. But it was the sensitive, private Nixon who was battered by the answering bombardments. He suffered grievously, intimates said, from the shell fire.

I honestly tried to understand this lonely, suspicious president who fought so hard for public approval and was rebuffed so often. After Nixon ascended to the White House, I espoused the spirit of cartoonist Herb

Block who gave him a free shave and made him look more presentable in the *Washington Post* cartoons. I, too, tried to humanize Richard Nixon.

I must have betrayed enough sympathy to raise hopes within the White House. For Nixon made an awkward attempt to woo my favor. He dispatched Murray Chotiner, his political tutor, to call on me and propose a truce. I suspect it was Chotiner's idea. It had always been too difficult for Nixon to extricate grudges that got stuck in his craw. But Chotiner was trying to teach the new president the political advantage of letting bygones be bygones.

"Dick wants to be friendly," Chotiner told me. I doubted that, but I listened. "He's willing to give you any help that he can, and he's asked me to be the liaison." All I needed to do whenever I had to reach the president or wanted hard-to-get information was to call Murray. Of course, I had no intention of selling out to the new Nixon administration. But Murray hadn't said anything about a quid pro quo, and my curiosity was aroused. I decided to test the Chotiner channel quickly before he changed his mind.

I had recently returned from an investigative foray into Alabama where I had wandered around the catwalks and country roads chasing a hot rumor. I had heard that a political crony of Alabama Governor George Wallace was taking kickbacks from liquor sales in state liquor stores and routing the payments through a Montgomery, Alabama, law firm with a famous partner—George Wallace. I nailed down enough evidence to write a cautious preliminary story. My report had raised eyebrows, I knew, inside the Internal Revenue Service. I was almighty curious to find out what the IRS, with its subpoena power, had uncovered. I told Chotiner that I wanted to see those investigative files.

In a few days, he called with an invitation to drop by his apartment in the Watergate complex on the Potomac River. There, spread out on a table, was the full report from the IRS to President Nixon on the Wallace case. I made good use of the information, and Chotiner probably thought a new friendship had been sealed. But not long afterward, I wrote some critical comments about Nixon on another subject. I got a plaintive call from Chotiner accusing me of violating our arrangement. "What arrangement? I made no agreement. I thought you guys just wanted to be helpful," I said. The olive branch was abruptly withdrawn.

I BORED INTO THE NIXON ADMINISTRATION with no more or less zeal than I had assailed its predecessors. I considered my investigative reports traditional stories such as I had always produced. I didn't know at first that I was involved in a mortal battle, that every damaging story I published was creating a frenzy within the administration, causing it to strike back in ways that soon exceeded the limits of the law.

In October of 1970, I took a swipe at Nixon in the column for secretly trying to get the presidential retirement pension increased. He ordered his chief of staff H. R. "Bob" Haldeman to find out who was feeding me derogatory information. At the instigation of the White House, a dragnet was laid out to snare my informants. Anyone who was caught should have his or her head hoisted on a spike, the White House instructed, as a warning to others who may be tempted to talk out of school.

Months later, I got a call from a stranger—a $13,500-a-year Pentagon clerk by the name of Eugene Smith. "Do you know me?" he asked.

"No, I don't think so," I said, thinking I must have forgotten some chance meeting with this faceless bureaucrat.

"Have I ever talked to you?" he pressed me.

"No," I said.

"Well, I'm under investigation and about to be indicted for giving you secrets. Would you please tell them that I never talked to you?"

I sympathized but explained: "Even if you were my source, they know I would deny it, so I don't think they're going to take my word for it." I didn't even have to ask who "they" were. A White House source had already informed me that Haldeman was beating the bushes looking for people who had talked to me.

The story that was mistakenly blamed on the unfortunate Gene Smith appeared on December 21, 1970. It described a meeting at which Pentagon officials had sat around laughing and telling smutty stories while they decided who should be fired at Christmastime. I had a clandestine tape of the closed-door meeting, so when the Pentagon brass denied the story, I offered to play the evidence. They backed off and instead poured their energy into finding out who had secretly taped the meeting, invoking an obscure law that prohibited the "aural acquisition" of conversations in government buildings.

Now that there had been an actual violation of a law, Haldeman went after poor Gene Smith, with an eye toward sending him to jail. All the while, Nixon was engaged in the "aural acquisition" of every word that was spoken in the Oval Office. And Haldeman, as Nixon's alter ego, was entrusted with this knowledge.

This didn't prevent him from going after Smith's scalp for the same offense. Investigators combed Smith's neighborhood, knocking on doors, gathering intelligence. Under bright lights, Smith was interrogated by military investigators who badgered him in language laced with obscenities. They behaved like caricatures from a B-grade movie. "Do you know Anderson?" they demanded. "Anderson must be stopped!" they repeated over and over again.

Smith was fired from his job in a phony reduction of force. Debilitated by inflamed ulcers and high blood pressure, he was summoned before a federal grand jury in Norfolk, Virginia. When Smith denied the charges, U.S. Attorney Brian Gettings told Smith that he would nail him either for the illegal taping of the meeting or for perjury.

I called Gettings who, unbeknownst to me, was gradually beginning to realize he had the wrong man. "You may not believe what I'm about to say," I told him, "but it's the truth, and if it will help, I'll take a lie detector test because I don't want to see this person hurt." I told him I had never met Gene Smith, nor had I ever received any information from him. "We probably do have the wrong man," Gettings said. He would admit only that a "federal agency" had suggested he investigate Smith. Smith never got his job back, nor did he get an apology from the White House.

Up to that point, I had merely scratched the surface of the Nixon administration. I was about to lay my hands on a story that would go much deeper. The details came from documents that were highly classified. I have always published what I thought the American people ought to know, never for pure titillation and never, I hope, for the sake of scooping my peers. Occasionally the decisions have been agonizing ones. But usually, when something has come across my desk classified as a national security secret, it has involved the misdeeds and manipulations of people who had abused the public trust and then had swept the evidence under the secrecy stamp.

Such a case came into my possession in late December 1971, delivered by a source who could no longer abide the deception. The source asked me to meet him at a drugstore near the White House. Both of us were to pretend we were perusing the Christmas cards. Such Hollywood spy games are not my usual style, but my source ranked high in the Nixon administration, and he had learned that telephone conversations were not always private.

As we browsed among the cards, he lingered close enough to me to mumble a message. On December 10, President Nixon had ordered a powerful navy flotilla into the Bay of Bengal to intervene in the war between India and Pakistan—a war in which, publicly, Nixon had sworn neutrality. National Security Adviser Henry Kissinger was bullying the biggest names in the State and Defense Departments to secretly support Pakistan, a military dictatorship, and spurn India, the world's largest democracy. The nation of Bangladesh, once East Pakistan, was about to be born out of that struggle.

REGRETS

ON THE LIST OF STORIES I would do differently is a flimsy case of implied homosexuality. With the hindsight of thirty years and the mellowing that comes with age, I now believe I was wrong to run it the way I did.

The subject was James Rand "Randy" Agnew, newsworthy only because his father was the soon-to-be-disgraced Vice President Spiro Agnew in an administration that was hard-nosed about sexual deviation. In 1970, Les Whitten had heard a rumor that Randy, twenty-four, had left his wife and child and moved in with a Baltimore man who made his living as a hairdresser, running a salon with his mother. Randy worked as a weight-lifting instructor at a health spa, and he and the hairdresser were reportedly sharing a tastefully decorated town house in a gentrified neighborhood in Baltimore.

In the enlightened 1990s, the combination of "male hairdresser," "weight-lifting instructor," and "tastefully decorated town house," would bring a shrug and a "So-what?" But two decades earlier, the story was guaranteed to raise eyebrows and cause snickers. I much prefer the 1990s, but we were living in the 1970s at the time. I jumped into the Randy Agnew story encumbered by the prejudices of the day and driven by my enthusiasm for a scoop.

Les didn't want to do the story himself because he was afraid his involvement would betray the source of the tip. We agreed that Brit Hume would be the best person on our staff to check out the Agnew tip for two reasons—he had worked in Baltimore and he had expressed strong misgivings about the newsworthiness of the story from the beginning. We figured he would be the most cautious legman we had on this subject. He reluctantly agreed and set out for Baltimore.

Brit accomplished his mission. He had dropped by unannounced at the town house of the hairdresser Buddy Hash, rumored to be the place where young Agnew had moved when he left his wife. Randy had come to the door barefooted, wearing white pants and an open-neck shirt. He received Brit cordially and explained that he had just stopped in to pick up some of his things and take a shower because the plumbing in his own garage apartment was on the fritz. He had lived with Hash for a month when he first left his wife, he said, but now was on his own.

Brit had more stops on his agenda. At the Baltimore police department he learned that Hash had a minor police record—two charges of possession of marijuana, and maintaining a "disorderly house." He had been cleared of both charges.

Next on Brit's route was Hash's beauty salon, where Brit was also received politely. He could hardly expect the cordiality to continue if he came right out and asked if Randy and Buddy were lovers, so Brit pursued another angle from the original tip—that Randy Agnew had become a societal dropout, a peacenik living a bohemian existence. That would have been a compelling peg for a story about the vice president's son, given the uptight Nixon administration and the passion about the Vietnam War that was gripping the nation's young people. But it wasn't true. "Randy's nowhere near the hippie type," Hash told Brit. "He's really very goody-goody."

I listened to Brit's report and weighed the facts. I felt that the lives of the vice president's children constituted news, especially since the vice president had made proper parenting an issue in his public discourse. The marital split was news, but how should I handle the question of possible homosexuality? As is my habit, I called in my senior staffers for advice. Predictably they were divided, with Les and I leaning toward using the details that would hint at homosexuality, and Brit and Opal Ginn feeling uneasy about that angle. Opal was an enthusiastic tale swapper in the office, but she was also the most adamant supporter of a person's right to privacy.

I decided to pursue the story delicately and placed a call to Spiro Agnew. We were on a first-name basis, and he took my call. I apologized for approaching him about a delicate family subject, and then launched into what I knew about Randy's marital split, leaving out the part about Buddy Hash. Agnew was the model of political decorum: yes, his son and daughter-in-law had split, but it was an amicable separation; no, there were no hard feelings between father and son. I asked Agnew if he knew about Randy's living arrangements. "He is living in a converted garage," Agnew said. "I have never seen this place, but I know where he is living."

The decision was in my hands, and I opted to tell all. The column announced the split and put the "male hairdresser" roommate prominently in the first paragraph so no one would miss the story between the lines. There were plenty of references to "elegant decor" and "arty paintings" in the town house. The readers learned that Buddy Hash had a goatee and that Randy Agnew answered the door barefooted. In retrospect, I realize all of this detail was short on news value but weighty with double entendre and the silly euphemisms of the decade. My apologies to Randy and Buddy.

These were countries half a world away from the United States; Americans were only mildly interested in such distant turmoil. But what was carefully concealed from them was an approaching confrontation between the Soviet and American navies in the Indian Ocean. President Nixon had brought the United States to the edge of war. His actions were deliberate; he operated in secret; and he lied to the American people about his actions.

Here are the bare bones of the story: The Pakistani Army had used brutal force to put down a Bengali rebellion in East Pakistan. This did not stop but, rather, escalated the war of secession. Congress had forced Nixon to cut off the pipeline of military supplies to Pakistan, and the majority of Americans wanted the United States to stay out of the mess. This public and congressional resolve deepened as the playing field widened. India moved in to defend its neighbor, the secessionist East Pakistan. Then the field became a playground for superpowers with the Soviet Union pledging to put its muscle behind India, and China lining up behind Pakistan.

It had been my suspicion that in his heart Nixon was not neutral on this issue. But the message whispered over the Christmas card rack was the first evidence that the president was following his heart with U.S. ships and guns. "Task Force 74," as the flotilla was called, was led by the U.S.S. *Enterprise*, a nuclear-powered aircraft carrier that was then the world's most powerful ship.

There was already acknowledged U.S. Navy activity in the Bay of Bengal, but the cover story put out by the administration was that ships had been sent to evacuate American diplomats left in East Pakistan. The American public knew nothing at all about "Task Force 74." My source told me that the secret mission was intended as a show of force staged for the benefit of the Soviets who already had a fleet of warships in the bay and were standing by to support the Indian thrust into East Pakistan. The U.S. Navy was about to confront the Soviet Navy over a regional skirmish in which Congress had ordered neutrality. It could have been World War III in the making.

I wasted little time in soul searching over the issue of disclosing national security secrets. The only thing holding me back was the need to get enough proof from my source so my word would not be questioned.

I needled my source until he reluctantly gave me some paperwork documenting his assertions. The proof was in the minutes of the Washington Special Action Group (WSAG), the crisis-management team of the National Security Council. It was chaired by Henry Kissinger and made up of representatives from the Joint Chiefs of Staff, the CIA, and the Defense and State Departments. It met in the White House "Situation Room" to hash out foreign policy strategy for the president to consider. At least, that was what the group was intended to do. The minutes passed to me in manila envelopes showed a different method of operation. Most of the hot shots in the WSAG meetings would sit in cowed silence while Kissinger told them what Nixon wanted. Then, like whipped puppies, they would nod their heads in agreement. Nixon and Kissinger had already made up their minds. The brain trust was there to affirm or shut up.

The minutes, stamped "Secret Sensitive," were held so closely to the vest by the members of WSAG that I feared to quote from them lest I pinpoint my source, cost him his job, and maybe land him in jail. So in the first column I spoke only in general terms, accusing Nixon of tilting toward

Pakistan and citing Kissinger's posturing in secret meetings as proof. The story got about as much attention as yesterday's horoscope.

I was determined not to let Nixon get away with this deception, so I tried again. The next column rephrased what I had already written, but this time, with permission from my source, I quoted directly from the minutes. The reaction was immediate. Kissinger, perhaps assuming that I couldn't possibly have the secret minutes, claimed he had been quoted out of context. The *New York Times*, already embroiled in a legal mess of its own about publication of the secret Pentagon Papers on the Vietnam War, recognized a kindred spirit. Though my column did not run in the staid *Times*, a *Times* reporter called me anyway, asking for my comment on Kissinger's claim that he had been quoted out of context. Impulsively I responded, "I'll show you the context. Come on over and read the documents for yourself."

I had the staff retype the minutes lest my copy might in some note or doodle betray my source. I shared the retyped version with the *Times* reporter, and laid out an array of supporting, secret documents. The next day, more than a full page of the *Times* was given over to a reprint of the minutes and excerpts from the documents. Other reporters asked to see the secret papers, and their reports contributed to a growing hullabaloo. Kissinger could no longer claim he had been misunderstood. Instead, the administration was giving the response that speaks volumes: "No comment."

No comment was needed. Kissinger's words spoke for themselves. At the December 3, 1971 meeting of WSAG, he railed, "I'm getting hell every half hour from the President that we're not being tough enough on India. He has just called me again. He does not believe we are carrying out his wishes. He wants to tilt in favor of Pakistan. He feels everything we do comes out otherwise."

The December 6 minutes said, "Dr. Kissinger also directed that henceforth we show a certain coolness to the Indians; the Indian ambassador is not to be treated at too high a level."

When the group met again on December 8, the minutes noted: "Dr. Kissinger said that we are not trying to be even handed. There can be no doubt what the President wants. The President does not want to be even handed. The President believes that India is the attacker. We are trying to get across the idea that India has jeopardized relations with the United States."

When reporters began to realize that they had been duped by Kissinger, the story snowballed. The big lie had begun rolling off his tongue on December 7, 1971; it started with a "background briefing"—one of those Washington institutions that strains credulity. A top administration official holds a press conference on the condition that he or she be quoted only as a "high-ranking" official, or a "top" official, or a "highly placed" source. The source chooses the designation, and the reporters agree to the terms or leave the room.

On that fateful December 7, Nixon's press secretary Ron Ziegler introduced Kissinger as the surprise guest, to be referred to only as "White House officials." The reporters complained that Kissinger should go on the record, but Ziegler said the session would be more productive for them if Kissinger could speak anonymously.

"First of all," Kissinger began, "let us get a number of things straight. There have been some comments that the Administration is anti-Indian. This is totally inaccurate. India is a great country. It is the most populous free country. It is governed by democratic procedures." This was a day after Kissinger had told WSAG to give the Indian ambassador the cold shoulder. The background briefing continued with whopper after whopper, and the reporters present were none the wiser. However, the U.S. ambassador to India, Kenneth Keating, knew a fish story when he smelled one. A lengthy account of the background briefing was published by the U.S. Information Service's official wire service and thus fell into Keating's hands. He was outraged.

From New Delhi, Keating dashed off a cable to his bosses at the State Department spelling out point by point how the account of the anonymous "White House official" differed from reality. "While I appreciate the tactical necessity of justifying our position publicly, I feel constrained to state elements of this particular story do not coincide with my knowledge of the events of the past eight months." He said the pussyfooting did nothing to enhance America's position or credibility.

It was inevitable that Keating's cable would be slipped to me, and I printed excerpts, letting the State Department's own expert bear witness to what I had been saying in print. I couldn't have put it any better myself. Perhaps Keating knew that the pipeline would eventually carry his words to me. In any event, sources close to him were quoted in the *New York Times* as saying he was "not unhappy" that his cable had been leaked.

When Kissinger was exposed as the anonymous pontificator, the White House blustered that the distinguished statesman had been libeled. Herbert Klein, White House communications director, went on national TV to say, "My interpretation is that Dr. Kissinger has been libeled when he was accused of lying and distorting the facts. I think the people are getting the wrong impression." In reality, the public was finally getting the correct impression of the credibility of the Nixon White House.

I don't claim to have read Nixon's mind as to why he took Pakistan's side against the impoverished people of Bengal, who had been abused by nature and by their Pakistani neighbors. All they wanted was freedom from tyranny—in other words, independence from Pakistan. But I do know this much: Nixon was beholden to General Agha Mohammad Yahya Khan, the military leader of Pakistan and a friend of China. Nixon was eager to atone for his early years as a rabid anti-Communist. He had come to believe that his own intractability in Congress and as vice president had contributed to the enmity between the United States and China at a time when Chou En-lai and Mao-Tse-tung had sought reconciliation. When Nixon moved into the White House, Yahya offered to act as power broker in the rapprochement, and when Kissinger made a secret trip to Beijing to begin the process, Yahya acted as his host.

Yahya was a drunk and a womanizer who carried a swagger stick and ruled by fear and intimidation. But Nixon preferred Yahya's company to that of India's Indira Gandhi who repeatedly outwitted him in their diplomatic encounters and, worst of all, was an uppity woman. So Nixon tilted toward Pakistan, without telling Congress or the American people.

What emerged from the WSAG minutes was a pattern of obvious deceit whether taken in or out of context. Kissinger leaned on WSAG to find a way to get weaponry to Pakistan. He suggested that King Hussein of Jordan might be willing to send some of his U.S.-made jets to Pakistan if he could be guaranteed that the United States would replace them. WSAG members expressed their doubts that such a ruse would work. I would later find out that Nixon got word to King Hussein that the transfer of ten planes to Pakistan would be in the best interests of everyone concerned. Hussein visited Washington in April, 1972, and was promised new American jets.

For a few days, the world breathlessly approached the brink of a possible world war. Fortunately, the Pakistani army fizzled, Bangladesh secured its independence, and the skirmish was relegated to a footnote in the history books.

But for Richard Nixon, the war was not over. He was determined to find the sources who gave me the WSAG papers. When I first printed excerpts from the minutes, the FBI immediately began an investigation to locate the leak. The Pentagon started its own investigation; so did the State Department. My sources let me know that all those probes were being coordinated by Robert Mardian, the assistant attorney general in charge of internal security at the Justice Department. His plan was to stake out my house and follow me around, hoping I would lead his gumshoes to my mysterious sources.

I was aware that I had become the object of certain discomforting attentions. I didn't know then that the White House was developing an "enemies list," but I did know I was on someone's list. People in key posts

SO WHAT?

MY FELLOW COLUMNISTS SPILLED PLENTY OF ink in the debate over whether I had done the right thing in publishing the India-Pakistan papers. Typical of my critics was columnist Joseph Kraft who took a position that I found sadly indicative of inside-the-beltway cynics. He claimed it was not news that the administration would say one thing and do another. Kraft said the tilt toward Pakistan was "known to everybody in touch with the State Department and the White House at the time of the crisis." The remark was a symptom of the Washington elitism that has alienated the press from the people it is supposed to serve—the people who are not "in touch with the State Department and the White House," the people who want to believe their president when he says he is neutral. It was one thing for political analysts and pundits sitting around a table to speculate on which way the administration was tilting. It was quite another to have the proof in writing—the words of the esteemed Dr. Kissinger as he petulantly lectured the government's top military and foreign policy leaders for not toeing the line.

Joseph Kraft's second complaint was even more disturbing: "But so what?" Everybody knows the government lies, he said. I had done a great disservice by flushing out the liars, he claimed. In the future they would simply be more clever. History has now confirmed what I suspected then about the integrity of Richard Nixon and the people who surrounded him. I do not regret having flushed them out. They did not become more clever in hiding their lies. On the contrary, they became sloppier.

New York Times columnist Russell Baker spent his ink on this subject making what I thought was the key point—that people in a democracy cannot afford to let their leaders do the thinking for them. "Back in the days of Lyndon Johnson," Baker wrote, "the White House used to twit the rest of humanity for having an opinion about the Vietnam War because only the President, they used to say, had access to all the facts. The rest of humanity was urged to bear this in mind and discount accordingly the value of any opinions that disagreed with the President's."

Generals and admirals and presidents have often stumbled when they sought to go beyond the mandate of the people. Johnson had campaigned on a peace platform, saying he did not intend "to send American boys to do what Asian boys should be doing." Not until seven years later with the leak of the secret Pentagon Papers did Americans find out that Johnson had been making contradictory plans in private. More than fifty thousand Americans died in a war that was planned and escalated without any real public understanding of the facts.

Johnson's war began with a deception. In 1964, he decided to stop the fall of Communist dominoes in Vietnam and needed an incident on which to build national solidarity. When Communist patrol boats raided American destroyers in the Gulf of Tonkin, Johnson saw his opportunity. He treated the event as an incident of significance, even though there were no casualties and no property was damaged. I obtained the secret naval documents that gave me enough evidence to report that the incident had been contrived, but it was too late to avoid a war with no satisfactory exit.

In 1961, the *New York Times* learned about the pending Bay of Pigs invasion of Cuba, but, in the name of national security, did not run the story. Later, a bitter President Kennedy told the paper's publisher Orville Dreyfus, "I wish you had run everything on Cuba." Kennedy realized that if the plan had been exposed to the light, it would have been seen for what it was: a very bad idea.

During the Korean War, Americans were not warned of the dangers the elite knew—that China would intervene in the war if U.S. troops crossed the 38th parallel. There was no public wisdom then to stop General Douglas MacArthur from crossing the line and inevitably drawing the Chinese response.

I made my own mistake in 1986 when I found out that the Reagan administration was trading arms for hostages in Iran. At Ronald Reagan's urging, I chose not to run the story in the name of national security and the good of the American hostages. Only later, when the full iceberg rose to the surface, did I realize I was wrong to keep it from the public. I had forgotten that the best judge of public policy is the people.

in the White House and Pentagon, suspected of having contact with me were subjected to phone taps, lie detector tests, and other indignities. My house came under surveillance by men with binoculars in parked cars, and I was conscious of being tailed.

As evidence that I had not become paranoid, the *Washington Post* published a feature story, based on its sources within the federal apparatus, detailing how the White House was "coordinating a continuous effort to discredit Anderson." All told, dozens of government agents, presidential aides, and political flunkies were assigned to investigate my operation, to prepare attacks on us, and to plant stories in the media against us.

One of them, Admiral Robert O. Welander, waggled an accusing finger at a navy yeoman Charles Radford. The admiral, who was the liaison between the Joint Chiefs of Staff and the National Security Council, agonized to higher Pentagon brass that his assistant, Radford, must have been my source. Thereupon, an incestuous tale of government spying began to unravel.

YEOMAN FIRST CLASS RADFORD SUDDENLY HAD reason to regret the day he met my parents in India. They were globe-trotting and found their way to New Delhi on a Sunday. They tracked down a local gathering of Mormons from America and joined them for church services. Chuck Radford, assigned to the American Embassy, attended that service. He took an instant liking to my parents and offered to show them the city.

My parents, whose main hobby was collecting friends, kept up a correspondence with Radford after he was reassigned to the Pentagon. On a visit to Washington, my parents suggested we invite the Radfords over for dinner. My interest was piqued when I learned that Radford worked on the Joint Chiefs' liaison staff with Henry Kissinger. I later learned that Radford had been along on Kissinger's first secret trip to China and had easy access to Kissinger's office. Suddenly I began to view our dinner guest as the main course.

Thereafter, the Radfords invited us to dinner occasionally, and of course, I tried to pump him for information. He was cordial but kept his guard up. My wife Libby, meanwhile, found she had a lot in common with Radford's wife, Tonne, including their interest in genealogical research.

While we exchanged dinner invitations and our wives traded family history research tips, the White House put a tap on Radford's phone, hoping to catch him in a clandestine conversation with me about national security secrets. The decision to tap his phones bypassed all the usual legal safeguards. Attorney General John Mitchell approved the taps verbally but never put the order in writing. And the FBI, in carrying out the order, exceeded its legal authority because it wasn't conducting its own investigation of Radford. Instead, the Bureau became a tool of the president's paranoid policies by turning the wiretap summaries over to Nixon aides David Young and John Ehrlichman, no questions asked.

When the phone taps yielded nothing, Nixon's minions strapped Radford to a polygraph machine. The test showed that he had indeed pilfered documents and that he did indeed know me. Radford had been spying on Henry Kissinger, all right, but for someone else. Guess who: He had swiped hundreds of documents from the NSC files and slipped them to his boss, Admiral Welander, whom Radford had understood was passing them along to the Joint Chiefs of Staff.

Not only did Richard Nixon distrust the media, the millions who composed the permanent government were suspect, too. The highest military officers were denied the kind of critical information it was previously considered essential for them to have. To carry out military policy, the Joint Chiefs at least needed to know what it was. That meant gathering inside intelligence from someone who did know. Aside from the president, only Kissinger seemed to have much idea what was going on.

For the record, Admiral Thomas Moorer, the Joint Chiefs chairman, denied that he had been on the receiving end of Radford's pipeline. Moorer said he didn't need a lowly yeoman to slip him documents to which he already had legitimate access. The truth is that he had a legitimate right to the information but had to use backdoor means to get it.

Pentagon investigators put Radford under the microscope for three weeks trying to get him to say he had leaked national security secrets to me. I didn't know what he had been put through until 1974 when the Senate Armed Services Committee conducted an inquiry into the episode. The investigation was deliberately shallow and left many questions unanswered. But at least Radford got his day in court.

Responding to questions from Iowa Senator Harold Hughes, Radford described one grueling polygraph session under interrogation by White House inquisitor David Young and chief Pentagon investigator Donald Stewart.

"Mr. Stewart is the one who used the profanity," Radford began, haltingly. Stewart called Radford a traitor. "He told me, did I know that I could do a long prison sentence for this . . . and he called Jack Anderson and his kind sons of bitches and bastards, and he was very profane. . . ."

Stewart inexplicably accused Radford of contributing to the deaths of soldiers fighting in Vietnam. "He used a lot of other words, just the whole list, string of gutter language˙ that you can imagine," Radford continued.

Young and Stewart varied the inquisition, alternately hooking Radford up to the polygraph and then taking him away to another room for more verbal abuse. "Did they use the rubber hose on you?" Senator Hughes asked.

"No, but I would not have been surprised. [Stewart] was pretty angry. He was almost hysterical. . . . His eyes were bloodshot, and he looked like he was mad."

"Were you physically threatened in any way?" Hughes asked.

"No, he did not lay his hands on me in any way. He pounded the desk. He made motions like, I suppose, he would leap across the desk at me at any moment. But he did not touch me in any way. He did not physically harm me."

Senator Hughes asked if this interrogation while on the polygraph put Radford in an emotional state.

"Yes, sir, I was rather upset. . . . After I broke down, that is when they let me go home. That is when it ended, after I told them that I was passing information from [the White House] to the Pentagon. Then they stopped. Then they let me go home."

"You broke down and cried?" asked Hughes.

"Yes, sir."

Admiral Welander was detailed out to sea duty, and Radford was transferred almost overnight to Salem, Oregon. Neither of them was prosecuted. That would have shone too bright a light on the whole sordid incident. Libby and I knew that the Radfords were gone, but we didn't know where until Tonne Radford called us after they got settled in Salem. The FBI was still tapping Radford's phone wherever he went, and two calls to my house were recorded. The first was between Tonne and Libby in which they passed nothing more secret than their news about genealogy and kids. The second was a call from Chuck to me to congratulate me on winning the Pulitzer prize for my India-Pakistan coverage. If this was my secret source, then I behaved oddly, because the FBI's own surveillance notes on that bugged conversation begin by saying that I didn't seem to know who Chuck was when he introduced himself. When my memory kicked in, we made small talk and then turned the phones over to Libby and Tonne. I was chagrined at having forgotten someone who had paid such a high price for befriending the Anderson family.

IT HAD BEEN TWO YEARS SINCE Drew Pearson's death, and I had worked hard to fill his enormous shoes. I felt he would approve of the India-Pakistan story, which came to be known as the "Anderson Papers." As Les Whitten put it in an interview with the *Washington Star*, "The measure of having arrived is that comedians now are making jokes about Jack. That's when you know you've broken through."

In May of 1972 I learned that I had broken through another barrier, the Pulitzer prize. My pleasure at finally being recognized by my peers belied the indifference I had always displayed toward the awards during the many years that Drew and I were passed over. Drew would have been amused, not so much in the winning, but in the backhanded way in which the prize was awarded. All things considered, the committee would rather have given it to someone else.

The Pulitzer prizes are chosen by Columbia University in a process that begins with a selection committee made up of news executives. They submit a list of nominees to the Pulitzer trustees, who can veto an award, but cannot substitute someone of their own choice.

In 1972, the trustees announced the winners along with a tersely worded caveat: "In the trustees' deliberations of the 1972 Pulitzer Prizes, a majority of them had deep reservations about the timeliness and suitability of certain

FANCY MEETING YOU HERE

THE FAMOUS AND INFAMOUS ARE SOMETIMES not happy to see me. I was frequently welcomed at the offices of Teamsters boss Jimmy Hoffa in Washington, but when I bumped into him in Acapulco, I was the last person he wanted to see.

Libby and I were invited to Mexico by friends who owned a luxurious home in Acapulco. They only had time to enjoy the house for about one month each year, so they decided it would be wiser to sell it and rent a vacation villa occasionally. The house was being advertised when Libby and I visited, and one afternoon the realtor arrived with a prospective buyer from Detroit, none other than Jimmy Hoffa.

I don't know who was more surprised to see whom, but Hoffa was definitely more dismayed than I. Part of Hoffa's carefully crafted image as a man of the people included his modest $6,800 house back home in Detroit. This elegant villa in Acapulco didn't fit that image, and I could tell by the look on his face that he had no desire to let the rank and file of the Teamsters Union know about it.

We exchanged strained pleasantries, and he made a cursory tour of the house, explaining that he was looking at it for a friend, not for himself. My hosts were amused and kindly never blamed me for losing the sale. My regret was that I had ever believed Hoffa's man-of-the-people act. In an earlier article for *Parade* magazine, I had said that he lived simply despite his huge expense account and that he was so ordinary he carried his own luggage when he traveled. I didn't realize then that he planned to carry his luggage to a secret luxury villa in Acapulco.

When he disappeared and was presumed dead in 1975, I wondered idly whether he had ever purchased another hideaway. I subscribe to the theory that Hoffa was murdered by the Mafia because he refused to retire gracefully. The mob sealed its control of the union when Hoffa went to prison for jury tampering and fraud in 1967. When he was paroled in 1971, he was supposed to sit quietly on his porch and enjoy retirement, but he refused to stay home.

Hoffa traveled the country giving speeches about prison reform, but his real agenda was to rally support for his bid to take back control of the union. In each city where Hoffa spoke, the local godfather would call on him and give him the same friendly advice. "You've had a great life, Jimmy. It's time to retire. We'll take care of you and your family. You need money? We'll give it to you. You want to travel? We'll pay the bill. You've had a lot of hard knocks. Why not retire now and lead the good life?"

Hoffa ignored the spiel from a half dozen godfathers and was killed.

of the journalism awards. Had the selections been those of the trustees alone, certain of the recipients would not have been chosen."

The trustees didn't name names, but they didn't have to. The community of my peers assumed it was either me or the *New York Times* or both. I had won in the national reporting category for the India-Pakistan story. The *Times* won that year in the public service category for its publication of the Pentagon Papers, the secret and sordid Pentagon history of U.S. involvement in the Vietnam War. The Nixon administration had tried unsuccessfully to stop publication of the papers by appealing all the way to the U.S. Supreme Court.

Speculation was rampant in the press that the Pulitzer trustees were squeamish about bestowing honors on someone for publishing national security secrets. If the Pulitzer committee was going to be queasy about secrets, then it was in for a prolonged bout of nausea as long as Richard Nixon was in the White House.

CHAPTER 12

AS PRESIDENT, RICHARD NIXON WAS AN introvert in an extrovert's shoes, harried by a suspicious nature and dogged by a sense of grievance that all too often had been confirmed. He had cut and had been cut; he had suffered and had survived and had won. Now he had a desire for solitude and a craving for an orderly environment undisturbed by trivial interruptions or internecine discord.

In the past, he had made mistakes and had lost elections by trying to direct everything personally. With the 1972 elections just around the bend, he would never again spread himself too thin. He would encapsulate himself from unnecessary turmoil, dealing regularly only with those select few who had learned not only to resolve conflicts but to modulate their personalities so as not to jar his sensitive vibrations.

And so he came to act through other men who aped him and tended, in the way of young men, to out-Nixon Nixon. They formed a grim offensive line that was ready to crush anyone who came after their quarterback. A statement attributed to aide Egil Krogh reflects the attitude inside the White House: "Anyone who opposes us we'll destroy. As a matter of fact, anyone who doesn't support us we'll destroy."

This defiant attitude caused them to commit first the blunders and then the crimes that produced the greatest political scandal in American history—Watergate. But before Watergate, there was ITT. It turned out to be a dress rehearsal for Watergate—same cast, same tactics, same dirty tricks. And I was the guy they tried to destroy.

They manipulated the political machinery during the 1972 campaign through a series of dangerous, unnecessary gambles. Had they limited themselves to the usual bag of tricks, they could have won the election by a landslide, without risk. But Nixon wanted guarantees in a business where there are none.

He decided a year in advance that the 1972 GOP nominating convention should be held in San Diego. He considered it his lucky city—his old stomping grounds where voters still liked him. But there was a rub. San Diego was a tourist Mecca that was booming year-round; the city, therefore, did not want or need another convention. Tradition dictated that the political party, be it Republican or Democrat, shake down the chosen city for money to subsidize the costly convention—all in the name of stimulating the local economy. But San Diego wasn't about to be fleeced.

Not willing to disappoint the president, Nixon's underlings set out looking for corporate sponsors to underwrite the festivities in San Diego. In early July 1971, San Diego was formally anointed as the GOP convention site. Eight days later, the Justice Department announced it was dropping a massive antitrust lawsuit against multinational conglomerate International Telephone and Telegraph, the biggest antitrust case in U.S. history. I didn't put the two announcements together until September when news broke that ITT had deposited $100,000 in the GOP convention kitty.

ITT was more than just a business. It was a nation unto itself with 331 major subsidiaries and another 708 minor offspring. Its 390,000 employees were spread over 67 countries on six continents, generating annual sales of more than $7 billion.

The pro-business Nixon, perhaps merely for window dressing, had appointed as head of the Antitrust Division of the Justice Department a zealous trustbuster in the person of Richard McLaren. Unaware apparently that he was supposed to go easy on corporate America, McLaren had aggressively pursued companies growing too big for their breeches and too big for the good of a competitive marketplace. His largest target was ITT, which he had ordered to give up some of its favorite subsidiaries.

Although McLaren's three lawsuits against ITT had not fared well in the lower courts, he was poised in the spring of 1971 to argue an appeal before the Supreme Court. Experts on both sides agreed that the case was in the bag for McLaren. The pattern was well established in monopoly cases—defeat in the early rounds and victory when it counted. The government had not lost an antitrust case before the sympathetic Supreme Court in twenty years.

The presence of Snow White among the seven dwarfs had already aroused my curiosity. Then came McLaren's sudden and unexpected out-of-court settlement of the ITT suit, followed quickly by ITT's generous donation to the GOP cause. None of us in the press had anything but our natural cynicism to nourish ugly suspicions. But then in November, McLaren abruptly resigned. He reappeared a couple weeks later as Nixon's nominee for a federal judge-

OPAL

THE CLOSE QUARTERS AND LONG HOURS in our office made for the kind of squabbles one finds in large families. History should record that the reason Brit Hume ended up working the ITT story was that the woman at the hub of my office for nearly four decades, my assistant Opal Ginn, was feuding with Les Whitten. When the ITT tip came in over the transom, Opal, the traffic cop for assignments, passed it on to her pet staffer, Brit, instead of Les, who was my top reporter.

Anyone on the outs with Opal could count on going weeks without receiving mail, phone calls, or news tips. Opal once demanded that I fire an intern, Murray Waas, because his fountain pen had leaked on her newly upholstered chair. I didn't let him go, because Les pleaded his case as an able reporter and then reported triumphantly to his nemesis Opal that Murray would stay, no matter how much he inconvenienced her.

One way reporters proved their metal was by winning over the cantankerous Opal. When they did, they discovered her generous heart. I was aware that she frequently bought groceries for the elderly ladies in her apartment building while they waited for their Social Security checks. She once gave a cab driver fifty dollars because he told her if he had some money he would have been at the horse track that day rather than driving her to work. The cabbie won a bundle at the races and formed an unbreakable friendship with Opal, becoming her personal chauffeur for years.

ship. The nomination was sent to the Senate for approval that same day. Four hours later, without benefit of hearings, McLaren was a judge. The odor had grown strong enough that, on December 9, I published a column, citing the curious chain of events. The column was more rumination than news, but my purpose was not to air the facts I already had. Rather, I wanted to draw more facts out of the woodwork. I was convinced that somewhere in the massive ITT bureaucracy there was an honest soul who possessed three key qualities— inside information, righteous indignation, and a Xerox machine. The column was my signal that the door was open.

It took almost three months, but someone, whom I still cannot name, finally walked through that door. On February 22, 1972, this insider delivered the smoking gun—or, more accurately, a smoking memo, for it was a scorcher. It was dated June 25, 1971, and addressed to ITT Vice President Bill Merriam from the company's Washington lobbyist Dita Beard. "Subject: San Diego Convention."

Beard began by complaining about loose lips. Other than a few insiders, she said, no one knew "from whom that four hundred thousand commitment had come." Among those who did know, she confided, were Nixon and Attorney General John Mitchell. Beard's memo discussed whether the $400,000 should be made in cash or services. Then she wrote: "I am convinced because of several conversations with Louie re Mitchell, that our noble commitment has gone a long way toward our negotiations on the mergers eventually coming out as Hal wants them. Certainly the president has told Mitchell to see that things are worked out fairly. It is still only McLaren's mickey-mouse we are suffering."

I didn't know who "Louie" was, but I figured "Hal" was Harold Geneen, the president of ITT. Tough and abrasive, he had risen by dint of ferocious single-mindedness from night-school accountant to the world's highest-paid executive. He ruled the ITT empire with crotchety tyranny. He opened one meeting of ITT executives by saying: "Gentlemen, I have been thinking. Bull times zero is zero bull. Bull divided by bull is infinity bull. And I'm sick and tired of the bull you've been feeding me."

The memo made it clear that ITT's investment in the GOP convention had been upped from the announced $100,000 to a secret $400,000. Beard ended her memo thusly: "If it gets too much publicity, you can believe our negotiations with Justice will wind up shot down. Mitchell is definitely helping us, but cannot let it be known. Please destroy this, huh?"

I had heard the name Dita Beard only once before. My assistant, Opal Ginn, had been invited to a retirement party for her friend Bill Burazer, a bartender at the Sheraton-Carlton Hotel in downtown Washington. I didn't know Bill, but Opal told me he was a fan of the column so she asked me to make an appearance at the party and present him with a plaque. I was in a hurry and left Libby waiting in the car while I popped in for the ceremony. I didn't meet Beard, who also attended the party that night, but Opal had an encounter with her. During the recurring rounds of introduction, Opal was presented to Dita Beard with the identifying tag line, "Opal works for Jack Anderson."

Beard replied, "Your boss is a son of a bitch. I wouldn't touch him with a ten-foot pole." I'm confident that Opal came up with some pithy rejoinder, and the two women avoided each other the rest of the night.

When Opal came into the office the following morning, she asked what I had done to offend Dita Beard. I didn't know her, but in my business that isn't a prerequisite for offending someone. I stored the name and her ITT connection in the back of my head. Now Opal and I reread Dita Beard's ITT memorandum and considered how best to proceed. Beard was a hard-drinking woman who knew how to curse and prided herself on being able to best the men around her at their own sports. Opal and I decided that my associate Brit Hume, young, with a transparent face, would be the best one to make contact with Beard. She might make a mistake and underestimate the gentlemanly Brit, unwittingly giving him the advantage.

Brit secured an appointment with her at the ITT offices and arrived with the memo in hand. Her appearance was dowdy—rumpled yellow slacks and a sweatshirt—but her personality was dynamic, Brit reported afterward. He thought she must be a powerful woman to dress with such carelessness for a day at the office. Hovering around her were two ITT public relations men. Brit didn't welcome their presence as censors, but he forged ahead.

His objective was to get Beard to admit the memo was authentic. Our source dared not testify, so we needed to establish what we knew but couldn't prove—that it was a real memo straight out of ITT's confidential files. The best strategy, we agreed, was to behave as if there was no question about it. Brit handed her the document and waited. Beard read it over and over, commenting on this phrase and that sentence and even acknowledging the initial by her typed name as "my own little 'd.'" Then, with an air of resignation, she said: "All right. What do you want to know about it?" The two PR men were aghast as Beard went over the memo line by line with Brit, never once questioning its authenticity. Brit needed to see her alone, so he left some issues still unresolved, promising to contact her again.

Brit had an appointment out of town, but when he returned the next day, there was an urgent message from Beard to call him. It was late at night, and she had been brooding. She wanted to come clean. Brit called me at home and suggested putting off the encounter until morning when he would be fresh. "She may not want to talk to you in the morning," I warned. "Go now."

Brit found Beard at her home in Arlington, Virginia, surrounded by her son, her secretary, her doctor, and a personal friend who also worked for ITT. Brit managed to pry her away from the entourage and into the kitchen where they spent two hours—Beard crying, drinking, chain smoking, and pouring out her guts, Brit fearing to take notes lest he spook her into silence.

The facts that spilled out that night were astonishing. In May of 1971, at Kentucky Derby time, Beard had gone to a party hosted by Kentucky Governor Louie Nunn (the "Louie" mentioned in the memo). She knew Attorney General John Mitchell, Nixon's political fixer, would be there. ITT officials briefed her in advance on what the company wanted from any court settlement—just in case the issue should come up with Mitchell over cocktails.

(Mitchell had publicly excused himself from any dealings on the ITT case because of a conflict of interest involving his old law firm. McLaren was supposed to be reporting instead to Richard Kleindienst, who was by then Nixon's nominee to replace Mitchell as attorney general. Mitchell was bowing out to run the president's reelection campaign.)

Brit listened attentively as Beard recounted how Mitchell had unexpectedly drawn her aside for an hour. He had told her that even the president wanted the Justice Department to "lay off" ITT. Brit was so shocked by the implication of those two words, "lay off," that he asked Beard if she was sure that's what Mitchell had said. Well, she allowed, maybe Mitchell had said Nixon wanted to "make a reasonable settlement" with ITT.

Then Mitchell asked her: "What do you want?" She took that to mean, what does ITT want in the way of a settlement of the lawsuits. Beard said the conglomerate wanted to keep its huge subsidiary, Hartford Fire Insurance Company, plus a part of the manufacturing concern, Grinnell Corporation. McLaren had ordered ITT to divest itself of both. By the time the party ended, Beard felt she had an informal deal with Mitchell to keep them.

Throughout her teary confessional with Brit, Beard insisted that the settlement of the ITT case was not related to the subsidy of the Republican convention. But midway through her crying jag, she dropped the bombshell: Brit's visit the day before had caused such panic at ITT that a security crew had beaten her to the office the next morning. She found them feeding documents from her files into a shredding machine.

Brit was carefully noncommittal about what he would do with the information Beard was spewing forth. Her doctor then told Brit that Beard had a heart condition and was too upset to continue. Sloppy from drink and red-eyed from tears, Beard gave Brit a motherly hug at the door. He rushed home and poured out on paper everything he could remember about the remarkable interview.

Within a few days, we had tied up enough loose ends for three columns: the first reporting how Dita Beard had put the fix in with Mitchell; the second revealing that Kleindienst himself had held half a dozen secret meetings with a director of ITT before the settlement had been reached; the third proving that Mitchell had known about the $400,000 pledge to the convention before the ITT case was settled. There were denials all around, but our information was solid.

Before our second column hit the print, Dita Beard disappeared—ordered by her superiors to get out of town. Before our third column appeared, the Senate Judiciary Committee had opened hearings on the scandal. Believe it or not, the hearings were Kleindienst's idea. He had already received the endorsement of the Judiciary Committee to be attorney general. The confirmation hearings had been swift and uneventful. Now he felt his name had been sullied, and he impulsively demanded to clear it before the committee. Over at the White House, members of Nixon's palace guard were fuming over Kleindienst's stupidity; he should have left well enough alone. But they clung to one glimmer of hope. The chairman of the Judiciary Committee, Mississippi Senator James Eastland, was Nixon's most steadfast ally on the Democrat side of the Senate.

I knew Eastland to have all the grace of a fluid crocodile who lolled quietly in the swamp waiting for his next meal to happen by. Outwardly, he was a southern gentlemen given to elaborate displays of courtesy and deference. But his eyes were always on the prey. I could play that game, too. So I called upon Eastland and offered my services as a witness to tell what I had uncovered.

Round-faced and tight-mouthed, blinking through glasses, he had the knowing look of a stuffed owl. With a great show of concern, he thanked me. "Jack, now you understand that I want your testimony. I want you to tell the committee whatever you wish to tell them. Feel free and comfortable and at ease. We're not going to try to block you," he said grandly. "But, you understand, we have to follow protocol. We're going to have to hear the government witnesses first." I knew immediately what he intended to do—save my testimony until the hearings had become back-page news.

"I know you're a fair man, Senator," I responded, with an equal dose of saccharine, and I thanked him for his time. Out in the hallway, I turned to Brit, who had accompanied me. "They're going to screw us," I said. I had expected no less. But I had a plan to confront Mitchell, Kleindienst, & Company even if we weren't on the witness stand. We would respond outside the committee room, in the hallway, where banks of cameras and microphones would be set up. Unless I missed my guess, the administration's witnesses would brush past these cameras, with a muck-a-muck's disdain, having said all they had to say in front of the committee. The hallway would make a perfect stage for Brit of the honest face and innocent eyes. I wanted him to appear awed by the process of democracy at work, respectful of the statesmen on the committee, eager to put the truth on the public record. "Don't give in to your natural temptation to snarl," I advised him. "I'll do the snarling. I'm the columnist. You're just a young reporter, concerned about the facts. Stop and reword your statements to find the most correct phrase. You should come across as someone who is so concerned about getting the story straight that you correct yourself as you go. You're simply telling what you saw and heard."

The strategy worked. While Brit and I held court in the hallway, the government witnesses skulked in and out of the hearings, evading the cameras, behaving as if they had something to hide. After one exit, Mitchell was in such a hurry to avoid reporters that he nearly knocked over a woman with a microphone. "Watch your arm!" he growled, as the woman tried to right herself.

The odds inside the Senate Judiciary Committee room were stacked against me. Of the fifteen men hearing the evidence on ITT, at least ten of them had reason to do me no favors. One of the risks of muckraking is that inevitably you will cross paths with those whose secrets have been turned over by the muckrake. There was Ted Kennedy, for one, still smarting from Chappaquiddick. And there were others guilty of one or more lesser offenses such as junketeering, profligate spending, taking money from shady campaign contributors, accepting gifts from special interest groups, influence peddling, nepotism. They were arrayed before me now, eager to prove me a liar.

At one point during the proceedings, committee bulldog Senator Marlow Cook accused me of conspiring with Ted Kennedy to discredit government officials. Although Kennedy understood the political psychology of turning the other cheek, he and I were unlikely bedfellows given my reports on Chappaquiddick.

I took some comfort in the presence of the venerable Senator Sam Ervin who could remain a gentleman in the southern tradition while delivering a verbal knockout padded by little homilies. At one point, after listening to one too many ITT executives reciting what they didn't remember, Ervin drawled, "Some people are good rememberers and some are good forgetters ... perhaps a good forgetter is better than a good rememberer. We have witnesses here who possess both or neither of these qualities."

ITT had hired the famous detective agency Intertel to search for skeletons in my closets, and they turned up a photo taken at the bartender's going-away party at the Sheraton-Carlton Hotel a year earlier. It was a photograph of a small cluster of partygoers, including Dita Beard and Opal. The two women appeared far enough apart to suggest that they had already had their cat fight and were keeping each other at arm's length. This seemed to be photographic evidence that White House aide Charles Colson might be on to something. He had picked up a tip from Nixon's barber, whom I had carefully selected to be my barber, too. This chatty hairstylist turned out to be a two-way information channel, passing tidbits to each of us about the other. But he gave Colson some misinformation, confiding that Opal and Dita were drinking buddies. Drinkers, yes; buddies, no. The photo was slipped to Senator Cook, who fleshed out the details in grand fashion. Opal and Dita had cohosted the party, he claimed. I had been the master of ceremonies. We were all old friends, now in collusion to ruin ITT and smear Nixon.

Opal began spitting nails when I recounted Cook's revelation. We both drew up affidavits, swearing to high heaven that we had been casual guests at this no-host party. We also tracked down the bartender who verified that he had never seen the two women together before that night. I demanded that Senator Cook read into the hearing record a letter from me giving our side of the story. He complied, through clenched teeth. He promised to apologize in the future, if necessary. But in the meantime, he said, proof of his version of the bartender's bash was forthcoming. It never came.

Nor did I ever get an apology. What I got, after I reported he was in the pouch of the tobacco industry, was a different kind of statement. "Jack Anderson has to be the most malicious man that ever walked the earth," declared an annoyed Senator Cook. But I could always go back to more nostalgic times, predating the ITT scandal, when he had said of me, "This country needs someone like Jack Anderson around. He does a lot to keep people honest."

ITT's EARLY STRATEGY WAS TO JETTISON the expendable Dita Beard—to portray her as a lush and a pathetic lunatic who fabricated memos to puff up her own importance. The administration's strategy was to claim that everything in the ITT settlement had gone by the book. Witness after witness took the stand, each adding a small stretch to the truth. John Mitchell and Louie Nunn claimed that Beard had been looped at the Kentucky Derby party, where she had hounded the poor attorney general around the buffet table until she finally passed out on the floor. Kleindienst admitted to repeated meetings with ITT executives, but said that nothing in those meetings could be construed as "negotiating" a settlement. Dita Beard's claim was, he added sadly, "a memorandum written by a poor soul."

McLaren, the once trusted trustbuster, said he had settled with ITT because he became convinced that forcing the company to lose some of its subsidiaries would be a financial hardship—an argument that the Supreme Court had already disallowed in other monopoly cases. Mitchell said he had met with ITT President Harold Geneen, all right, but that the two hadn't talked about ITT. They had merely passed the time in philosophical discussion of antitrust policy. Other than that, the attorney general didn't know anything about anything.

Finally it was our turn. Brit and I were allowed to testify after the hearing had nowhere else to go. I used my time to point out the gaping holes in the testimony of others, just to remind the committee members of what they could hardly have missed themselves. The evidence of perjury was plastered throughout the newspapers each day as reporters did their homework and exposed contradictory stories and shifting accounts of who knew what and when. I wound up with my big finish: "This country needs as its top law enforcement officer a man who understands the law and respects the truth. Richard Kleindienst is not such a man. He is unfit to be attorney general." Then I turned most of the questions over to Brit, who played the nice cop to my nasty cop.

Loitering around the hearing room each day had taken Brit and me away from the daily grind. He had cultivated a source of his own within ITT who had given him a stack of documents that we hadn't yet had time to sift through. So we turned them over to an office intern to mine for tips. What he found was several sizes larger than a mere tip. It was a delicious tandem scandal.

The document cache included a series of internal ITT memos from 1970, proving beyond any doubt that the company had considered participating in a plan cooked up by the CIA to wreak economic havoc on Chile in an attempt to stop the election of Marxist President Salvador Allende. Allende was threatening to nationalize Chile's big corporations, and ITT stood to lose $225 million in investments, including a 60 percent ownership in the Chilean telephone company.

The plans were a cutthroat fantasy that, in the end, even ITT couldn't bring itself to participate in. William Broe, the CIA's director of clandestine operations in Latin America, spelled out a strategy of economic strangulation in the weeks leading up to the Chilean election. The plan was for American banks to deny credit to Chilean clients, for American companies to "drag their feet" in paying bills and sending materials to Chile, and for corporations with assets at risk in Chile to apply a variety of other pressures to deflate the national economy.

In one memo, ITT Vice President Edward Gerrity reported to President Harold Geneen about a meeting with Broe, referred to cryptically in the memos as "the visitor" or as the contact at the "McLean agency." (The CIA is headquartered near McLean, Virginia.) Broe suggested certain economic disincentives and gave Gerrity a list of other companies that might cooperate in the plot, with a little arm-twisting from ITT. Apparently Broe had not had a lot of luck in selling his plan to corporate America. Gerrity wrote, "I was told that of all the companies involved, ours alone had been responsive and understood the problem. The visitor added that money was no problem." It was reassuring to know that most American companies when asked to participate in the economic ruin of another nation would politely decline.

As the election approached and Allende's victory appeared to be in the bag, the ITT memos gave off a note of despair. There were references to the possibility that the CIA could spark a military coup since throwing the nation into poverty wasn't going to work. "Approaches continue to be made to select members of the Armed Forces in an attempt to have them lead some sort of uprising—no success to date...," wrote ITT Washington chief William Merriam in a memo to ITT Director John McCone. The latter was somewhat familiar with clandestine dirty doings. He had been director of the CIA under John F. Kennedy.

AL CAPP

AN UNSIGNED LETTER LANDED ON MY desk in 1971 containing almost unbelievable allegations about one of my favorite cartoonists, Al Capp.
The anonymous source claimed that during a visit to the University of Alabama
on the college lecture circuit, Capp had told his student escorts that he was
doing a survey for NBC about sex on campus. With that as his justification, he
quizzed female students privately about their sex lives and then demanded that
the girls take off their clothes and perform various sex acts. One girl reported
the incident and the police escorted Capp out of town.

The letter made me queasy. I had admired Capp and was a big fan of his
cartoon creation, "Li'l Abner." At sixty-one years of age he was a respected
political commentator and a fellow syndicated columnist. He had overcome the
loss of one leg in a streetcar accident when he was a boy and walked confidently
on an artificial limb. He was a sympathetic and popular character—the toughest
kind to accuse of sexual impropriety.

I gave the letter to Brit Hume, and he ignored it for several months, being
as loathe as I was to touch the subject. Finally Brit got on the phone and with
good detective work located four female students whom Capp had allegedly
frightened with his advances. In the most bizarre case, the woman said Capp
had stripped off his clothes and even removed his artificial leg before shoving
her to the floor. She managed to get loose and lock herself in the bathroom,
where she screamed until Capp agreed to let her go free.

Brit asked the women to put their accounts in writing and sign them as
affidavits. Three of the four agreed. It was time to take the evidence to Capp.
Brit called him in Boston and got a blanket denial from an obviously shaken
man. Then, fifteen minutes later, Capp called back. He had booked the next
flight to Washington. Could he meet with me? Brit said we would be waiting.

I cleared my afternoon calendar and Capp was there in less than two hours.
I had decided to plead ignorance of the story, and let Brit spell out the tawdry
details with Capp sitting across the desk from me. I had no trouble maintaining
a sympathetic expression until Capp made a desperate gamble. The "babes"
on the lecture circuit were aggressive groupies, he said. Surely I must know that
from my own experience speaking at colleges. I cut him off with a frozen stare.

Capp stood up, strode into the hallway, and pulled off his artificial leg. Then
he proceeded to hop up and down the hallway to show how tough it would be
for him to catch a coed. I invited Capp to come back into my office, where he
put on his leg and paced across my carpet with an exaggerated limp, pleading
for my understanding as a father. He did not want his children to learn the truth.
I was almost persuaded to forget the matter. He wasn't a politician or a public

servant, just an old man with enormous talent, some celebrity, and a dark secret. Maybe it should remain his secret. I told him I would think about it.

As soon as Capp was out of earshot, Brit made his case that Capp was possibly guilty of sex crimes and at the very least had victimized young people who trusted and admired him. Brit tipped the scales toward publication with his argument that Capp had been pounding the pulpit about sexual promiscuity on college campuses. We wrote the column and toned down the description of the sexual encounters, in part to make the column suitable for daily newspapers and in part to go easy on Capp. He issued a denial, raging with charges of a left-wing conspiracy against him and dripping with self-pity about his physical handicap.

Only about half of my subscriber newspapers ran the column. The rest, including most of the largest metropolitan daily papers, either didn't believe it, didn't think it was suitable for a family audience, or feared the repercussions from readers. Those repercussions reverberated in my mail for weeks. But interspersed with the caustic letters from Al Capp fans were a handful of letters from other women who claimed to have been aggressively propositioned by him.

One incident had occurred in Eau Claire, Wisconsin, just three weeks before we wrote about Capp. The woman had wanted to press charges, but until she read our column, was afraid no one would believe her. The local prosecutor also was pushed off dead center by what he read, and Capp was called to Wisconsin to answer the charges. More alleged victims broke their silence and university administrators and police who had kept the secret were forced to do some soul-searching.

I noted with mixed feelings of satisfaction and regret that Capp pleaded guilty to attempted adultery and was put on probation—satisfaction because the newspapers that refused to run the column were now running stories about the case in Wisconsin, and regret because I had been the instrument that ended the career of a talented but troubled man.

Brit had been right in pushing me to publish the story. If we hadn't done it, Capp might have continued his campaign of aggression against selected young women, and those women would have been twice victimized—once by him and a second time by a system that dismissed what happened to them as inconsequential.

When news of the ITT plot broke in Chile, its subservient press seemed more interested in who my sources were than in the facts. That an American company had plotted the overthrow of their government, it seemed, was of less consequence. Chilean newspapers began to speculate that we were getting our secret memos from Orlando Letelier, the Chilean ambassador to Washington. There was even a wild rumor in the highly excitable Chilean media that Letelier had paid me $70,000 to publish the ITT memos. More than a year later, I heard from Letelier's anguished wife that he had been thrown into prison by a military junta, which had seized power from Salvador Allende. Letelier's wife pleaded that his life was in danger. She was convinced that the junta, and its leader Augusto Pinochet, had retaliated against her husband because they suspected he was my source on the ITT papers. I did what I could; I lodged a protest with the highest-ranking Chilean diplomat left in Washington after the coup; then I swore out an affidavit declaring that neither Letelier nor his associates had leaked the papers to us.

Letelier was not destined to be murdered in a Chilean jail. His enemies picked a more intriguing venue—Washington D.C., where he lived in exile after his release from prison. On September 21, 1976, Letelier was blown up by a bomb planted in his car. A year later, I was the first to accuse Manuel Contreras, head of the Chilean secret police, of ordering the killing. At the time, our Justice Department said I was "totally incorrect." It took nineteen years to write the end of this tragedy. In 1995 a Chilean court finally convicted Contreras for the assassination.

WE PLAYED OUT THE ITT-CHILE DIVERSION in a series of columns that kept the company hopping. Then ITT came up with a surprise. The exiled Dita Beard turned up in a hospital in Denver, suffering, she said, from chest pains. Her doctor said she might be able to testify, but only if the committee came to her bedside. It occurred to me that if ITT was permitting Beard to come out of hiding and testify, they must have something up their sleeve. While the committee members were readying for their trek west, Beard announced to the press that the memo I had published was not hers at all but a blatant forgery. ITT's transformation of Beard from boozy perpetrator to stricken victim had begun.

Beard's disappearance, and then her sudden resurrection, was the work of a peculiar White House undercover unit that specialized in committing blunders and staging fiascos. They called themselves the White House Plumbers. Their mission was to stop leaks to the media. But the ITT case would not make their reputations. That would come later during the Watergate fiasco.

As a test run, the plumber in chief, G. Gordon Liddy, undertook the assignment of spiriting Dita Beard out of state and out of sight. Her cover story was that she had caught a plane for Yellowstone National Park for a needed rest but had had to disembark during a Denver stopover because of chest pains. She was kept under wraps in a Denver hospital until ITT decided what to do with her.

Yet another Plumber, ex-CIA operative Howard Hunt, was sent by

Charles Colson to hustle Beard out of hiding. Hunt's clandestine training, or the lack thereof, compelled him to wear a cheap red wig, awkwardly askew, and use a voice modifier. The first rule of espionage is to be inconspicuous. Yet Hunt showed up at Beard's hospital bedside, in his vaudevillian disguise, as the lone, late-night visitor. Hunt's secret mission, should he accept and manage to keep his red wig on, was to persuade Beard to disassociate herself from the memo and to find some way to smear me.

Brit began to suspect that his copy of the memo, which he had dutifully turned over to the committee, may have fallen into the wrong hands. He called the chief lawyer for the committee and was stunned to learn that the memo had been turned over to the FBI for an analysis by J. Edgar Hoover's lab. I thought we were sunk. Hoover would surely be delighted to get his hands on evidence that he could turn against me.

Yet the results from the FBI lab tests were so conclusive that Hoover couldn't risk saying otherwise. The memo was legitimate, all right—from Beard's typewriter at approximately the time it was dated. So Hoover, opting to protect himself rather than the president, released the truthful findings.

White House lawyer John Dean later wrote that the mood at the Oval Office was surly when word came over from the FBI that the memo was legitimate. Chuck Colson insisted that Hoover change the wording on his cover letter at least to take a middle-of-the-road stance, but Hoover refused. Dean recorded in his memoir, *Blind Ambition,* that when Nixon was told of this turn of events, he said, "I don't understand Edgar sometimes. He hates Anderson."

Dean was orchestrating the ITT plot, as he later did Watergate, behind the scenes. He tried one more ploy. He requisitioned the memo out of the hands of the FBI and turned it over to ITT. They had their own expert eagerly waiting to prove it phony. Predictably, ITT's document analyst concluded that the memo was bogus, but by the time the company triumphantly released its findings, the FBI had already declared it legitimate. The ITT announcement hurt only ITT.

With all the lies swirling around the ITT case, I decided it would be good strategy to wire up Brit to a polygraph machine and show the world that he was telling the truth. I've always had a fondness for lie detector tests. They appeal to my dramatic flair and they tickle the public's fancy, even if they are not admissible in legal proceedings. Occasionally my peers have lifted their noses when I have resorted to the lie detector. I confess that makes me love the gadgets all the more.

I asked Les Whitten to find us a polygraph expert, and his choice showed his own theatrical flair. Les picked Lloyd Furr, who back in 1958 had worked as a private detective for Bernard Goldfine, the industrialist I

"WING IT, JACK"

BRIT HUME HAD THE GIFT OF multiple voices, which he sometimes used to bedevil others. When Brit read that Nixon aide Charles Colson had made an intemperate remark about his willingness to walk over his own grandmother's grave to accomplish his ends, Brit picked up the phone and dialed Colson's office. In the perfect quaver of an old woman, Brit introduced himself as Colson's grandmother and demanded to speak to him. A sputtering secretary said Colson was out, but she delivered grandma's indignant message to "the disrespectful little whipper-snapper."

Brit wasn't finished. He waited a few minutes and then called Colson's secretary again, this time announcing himself in a deep voice as the Associated Press bureau chief in granny's hometown: "Mr. Colson's grandmother has called us with a statement and I'd like his response." Brit waited a few minutes and then called again, this time as the United Press International bureau chief with the same request. When Brit called in behalf of the *New York Times,* Colson's office had prepared a written statement disowning "granny" as an impostor.

Brit has carved an impressive niche for himself in TV news, and each time I see him doing a standup from the lawn of the White House, I think back to the few months when I made him my TV editor and watched him chafe under the assignment. Brit loved a long investigation exposing a big scandal, but he had little patience for stories that were news one day and birdcage liners the next. As my TV editor, he had to produce scripts for five news spots a week for the Metromedia network. On Mondays I would go to the studio with five changes of clothes and record five exposés for the week—exposés that Brit was supposed to have supplied by the previous Friday. One Friday afternoon I saw Brit leaving for the day and I called to him at the door, "Do you have the TV scripts?"

"No, I couldn't come up with anything," Brit said as he pulled on his coat.

"What are we going to do?" I asked, already knowing the answer.

"I guess you're just going to have to wing it, Jack." Which is what I did.

was snooping on at the time. It was Furr who had caught me and House investigator Baron Shacklette with our ears to the wall, eavesdropping on Goldfine's hotel room. With Furr as our polygraph examiner, no one could say that the fix was in. Brit sat nervously through five polygrams, after which Furr pronounced him to be telling the truth about Dita Beard and her memo.

Meanwhile, the senators on the Judiciary Committee packed their bags and headed for Denver to set up a makeshift hearing room at the foot of Beard's bed. Propped by pillows, surrounded by doctors, tubes up her nose, the once gritty lobbyist had been reduced to playing the dupe. Someone had concocted the memo to ruin her and ITT, she claimed. And why had she not mentioned this before to Brit, to her bosses, to anyone? When she first saw the memo, she had read it too quickly to notice that it was not authentic, she said. She had begun to have her doubts the next day.

And what about her claim that the memo was initialed with "my own little 'd,'" as she had told Brit? Well, it had looked like her own little 'd,' until she saw it again later in a TV closeup. She had just been moved from the intensive care unit in Denver and was watching *60 Minutes* when the memo had come up on the screen. "I just nearly jumped out of bed. I called the children. I called everybody to look at that. That is not mine."

Why had she not exposed the memo as a fraud earlier? Because, "I had absolutely no one to turn to." Apparently Beard thought no one would believe her. I couldn't fault her there.

The committee, mindful of her delicate condition, eased Beard into dangerous waters—her encounter with Mitchell at the Kentucky Derby party. But the interrogation was not to be. Suddenly, she swooned back onto her pillows. Her doctors swarmed over her, the senators scurried out, and the hearing was over. Beard's lawyer emerged to say she had suffered a "near-massive heart attack." Her doctor added, "She will probably never be able to testify as long as she lives." Three days later Beard had recovered enough to grant an interview to *60 Minutes,* outside the hospital. And a week later she checked out for good.

The hearings were effectively over. All had spoken their peace, a few had perjured themselves. For the Nixon White House, it was a prelude of things to come.

I took some satisfaction in the fact that though the White House had tried to destroy my credibility, my face appeared on the cover of *Time* magazine the week that Dita Beard performed her swan song from her hospital bed. The largely flattering five-page story called me, however, "a college dropout with no intellectual pretensions . . . a relentless square whose biggest indulgences are a Sunday-afternoon nap and a second ice-cream cone for dessert, a clumsy writer who has yet to put together any memorable combination of words." My column was a "mishmash," according to the scribes at *Time,* and I was on no one's fashionable guest list. The story said the more staid members of my church would "choke on the words" when they had to call me "Brother Anderson."

I read it with some satisfaction. All things considered, I was where and who I wanted to be.

CHAPTER 13

THE THOMAS EAGLETON AFFAIR HANGS OVER my head like a toxic cloud. I have not forgotten those few days in 1972 that left me apologizing in public and nursing a bruised ego in private. But when a reporter pulls a whopper, he has an obligation to explain, if he can.

The story really began in 1968 when an old friend, True Davis, called me for advice. True had been an ambassador to Switzerland during the Kennedy administration and an assistant Treasury secretary under Lyndon Johnson. In 1968 he was running for the Senate from his home state of Missouri, and his toughest competitor for the Democratic nomination was the charismatic lieutenant governor of Missouri, Tom Eagleton. True confided in me that he had some dirt on Eagleton, but didn't know whether it would be smart to use it.

A man in civilian clothes, claiming to be a Missouri highway trooper, had approached True at a political rally with a handful of photocopies of arrest citations for drunken and reckless driving. The name on those citations was Thomas Eagleton. True didn't know if the citations were real or fabricated, and he didn't know if the messenger was really a trooper, or perhaps a dirty trickster.

I advised True to file away the derogatory information under lessons painlessly learned. If he spread the documents around, they could turn out to be false. And if they were real, the ploy could still backfire against True. A politician who drinks is not news, and my rule has always been to ignore such stories unless the politician became a drunk on the job.

I watched the victorious Senator Eagleton over the four years that followed, looking for signs of boozing above and beyond what would be considered tolerable in Washington. I came to admire his work in the Senate and all but forgot about the drunken driving allegations. My memory was triggered, however, at the Democratic National Convention in Miami in 1972 when presidential nominee George McGovern picked the likeable Eagleton as his running mate. Suddenly, wherever I turned, there was someone eager to whisper in my ear that Eagleton had a dark secret—a drinking problem that had run him afoul of the law in Missouri.

A rumor does not become true simply because it is heard from more than one source. My instinct told me to investigate what I was hearing, but I talked myself out of it, reasoning once again that a public figure's drinking habits were not a matter of public business unless they affected his work, so once again I stored the information in the inactive file.

Then, on July 25, 1972, Eagleton called a press conference to drag his own skeletons out of the closet. He admitted that he had checked himself into mental hospitals three times during his adult life for fatigue and exhaustion. Twice he had undergone electric shock therapy. He had kept the secret, even from McGovern, until that day. But two reporters from the *Detroit Free Press* had painstakingly followed a rumor and turned up the proof. They were about to print their story, so Eagleton had decided to beat them to the front page with his version.

I was as surprised as poor McGovern was to hear that the man who wanted to be a heartbeat away from the presidency had a history of choking under stress. Eagleton went on to explain that he was now mentally sound and careful to pace himself and manage the stress in his life. Then he mentioned something, almost as an afterthought; he volunteered that his stays in the hospital had never had anything to do with alcohol.

I immediately picked up the phone and called True Davis. Did he remember our conversation of four years earlier? Yes, but he didn't want to talk about it. Besides, he had destroyed the photocopies of the drunken driving citations, so he couldn't help me with proof.

Twice I had ignored this story, but a voice in the back of my mind was nagging me not to ignore it a third time. I interpreted this mental prodding as keen reportorial instinct. Instead, I should have recognized it as pure competitiveness. The two sensations are almost indistinguishable at times, but instinct tends to encourage careful reporting, while competitiveness more often causes carelessness.

With the help of a Missouri stringer whom I trusted, I got the names of three state troopers who might talk. Two were on vacation and not reachable. The third seemed to know what I was talking about, but he was skittish. In the middle of telling me stories he had heard from other troopers, he abruptly stopped and said he couldn't help me any more.

A former high official in Missouri government gave me names of more troopers; with one, I thought I hit pay dirt. He said that in 1968 his captain had come to him with a secret assignment—to quietly collect from other troopers any copies they might have of traffic citations issued to Eagleton while he was attorney general and then later lieutenant governor of Missouri. The captain reportedly was peeved because he had heard of troopers who had flagged down Eagleton and had written him tickets, only to have those tickets mysteriously disappear from the public record.

The trooper I talked to said his assignment was to find out if other troopers had kept copies of their citations. He told me that he asked around and came up with about a dozen tickets, some for drunken driving and some for careless driving and speeding. My source said the captain then ordered him to make three copies of each citation and deliver them to three people who might care—the Republican candidate for the Senate seat, Thomas Curtis; and the two men running against Eagleton for the Democratic nomination, Ed Long and True Davis.

I called True back again and told him I thought I had found the man who had delivered the photocopies to him at that political rally in 1968. It was enough to get him talking. He said he remembered examining ten or eleven citations and he thought three or four of them involved intoxication. I reached Ed Long who confirmed that one of his aides had received an envelope with copies of arrest records, but that Long had taken the high road and refused to look at them. Tom Curtis could only vaguely remember hearing something about Eagleton's traffic record during the campaign.

The trooper who claimed to have handed out the records refused to name his captain, who had initiated the search, but he promised me he would call the captain to see if he would talk to me. The captain refused. I left the office that night frustrated. Yet I was confident that the documents existed and that I would soon lay my hands on them.

When I face death, I am sure there will be moments of my life that roll before my eyes like a movie reel showing a rapid succession of what I will wish were outtakes. Chief among those moments will be July 27, 1972, when I sat in the Washington studio of the Mutual Broadcasting Network putting the finishing touches on the copy for my daily radio broadcast. In my hands was a short item prepared by one of my staffers reporting as much as he thought we could safely reveal about the drunken driving rumors—that reporters were swarming over Missouri trying to determine if they were true. It didn't seem strong enough, given what I had learned from the trooper the day before, so I penciled in a line. "Eagleton has steadfastly denied any alcoholism, but we now have located photostats of half a dozen arrests for drunken and reckless driving."

My source indeed claimed to have located copies of the citations and promised to put them in the mail. Yet the line was wrong and I was ready to admit it by the time I arrived back at my office. I walked in the door and headed straight for the phone to call Mutual and tell them I was going to retape the spot, but the phone lines were already lit up with incoming calls. It was only 9:50 A.M. and Mutual was not supposed to put my broadcast on the air until 10:15, but the producers had been so excited about my story that they had sent it out immediately. In the few minutes it had taken me to walk back to my office, my words had already begun bouncing across the country, and eager reporters were on the phone to ask me if I planned to release the documents they thought I had.

I huddled quickly with my staff, and we decided to send out a correction. I had not strictly "located" nor yet seen any documents. I had "traced" them, the correction said. It wasn't enough of an admission, and I should have realized that. But I was acting on a gut feeling that I would soon be able to obtain the arrest citations from the state trooper who had promised to send them, and I wasn't about to retract what I believed was a true story.

Eagleton, who was vacationing in Hawaii, assembled a press conference and called my report a "damnable lie." Either he was risking a monumental bluff or he was telling the truth. My staff spent the rest of the day trying to track down the arrest citations, but it was too late. Even the trooper who had been cooperative the day before was now spooked by the massive attention my stupid mistake was receiving. It was time for another mea culpa.

The next day was Friday and I issued a longer statement, admitting that competitiveness had pushed me to rush the story out too fast and that "I should have waited until I could authenticate the traffic citations personally." I was still not ready to make a full retraction.

On Friday morning, the *Washington Star* reported that Eagleton had shown up drunk and boisterous in a Columbia, Missouri, hotel lobby in 1960 and had been ordered out by police. Two weeks after the incident, Eagleton had checked himself into a psychiatric hospital and had not emerged again for a month, appearing just in time for his swearing in as Missouri's attorney general.

On the same day that I broadcast my blunder, the *St. Louis Post-Dispatch* ran a story quoting a former state highway patrol official saying troopers had stopped Eagleton for alleged traffic violations. The newspaper offered no proof and did not identify its source.

All around me, other reporters were filing their own stories citing anonymous sources who claimed to have seen arrest records or heard of drunken driving problems. The difference between their stories and mine seemed small but was undeniably large. They were reporting hearsay and calling it such. I had led people to believe that the sought-after documents were within my grasp.

The most damning news came on Saturday when the *Washington Post,* my flagship paper, published a story by society reporter Maxine Cheshire. She had received the same drunk-driving tip earlier in the week, and she related step by step how she had tried to verify the information but had come up dry. It was painfully obvious from her story that True Davis had been her source, too. The same True Davis from whom I had coaxed information three days earlier had gone to a cocktail party that night and, without any coaxing, passed on his tidbits about Eagleton to a gossip columnist.

Cheshire's story was devastating. Adding to my misery was a story on the same day in the *New York Times.* Their reporter had interviewed True Davis, on conditions of anonymity, and also had been unable to verify that the arrest citations existed. True himself delivered the worst blow late Saturday when he appeared on network television to say, "I have come to the reluctant conclusion that I am Jack Anderson's source." Then he mentioned our original conversation in 1968 and said nothing of my revisiting the story with him only two days before. The affect of his mea culpa was to make it seem that I was basing my report on a four-year-old conversation and nothing more.

I GOT UP SUNDAY MORNING AND drove to the CBS studio in Washington where I was to appear on *Face the Nation* with a panel of reporters questioning Eagleton. It was time to apologize again, this time face-to-face with Eagleton. "I violated my own rules," I told him as soon as the panel got rolling. "I did not authenticate whether or not these tickets were genuine. Using these sources, I went ahead with a story that I should not have gone ahead with and that was unfair to you. And you have my apology."

Eagleton thanked me graciously and appeared ready to let bygones be bygones. Had I left it alone at that point, I believe the brouhaha would have died down. But, when the moderator of *Face the Nation* referred in passing to my statement as a "retraction," I couldn't let it sit. I still believed the story was true. All I was willing to admit at that point was that I had rushed to tell the story without the proof in my hands. "Well, Senator," I slipped my foot into my mouth, "I would like nothing better than to dispose of this issue right here and now and I wish I could retract the story completely. . . . I cannot in good conscience do that."

When the show ended, I was in a worse position than when it had begun. On Monday, McGovern dropped Eagleton as a running mate, and on Tuesday I presented myself at Eagleton's Senate office. We talked privately for a few minutes while the hallway outside filled with reporters and photographers. I told him what evidence I had against him and acknowledged it was not enough. I owed him a full retraction. Noting that we had an audience outside, he suggested that we get it over with immediately. We stepped out into the hallway and up to a bank of microphones and I issued a full retraction, saying I had exhausted my investigative abilities and come up dry. "I think the story did damage the senator and I owe him a great and humble apology for that." To his credit, Eagleton, who just the night before had seen his chance at the vice presidency snatched away, was magnanimous and gentlemanly. "The book is closed as far as I'm concerned," he said.

It had been only a week, yet the time that had elapsed seemed like an eternity. I was excoriated on editorial pages across the country. The volume of criticism caused my peers to assume that my blunder cost me heavily in newspapers that carried my column. In fact, only six papers canceled the column, and I quickly gained twelve more to make a total of 946. The gains did not wipe out the painful lesson I had learned though, nor did they stop the questions.

For years I would be dogged on the lecture circuit with the Eagleton accusations. Sometimes I repeated my apology, we make mistakes and we learn tough lessons. Sometimes I defensively asked, where were the sinless reporters who were qualified to cast the first stone?

CHAPTER 14

THOMAS JEFFERSON DIDN'T KNOW RICHARD NIXON, but he saw him coming. To a friend, Jefferson wrote, "Of future presidents, we can have no confidence in the man. We must bind him down in chains, the chains of the Constitution."

Nixon strained against those chains, especially the First Amendment restraints that protected journalists. He came to power with the conviction that he had gotten there by circumventing the working press. He drew a curtain of secrecy between his internal operations and the outside world, a veil that was unprecedented in the memory of Washington observers. He did not want the acts and policies of his administration to reach the people through what he considered the distorting prism of the media.

Since he could not stop the publication of news, Nixon tried to stop the hemorrhaging of classified information. He sought to have reporters thrown in jail for refusing to reveal their sources. Not since 1735, when John Peter Zenger had been hauled to prison for criticizing the British governor of New York, had reporters been given such cause to fear that they would be dispatching the news from behind bars. "We've got to take care of these people!" Nixon once exploded in reference to the *Washington Post*.

THERE WERE SO MANY ENEMIES FOR the president to keep track of that White House counsel John Dean proposed keeping a formal list of those who had given the president a "hard time." In a memo dated August 16, 1971, Dean said, "This memorandum addresses the matter of how we can maximize the fact of our incumbency in dealing with persons known to be active in their opposition to our administration. Stated a bit more bluntly—how we can use the available federal machinery to screw our political enemies." Other politicians tended to call their political rivals "opponents," and journalists "critics," but viewed through the screen of Nixon's paranoia, these people were all enemies.

The original shortlist identified Nixon's top twenty enemies, and perhaps for alphabetical reasons, my name led the others. The existence of the list outraged me, but all the same I would have been disappointed not to have been on it.

It was the job of Charles Colson, Nixon's ardent counsel, to manage the dirty tricks against the president's enemies. At one point Colson discovered that I had once been caught in a hotel room with wiretap equipment. The information—stemming from my 1957 investigations of Eisenhower's chief of staff Sherman Adams—was so old and worn to render it comical lore from ancient history.

When the old wiretapping charge proved to have no legs, Colson fabricated something juicier. He claimed that I been paid $100,000 in 1958 to write favorable stories about former Cuban dictator Fulgencio Batista, the predecessor to Fidel Castro. Colson wrote triumphantly in a memo to Dean that finally he had the ammunition to "destroy" my credibility. Of course the truth was that I had never had a nice thing to say about the tinhorn Batista, in or out of my column. When I learned of Colson's lie, I offered to pay $100,000 to anyone who could prove I had ever coddled the Cuban dictator. There were no takers.

Nixon's list of top enemies grew and grew to about two hundred names. The punishments prescribed for these assorted enemies ranged from smear campaigns to IRS audits to denial of federal grants and contracts. There was also a "B" list of as many as 1,500 people who were to be refused White House favors including government jobs and invitations to dinner.

I discovered the existence of yet another list—this one a shortlist of senators who were on the outs with the White House. It was subject to change every few months depending on the senators' voting records. These poor outcasts couldn't even arrange White House tours for tourists from their home states. Nixon didn't keep a similar list of House members, only because it was too time consuming to track their voting records and update their status as friends or foes.

MY WHITE HOUSE SOURCES KEPT ME informed of the high jinks of Nixon's Keystone Kops, sending me new evidence almost daily. One White House source told me that Nixon's shadow, Bebe Rebozo, was collecting cash contributions for "walking-around money" for the president.

CONDUCT UNBECOMING

DIPLOMACY, WITH ALL THE DIGNITY THE word implies, makes stories about undiplomatic conduct all the more compelling. Joe Spear was in the office one day in 1971 when a man who worked in the cable room at the State Department showed up at our door with a tip. It was a cable from the U.S. ambassador to Kenya, Robinson McIlvaine, to the head of the Agency for International Development in Washington, John Hannah. The cable complained about the conduct of an AID employee in Kenya, who had thrown protocol to the wind during a visit to Kenya by Vice President Spiro Agnew. The man had crashed the vice president's party at a game preserve called Treetops and proceeded to get annoyingly drunk.

Treetops was a luxury spot built on stilts so the guests could sit on the deck and sip martinis while watching wild animals roam below them. Late in the evening, as the party wound down—Agnew had gone to bed—the AID worker grabbed Agnew's secretary, made a pass at her, and, in the words of the cable, tried "to drag her down the steps to meet an elephant at ground level." The next morning, the hungover employee woke up after most of Agnew's entourage had departed. He carjacked the one remaining Secret Service car, leaving some of Agnew's guards stranded at Treetops.

Joe called John Hannah at AID to tell him we had the cable and to ask for comment. "How did you get that?" Hannah sputtered. "That was top secret!" He launched an investigation, but never discovered Joe's source. Hannah put a lock on the copier to discourage more leaks.

It has been my experience that for every public servant who makes a drunken fool of himself, there is at least one witness who thinks the incident deserves airing. More than one person was eager to tell me when one particular diplomat stumbled.

In 1972, while enroute to China where he was to plan delicate trade negotiations, this diplomat put on quite a show for the passengers and crew of a Pan Am jet. Drinking and shouting for more booze, he pawed female flight attendants and tried to stuff money down their blouses. His curious revelry stopped when he passed out in the first-class lounge.

I heard the news from the flight crew, despite the fact that they had been ordered by airline officials to keep their mouths shut. One stewardess filed a complaint about the passenger's unseemly conduct. Witnesses told me that he had been drunk before he boarded the flight, that he had ignored the "no smoking" signs, and that he had demanded a Bloody Mary before the plane left the ground. When the stewardess had refused to bring around the mini-bottles during takeoff, the diplomat had called her a bitch and threatened to have her fired. Two State Department aides met the plane at Dulles Airport in Virginia, helped the man off the flight, and whisked him away.

I learned this was not the first time this diplomat had carried the festivities a bit too far in the friendly skies. On another Pan Am flight, this one from Washington to Paris, he told a stewardess he wanted to expedite the sexual development of his teenage son and asked her to help with the boy's training. When she declined the role of mistress to an adolescent, he lobbed grapes at her.

It was a case of decidedly undiplomatic conduct, but one I would normally downplay, were it not for the fact that the Chinese trade talks hung in the balance. I knew that the Chinese considered drunken behavior shameful and that America should not risk using such a bibulous diplomat on such a sensitive mission. Sure enough, a month after I first reported on the man's midair antics, Chinese diplomats in New York were discreetly asking around about his behavior, implying that his presence as a negotiator was an insult to China.

The Senate Foreign Relations Committee got nervous but was calmed by reassurances from the CIA and State Department that there was nothing to the story, even though members of the flight crew were questioned on Capitol Hill and confirmed what I had written. To calm the Chinese, the State Department assured them that the offender would not be a big player in the trade talks.

No records were kept of the gifts, although Nixon would occasionally make a thank-you phone call to a donor. In August 1971 I reported on the first of these cash gifts that I was able to confirm—$100,000 from billionaire Howard Hughes. But, it took another two years to flesh out all the details of the story that the White House repeatedly denied.

The $100,000 was siphoned like a sip of champagne from the Silver Slipper, one of Hughes's Las Vegas casinos. The secret transaction was handled for Hughes by his fix-it man, Robert Maheu. I suspected that Hughes was simply using his money to influence the outcome of the 1968 election so he could ask the new president for favors. Hughes had a pathological fear of nuclear testing in the Nevada desert, next door to his abode atop the Desert Inn in Las Vegas. He not only thought Nixon would oppose the testing, but he felt Nixon's election would pave the way for another future Republican president, Nevada Governor Paul Laxalt, who was even more likely to do Hughes's bidding.

But my theory about Hughes's political motives quickly dissolved as I pieced together the timetable of his donations. The first half of the gift— $50,000 in $100 bills—had been delivered to Bebe Rebozo at Rebozo's bank in Key Biscayne, Florida, in 1969, after Nixon had already won the 1968 election. The second installment, also in $100 bills, was handed over to Rebozo at the "Western White House" in San Clemente, California, in early 1970.

Richard Danner, the Hughes executive who had made the deliveries, insisted that the cash was intended for distribution among Republican congressional candidates for the 1970 election. But I was intrigued by the fact that shortly before the first bundle of cash was delivered, Nixon personally approved Hughes's purchase of Air West airline. And around the time of the second installment, the Justice Department reversed itself in an antitrust ruling and allowed the expansion of Hughes's casino empire in Nevada.

The Air West matter had the fingerprints of Nixon's brother Donald all over it. Drew Pearson and I had already embarrassed the Nixon brothers in 1956 when Richard Nixon was vice president. We had uncovered a $205,000 loan Hughes had made to Don Nixon to run a chain of hamburger stands. The loan had been secured by a mortgage on Nixon family land in Whittier, California, land that was valued at only $13,000. A few weeks after Donald Nixon had received the "loan," the IRS had granted tax-exempt status to the Howard Hughes Medical Institute, a designation that had twice before been denied.

Donald Nixon never repaid the money, and Richard Nixon never forgot that I was the one who had uncovered the story. He also never forgot that his brother could get him into trouble. When Nixon learned that brother Don was again consorting with Hughes's aides, the president had Don tailed and ordered his phones tapped.

When Hughes decided to buy Air West, Maheu's first move was to contact Don Nixon, who put Maheu in touch with an Air West board member. The Securities and Exchange Commission suspected that Hughes then manipulated Air West stock by pressuring selected board members to dump their stock at cheap prices, promising he would make good on their losses. When the stock prices tumbled, the board panicked and voted to sell the company. Hughes was there with the check, and President Nixon was there to approve Hughes as the buyer, despite Hughes's poor record managing Trans World Airlines.

Don Nixon later groused to my reporter George Clifford that Hughes should have at least given him a "finder's fee" for his work on the Air West deal. Or, it would have been fair, he said, for Hughes to give the catering contract for the airline to the Marriott Corporation, which, at the time, employed Don as a vice president. Instead, it was Richard, not Don, who got $50,000 in cash from Hughes, with more to come later.

The second $50,000 delivery coincided suspiciously with a decision from the Justice Department that allowed Hughes to become the biggest casino magnate in America, even after the antitrust section of the Justice Department had already blocked him from adding the Stardust Hotel in Las Vegas to his growing empire.

In January and February of 1970, Richard Danner, Hughes's bagman, flew to Washington for meetings with Attorney General John Mitchell. Danner made a pitch: Let Hughes buy the Dunes Hotel in Las Vegas instead of the Stardust. Mitchell followed up with a call to Richard McLaren, the antitrust chief with whom I had crossed paths in my ITT investigation. Mitchell laid it on thick, according to my sources, telling McLaren that Nevada Governor Laxalt had complained the Dunes was owned by hoodlums and that granting title to Hughes would help clean up Las Vegas. Laxalt later said that he never spoke to Mitchell about the Dunes, that he didn't believe it was run by mobsters, and that he would not have supported Hughes's purchase. But McLaren didn't know that at the time. He passed the message from his boss Mitchell on to the attorney handling Hughes matters. That attorney said Hughes's casino empire was already too big by antitrust standards. The lawyer even put his objections in writing, and McLaren dutifully took the opinion back to Mitchell. Imagine their surprise when Mitchell subsequently met with Danner and told him Hughes could go ahead and buy the Dunes. (The deal later fell through when Hughes looked at the hotel's profit and loss data.)

Richard Danner insisted that he never mentioned the hotel deals to Bebe Rebozo when he delivered the cash payments for Nixon. Danner also said he never talked to Mitchell about the money when he was negotiating hotel deals with the attorney general. As for Nixon and Mitchell, they adopted the standard stratagem of high officials under fire. Whatever the alleged crime, if it was committed at all, expendable subordinates must have done it while their unknowing superiors were tending to higher responsibilities.

There was no record in the president's campaign finance reports that the money was ever received. That was because, explained Rebozo, he kept the cash in a lock box at the Bank of Key Biscayne for three years while he fretted over the wisdom of accepting it. At that point, Rebozo said, he tried to give it back to the Hughes organization. Danner wouldn't take it back, Rebozo said, so he gave it to a Hughes lawyer. The only action the money saw during those three years, according to Rebozo, was when he tore off the wrappers because they were imprinted with "Las Vegas."

I never believed the money was idle. I got a tip that Rebozo had divided it among Nixon's brothers Donald and Edward, and Nixon's secretary Rose Mary Woods. Rebozo had then reportedly gone to the president's lawyer Herbert Kalmbach for advice after the fact. My source was reliable, but I couldn't verify his information, so I passed it on to someone with subpoena power—the Senate Watergate Committee. The committee's investigator Terry Lerner summoned Kalmbach and Rebozo to give depositions in secret.

Rebozo refused to talk and Kalmbach claimed attorney-client privilege. But when the chairman of the Senate Watergate Committee, Senator Sam Ervin, threatened Kalmbach with contempt, the lawyer opened up. He said Rebozo had come to him on Nixon's advice and had admitted that he had divided the money among the Nixon brothers, Woods, and "others."

Rebozo still stuck to his story about returning the Hughes money, even after the Watergate committee found proof that he had personally paid for work on Nixon's vacation homes from a secret trust account that had been deposited in the form of $100 bills. From the same account, Rebozo had bought a $5,660 pair of earrings for Pat Nixon's birthday. The first lady thought the baubles were a gift from her husband, and Nixon thought so too. He had, in fact, asked Rose Mary Woods to select some jewelry for his wife. Rebozo had also been shopping for a gift for her and had asked Woods to keep an eye out for something nice. Woods put Rebozo together with a jeweler, and the earrings were delivered to Pat Nixon. Nixon assumed they were the gift he had asked his secretary to purchase. It was the Senate Watergate Committee that finally solved the mystery of the first lady's earrings. The Hughes slush fund had paid for them.

Even while Rebozo was taking Hughes's money, incredibly, the White House gang was trying to double-cross the billionaire. I got hold of confidential White House memos that revealed that White House Chief of Staff Bob Haldeman had planted stories in the press linking Hughes to Democratic National Chairman Larry O'Brien. Haldeman sought Rebozo's help in exposing Hughes's ties to the enemy. It wasn't clear from the exchange of memos whether Rebozo cautioned Haldeman that the president was beholden to Hughes.

In any event, Haldeman decided to go ahead with the smear of O'Brien. He had the courtesy to tell John Dean to "keep Bebe out of it at all costs," according to their exchange of memos. Rebozo's intelligence from the Hughes organization fed the smear campaign. He informed Dean that the top democrat O'Brien had been on the Hughes payroll at a time when Hughes was feigning friendliness toward the Republicans.

Haldeman decided to leak what he knew to a reporter. As I dug deeper into this caper after the fact in 1973, I discovered the identity of that reporter. He was me. In 1971 the White House had tipped me off that Hughes had offered to pay Larry O'Brien's salary as Democratic National Chairman during the 1968 campaign. At the time, O'Brien told me that he had never taken a dime from Hughes during the campaign, and I believed him.

In his memoir, *Blind Ambition*, John Dean said that around the White House, Larry O'Brien was second only to myself "as a target of ugly thoughts. . . ." So, in a dirty trick of delicious irony, Nixon had tried to use me, number one on the list, to smear O'Brien, number two on the list. It must have cankered the president's men when I reported that there was no truth to the rumor they had slipped me. But I also reported that after the campaign, O'Brien had joined the Hughes payroll as a sometime consultant making $180,000 a year. That news caused sheer panic inside the White House. This would give O'Brien access to Hughes company files; he might find out about the money Hughes had given to Nixon. Haldeman ordered O'Brien's phones to be tapped.

In the years since the Watergate scandal, I have had reason to wonder whether the burglars who broke into the Democratic headquarters in the Watergate complex under orders from the White House were trying to find out how much O'Brien knew.

Clue No. 1: The same burglars broke into the safe of Hank Greenspun, publisher of the *Las Vegas Sun*. The only link between the two break-ins is the Howard Hughes money. Hank also happened to be collecting evidence of the cash gifts and trying to prove that Rebozo had spent the money refurbishing Nixon's vacation houses. Locked in the safe the White House burglars tried to open was a stack of confidential, handwritten memos from Hughes. Hank showed them to me.

Clue No. 2: Having been badly burned by my exposé of the Hughes loan, Nixon was particularly sensitive about the Hughes connection. He didn't want to be burned again.

Next to stories about Hughes, Nixon was most sensitive about stories that exposed the fiction of his Vietnam policy. He had promised during the campaign that he had a secret plan to end the war, but there was no plan. Nixon simply escalated the U.S. presence in Vietnam, chalking up losses that nearly matched those of the Lyndon Johnson years. One-third of the U.S. casualties for the entire war fell on Nixon's watch, and more American bombs were dropped during Nixon's term than during Johnson's.

In the spring of 1971, while Nixon claimed he was winding down the U.S. role in Vietnam, I exposed detailed plans for bombing North Vietnam and mining Haiphong harbor. A week later, after Nixon denied that American ground troops were continuing to operate in Cambodia and Laos, I published the exact number of Americans killed during those incursions. Perhaps my story out of Vietnam that caused Nixon the most embarrassment was the revelation that the National Security Agency was intercepting the private communications of a U.S. ally, South Vietnamese President Nguyen Van Thieu, and passing the transcripts along to the White House.

UNDER THIS BOMBARDMENT OF HEADLINES, NIXON'S
aides escalated their war on the media. Charles Colson, the chief aide in
charge of plugging the news leaks, sought reinforcements. It was time to call
in the Plumbers. This goon squad, assembled by Colson, also had an aux-
iliary mission: planting bogus news tips to embarrass the president's critics.
Carl Bernstein and Bob Woodward, the *Washington Post*'s crack Watergate
investigative team, claimed in their book *All the President's Men* that their
legendary source "Deep Throat" suspected my reporting on Senator Eagleton
was tainted by information manufactured by the Plumbers. To this day I
don't know if that was the case, but with the Nixon trick-or-treat gang,
anything was possible.

The masterminds behind the Plumbers were David Young, who transferred over from the National Security Council, and Egil Krogh, who had
been groomed, in his own words, to "destroy" anyone who got in Nixon's
way. The brawn for the Plumbers was supplied by a quirky duo: Howard
Hunt and Gordon Liddy.

Hunt had a background in covert action and counterintelligence work
for the CIA. He was a natural spook. If given a choice between doing his
research from nine to five or donning a kooky wig and venturing out in the
middle of the night, he would choose the wig and cover of darkness every
time. Whenever Hunt was temporarily out of the action for any reason, he
found an outlet for his spy fantasies in writing. He authored forty-five
obscure novels.

Colson met Hunt through their Brown University alumni club in Washington and became enamored with his style. No one could talk a better
game. When it became clear that the White House urgently needed someone
to do dirty work, Colson thought of Hunt.

Liddy's official title was legal counsel for the Committee to Reelect the
President, but that didn't come close to explaining his unwritten job description—bag-jobs, forgeries, frame-ups, break-ins, and buggings. An ex-
FBI agent, he had first joined the Nixon administration at the Treasury
Department where he worked on antidrug policies, but he was ill suited for
a policy-making position. As one of his co-workers told me, "He's much
too, uh, inventive for that."

A glowering and cheerless man who thrived on conspiracy, Liddy
worked hard to cultivate a macho image. Once, while recruiting some men
to work for him at the Republican Convention, Liddy held his hand over
a candle flame, without so much as a twitch of his heavy mustache, until
his flesh burned. He wanted to illustrate for his recruits what kind of men
he wanted them to be.

This bantam Groucho Marx in a three-piece suit strolled through the

Nixon circus with no apparent realization that he was different from other men. He once stopped to talk with the wife of Republican official Robert Odle outside GOP campaign headquarters, and the conversation drifted toward the safety of women on the streets of Washington. Liddy advised her that she should carry a sharpened pencil to use as a stiletto. "Be sure the eraser is in good condition," he warned. "It will protect the palm of your hand when you drive the pencil into the attacker's throat."

A man of action, Liddy once leaped out of a taxi to rescue a pedestrian who was being mugged. Liddy was beaten senseless by the mugger. It was a rare occasion when he was bested. Usually Liddy was prepared for battle. While casing Senator George McGovern's campaign headquarters for a possible burglary, Liddy whipped out a pistol in quick-draw fashion and shot out a street light that he thought might illuminate the scene of the crime.

During the 1972 presidential campaign, Nixon's treasurer Hugh Sloan asked Liddy to escort him to the bank with $350,000 in Sloan's briefcase. Liddy had a surprise in his own briefcase—a gas-operated pellet gun. After the bank, the two men stopped at a restaurant for lunch and Liddy began to worry that the gas pressure in his gun would build up and the weapon might accidentally discharge. Sloan started to sweat, but Liddy was cool. He strode into the men's room, walked into the first stall, and fired the gun into the toilet. The reaction of the man in the next stall was not recorded.

My reporter Jack Cloherty made the rounds in Liddy's neighborhood to find out more about him. The neighbors said Liddy sent his own children to bed before dark and could never understand why other parents didn't do the same. Liddy became so annoyed by a group of neighborhood youngsters talking loudly after dark that he perched on a garage roof and waited for them. When they passed within range, he leaped from the roof like Batman, grabbed the kids, and slapped one of them. A delegation of parents decided it was time to negotiate, but their resolve to soften Liddy weakened when they arrived at his house and saw his guns prominently displayed on the dining room table.

Nixon, in a conversation with Haldeman, admitted that he thought Liddy "must be a little nuts." "He is," Haldeman agreed. But neither seemed to think Liddy was too nuts to be carrying out orders from the president of the United States.

When the Watergate burglary was bungled and the intruders were arrested, Liddy felt personally responsible. In all seriousness, he invited John Dean to have someone shoot him down in the street, gangland style, as punishment. Dean said that wouldn't be necessary.

MISSION IMPOSSIBLE

DONALD STEWART, THE PENTAGON SECURITY CHIEF who was assigned to help the Plumbers find my sources, told me after the furor of Watergate died down that he had overseen eleven separate investigations of me during the Nixon years. Whenever he needed money to continue the work, he said, all he had to do was let the White House know he had a hot lead. "They'd give me all the money I wanted," he told me, his words tinged with wry humor.

When the Pentagon brass figured out that I knew Yeoman Charles Radford, there was panic in the White House and Defense Department. They suspected incorrectly that Radford had leaked the secret papers about Nixon's tilt toward Pakistan in the India-Pakistan war. But Radford also had access to a motherlode of other secrets through Henry Kissinger. Would he feed me those?

On December 23, 1971, Stewart met in the Plumbers' hangout in the basement of the Old Executive Office Building with David Young, the Nixon aide in charge of the goon squad. Young had an assignment for Stewart—to prove that I had an ongoing homosexual relationship with Radford. The order was not simply to find out if such a relationship existed. Stewart said he was supposed to "ensure that I found a homosexual relationship" whether it was true or not.

It was mission impossible—to prove that I, married for two decades and the father of nine children, was having an affair with a man that I had met through my church, one of the more puritanical religions on the planet. Stewart said, no, he wouldn't do it. Young repeated the order emphasizing that it had come from the president. Stewart still refused. Young was livid. "Damn it, damn it! The president is jumping up and down and he wants this and we're always telling him everything can't be done. The president is mad at us and we're telling him it can't be done." Stewart was unmoved and Young dropped the subject.

Stewart was on vacation in Florida in January of 1972 when he was summoned back by his boss, J. Fred Buzhardt, the general counsel to the Defense Department. Buzhardt wanted Stewart to find out just how much Radford knew about secret peace talks with North Vietnam. Kissinger had made thirteen trips to Paris to meet secretly with Communist leaders, and Stewart soon determined that Radford knew all about those trips.

Nixon was gripped by the fear that I would break the story of the talks and thereby preempt his own announcement. So he called a press conference and revealed that the talks had been taking place for thirty months. He proudly announced, seemingly out of context, that there had never been a leak about the talks. Privately, officials at the Defense Department wondered why Nixon had chosen that moment to make public the peace plan. Stewart said it was because the president feared I would scoop him. He was right. Had I known about it, I would have broken the story. But Radford never told me.

The Plumbers set up shop in room 16 of the basement of the Old Executive Office Building next to the White House. Young and Liddy had desks there, but Hunt preferred to float in and out, phantomlike. A corkboard showing their current targets was kept up to date by Egil Krogh. Reports coming out of the office were stamped with the code name "Odessa." When *New York Times* reporter Seymour Hersh managed to get access to the room (he wrote the first story exposing the existence of the Plumbers unit) he found my name scrawled on the wall, presumably to inspire them on against the foe.

But I was not the first target of the Plumbers. That honor went to Daniel Ellsberg, the antiwar activist who had leaked the Pentagon Papers to the *New York Times* in June of 1971. Nixon wanted to discredit Ellsberg, so the Plumbers began prowling for dirt. According to rumor, FBI investigators had already pumped Ellsberg's psychiatrist for information. Why stop there, Krogh and Young asked. Why not burglarize the psychiatrist's office and get the complete file? John Ehrlichman later admitted that he gave the final approval for the burglary, but only after getting the go-ahead from Nixon himself. The burglary netted nothing, but it whetted the Plumber's appetite for covert action.

CHAPTER 15

HAD I TORMENTED POOR RICHARD BEYOND his endurance? Had he decided that the only way to silence me was permanently? Did the president of the United States mark me for murder? I don't really think so, but I do know that the tantalizing subject was discussed more than once. Gordon Liddy had offered his services as general-purpose assassin. One day standing on the front steps of the Old Executive Office Building, Liddy told White House aide Egil Krogh that if the administration wanted anyone dead, he stood ready to do the deed. Krogh smiled politely. "Look, I'm not kidding," Liddy insisted.

"Yeah, I know you're not, so I'll let you know."

Twenty years after Watergate, Liddy took pains to explain to me that he was pulling Jeb Magruder's leg the day in 1971 when Liddy strode out of the White House with my name at the top of his hit list. But I think his memory may have been softened by the years. In 1971 and 1972, Liddy was convinced that I was public enemy number one.

There was a bit of fiction running through Liddy's head, planted there, I suspect, by Howard Hunt. Liddy thought that something I had written had led to the death of an American agent abroad. Liddy told the story repeatedly in the post-Watergate years when he became a media celebrity. Sometimes he would say the agent had been killed, sometimes just tortured. He didn't know the man's name, or even the country where this alleged betrayal had taken place. He only knew that something I had written had blown a man's cover. I never had any idea what Liddy was talking about.

Once a radio station had Liddy on the air as a guest and called me for comment on the worn-out story. Liddy refused to engage in a dialogue with me, so I issued a challenge. "You tell him he can put up any amount of money he can afford, and if I have to borrow it I'll go get the same amount of money and we'll put it in neutral hands. All he has to do is supply the name of the agent and the evidence that the story is true. If he can even supply a name, I'll be surprised. If he can do that, he gets to keep the money. If he can't, I get to keep his money." Liddy didn't take me up on the offer.

AS EVIDENCE OF HOW TIME HEALS all wounds and softens some murder plots, Liddy and I were finally brought together by *Good Morning America* to joke about his plans to do me in. But Liddy may not have been the only one with my murder on his mind. On September 21, 1975, the *Washington Post* published a story by Watergate reporter Bob Woodward alleging that Howard Hunt had been under orders to kill me in the winter of 1971–72. This came as a surprise to me. At the time I read the story, the Nixon years were over, but for the pontificating. I thought I already knew all the various and sundry ways the Plumbers had tried to embarrass and discredit me. And I sincerely thought murder had been nothing more than Liddy's brief fantasy. Now here was word that Hunt had also considered killing me, under orders from "a senior official" in the White House.

Hunt, who was by then in prison for his Watergate crimes, denied there had ever been a plot to assassinate me. Charles Colson, mellowed by Christianity, wrote me a "Dear Jack" note and assured me, "As best I remember, none of this ever happened."

But the way Hunt and Liddy had originally told it, Colson had forgotten quite a bit. In the spring of 1972, Colson summoned Hunt to the White House for a new assignment. Colson looked agitated, Hunt said, indicating that he had just come from a meeting with Nixon. The president was positively seething over leaks of information to my column. Having failed to prove me a homosexual, Colson was ready to venture into the "twilight zone." "It would be great to make it look as though he's blown his mind," Colson told Hunt. He pondered trying to get me drunk just before one of my radio broadcasts, or slipping me something that would make me seem drunk. Colson wondered if Hunt, who was ex-CIA, might know someone at the Agency with a recipe for an appropriate potion.

Hunt reminded his boss that the CIA had lost confidence in the Plumbers following the messy break-in at the office of Daniel Ellsberg's psychiatrist. But Colson was not dissuaded. Surely Hunt must know someone who could help apply a little CIA technology against Anderson. Hunt agreed to revisit the CIA's dirty tricks department. He remembered that Liddy suggested using sedatives and hallucinogens on antiwar activists who might disrupt the 1972 GOP nominating convention. And Hunt just happened to know someone with expertise in slipping Mickeys to unsuspecting dupes—a former CIA colleague, Dr. Edward T. Gunn. The aforesaid Gunn had worked for a while in a CIA lab experimenting with chemicals and their use in covert actions.

Hunt rounded up Liddy, and, in the name of the president, they invited Dr. Gunn to meet them for lunch at the pricey Hay-Adams Hotel across a small park from the White House. Over soup and salad, Hunt introduced Liddy by his favorite alias, "George Leonard," and explained that they were working on a White House project.

The idea-swapping was kept on a hypothetical level, with my name discreetly left out of the conversation. Hunt asked about slipping the hallucinogen LSD to somebody to compromise the victim's capabilities, but Dr. Gunn waved away the idea. "Too unpredictable."

Suppose the intended victim had a radio broadcast. Was there something that could be administered before he went on the air to make him sound stupid? Gunn dismissed that idea as foolishness. They would have to drug the man, drive him to the studio, carry him inside, and prop him up in front of the microphone in full view of the production crew. Somebody was bound to notice. (Had they thought it through, they would have realized that my show did not air live, and the producers were unlikely to put an incoherent tape on the air.)

Liddy was getting impatient. As he has related the story, he interrupted their speculating. "I really think the way to go about this is that the man just be eliminated." Gunn and Hunt paused midbite and thought about that idea for a while. How best to do it? Somebody suggested aspirin roulette—a bottle of medication would be spiked with a drug and planted in my medicine cabinet. Except that I had a wife and nine children, and nobody wanted to risk the chance that one of them might get a headache.

Dr. Gunn said there was an auto-accident technique quite popular among covert agents abroad—to hit the victim's car at a particular spot on the rear bumper while the car was turning at a certain angle and going at a specific speed. Liddy and Hunt demurred that they didn't know any hit men in the United States who were familiar with the technique. Gunn was surprised, because it was all the rage overseas.

The good doctor remembered one case where the steering wheel of a victim's car had been painted with a hallucinogen that was supposed to seep into the skin and from there into the bloodstream. Alas, the intended victim's sweaty palms had diluted the mix. The method wasn't foolproof. How about slipping a pill into my drink at a cocktail party? Liddy and Hunt shook their heads. I was a teetotaler. The Plumbers thanked Dr. Gunn for his help and Liddy slipped Gunn a wad of money for the consultation.

On the walk back to the White House, Liddy and Hunt were discouraged. The one decent option was the steering-wheel potion applied in cold weather so I wouldn't sweat it off, but they theorized that a man in my line of work probably had a chauffeur anyway. They had an inflated view of my financial position. My only chauffeurs were teenagers with learner's permits.

Liddy was angry, thinking as he always did when my name came up of the mythical agent who had been tortured to death because of my reporting. Then he hit upon an idea. This was Washington, D.C., after all. Why not just have me murdered in a common street mugging. Take my watch, take my wallet, and leave me on the sidewalk as just another statistic. Hunt said he would ask his superiors. Later Liddy pressed him for an answer. "We can forget that," Hunt told him. Liddy was becoming increasingly annoyed with these spineless desk jockeys.

Hunt reported back to Colson that the ideas gleaned from the doctor were unworkable. Colson was disgusted. At the very least, he said, the Plumbers could flatten my tires to send me the message that my column was not universally popular. But such a menial prank was beneath Hunt.

MEANWHILE, THE PRESIDENT WAS OPENING HIS newspaper every day to find yet another installment of my International Telephone and Telegraph story. I was threatening to spoil his big convention in San Diego by revealing that ITT may have subsidized the site in exchange for favors from the antitrust division of the Justice Department.

Liddy was dispatched by the White House to hustle ITT lobbyist Dita Beard out of town. When she surfaced at a hospital in Denver, Hunt was sent to persuade her to change her story and say she had never written the incriminating ITT memo. Hunt never denied he made a midnight visit to Mrs. Beard, but he was insulted by references in the press to the fact that he wore the now famous cockeyed red wig. It wasn't red, he said. It was blond.

ITT concluded that the White House Plumbers were rank amateurs, and the company turned to a professional detective firm, Intertel, to investigate me. But Intertel couldn't turn up any dirt either.

In March 1972, White House lawyer John Dean figured it was time to pull out the big gun: the FBI. *Newsweek* magazine was preparing a story on Brit Hume and myself. Dean told FBI officials that he feared the magazine would paint me as "the all-American boy." He wanted to know if in J. Edgar Hoover's vast arsenal of files there was something "relating to Anderson or Hume which the White House could use through unidentified channels to get across a more balanced picture of Anderson," according to an FBI memo about the conversation.

The FBI responded that Colson had already been given my file once during the Senate ITT hearings and that there was nothing new in it. For some reason, Hoover didn't turn over my complete file on the two occasions when the Nixon White House asked for it. The first time, Colson got only a slim collection of newspaper and magazine clippings. The second time he got nothing. Yet I know that by 1972, the file, which dated back to 1940, was several inches thick, and included at least one lengthy surveillance, plus the details of my burlesque countersurveillance of Hoover in 1970.

NIXON'S MINIONS TURNED TO THE TRUSTY IRS for help. I was on the president's Enemies List, and a favorite tactic to make life miserable for the enemies was a tax audit. In my case, the IRS was more than willing to comply. My wife does our personal and business books, and a more meticulous, penurious person could not be found for the job. It should have taken the IRS about twenty-four hours to audit us. Instead, Libby endured four years of correspondence, threats, and wasted time. Finally the IRS zeroed in on my financial relationship with my aging father.

I owned a piece of land in Salt Lake City at the mouth of a canyon. On the property were two buildings—a huge, graceful house and a small caretaker's cottage. Predictably, when I asked my parents if they wanted to live on the property, my father said they would settle in the spartan cottage. The state highway department had already purchased the big house as part of the right-of-way for a future highway, but they didn't need it yet, so I rented it back from the state and my brother moved in. As part of the expenses, I included a pittance of a salary I paid my father to maintain the property. As was his habit, he worked from sunup to sundown irrigating the land, mowing the grass, and tinkering with the upkeep of both houses. He was a bargain, but the IRS wouldn't allow the expense, even when I proved that the prior caretaker on the property had been paid much more.

After two years, my lawyer said the IRS was ready to settle. I wanted to stand my ground against this harassment, but the price of getting them off my back was only about $600 in taxes, so I paid it.

I was not the only enemy Nixon had audited, but to its credit, the IRS did not always roll over for the president. My old reporter friend Clark Mollenhoff, who had become a White House aide during the Nixon administration, told me a heartening story. In the spring of 1970 Haldeman warned Mollenhoff to expect a list of ten to twelve names that he was to deliver to the IRS with the order that those people be audited. Mollenhoff had been a messenger from the White House to the IRS on other occasions to get tax information for the president, but he said there was something different about the new requests.

Mollenhoff was skeptical, but he followed orders and forwarded the list to IRS Commissioner Randolph Thrower. That's where the buck stopped. Thrower said he wouldn't have minded if the president had specified some suspected problem with these particular tax records, but this request had the look of "handpicked targets." Thrower sent the White House a delicately worded memo refusing to audit the names.

But Haldeman was undaunted. He put Murray Chotiner on the job. Chotiner called the Treasury Department's law enforcement director, Martin Pollner, and invited him to the White House. "If it's at all possible, as a public service," Chotiner said, "these are people I suggest." Then he handed Pollner the list of a dozen names on a piece of paper with no letterhead.

Badly shaken, Pollner left the White House and headed across the street to his own office. But as soon as he was out of Chotiner's sight, he ripped the list into tiny pieces and stuffed them in a trash can. Chotiner called Pollner at least twice to ask about the progress of the audits, but Pollner begged off, saying he was busy with other pressing matters.

At one point Nixon ordered audits of every member of Congress. His use of the IRS as a weapon against his enemies was listed in the articles of impeachment drafted against him by Congress.

POLLNER WAS A REFRESHING EXCEPTION TO a depressing rule: that if Nixon had a dirty job to do, there was no end of volunteers to help him. To my surprise, Nixon even recruited a friend of mine, respected newsman Seymour Freiden, to spy for him. Freiden had worked for the *New York Herald Tribune* and would eventually work for Hearst newspapers in London. But he was between jobs when Murray Chotiner approached him with an offer—to follow the campaigns of Nixon's challengers first in 1968 and then in 1972. Freiden's job was to pick up tidbits of gossip or campaign strategy and relay them to Chotiner for $1,000 a week.

Freiden was following the George McGovern campaign in 1972, ostensibly as a freelance writer, when I bumped into him at the Democratic Convention in Miami Beach. Freiden asked if I would take on his son Josh as an intern during the convention and I agreed without hesitation. I put Josh to work under Joe Spear to find out whether any of the Democratic bigwigs at the convention were being treated to luxury accommodations in

Miami Beach as the guests of big corporate interests. Gut instinct told me that someone was taking favors when they shouldn't be.

Joe sent Josh to the waterfront to knock on the door of every fancy yacht and ask outright if any Democratic officials were guests there. Joe didn't have much hope that the inexperienced Josh would come up with anything, but the assignment would keep the boy out of our hair. Much to our surprise, Josh struck paydirt. On one $200,000 corporate yacht, two bronzed crewmen opened up to Josh. They had been waiting hand and foot on Democratic Chairman Larry O'Brien all week and were sick of it. They complained about his drinking habits, his companions, and his expensive meals. Josh reported back to Joe, who wrote a stinging column about O'Brien's excesses.

Only later did it occur to me that the elder Freiden, who had easy access to our operations during the convention, might have been spying on us for Nixon. Perhaps his son the intern was moonlighting, too.

EVERY TRICK THAT THE NIXON WHITE House tried against me was a bust. In desperation, Haldeman appealed to the Justice Department to find me guilty of a crime, any crime. But short of a few traffic tickets, there was no case they could make against me. Time to turn to the dirty tricksters of last resort—the CIA. By early 1972, the agency was glad to cooperate. The spooks were furious at me for intercepting and publishing intelligence reports intended for the president's eyes only.

The most galling was the news that the Soviets had threatened to confront the naval task force Nixon secretly sent into the Bay of Bengal to support Pakistan during the India-Pakistan war. Nixon's private tilt toward Pakistan risked an ugly incident between superpowers. Then I exposed that the strongman Nixon was backing in Cambodia, Lon Nol, was physically and mentally ill. The CIA began an exhaustive search for my sources, grilling 1,566 CIA employees without drawing a single confession or clue. I was unaware of the interrogations, which didn't stem the flow of intelligence to me from my CIA sources. Those sources didn't warn me about what was to happen next.

Instead, the warning came in late March 1972 from a friend who lived about a mile from me as the crow flies. He began to notice cars loitering in the parking lot of the Concord Methodist Church, which was located on a rise in his neighborhood. Men in heavy coats carrying binoculars and cameras would emerge from those cars and study something off in the distance. My friend naturally become curious about what they were watching.

TREASURE HUNT

LES WHITTEN HAD A FLAIR FOR the dramatic that served him well in his second career as a novelist. Whenever an investigation required a touch of melodrama or feats of derring-do, Les always came through. In 1971 he got a tip from former army captain Bradley Ayers that led to a wild-goose chase well suited to Les's sense of adventure.

In 1963 the army loaned Ayers to the CIA to train Cuban exiles for secret operations against Fidel Castro. One of their targets was Cuba's key oil refinery. Ayers did his best to turn his ragtag Cuban cadre into guerilla fighters, with training maneuvers in the Florida Keys. But on the day of their final dress rehearsal, President Kennedy was killed and the CIA ordered Ayers to shut down the operation.

In 1971 Ayers was busy working on a book about his adventures and came to us with a teaser story. Les was intrigued by the fact that the Cubans were paid by the CIA in bundles of cash, and that some of the cash was rumored to be buried and forgotten in the Florida Keys. Ayers claimed he had found one cache of molding $20 bills in a half-buried suitcase in a mangrove thicket on upper Key Largo. He said he took a few of the bills home to pass them through his bank as a test to see if they were counterfeit. He left the rest in the suitcase in the spot where he had found it, thinking that no one else would be digging through the underbrush. Ayers invited Les to return with him and collect the suitcase.

Les didn't have to be asked twice. The two of them, along with Ayers's wife, flew to an airstrip on upper Key Largo and borrowed a boat to make their way through the sluggish canals and treacherous swamps. When they were sure they weren't being followed, they abandoned the boat and plunged into underbrush so thick they couldn't see more than a few feet in front of them. In the spot where Ayers had left the suitcase, they discovered that the ground had been dug up for ten yards in every direction and the grass had been trampled down as if by many feet. The suitcase was gone. All that was left were a few pieces of money and a scrap of a road map that Ayers said had been used as a wrapper for the bills.

The trio headed back to the airstrip and as they neared the remote landing site, Les heard what sounded like a helicopter. Before leaving Washington, Les had told a CIA source about his mission, so when he heard the helicopter, he immediately feared he had been followed—not an irrational fear in those days of runaway covert CIA skulduggery. Ever resourceful, Les wrapped the money scraps in a piece of plastic and hid them where only a medical professional would dare to look. When Les arrived at the airplane, there was no helicopter and no CIA welcoming committee.

Ayers's story about the CIA operation checked out, but Les and I were skeptical about the buried treasure. A few months later, Les and I were in Miami on other business and I had brought Libby along. We decided on a whim to take time out to go treasure hunting. A wealthy friend of mind provided a yacht and we sailed down to the Keys to search another site that Ayers had pointed out as a possible hiding place for more money. The cash, he said, was rumored to be stashed in a waterproof canister. It might be buried in the bottom of a dry cistern near the ruins of an old building on a deserted stretch of upper Key Largo, or it could be anchored to a pilings of a private dock near the site.

We found the cistern and while I fretted about snakes, Les threw caution to the wind and jumped in. He kicked around the leaves and debris and found neither snakes nor money. Inspired by his bravado, I was the one who later leaped off the dock and swam down to search at the base of the pilings. Les wondered whether the CIA might have attached explosives to the canister to foil pirates like us. We were two middle-aged buccaneers who had spent too much time in the sun that day.

There was no canister, but we did find scraps of a few bills lying in the dirt near a spot Ayers had described. We were elated until Libby burst our bubble. While Les and I were congratulating each other, Libby had examined the bills. The dates on them showed they were printed years after the Cuban guerrillas had supposedly trained on the island. To this day I don't know who salted the money there or why, but it wasn't the CIA.

After they had driven off one evening, he strolled over to the parking lot and looked out across the landscape. Below, in full view, was my house. He hurried back home and gave me a call.

Thus alerted, I began keeping an eye on the rearview mirror. Sure enough, I noticed my car being tailed, awkwardly and conspicuously, by a series of other cars. Memorable was the yellow sedan. It was the most colorful car on any block and gleamed under the noonday sun. I could almost hear it go "chitty, chitty, bang, bang." I toyed with the driver of the car, speeding up and slowing down for no good reason, making last-second turns. Sometimes my moves were so abrupt as to betray the game, and the yellow car would speed away. Then the next day it would reappear in all its splendor.

By their immaculate dress and their curious taste in cars, I knew the men following me had to be federal agents, but which agency? The FBI? The Pentagon? Certainly not the IRS. We had a debate in the office and decided the chief snoop behind the operation must be Robert Mardian, the security chief at the Justice Department whom my White House sources told me was orchestrating the search for my sources. I assigned an intern to follow Mardian to give him a taste of his own medicine. This junior reporter tailgated Mardian wherever he went, staying conspicuously at his heels, occasionally whipping out a notebook and dramatically scrawling notes in full view of his prey. Mardian was outraged, and rightly so. It turned out that he was innocent, at least of this latest caper. The guilty agents were CIA spooks. Trained to skulk around the bazaars of the Middle East or the backstreets of Moscow snooping for intelligence to make the world safe for democracy, my CIA shadows were dunking donuts and sipping coffee in a church parking lot in suburban Washington and taking pictures of my yard full of bicycles.

The CIA gave the operation a code name—"Mudhen." This was an appropriate name since the mudhen is known for scratching around in the mud and clacking obstreperously when it is riled. I doubt that the code name was meant to be flattering, but I liked the ring of it. The snoops called me "Brandy," although a more fitting moniker for my vices might have been "Ice Cream." Each of my staffers was called by a drink. Opal Ginn was "Sherry," Brit Hume was "Eggnog," Joe Spear was "Champagne," and Les Whitten was "Cordial."

What the CIA didn't know was that I had my own trained spooks at home, nine of them, plus their sundry teenage friends, all with time on their hands and spring fever. I turned my katzenjammer kids loose on the CIA with the most sophisticated surveillance equipment we could find around the house—a bulky home movie camera in the days before minicams, and a 35-millimeter camera. In the end, we outclassed them in style and stealth, if not in electronics.

We never tried to hide the fact that we were "surveillance conscious," as the agents put it. As soon as the kids knew we were being watched, they scrambled up the hill to the Concord Methodist Church parking lot with their cameras and skulked around taking pictures of the surveillance teams.

On March 27, two CIA cars were idling in the parking lot when my junior sleuths pulled up in a station wagon. The CIA report records that an "unidentified female" behind the wheel rested a camera on the dash and photographed the front end of the surveillance cars. Then "she" whipped the wagon around in a circle behind the agents' cars, took more pictures from that angle, and peeled out of the parking lot. Not to be bested, the agents took off in warm pursuit. The "unidentified female" stopped at my street, hopped out of the station wagon, and shot footage of the agents with a movie camera as they cruised by in their cars. "All units were withdrawn from the area," the agents' report noted for that day. They dutifully recorded the movements of the "unidentified female" with a tidy drawing of the church parking lot and arrows indicating the path taken by the station wagon.

My children got a huge laugh when they later read the report that a double agent delivered to me. It had not been a woman at all, but my daughter Laurie's boyfriend and future husband Peter Bruch, who wore his hair long in the fashion of the day.

For six weeks, I was accompanied near and far by my CIA shadows. Twenty men were assigned to the Mudhen team. They set up a photo observation post near my office, which they called the "Nest." They rushed with me to catch a shuttle to Newark, where they noted that some conspiratorial youths hustled me into a car and drove me along the backroads of South Orange, New Jersey. These were students from Seton Hall University who were taking a circuitous route to avoid traffic and deliver me on time to a campus lecture.

I was photographed with various unidentified persons going into my office, coming out of my office, going into restaurants, coming out of restaurants. At one point CBS was also following me, with my permission, taking footage for an episode of *60 Minutes.* I posed in front of the Justice Department, the White House, and the Pentagon. The caravan of cars going from place to place must have made quite a ring-around-the-rosy—with me in the lead, the CBS crew tailing me, and the CIA bringing up the rear.

MY SOURCES NEEDED A SUITCASE TO contain the Mudhen files, which, nevertheless, were smuggled to me. They were full of tidbits reflecting the cloak-and-dagger mentality of my shadows. I was suspected of having "connections with unidentified officials of the *New York Times.*" That must have been my paper boy. I was known to be a "rather flamboyant, confident individual," who "conducts his professional activities in an overt manner." I ate sandwiches at my desk and avoided the "cocktail party and embassy circuit," choosing instead to spend most nights and weekends at home. The CIA even recorded that I normally went to bed about 2 A.M. "He readily admits to being a publicity seeker," the Mudhen files say of me, "and is apparently basking in the focus of attention which has come his way as a result of his recent disclosures of classified (SECRET/SENSITIVE) U.S. Government documents regarding the India/Pakistani conflict."

I was "unconcerned with parking violations," and was "a fast and somewhat careless driver" who often broke the speed limit. That was a shade better than the CIA's indictment of Les Whitten who "seems possessed of a great deal of nervous energy. He operates his personal automobile in a fast, impatient manner and will deviate from normal routes in order to avoid minor traffic delays."

The CIA even attempted a bit of pop psychoanalysis, concluding that I was so ego driven that I would never allow my subordinates to "continually receive choice assignments or to build up a reputation which might conceivably compete with Brandy's image." The reason that I had kept Opal Ginn so long as my assistant, the sleuths surmised, was her lack of ambition to outshine me. "The fact that she is only listed as a long-standing clerical employee might well comfort Brandy that she has no personal ambitions to gain professional recognition," the Mudhen reports said. I would like to have seen them say that to Opal's face, especially on a day when the "Opal Meter" we posted outside her door had the arrow in the red zone warning of imminent danger to anyone who crossed her.

My chosen venue for meeting secret sources, according to the CIA, was the Madison Hotel near my office. As proof of this, they offered the information that I parked my car in the Madison garage and was well known to the garage attendants. Besides, the Madison management was extremely discreet, the CIA concluded. Thus the hotel was a perfect place for keeping secrets. The Mudhen crew hypothesized that I probably was on such tight terms with the hotel's staff that I could lean on them to help me do my job.

The CIA figured that was why I chose the Montpelier Room at the Madison for a March 17 lunch with the most interesting "source" the sleuths ever saw me interview during their surveillance—CIA Director Richard Helms. He told the Mudhen team that the lunch had been arranged at his request, and they began their feverish preparations, staking out the hotel lobby and restaurant, sizing up the waiters to see whom I might suborn, speculating on what kind of tape recorder I might have strapped to my body. They had read about the Bernard Goldfine caper in 1957 when Baron Shacklette and I eavesdropped on the hotel room next door. "Brandy may still be utilizing audio equipment in his professional operations," the Mudhen reports warned. "This would certainly include bodily concealed recorders and/or concealed transmitting devices." The notion that I might arrive wired would bring a chuckle to anyone who knows that I rarely carry a notebook, let alone bother to strap tape recorders to my body.

At the appointed hour, Helms and I faced each other across the table. He wanted to talk me out of publishing a bit of espionage trivia I had uncovered—that the United States was monitoring conversations in the Kremlin by eavesdropping on car telephones. While the telephones within the Kremlin itself were secure, the Communist Party hierarchy could be overheard talking business and making dates with mistresses during calls

MYSTERY MAN

OPERATION MUDHEN SHOOK MY FAITH IN the investigative abilities of the CIA. When I read the files after the fact, the things the CIA had not been able to find out about me far outweighed all the trivia the agents had recorded during months of surveillance.

I pride myself on leading a rather predictable private life, so the chance of the CIA finding something really juicy was slim. But I certainly expected them to be capable of confirming the basics. The final Mudhen reports show that the agency's best and brightest were able to find no record that I had ever been in the Merchant Marine or attended the academy in San Mateo. Why they think I would lie about something so unremarkable eludes me. They also disputed that my ship, the *Cape Elizabeth,* served the Merchant Marine during the war—a contention that would surprise the captain and crew.

The CIA could find no evidence that I had ever worked for the *Stars and Stripes* in Shanghai. Had they asked me for my bylined clippings from those days, I would have gladly supplied them from the cache that my father kept, along with photos of the staff, myself included, at work around the copy desk.

Most remarkably, the CIA could find no record that I joined the army while in China when my draft board gave me no option. I claim no nobility in that forced induction. And had I the inclination to make up a military record, it would certainly be more swashbuckling than the reality of washing jeeps and selling socks in the quartermaster's haberdashery. I will be forever grateful to my father for saving my discharge papers in case I am ever personally called upon to prove that I did my duty, however inconsequential, for Uncle Sam.

To its credit, the CIA did not dispute that I had been a Boy Scout and a Mormon missionary. The spies did, however, unearth an old rumor that while in China I had written seditious and mutinous editorials for an underground GI newspaper called *China Lantern,* a publication I had never heard of until I read the Mudhen files. I hope some day to meet the Jack Anderson who did write those editorials so we can swap war stories.

from their limousines. The Kremlin had already figured out that the United States was intercepting their car phones and had sharply curtailed the loose lips in limos. I made the argument to Helms that the only ones who didn't know about the eavesdropping at that point were the American people. He responded, lamely I thought, that he didn't want to remind the Soviets of our capability on the off chance that they might forget about the eavesdropping and get careless. It was not worth going to the mat over, so I agreed not to publish the information.

HELP

I WAS BORN TOO EARLY TO call myself a Beatles fan, but I couldn't help coming to John Lennon's defense when the Nixon administration used McCarthyite techniques to try to run him out of the country. In 1972 the Justice Department began inexplicably treating Lennon like public enemy number one just because he had a minor drug offense on his record in England. An effort was made to deport him but Lennon fought back, tying up the deportation in the courts.

In 1974, I learned that the White House was behind the attempted deportation. The Senate Internal Security Committee, the last bulwark of McCarthyism on Capitol Hill, concocted a memo falsely linking Lennon to radical groups that planned to disrupt the 1972 Republican Convention. It was the kind of paranoia that festered in the antiwar climate of the Vietnam years. Republican Senator Strom Thurmond mailed the ridiculous memo to a White House aide, and sent a copy to Attorney General John Mitchell with a personal note: "Dear John. This appears to me to be an important matter, and I think it would be well for it to be considered at the highest level. . . . Many headaches might be avoided if appropriate action be taken in time."

"Appropriate action" was taken by the Immigration and Naturalization Service, which began throwing legal roadblocks in the way of Lennon's plans to stay in the United States with his wife, Yoko Ono.

When I got a copy of the Thurmond letter and memo, and began asking around about them, the original of the memo mysteriously disappeared from Lennon's immigration file. I wrote a column exposing the political manipulations behind the case. That, combined with the superb legal work of Lennon's lawyer, Leon Wildes, who proved the United States harbors far more dangerous felons than a rock star, convinced the government to leave Lennon alone.

Much to my surprise, I got a thank-you note from Lennon.

Our conversation was "animated," according to the agents posted like potted plants within view of our table. Outside, another team scanned the streets to make sure no one was spying on the spies.

During our lunch, still another team was keeping a wary eye on Les Whitten and Brit Hume back at the office because, "if there is to be any counter-surveillance, audio or photographic operations against the director, either of these individuals would necessarily play a major role." There was no explanation as to why Brit and Les might spend their lunch hour taking pictures of me eating with Richard Helms.

My conversation with Helms might have been a lot more "animated" had I known then that it was his men who were spying on me in flagrant violation of federal law, which bars the CIA from domestic espionage. I didn't find out which federal agency was responsible for Operation Mudhen until a few days after our lunch.

The surveillance fell apart shortly thereafter. On April 2, the snoops recorded that I drove from my house to my church with an "unidentified female," and when I arrived there, two other females came up to my car and then scanned the area. "The two young females seemed to be staring at the surveillance vehicles and one surveillance unit reported that the two girls waved at them." The report concluded that this may have been "a further indicator that Brandy and members of his family may be becoming 'surveillance conscious.'" Apparently the subjects of surveillance don't normally wave at the spies, but I could not control my daughters' friendliness.

The CIA could no longer stand this game of cat and mouse, especially when the mice were having so much fun. The day after my daughters hailed the agents with a wave, the surveillance ended. The CIA's after-action memo summed it up: "Due to the length and rather unproductive results of the surveillance coupled by the suspicion that the subject was aware of the operation, orders were verbally given by senior Office of Security officers to terminate all surveillance activities. . . . The surveillance failed to establish the existence and/or identity of any individual who might have been supplying the subject or any of his employees with classified government data."

CHAPTER 16

LONG BEFORE FRANK STURGIS JOINED THE world's most celebrated burglary crew and broke into the Watergate office building, he was
my friend. I knew him as an idealistic soldier of fortune, a daredevil pilot
and a gunrunner, a romantic who bloomed out of his time, an adventurer
who fought the good fight against a humdrum existence.

After Frankie and four others were arrested at gunpoint inside the Democratic National Headquarters in the Watergate complex, he was pictured
in the press as a petty thief, a bungling second-story man who couldn't pull
off a simple heist of political paperwork. That image did him an injustice.
He was the type of man you would want to share your foxhole, but not
the best pick to burglarize the Democratic National Headquarters. He would
gladly do both if he believed in the cause. Never a petty gun-for-hire, Frankie
was an anti-Communist Don Quixote, drawn irresistibly into causes that
became calamities.

In his youth, Frankie confounded the odds and became one of the
ragged few who persevered in the mountains of Cuba with Fidel Castro
until they could overthrow the dictatorship of Fulgencio Batista. After their
incredible victory, Frankie could be seen on the streets of Havana in the
regalia of an air marshall, and for a brief time his job for Castro was to
run the "liberated" gambling casinos and luxury hotels.

Frankie became a long-shot gambler against the house when he broke
with Castro as a matter of principle, having to do with repression. He
escaped from Cuba, and thereafter dedicated himself to the doomed ventures
of exiled Cuban freedom fighters. I met him while covering the Bay of Pigs
invasion, in which he played a shadowy role, and I liked him immediately.
His constant companion at the time was fellow exile Major Pedro Diaz-
Lanz, formerly commander of Castro's air force. Their positions as high-

ranking defectors and their insights into the Bay of Pigs fiasco made them both important sources. To break down their barriers, I needed to get to know them both better. Libby and I invited them to move into our house for a while. Being footloose and without a revolution to fight at that moment, they accepted the invitation.

In later years, Diaz-Lanz took an ideological turn to the far right and no longer approved of me, but my friendship with Frankie persisted. In 1967 he coauthored an article with me for *Parade* magazine on Cuban freedom fighters. By then he was living near Hollywood, Florida, where my children loved to vacation. We would stay at the Diplomat Hotel and Frankie would come to visit, always bringing news of some new crusade.

Frankie's plot du jour when I saw him in Florida in 1968 was a mission to hijack a Soviet freighter on the high seas. I struggled to stifle my amusement as he told me the details of the caper. A soldier who was a total stranger to Frankie had approached him to lead the mission. The man wouldn't say whom he represented, but it was altogether characteristic of Frankie to accept once he heard the noble purpose—to hold the Soviet ship hostage for the return of the U.S. spy ship *Pueblo*, which the North Koreans had captured in January 1968.

Frankie had seen the movie *The Dirty Dozen*, and liked the notion of recruiting his own dirty dozen drawn from a pool of the toughest applicants. So he advertised in the newspapers for adventurers and, without a careful check of their references, selected an even dozen and ordered them to rendezvous with him in Mexico. They were to get there by whatever means they could. Frankie bought himself an airline ticket, but his recruits were more creative. They rented cars, drove to Mexico, and then sold the rentals for drinking and gambling money.

When Frankie arrived in the flyspeck town chosen for the rendezvous on the east coast of Mexico, he realized he had not told his men precisely where to meet. But Frankie knew where to look. He systematically rounded up his undisciplined band from the local bars and bawdy houses.

The men spent two weeks training under Frankie's tutelage, then set out for a secret meeting with a gunboat that he had been told would assist them in the hijacking. Alas, their own rickety boat developed engine trouble off the coast of Honduras. Frankie realized he could not let his boat limp into port for repairs with a dozen armed desperadoes on board, so he unloaded them on a small island in the harbor and went ahead himself.

Unbeknownst to Frankie, a shore patrolman with binoculars had seen the men and their machine guns unload onto the island. The coast guard met Frankie and rounded up his men, and their mission impossible ended in a Honduran jail. The gang was deported back to the United States where they all had to answer for the rental car theft charges. Frankie hadn't been involved in any car theft, but rather than let his men take the rap alone, he characteristically sat through the trial tight-lipped, without testifying in his own defense, and was convicted of transporting stolen cars to Mexico.

ON JUNE 16, 1972, I WAS making my way through National Airport in Washington to catch a plane to Cleveland when I spotted Frankie with a group of suspicious-looking characters—some of his Cuban vigilante friends, I guessed. He seemed chagrined to meet me, so I suspected something was up. "Private business. Top secret. Top secret," he explained tersely, with a conspiratorial smile. I didn't have time to pump him for information, but I made a mental note to check up on him when I got back to Washington. The next morning I read the newspapers: Five middle-aged men in business suits had been caught in a burglary at the Democratic National Committee's offices.

They all gave aliases, but I knew immediately what Frankie's "private business" had been. When I landed back in Washington I hustled to the old redbrick building that housed the District of Columbia jail. He had told the police his name was Edward Hamilton, but it was Frankie all right. We huddled in the visitors room and I pumped him for information, but he was tight-lipped. "We're sticking together," he told me, predictably. I knew if I could get him alone, he would loosen up. "Frankie, I hate to see you sitting here in this jail. You're a friend of mine. I'll get you released into my custody."

I went through the formal legal motions of asking to have Frankie released to me. Sitting in front of the judge, I could barely keep a straight face. "It was only a cheap burglary," I said. "I hate to see him in jail." An audible groan of cynicism rolled through the press ranks. The judge looked uncomfortable and eyed the prosecutor for help. The prosecutor came through, insisting that, considering the circumstances, it wouldn't be a good idea for Frankie to waltz out of jail on the arm of Jack Anderson. At that point, no one outside the White House was quite sure what those "circumstances" were, but we all knew this was more than the "second-rate burglary" the Nixon people were calling it. The judge looked relieved and slammed down his gavel. "Motion denied."

CHAPTER 17

MY BRUSH WITH THE WATERGATE BURGLARS at National Airport was not the first advance hint I got of their pending skulduggery. Two months before the burglary, I picked up a tip that the Democratic Party headquarters was about to be bugged by Nixon operatives, but the information I had received was distorted just enough to render it unbelievable. Had I been graced by better luck, I might have blown the plot and prevented the Watergate that was.

On April 15, 1972, William Haddad, a New York entrepreneur, sent me a tantalizing letter. A private investigator had told him that agents of the Nixon reelection apparatus were going to tap the telephones of the Democratic National Committee, specifically Chairman Larry O'Brien. As Haddad heard it, the bugging would be done by the November Group, an advertising consortium under contract to the Nixon campaign. That was the clinker in the tip. It didn't make sense to me that admen in pin-striped suits would want to bug O'Brien's phones to craft a better ad campaign for Nixon's reelection.

Haddad had gotten the facts mixed up, and the truth was even more bizarre. The leak came from James McCord, ex-CIA agent, soon-to-be burglar, whose formal title was security director for the Committee to Re-elect the President. He had been sent to the offices of the November Group to sweep their telephones for bugs. Thinking he was in the bosom of Nixonites, he let it slip that his next assignment was to bug O'Brien's office. "We tap them, they tap us. This is routine," he said, almost boastfully. Not all the admen working for Nixon were sympathetic to his politics. One of them, who overheard McCord's remark, thought he should tell someone. Haddad was a power in the Democratic Party, so the adman contacted him. Haddad tipped off two people—myself and the intended victim, Larry O'Brien. I don't know whether O'Brien paid any attention to the warning. In my case, I learned more about the November Group than I really wanted to know and found nothing that added up to skulduggery. To my everlasting regret, I dismissed the tip.

The burglary, planned as it was by Gordon Liddy and Howard Hunt, was doomed from the start. I later discovered that Liddy, never too subtle, had flashed his White House pass as identification when he had tried to buy pistols from a Virginia gun shop. Unfortunately for Liddy, the gun dealer had recently gotten into trouble for selling an antitank gun to a man who had used it to stick up a Brinks vault. The dealer was being extra cautious the day Liddy came in. He decided Liddy was a tad too "flaky" and refused to make the sale. Then he called the Treasury Department's gun-control unit to report the attempted purchase, but nothing came of the report.

While Liddy was shopping for hardware, Hunt's job was to recruit the second-story crew. A year before the burglary, he had anticipated that the president one day might need a few good men to carry out a covert mission. He had already handpicked his men from the Bay of Pigs fiasco. Hunt had been their CIA handler; they knew him as "Eduardo." Frank Sturgis had spoken to me often about a heroic figure—a mystery man called Eduardo. On one of my Florida visits, Frankie had introduced me to another burglar-to-be, Bernard Barker, and they both had spoken admiringly about this Eduardo. Not until the Watergate bubble had burst did I learn that Eduardo was none other than the bewigged Howard Hunt.

While investigating Watergate, I turned up rumors that the burglars may have practiced their skills on the Chilean Embassy in Washington and the New York apartments of three Chilean diplomats. Those burglaries coincided with ITT's troubles with Salvadore Allende who was hell-bent on nationalizing ITT's holdings in Chile. The Senate committee investigating ITT's operations in Chile was never able to gather anything more than circumstantial evidence linking the Watergate burglars to the embassy break-in several weeks earlier. I don't think Frank Sturgis would have lied to me. He denied having anything to do with that particular embassy job, although he volunteered that he had once broken into the Chilean embassy in Havana.

The burglary team also staked out George McGovern's campaign head-quarters and considered bugging it. But Hunt already had an insider in the McGovern campaign—a naive Brigham Young University student named Thomas Gregory whom Hunt had recruited to pose as a McGovern campaign worker. Gregory, a straight-laced Mormon, became increasingly uncomfortable with his undercover work, especially when Hunt ordered him to work late one night and leave the door open.

JACKGATE

ONE OF THE STRANGEST CLAIMS EVER made about me was that I knew about the Watergate burglary in advance and kept it a secret for reasons undisclosed. Fred Thompson, the minority counsel for the Senate Watergate Committee who later made a career in the movies before being elected to the Senate himself, got caught up in the conspiratorial mind-set of Watergate that led to an investigation of me.

Thompson was curious about my long friendship with Frank Sturgis and the fact that I had seen Sturgis in the Washington airport the day before the burglary. Thompson's conspiracy theory was fed by one of Frankie's mysterious Cuban friends who called the Senate Watergate Committee with a hot tip. He claimed he had overheard Frankie discussing with me on the phone a ''big project'' in Washington that was going to net the anti-Castro soldiers of fortune enough money to liberate Cuba. In truth, Frankie might have said something like that to me dozens of times over the course of our friendship, but I usually tuned out his scheming. I would have remembered, however, if he had told me he was planning to bug the Democratic Party headquarters.

The Cuban tipster also claimed that after Frankie got out on bail, he visited me at a hotel in Miami and came out carrying a big stack of $50 bills. Aside from the fact that I have never seen a big stack of $50 bills, and would never be foolish enough to give one away, the bigger question was why I would sit on the Watergate story. Even Thompson couldn't figure out the answer to that one.

He similarly smelled a rat in my admission that Bill Haddad had warned me in advance that someone was going to be bugged. Haddad had sent me a packet of information telling everything an acquaintance of his had overheard at the November Group. When Fred Thompson called me in and asked what had happened to that packet, I told him I had lost it, twice. He couldn't believe that the legendary Jack Anderson would misplace something. (He had obviously never seen my desk.)

Thompson and his aides wrote up their suspicions and fought hard to get the report included in the official Watergate Committee conclusions. Committee Chairman Sam Ervin decided that it was too far-fetched, so the report never saw the light of day. I think Thompson was haunted by the possibility that Haddad and I had warned the Democrats of the pending burglary and then, together with the Democrats, decided to let the burglars do their job so they could be set up for capture, all to embarrass Richard Nixon. I liked and admired Thompson as an investigator, but his imagination clearly lent itself to the big screen.

Gregory confided his dilemma to a friend, Washington public relations man Robert Bennett, son of Utah Senator Wallace Bennett. Les Whitten got the story from young Bennett, who would one day become a senator himself. As Bennett recalled, Gregory told him Hunt was "reporting to someone higher up." Gregory had been impressed by Hunt's White House credentials and had assumed Hunt wouldn't steer him wrong because Hunt had a full-time lawyer advising him. That lawyer was the person most in need of one—Gordon Liddy. Bennett advised Gregory to "get out," and he did, two days before the Watergate burglary.

If Hunt was trained by the CIA in covert operations, he should have taken a refresher course. He let James McCord, who could easily be linked to Nixon, join the crew of Cuban burglars—Sturgis, Barker, Virgilio Gonzalez, and Eugenio Martinez. McCord gave an alias, Edward Martin, when he was arrested during the break-in, but later at the police station, a policeman recognized him. The police noticed something else about McCord: He was the only burglar whose pockets weren't stuffed with crisp, new $100 bills. It was McCord's direct participation that touched off a firestorm of speculation, which grew into an investigation, which blossomed into a cover-up and ultimately brought down a president.

While the burglars were sitting in the slammer, Gordon Liddy was fast-feeding documents through a small shredder. He also phoned the press chief of the Committee to Reelect the President and told him they had a minor "public relations problem." Apprised of the "problem," the White House started issuing its denials and didn't stop for more than two years.

Hunt packed up eight cardboard boxes of documents and hastily deposited them in the basement of a friend, Roy Sheppard. When I found out later that they existed, I tried to cajole Sheppard through his nervous lawyer to let me see them. I had Les Whitten on round-the-clock alert to be ready to go to Sheppard's basement and comb through the papers should Sheppard give us access. But Hunt called Sheppard and reclaimed the cache before I could get my foot in the door.

I am occasionally asked why it took so long for the press to unravel the Watergate scandal and implicate Nixon in the cover-up. Five months after the burglary, Nixon was reelected by a landslide and wasn't forced out of office until two years later. Those events are now compressed by history into a single incident called Watergate, but the Watergate I lived through was a day-after-day, tooth-pulling process that changed reporting in this country.

Before Watergate, the press in Washington had a bad case of "clientitis"; most reporters simply got too cozy with the agencies they covered. The correspondents who covered the White House were dependent on their sources for daily stories. The notion that they might be duped by those sources was unthinkable to them. "Investigative reporting" at most newspapers in those days occurred when someone covering a certain government agency got a tip about dirt at a rival agency. The biggest obstacle would come from their own staff when the reporter covering the accused agency would come to its defense. That is why, in the early days of the Watergate scandal, the three reporters who refused to let the story die were myself, who had no allegiance to any government agency, and Bob Woodward and Carl Bernstein of the *Washington Post,* who wandered off their normal beats to get the story and had to fight to break it.

The role of pariah was not new to me. On rare occasions when Woodward would call me to commiserate, we would celebrate each other's scoops, happy to see anything that advanced the story and gave it legitimacy. But we were intensely competitive, too. Though the *Washington Post* carried my Watergate columns faithfully, I know editor Ben Bradley would have been happier to have had his own team take credit for every exclusive.

Each morning when I picked up the *Washington Post,* I speculated privately about Woodward's and Bernstein's sources and their primary source, whom they referred to as "Deep Throat" in their Watergate book, *All the President's Men.* It was no mystery to me that Woodward and Bernstein were getting basic information, as I was, from the Washington Field Office of the FBI. I knew that because occasional mistakes in their reporting reflected exactly the same erroneous information that FBI sources had given me.

White House insiders proved to be useful sources as they watched the men closest to the president lose their ethical bearings. One aide fed me enough information for several columns on Nixon and Watergate. When my source became concerned for his own future, he told me he was going to quit, but I talked him into staying for another three months. "You owe it to the public," I told him. Eventually he came to me and said, "I don't want to be a part of this," and he walked away from the job just in time to salvage his own reputation.

My most fruitful source, whose identity I cannot reveal, was not at the FBI but elsewhere in the Justice Department where the fear was rampant that Nixon would shut down the Watergate investigation before the public had a chance to hear the truth.

Frank Sturgis was also a golden source for me, although I'm sure he would not like the characterization. He was determined not to break ranks from his fellow burglars and their vows of silence, but I persuaded him that Nixon's men were going to let him go to jail while they emerged from the scandal unscathed.

ON JANUARY II, 1973, ON THE eve of Frankie's trial on burglary charges, I took him to lunch at a Chinese restaurant in which I was
part owner. He was evasive early on, but I knew he would warm up by the
time the fortune cookies arrived. "Well, we're having a meeting," he finally
said, referring to himself and the three Cubans caught in the burglary. "A
White House representative wants to talk to us."

I contained my excitement at the news that the White House was sending an emissary to the burglars. "Oh? Where are you having the meeting?"
Frankie named the Arlington Towers, a hotel in suburban Virginia just
across the Potomac River from Washington.

"When?"

"Tonight."

I pressed on. "If I were nearby, would you come and tell me what
happens?"

Frankie ruminated for a moment, then, "Okay."

I called the hotel, reserved a room, and gave Frankie the number. That
night I waited in that room for what seemed like an eternity. Finally there
was a knock on the door. It was Frankie and he was in a hurry. The meeting
was still in progress but he had made some excuse to leave. The emissary
from the White House, he told me, was Howard Hunt. "They've offered
to pay all our legal expenses if we keep our mouths shut," Frankie said.
"And they said they would take care of our families while we were in jail."
Hunt himself was planning to plead guilty, and he wanted the others to
follow his example, with the understanding that they wouldn't have to spend
too much time behind bars.

The four Cuban burglars didn't have much reason to trust their benefactors at that point. The cash payments they had been getting all along
from Hunt had been used as leverage against them. The money had flowed
freely as long as Hunt thought they were being cooperative, but when the
four had demanded that the charges against them be reduced to misdemeanors, the money had stopped.

At the meeting they reminded Hunt that they had some leverage of
their own and would use it if they were abandoned. They could write books
about the experience, telling all. But Hunt knew what buttons to push with
these patriots. He spoke of "one for all and all for one," reminding them
of the good old days fighting Castro. Hunt cut a sympathetic figure. His
wife, who had managed the cash flow to the burglars, had recently died in
an airliner crash with $10,000 cash in her suitcase.

Frankie finished his report to me and returned to the meeting. Later he told me the upshot. After heated debate, the Cubans had agreed to stand mutely together and take whatever sentence the court handed down. Hunt and the four Cubans pleaded guilty to burglary. McCord and Liddy went to trial and were convicted of the same charge. In March 1973 while they were all waiting to hear what their sentences would be, McCord, who had a paralyzing fear of jail, forgot his vow of silence and sent a letter to the judge, John Sirica. He said the defendants had been pressured to plead guilty and keep quiet, that perjury had been committed during the trial, and that there were others involved in the break-in who had not yet been fingered. It was the breakthrough the investigators needed to pursue the case to the White House.

THE REACTION TO MY COLUMNS ABOUT Watergate stirred old hostilities inside the White House. Nixon was still as determined as ever to destroy his enemies in the press. This time the victim would be Les Whitten.

Our office had been consumed by the Watergate pursuit, but Les had still found time to follow the dramatic tale of the Broken Treaties Papers. In the first week of November 1972, a coalition of American Indian groups traveled to Washington to protest innumerable and timeless grievances. They ended up taking over the offices of the Bureau of Indian Affairs, eight-hundred-strong for seven days. Under the terms of the negotiated truce, Uncle Sam promised to put up $66,650 in travel expenses to get the Indians home if they would just leave peacefully. They went peacefully enough, but not empty-handed.

Unbeknownst to the police who escorted the forty-vehicle caravan of buses and vans to the city limits, those vehicles were carrying documents looted from the BIA—documents telling the story of betrayal by the federal government that came to be called the Trail of Broken Treaties. Not until the Indians had scattered did the FBI realize Uncle Sam had been robbed. A nationwide dragnet was organized to recover the documents. Finally, in St. Paul, Minnesota, the FBI made its move. The G-men swooped down on a lone green van identified by an undercover agent as the vehicle that carried the bulk of the loot. Inside, the FBI found a government typewriter and a notepad. Another raid in Oklahoma City was no more fruitful. Most of the documents—seven thousand cubic feet of paper—had vanished without a trace.

Les began his own search for the documents, convinced that if he could win the trust of the Indians, we could print the damning truth from those documents about how the Indians had been fleeced by their own government. Les made a connection with Russell Means, head of the American Indian Movement. When word came that the keepers of the documents would see Les, he had to leave for Tempe, Arizona, immediately, with the clothes on his back and only $5 in his wallet. Les was notoriously thrifty, but I knew he couldn't get by on $5, so I gave him what I had in my pockets—$100 and a credit card.

At a bowling alley in Tempe, Les met with Russell Means, who spoke only when the racket of the bowling balls hitting the pins would mask his words from anyone who might be eavesdropping. He said that others had offered to pay for a peek at the documents but he was willing to let us see them for free because of the work Drew and I and later Les had done on Indian grievances. Means assigned his brother and another Indian to escort Les to Minneapolis where some of the documents were stashed. My credit card got them all on the airplane and then into a cheap motel where Les spent a sleepless night with an armed guard outside his door.

The next day a courier delivered stacks of documents that Les pored over. They were photocopies of stolen documents that Les learned had been brazenly copied by the Indians on the copier in the local Bureau of Indian Affairs office. We began publishing stories based on those documents, much to the chagrin of the FBI. The agents had been unsuccessful in tracking them down even though an agent had infiltrated the Indian organization posing as an Indian named Johnny.

When Les returned to Washington, he contacted Henry Adams, the Assiniboin Sioux lawyer who had negotiated the Indians out of the weeklong occupation. Adams didn't approve of stealing the documents in the first place and was eager to arrange for their return—after letting us read some more, if it would help the Indian's cause. Les wanted to be on hand when the documents were returned, so he volunteered his car for the handoff.

At ten-fifteen on the cold morning of January 31, 1973, Les and Adams were loading boxes of documents into Les's yellow Vega in front of Adams's apartment building. Their destination was the BIA, but they never got there. FBI agents surrounded them, called Adams by name, and told him he was under arrest. When Les protested, they arrested him, too, cuffing his hands in front of him. Ever the reporter, Les reached for his notebook and pencil and began taking notes on the incident. The agents grabbed the tools of his trade, hustled both men into an unmarked car, and dumped them in jail.

The bust was not all the FBI had hoped it would be. The undercover agent "Johnny" had told them where to find Adams and Jack Anderson. I think the agents expected to be able to arrest me and make Richard Nixon's day. Instead they got Les, a gentle soul whose idea of excitement was translating Baudelaire poems from French to English. He spent five hours in jail that day, tormented by the thought that he might have more than enough time for Baudelaire in the very near future. The crime with which he was charged, receiving and possessing stolen property, was punishable by up to ten years in prison and a $10,000 fine.

While Les sweated, I was pounding on the doors of prosecutors and police with our lawyer Betty Murphy. Opal Ginn sent the word out through the press and printed up "Free Les Whitten" buttons, which she pinned to my reporters whom she marshaled for the bail hearing. We knew how to use the press, and we weren't about to let the Nixon administration arrest one of our own without setting up a howl that could be heard from the *Washington Post* to the *Los Angeles Times*.

Les was sprung to await his trial, and newspapers around the country vented their own outrage in editorials condemning the Nixon minions for going too far in their war against the press. Les was no thief. He had not stolen the papers; he was merely reporting on the return of the contraband. Every reporter in the country knew that the mission of the press was in grave danger if reporters could be arrested for covering the news.

It dawned on me that the arrest had little to do with the Indian papers and everything to do with Nixon's ongoing determination to bring me down. Within two days after Les was bailed out, the government secretly subpoenaed six months' worth of telephone bills for my office and Les's and my homes. Their excuse was that they needed to find out how we had tracked down the Indian papers so they could make the case against Les before a grand jury. But soon I began to hear from sources as far away as Arizona and Guam that FBI agents were poking around asking questions that had nothing to do with Indians.

The jubilant FBI had finally found a way to uncover my sources—a search that H. R. Haldeman had begun four years earlier. I immediately protested to the judge in Les's case, who happened to be the Watergate burglar's judge, John Sirica. He recognized the subpoena for what it was, a fishing expedition. First, the FBI had tried to learn from the phone records the identity of a B-52 crewman who had called me from Guam to complain about dangerous flight patterns by U.S. planes bombing Hanoi. Then the FBI contacted an assistant city prosecutor in Phoenix, whom I had called in reference to a report about a drunken driving incident involving a senator. Judge Sirica ordered the FBI to end its witch-hunt and destroy all copies of my phone records, which it had passed around to twenty-three FBI offices.

I arranged a luncheon appointment for Les and me with Interior Secretary Rogers Morton, the ultimate boss over the BIA. Our goal was to persuade Morton to ask the Justice Department to drop the charges against Les, but as we ate, I hit upon a different strategy. Les stood accused of reporting the highlights of BIA documents intended for official eyes only. If I could get Morton to give us more documents, the BIA would have a tough time making its case that Les had violated any law.

"You've done more for the Indians than any Interior secretary in history," I flattered Morton. "You should get some credit in the press for that. If you could slip me some confidential memos on what you've done, I could write a credible story. The memos would give it more credibility than an interview would." Morton was game. He turned to one of his lawyers who was present and ordered him to disappear and return with a secret memo from his files on some action Morton had taken on behalf of the Indians. The lawyer looked as if Morton had lost his mind, but he followed orders and soon returned with a document—the same class of information that Les was accused of having stolen. As Les and I left the restaurant, I turned to him and smiled. "Rogers Morton is going to make a great witness for the defense."

We never had occasion to call him to the stand because the government had no case against Les. The boxes he had helped Hank Adams carry were boldly marked with the name and phone number of the FBI agent that Adams wanted them to go to. He had an appointment that morning with a BIA official to give him the documents to pass on to the FBI. And the FBI's own undercover man, "Johnny," knew exactly what Adams was planning to do. The FBI tried to float a bogus charge that Les and I had offered to pay money for the documents. Had they checked, they would have found that I never pay for information, not only because it is unethical, but because I can't afford it. The only illegal act Les committed that morning was to double park his car.

Les lost twelve pounds in two weeks as he awaited the decision of the grand jury. Truth be told, I was enjoying the spectacle, albeit at Les's expense. He was particularly upset when I took the witness stand before the grand jury and asked the jurors—I may have used the word "beg"—to indict him. He was just doing his job, I said, and we were prepared to go to trial. The government doesn't own the news, I told them, adding that I didn't think any jury in the United States would disagree with that. I was ready to win a court fight that would set a precedent and make sure no one ever did this to a reporter again.

Two weeks after Les was arrested, the grand jury refused to indict him, despite my stirring plea. The case was dropped against Hank Adams as well, but I wasn't finished. Drew Pearson had taught me that if anyone ever trampled on the Constitutional rights of the column, I should hit back swiftly and with such force that the next person would be forewarned not

JUSTICE DENIED

LONG AFTER RICHARD NIXON GAVE HIS farewell salute and left the White House, his method of searching for my sources still haunted me. In 1976 I sued the ex-president, nineteen of his underlings ranging from Henry Kissinger to Gordon Liddy, and five government agencies. I accused them of running a five-year campaign of harassment against me. The point of the suit, which was actually instigated by a group of reporters interested in defending the First Amendment, was to make sure Nixon was taken to task for his actions against the press and to dissuade future presidents from similar behavior. My suit spelled out the phone tapping, the spying, the lies, the plots to poison me, harassment by the IRS, the arrest of Les Whitten, and all the various ways Nixon's men had amused themselves at my expense.

Ironically, I lost the case because I would not name my sources. The lawyers for Nixon and the others convinced the judge, Gerhard Gesell, that if there was a conspiracy against me as I claimed, they were entitled to know who the sources were who had told me about that conspiracy. They wanted to know who my source was on the India-Pakistan story, who on H. R. Haldeman's staff had told me about Haldeman's investigation of me, and who my sources were at the CIA. I refused to tell them and Gesell dismissed my suit.

It didn't surprise me that Nixon's first defense against my suit was to try to discover who had told me about his deceptions, crimes, and misdeeds. It was another attempt to destroy the very First Amendment rights I sought to protect.

to tangle with me. "If you don't," Drew said, "they'll descend on you like a flock of buzzards and pick you apart."

IN PRINT, I ACCUSED THE WHITE House of orchestrating Les's arrest. Press spokesman Ron Ziegler responded that I was "wrong, wrong, wrong." But my experience with Richard Nixon, and my sources in the FBI, told me that I was right, right, right. My suspicions fell on Patrick Gray, acting director of the FBI after J. Edgar Hoover's death, who was awaiting Senate confirmation of his appointment as director. He had already crossed me in the ITT case when he had been assistant attorney general to Richard Kleindienst. My sources had told me that it was Gray who had made sure that ITT got the copy of Dita Beard's memo in a failed attempt to prove it a forgery. When the Senate Judiciary Committee had tried to get the memo back, Gray had stalled to give ITT more time to discredit it. He repeatedly gave the committee documents that were favorable to his boss Kleindienst, but conveniently was unable to produce the documents they wanted that might have proved embarrassing.

Gray had been a Nixon lackey since the late 1950s and his loyalty to the president was legendary. I had to laugh when Nixon's press secretary, Ron Ziegler, in announcing the appointment of Gray as acting FBI director right after Hoover's death, made a point of saying how hard Nixon was working to keep politics out of the FBI, just as Hoover had. It was true that Hoover had not politicized the FBI. He had personalized it, making the FBI his own police force.

The appointment of Gray was pitifully transparent. His only qualifications were his bullet head and pugnacious jaw, which gave him the look of an FBI chief. Nixon installed Gray as acting director during the 1972 political campaign, but put off the formal nomination and confirmation process until after the election, so as not to sully the matter with politics, he said. Gray immediately began roaring around the country in air force planes on the pretense of visiting FBI offices. Almost everywhere he went, however, he took the occasion to be a cheerleader for the campaigning president. He was so rarely in his FBI office that people around the headquarters took to calling him "Two-Day Gray."

Gray assured newsmen that the FBI held no secret files on prominent Americans unless they had committed crimes. Of course, under Hoover the FBI had collected information on citizens simply because they opposed the policies of the men in the White House, or because they had exotic sex lives, or, in an astounding number of cases, simply because they were black. But Gray denied the files existed. "None of you guys are going to believe this . . . but there are no dossiers or secret files," he said.

Since Gray was new around the FBI, I offered, in my column, to tell him where some of the secret files were stashed. I named names and file numbers for Gray's convenience. Six months later, FBI agents were caught gathering intelligence on a Democratic congressional candidate in Ohio. An embarrassed Gray pleaded that the practice had "just come to my attention" and that he had ordered it stopped.

After Les's painful experience with Gray's FBI, I figured this was cause enough to follow Drew's advice and hit back. The Senate Judiciary Committee, run by Democrats, would conduct Gray's confirmation hearings, so I made the rounds of the Democrats. I singled out Ted Kennedy and Robert Byrd, who agreed to lead the anti-Gray movement. At first Byrd said he

Jack Anderson as a WW II correspondent.

Jack Anderson behind Japanese lines with Chinese Nationalist guerrillas.

The staff of the *Shanghai,* China, edition of *Stars and Stripes,* 1945.

General Dwight D. Eisenhower, candidate for the Republican
presidential nomination, April 17, 1951.
(UPI/CORBIS-BETTMANN)

Anderson brought the trustees of China's refugee relief to the White House. *(Left to right)* Jack Anderson, David Lee, Mme. Chennault, and President John F. Kennedy.

Federal Bureau of Investigation Director J. Edgar Hoover outside the FBI Building in Washington, February 6, 1950.

Charles "Lucky" Luciano on his way back to jail after the first day of his trial for operating New York's vast vice ring, May 11, 1936.
(UPI/CORBIS-BETTMANN)

Cuban Premier Fidel Castro and other government officials watch the funeral procession
for victims of an air attack on the Havana airport, April 16, 1961.
(Left to right) Cuban President Osvaldo Dorticos; Castro; Captain Emilio Aragonas;
Acting Foreign Minister Carlos Olvares; Public Works Minister, Major Osmani
Clenfuegos; and Labor Minister Augusto Martinez Sanchez.
(UPI/CORBIS-BETTMANN)

Mrs. Jacqueline Kennedy Onassis and her husband, shipping magnate Aristotle Onassis, on a Nile River boat during a private holiday in Egypt, March 28, 1974.

President Richard Nixon during a TV speech to the nation from the White House, April 30, 1970.

(UPI/CORBIS-BETTMANN)

Senator Joseph McCarthy *(right)* and lawyer Roy Cohn, May 6, 1954.
(UPI/CORBIS-BETTMANN)

Multimillionaire movie producer and aviator Howard Hughes in front of his B-23 converted bomber, September 11, 1946.
(UPI/CORBIS-BETTMANN)

Reformist Supreme Soviet Member Boris Yeltsin during a news conference in Tokyo, January 23, 1990.
(REUTERS/CORBIS-BETTMAN)

Teamster Union Chief James Hoffa at the Federal Prison at Lewisburg, Pennsylvania, where he was to serve an eight-year term, December 9, 1967.
(UPI/CORBIS-BETTMANN)

Jack Anderson standing at President Reagan's right at the launching ceremony
of the Young Astronaut program for which the president appointed
Anderson chairman, 1984.

President Jimmy Carter works on the first speech in the series of "Fireside Chats" to the nation, February 2, 1977.

Jack Anderson visiting with President George Bush in the Oval Office.

Jack Anderson spends an evening in the Royal Tent of Mu'ammar Gadhafi.

wouldn't go along with it. To twist his arm, I did something that I am not proud of. In fact, had my own staffers done it, I would have fired them.

"Bobby, I've got more newspapers in West Virginia than Pat Gray has," I said. My message was clear; If I ever found any dirt on him, I had an audience in his home state that would love to read about it. There was a pause and then he said, "All right. What do you want me to do?"

Once I had Byrd and Kennedy in my court, I wrote a column saying Gray lacked the qualifications to head the FBI, and I volunteered to testify against him at his hearing. Gray got the message. My friend Edward P. Morgan, a former FBI administrator, called me and said, "I've got a guy who wants to meet you, totally off the record." When I arrived at Morgan's house, he told me Pat Gray was waiting. The encounter lasted less than five minutes.

"Why are you doing this to me?" Gray asked me.

"Because you arrested one of my reporters."

"Oh, no, no. That wasn't me. I didn't order that," he said, almost desperately. "That happened at the lower echelons."

"You're the acting director of the FBI. I have to hold you responsible," I responded. And then, in a tone as even as I could muster, given my still-simmering anger over the treatment of Les, I told him, "Pat, do your successor a favor. Tell him that the reason you were never confirmed as head of the FBI was because you sent one of Jack Anderson's reporters to jail."

On April 5, 1973, with the Senate Judiciary Committee threatening to give him the kiss of death by postponing his nomination indefinitely, Gray withdrew his name from consideration. I was frankly pleased to have played a small role in keeping him out of the FBI. I believed that if he had been confirmed, it would have set a dangerous precedent and would have opened the door for a parade of political hacks into that office.

SHORTLY AFTER GRAY WAS LEFT TWISTING in the wind, I was handed my biggest Watergate scoop. A new source dropped by our office in April 1973 and offered to cut a deal. He spoke to one of my new young reporters, Jack Cloherty, claiming he had access to the secret transcripts of the grand jury investigation then in progress. He was willing to let us have them, but his motives were not entirely altruistic. He wanted money. I never pay for documents, but we had a fish on the line and I didn't want to lose him. I assigned Les to finesse the negotiations. We appealed to the man's patriotism, and he ultimately gave us the transcripts gratis.

BLACKMAIL

I AM SURE THAT CYNICAL OBSERVERS of my profession think that journalistic extortion to get information goes on all the time, but it does not, at least not in my experience. I have cut deals with sources—to soften a particular angle of a story, for example, if they will cooperate with me on getting information for a better angle. But only once did I ever imply that a person might get some negative publicity if they did not cooperate with me on an unrelated story. That happened when I needed Senator Robert Byrd to help sink the nomination of Pat Gray to head the FBI.

No doubt countless public servants, while awaiting a meeting with me, have considered all the things I might uncover about them. Some have probably imagined that I held a sword over their heads when I did not. The most personally upsetting of those incidents involved a Cabinet member who would later go on to become the president and prophet of the Mormon Church, Ezra Taft Benson.

Benson took a leave of absence from his full-time clergy duties in Salt Lake City to serve as Agriculture secretary to President Eisenhower. During Benson's stay in Washington, he and I occasionally crossed paths in church meetings. I wrote about the way he was handling his job, both favorably and unfavorably.

One day I stepped onto an elevator in the church headquarters in Salt Lake City and right into the path of Benson, who was by then the president of the church's Quorum of the Twelve Apostles. I stuck out my hand and introduced myself, thinking he might not remember my face. He remembered, and turned away from me without taking my hand.

I chalked it up to miscommunication. Later, at a meeting of the church public relations committee on which I served, another church leader approached me and asked if I would be willing to work out my "problem" with Benson. I eagerly agreed and found myself sitting across a desk from Benson listening to his accusation that I had tried to blackmail him while he was in Washington. I was stunned; what he thought had happened hadn't. Here was a man so above reproach as to not have any closets to hide skeletons in, yet years earlier I had left him with the impression that I was poised to write something scandalous about him. I apologized for the misunderstanding and went away with a renewed reverence for the power of the pen, even when it is not loaded.

I respected the sanctity and secrecy of grand jury proceedings, but I didn't trust Nixon to prosecute his own wayward aides. I had heard from inside sources that he looked upon the grand jury as a safe rug to sweep the Watergate scandal under. His intention, my sources said, was to lift a corner of the rug just enough to quiet the public clamor. He believed that as president he could control the prosecutors.

The revelations from the grand jury were startling—hush-money payments to the burglars, slush funds hidden away by the Nixon campaign, Liddy and Hunt skulking around planning dirty tricks, Nixon's hidden stash of office tapes, wiretapping and complicity at the highest levels of the White House staff. The incredulity of the twenty-three grand jurors fairly leaped off the pages. These people, chosen from every walk of life, witnessed the unmaking of a president. White House officials lied and cried. The mighty were humbled and careers were ruined. At first the jurors shied away from asking questions that might implicate Nixon himself, but eventually their outrage got the better of them; they concluded that the president was involved in the cover-up and the conspiracy to silence the burglars.

All hell broke loose when I began publishing the verbatim transcripts on April 16, 1973. A coalition of all federal judges in the District of Columbia signed an order directing the U.S. attorney to find out who gave me the forbidden transcripts. And reporters descended on my office.

Half a dozen TV and radio crews were camped in my reception room one afternoon, waiting for the latest developments, when the source himself unexpectedly walked in the door. Oblivious to the reason for all the excitement, he threaded his way through the throng to Les's office for a casual chat. "What's everybody here for?" he asked Les.

Les bolted from his desk, grabbed the man by the arm, and steered him out the back way. "Ask not for whom the bell tolls," Les whispered. "It tolls for thee."

More significant than the revelations in the transcripts was the effect the publication had on Nixon. He could no longer use the grand jury as an excuse for stonewalling. He had refused to allow his aides to testify before the Senate Watergate Committee or to cooperate with the committee's investigators. He had counted on the secrecy of the grand jury to allow him to choose what to make public and what to keep hidden. He was holding the Senate at bay, meanwhile, by warning senators not to interfere with the grand jury probe. But Nixon's strategy collapsed after I got hold of the secret testimony.

When I started publishing the testimony, a horrified Nixon placed a call to the Justice Department and got Assistant Attorney General Henry

Peterson on the line. "The only copy of the grand jury transcripts has been locked in the prosecutor's office," Peterson reported. "We haven't even tried to bring it over here for security reasons."

Nixon complained petulantly, "I would hope to keep the grand jury from leaking. . . ."

Peterson suggested it would only make matters worse to crack down too hard. "I don't want to go too far there," he said, "because I don't want to get into a diversionary battle with Jack Anderson."

"Oh, hell no," responded Nixon. "It would pay too much attention, I agree. I agree. Well, what I mean is, do the best to control it. We know that it . . . it . . . it is just . . . just wrong."

In another telephone conversation with Peterson the next day, the president vented his frustration. "Of course Jack Anderson has them . . . ugh . . . verbatim . . . Let me tell you. In view of this Jack Anderson thing, that may damage this grand jury . . ."

Shortly thereafter, Nixon abandoned his stonewalling strategy and announced at a Cabinet meeting that he would support a full investigation by both the grand jury and the Senate Watergate Committee. Then he mentioned with obvious irritation my reporting of the testimony. Attorney General Richard Kleindienst, in defense of his department, said that I must have gotten the papers from a grand juror or from the company that supplied the court stenographers. Nixon snapped back, "Cut the crap. We both know it came out of the Justice Department."

The fifteen judges that made up the U.S. District Court of the District of Columbia, including Judge Sirica, had ordered a separate grand jury to investigate who my source was. It is illegal for officers of the court to give out secret grand jury proceedings, but not illegal for me to publish them if I get my hands on them, although I could have gone to jail had I refused to name my source.

I asked Les to bring the source to my house to discuss our options. By then this noble man had completely forgotten his original pitch for money and become dedicated to the cause of truth. I explained to him that one of us was likely to go to jail—me for refusing to divulge his name, or him for confessing he was the source. I made it clear I was willing to serve time to protect his identity. But in an act that touched me deeply and brought Les to tears, the man stood, lifted his hand to his forehead in a small salute, and said, "I'll come forward at the jailhouse door."

I had one more card to play before I would let that happen. U.S. Attorney Harold Titus invited me to a meeting to negotiate a way out of this pickle. The fifteen judges expected Titus to settle for nothing less than the identity of my source.

DEEP THROATS

AN INVESTIGATIVE REPORTER IS ONLY AS good as his sources, and there would be no sources if people thought I would spill their names under pressure. For that reason, we had an office policy—we would go to jail if necessary to protect the identity of a source. Of course, that policy was noble but counterproductive if our whole staff was jailed and there was no one back in the office who could use the ink to make life miserable for our opponents. For that reason, it was also our office policy that we each keep our sources to ourselves. If only one of us knew the identity of a source, only one of us could be jailed.

Fortunately, I never had reason to regret the policy. My reporters have handled their own sources responsibly, and none have ever gone to jail for failing to reveal a source. There was, however, one close call.

Brit Hume was packing his bag and preparing to be fingerprinted one miserable day in 1975. The drama had begun on December 14, 1970, when we published a short item in the column about the mysterious disappearance of documents from the United Mine Workers headquarters. The Justice Department was, at the time, looking into the finances of the UMW. A woman told Brit that her father-in-law, a lawyer for the UMW, had seen UMW President Tony Boyle and the union's general counsel Ed Carey hauling boxes of documents out of Boyle's office. Not long afterward, Carey reported a burglary at the office and said a box of "miscellaneous items" had been taken.

Carey was infuriated by the column and sued us for libel. It took four years for the case to come before a jury, during which time Brit's source steadfastly refused to come forward.

Carey's lawyers were demanding to know who had given us the information, and it looked like Brit was headed for jail, when the woman dramatically stepped forward in the courtroom and announced that she was the source. We were still facing a libel judgment so gargantuan that it would have broken me and dissolved the column. The jury was out for two and a half hours before coming back and pronouncing us not guilty. A juror later told me they would have been back sooner, but it was lunchtime.

Playing my only card, I told him that newspapers all over the country were begging me for copies of the transcripts, that I was inclined to spread them around, but that I understood such widespread publication could queer the whole grand jury process. So I was willing to deal. Titus replied gravely that leaks from a grand jury were very serious business.

"Yes," I replied, "and the State Department feels the same way about

State Department leaks, and the White House feels the same way about White House leaks, and congressional committees feel the same way about congressional leaks. But I'm concerned about the public's right to know. We can't permit government to operate behind closed doors and withhold from the American people information that they are entitled to have."

We had a short philosophical discussion about my First Amendment right to protect my sources. Then he spoke bluntly. He had been ordered to discover my source, and he was prepared to call me before a grand jury. I responded with equal clarity, "You are not going to get that information out of me," I told him. "So we both understand that if you put me in jail, your only purpose will be to punish me. You can inform the judges that I will not identify my source and that jailing me would serve no purpose except to punish me. But if you punish me, then I will punish you. Every day I'm in jail I will write a story about this. You may win on your battlefield, but the press is my battlefield and I'll win there. Which is the more powerful? We'll find out. We'll see who can last longer."

Titus said he would report back to the judges. He called me the next day with an offer from the chief judge, John Sirica. The judges would let me off the hook if I would stop publishing quotes from the transcripts, which I would deliver to Sirica. I issued a statement to the press saying that "I have become convinced that further disclosures would not be in the best interests of the investigation." But, I added, "I have an obligation and a right to continue to report any and all pertinent information on this sordid scandal that so many people in high places have worked so hard to keep from the public."

We had kept Joe Spear in the dark about the source's identity so he could keep the column going if Les and I were hauled off to jail to protect the man's anonymity. Joe secretly lamented being excluded from the prospect of martyrdom. When I agreed to stop publishing the transcripts and turn our copies over to Judge Sirica, I first gave the stack of documents to Joe and instructed him to find the fastest copy machine in town and photocopy them in case we should want to refer to them again. Joe later confessed to the staff that while standing at the copier, he made a point of pressing his fingerprints liberally on the originals, so he might have a chance to go to jail, too.

WITHOUT THE WATCHDOGS OF THE PRESS, the Watergate scandal would have been swept under the rug of the Oval Office. Instead, the dominoes fell one by one until the president himself finally resigned in shame. I felt sorry for that shy, decent, inner Nixon, but my voice was among the loudest calling for the impeachment of his political alter ego.

And it seemed unfair that his coconspirators would up in jail when he retreated into wealthy retirement. I changed my mind after Gerald Ford became president and one of Ford's lawyers confided in me. The attorney, who consulted with Ford about whether to pardon Nixon, visited Nixon's retirement office in California. An aide asked the lawyer, please, not to mention Watergate, then ushered him into the office.

Nixon sat in sparse surroundings. He could have livened up the office with mementos, but he had chosen the spartan look. With seeming disorientation, he gestured around the room and said, "They've taken everything." Then Nixon reached into a desk drawer and brought out a cheap tie clip, the kind he once handed out as a campaign trinket. "This is all I have left," he said. "You take it."

The lawyer made some discreet inquiries among Nixon's friends and learned that the former president was making middle-of-the-night phone calls and talking gibberish. Nixon developed a strange inability to say the name of special Watergate prosecutor Leon Jaworski. He took Seconal to sleep. The lawyer reported back to President Ford that Nixon was a broken man who could not stand the rigors of a trial. Ford kindly pardoned him and put the matter to rest, absorbing a great deal of criticism himself for not holding Nixon accountable for his crimes.

I understood and appreciated what Ford did to spare Nixon and heal the nation. And I took no satisfaction in learning that Nixon was a broken man. I also predicted at the time that he would one day make a comeback and cast himself as a statesman, perhaps seeking appointment as an ambassador or presidential advisor. This dogged president with the tormented soul desperately wanted to succeed. He overcame his depression and, by sheer grit, rose from the ashes of Watergate. At his funeral in 1994, a sense of forgiveness and something akin to respect pervaded the service.

The president's men did not rebound so well. Most of them wrote their memoirs and then lived quiet, private lives. Gordon Liddy was the exception. I heard about his experiences in jail from a fellow inmate who called to bellyache that the guards were giving in to everything Liddy wanted. When Liddy was assigned to a bed near the TV room, he squawked that he couldn't sleep because of the noise. The guards banned TV after 11:30 P.M., which did not endear Liddy to the other inmates, who set his mattress on fire and threw his possessions out the door. He once got into an altercation with another inmate over a hairbrush and wound up with a cut ear and a bruised nose. At his lowest point, Liddy spent one hundred days in solitary confinement. Eventually the other prisoners came to respect him because he fought men twice his size, kept his vow of silence on Watergate, and handed out free legal advice. They called him "Watergate Liddy." After prison,

Liddy remade himself as only Liddy could—as a surly radio talk-show host, author, and sometimes-actor.

Charles Colson, the president's ruthless hatchetman, turned to religion. He had the round-faced, bespectacled look of an evangelist, and he became one. The most disliked aide among the White House staffers, Colson made his peace with the other Watergate figures and tried, without much success, to bring them all to Christ.

Before Colson served his prison term, he and I appeared together on a television talk show. Although he had masterminded the campaign against me from behind the scenes at the White House, he had always treated me with gentlemanly cordiality to my face. I rather liked the guy. While we waited for the TV taping to begin, I chatted backstage with his wife, Patty. She was understandably anxious about how she would fare while her husband was behind bars. I offered to help her out financially if I could, and both she and Colson were visibly touched.

I had watched Drew Pearson over the years as he had reached out to help those he had tangled with in print. I had learned from Drew that shooting and being shot at was the nature of our business, and that it rarely made sense to take things personally or hold long grudges. Colson mentioned my offer in his memoir, *Born Again*. But he never came to me for financial help.

Frank Sturgis spent thirteen months in prison and then resumed his scheming and dreaming and plotting to overthrow Fidel Castro. On December 3, 1993, one of Frankie's friends called me to say that Frankie was in the hospital with lung cancer and would be cheered up by a call from me. It was Friday and I had to hurry to catch a plane for a weekend speaking engagement. I made a mental note to call him when I got back on Monday. On Saturday he died in a Miami Veterans Hospital at the age of sixty-eight. I can imagine how our conversation might have gone. We would have traded reports on our respective families. He would have filled me in on his latest mission, training guerrilla fighters in case anyone wanted them to invade Cuba. Neither of us would have mentioned Watergate. I already knew he felt bitter and betrayed. In his mind, he had been serving the president.

LIKE MANY AMERICANS, I HAVE ALWAYS felt that the presidency is something special—the closest thing we have to royalty—and that the president is a father figure for the nation, a commander in chief. Our founding fathers were more realistic, so they set about restricting presidential power and separating the branches of government so that each could act as a check on the others. A large portion of the policing responsibility, however, has been left to the people and the press.

The Nixon coterie encroached upon the powers of Congress, trampled on the rights of the press, and violated basic freedoms. They sat in the witness chair in the Senate caucus room and asserted the president's right, in effect, to steal and wiretap and rig court cases. They goaded dissidents, encouraged demonstrations, and rejoiced over a report that there might be violence at a presidential function. "Good," scrawled H. R. Haldeman in response to the report that one group of demonstrators "will be violent" and will carry "extremely obscene signs." This would justify harsh measures to protect the nation from such people.

The language of the Constitution—the people, justice, tranquillity, welfare, liberty—would protect the people from the government. The language of the Nixonites—law and order, secrecy, surveillance, executive privilege—would protect the government from the people.

When we begin to equate citizenship with mere obedience, when we define patriotism as the singing of songs and waving of flags, then we risk getting a Watergate. When the threat comes, the system could fall if the press fails to expose, the opposition party declines to oppose, the public neglects to care, and the courts demur from the law. That didn't happen with Watergate, so the system held. The leader of the foremost nation of the world, the man who commanded great armies and treasuries, waited glumly upon the verdict of a free people in the case of a third-rate burglary.

The last time I saw Richard Nixon was in 1985 at the funeral of hotel magnate J. Willard Marriott. Because I was a friend of the Marriott family, they asked me to serve as chief usher at the funeral, which meant I was to stand at the entrance of the chapel and direct the distinguished guests to the seats that had been reserved for them. Nixon strode up to me to get his instructions, not paying attention. Then we made eye contact. When he recognized me, his face contorted into that old "hunted adversary" expression. "Hrrumph," he growled, and walked away.

CHAPTER 18

I HAD BEEN WITH DREW PEARSON only three months when he gave me a heady assignment—to instruct the mysterious magnate, playboy, aviator, power broker Howard Hughes on the workings of the U.S. Senate. Had I known that I would be tracking Hughes to determine whether he had been replaced by a double and that I would be close on his heels on the last day of his life in 1976, I would have taken detailed notes.

My first encounter with Hughes was awesome enough, given my limited experience as Drew's resident expert on the Senate. Hughes wanted my advice, however humble, about going up against Maine Senator Owen Brewster, a rascal who was preparing to fire a political broadside against the Hughes industrial empire. Hughes was supposed to have built two revolutionary aircraft for the Pentagon—a photo-reconnaissance spy plane called the F-11, and a giant plywood cargo seaplane nicknamed the "Spruce Goose." They were two wartime contracts that cost the taxpayers $40 million. Now it was 1947, the war was well over, and Hughes had not yet finished either plane.

Normally this would have been grist for Drew's mill—a defense contractor cheating the taxpayers, hints of political string pulling, two projects running way over budget. But Drew had satisfied himself that Hughes and his designers had done their level best to develop the two planes that were almost ready to fly. A passionate aviator and inventor, Hughes had an irrepressible emotional investment in both projects that went beyond the contracts. He was personally absorbing the cost overruns.

The real story in Drew's judgment was Brewster's motive. His political guns were aimed at the F-11 and the Spruce Goose. But his target was Trans World Airlines, and his objective was to defame its majority stockholder, Howard Hughes. Brewster was the chief water carrier in the Senate for the rival Pan American Airlines. The two giants of the air were duking it out for the exclusive right to fly international routes from the United States. Under a regulatory scheme called the "chosen instrument," one airline would be selected to fly the international routes and would be subsidized by the taxpayers. Brewster was pushing through a law to give Pan Am that worldwide monopoly, and Hughes stood in his way.

Hughes abhorred the spotlight, but when it became apparent that he could not dodge a summons to appear before the Senate to explain his performance on the defense contracts, he placed an emergency call to Drew Pearson. Hughes correctly assumed if anyone had the lowdown on Owen Brewster, it would be Drew. Over the phone, they agreed to share information. Between Hughes's investigators and Drew's contacts, they should be able to assemble a profile of Brewster's dark side.

Drew offered to coach Hughes for an appearance before a hostile Senate committee. Then he turned that assignment over to me, apparently assuming I had acquired his Washington wiles by osmosis. I telephoned Hughes's secretary and gatekeeper, Nadine Henley, who indoctrinated me on the elaborate procedure to establish communications with her boss. First I should make an appointment with Henley to place the call to Hughes at a specific time. She would give me an unlisted phone number that I must call not a minute early nor a minute late. She explained that Hughes was hard of hearing and took only scheduled calls on a specially adapted telephone.

I called at the appointed minute. Hughes answered and got right to the point: How should he handle himself when he testified? I gave him the benefit of my limited exposure to the Senate. I had learned that most senators become suddenly timid when they're caught in the glare of klieg lights. They abhor confrontations that force them to choose a side and alienate voters on the other side. They prefer to straddle the fence. I advised Hughes to come out swinging, to accuse them of violating his rights and treating him unfairly. He should play the angry, wounded patriot who had come to Capitol Hill to clear his good name. I told him his critics would pose as champions of the people, but he must portray them as tools of Pan Am. He thanked me for my advice and said he would see me in Washington. I noted that perhaps because of his hearing problem, he wasted no words.

In the weeks leading up to Hughes's appearance before the Senate, I took satisfaction in watching him follow my advice. From behind closed corporate doors in California, he lobbed daily press releases lambasting Brewster as a "mouthpiece" for Pan Am. He charged that Brewster had offered to drop the investigation—sheer blackmail—if Hughes would allow TWA to merge with Pan Am. From our bastion, Drew joined the bombardment.

Brewster issued a subpoena demanding that Hughes appear before his committee immediately, five days earlier than originally scheduled. But Hughes, a master at hide-and-seek, became temporarily incommunicado, so the subpoena could not be served. Hughes finally made the cross-country trip to Washington on his own schedule at the controls of his own converted B-32 bomber. Each leg of the trip was breathlessly chronicled by a press that had been whipped into a frenzy.

The night before Hughes was to testify, he checked into a suite at the Carlton Hotel in Washington and invited me to drop by. The invitation came at the last minute, so I had a date in tow, but I was pleased for the opportunity to impress her. "Mind if we stop at the Carlton for a quick meeting with Howard Hughes?"

Hughes ignored my date and left her in the reception area while he led me into his private quarters for a last-minute strategy session. He fidgeted and paced, sometimes drumming his fingers on the desk. Again I was intrigued by his succinct, incisive statements and quick wit. Yet in his eyes I saw no hint of joie de vivre.

The next day Hughes twisted the senators tightly around his little finger in a performance that remains unequaled before a congressional committee. He railed against injustice and unfairness; he pinned Brewster to the wall with accusation after accusation. I went to his hotel room again that night, but it was clear that he needed no coaching from me.

On the second day of his testimony, Hughes so fired up the spectators that the committee chairman, Senator Homer Ferguson, pounded his gavel and demanded that the sergeant at arms take out the rowdies. A police squad had been called in to keep the peace, so the head cop asked Ferguson who he wanted evicted. "Whoever demonstrated," Ferguson boomed.

"Well, Senator, I guess that's everybody," the officer responded. When the police squad tried to clear the room, the ensuing melee forced Ferguson to bang his gavel and rescind the eviction order.

On the final day scheduled for his testimony, Hughes arrived with a 400-page list of grievances he planned to read. But the senators' chairs were empty. In the middle of the night, the harried Brewster had called off the hearings, dismissed the committee, and hightailed it home to Maine.

Three years later Drew and I learned that Joe Shimon, a Washington police lieutenant, had bugged Hughes's room at the Carlton Hotel. Brewster had ordered the bugging and had paid Shimon's expenses. Despite Drew's hammering in the column, Brewster wriggled out of the accusation with a lame excuse about ordering the bugging out of fear for his personal safety.

But Drew was not finished with Brewster. For the two years before Brewster's next election campaign in Maine, Drew published no less than fifty columns assailing him. Then, not willing to let the democratic process take its course without some prodding, Drew cajoled Maine Governor Frederick Payne into running against Brewster. Payne agreed to run only if he got at least $50,000 in contributions from outside of the state.

Drew placed a quick call to Howard Hughes and the check was in the mail. Payne won the election. On the day after the election, lobbyist and Brewster ally Charles Patrick Clark punched Drew to the carpet in the lobby of Washington's Mayflower Hotel. "That's for what you did to Brewster," Clark said. Following the assault, still pumped with adrenaline, he positioned himself at the hotel entrance and reenacted his moment of glory, with lightning-quick jabs and fancy footwork. Drew was typically urbane when asked about the punch. "It hurt like hell, but the ringing in my ears was music."

I NEVER SAW HOWARD HUGHES AGAIN after the Brewster hearings. He told me to keep his phone number and call (by appointment of course) whenever I needed anything from him. Over the next few years I called him occasionally for his slant on stories. He was always polite, helpful, and laconic. In 1960, Drew and I exposed his loan to Richard Nixon's brother Don to finance a string of hamburger restaurants. I was unable to reach Hughes for comment. By 1971, when I revealed that he had given Richard Nixon a $100,000 campaign donation in cash, two years after the election, Hughes wasn't speaking to anyone except a tight circle of aides, most of whom never saw him face-to-face.

By then, the elusive billionaire had become my story instead of my source. I had friends in Las Vegas who, in the late 1960s, tipped me off that Hughes was buying up casinos as fast as they came on the market. Those friends included *Las Vegas Sun* publisher Hank Greenspun and Edward P. Morgan, the ex-FBI lawyer I had introduced to Greenspun. The two of them put me in touch with Robert Maheu, Hughes's chief factotum in Las Vegas. He told me Hughes was holed up on the ninth floor of the Desert Inn Hotel, never emerging to see the light of day. Despite the fact that Maheu ran Hughes's casino operations, the two men had never met face-to-face. Maheu communicated with Hughes solely through memos and telephone conversations.

Maheu described Hughes's intense, ever-increasing isolation. Even Hughes's wife, actress Jean Peters, had stopped trying to see him since the day in 1966 when he had made her stand in the hallway outside his hotel suite in Boston. Thought he adored her, he had a pathological fear of human contact. The man allowed no one into his room except a small core of

SAVIOR WITH A PROFIT MOTIVE

HOWARD HUGHES WAS FAR FROM BEING a humanist, a fact that was painfully clear in his memos to Robert Maheu. The memos revealed a completely different Hughes from the brilliant tycoon I had met and admired. In reality, he was a bigot, a political fixer, a greedy baron who tried to turn Nevada into his personal fiefdom, a man who considered his own accumulation of wealth paramount to the interests of the United States, a self-appointed savior with a profit motive.

In 1968, while most Americans were mourning the death of Dr. Martin Luther King Jr., Hughes had his own unique take on the tragedy. He was afraid the wave of national pathos might prompt Maheu to hire more blacks as casino employees.

With television as his primary source of information from the outside world, Hughes had watched with horror news reports about race riots in major cities. Fearing the contagion might spread to his own doorstep, Hughes wrote a memo to Maheu: "I certainly would not say these things in public, however I can summarize my attitude about employing more Negroes very simply—I think it is a wonderful idea for somebody else, somewhere else."

He referred to a race riot he claimed to have witnessed in his hometown of Houston where "Negroes committed atrocities equal to any in Vietnam." Acknowledging that his attitude was not politically correct, Hughes said he wasn't suggesting a resurgence of the Ku Klux Klan in Las Vegas. "But I am not running for election and therefore we don't have to curry favor with the NAACP either."

fiercely loyal male attendants known as the "Mormon Mafia," so called because most of them were Mormons, recruited by Hughes's Mormon chief aide Bill Gay.

It had been a few years since Hughes had taken my calls, but I thought I would test our relationship and check out Maheu's revelations. On a trip to Las Vegas in 1969 to investigate the rise of Hughes and the decline of the Mafia in that gambling paradise, I stopped at the Desert Inn and sent a message up to the ninth floor that I would like to see Hughes. Within minutes, a note with Hughes's signature was delivered to me, politely begging off.

Within a year I was back in Las Vegas, this time to investigate the mysterious disappearance of Howard Hughes. On Thanksgiving eve 1970, his aides lugged him down an outside fire escape at the Desert Inn, rushed him to nearby Nellis Air Force Base, and lifted him aboard a private plane that flew him to the Bahamas. Maheu had no idea Hughes had been spirited away until the next day. It was several weeks before Maheu was able to confirm what had happened to Hughes.

Hughes's right arm, Bob Maheu, was embroiled at the time in a power struggle with the left arm, Bill Gay. Maheu ran the casinos, but Gay controlled the palace guard. In the weeks leading up to Hughes's disappearance, his attendants had virtually cut off communications between Maheu and Hughes. Meanwhile, the billionaire, encouraged by the Gay faction, plotted Hughes's move to the Bahamas. He wanted to get out of the country quickly to avoid the IRS, which was closing in on him in a tax dispute.

When I arrived in Las Vegas, I pumped both sides for information. I also obtained a copy of a shocking memo submitted by a Las Vegas doctor to the police. What I learned was so outlandish as to be almost unbelievable—that the once vital playboy was now, at sixty-five, an emaciated invalid with white hair down to his shoulders, shaggy eyebrows, a straggly beard, and grotesquely long fingernails and toenails. He was a "basket case" who alternated between flashes of his old brilliance and long stretches of stupor.

The Bill Gay faction claimed that Maheu had been keeping Hughes a virtual prisoner in his own luxury hotel. The Bob Maheu faction countercharged that Gay and the Mormon Mafia had kidnapped the old recluse and hustled him out of the country against his will, though he was unfit to travel. Their purpose allegedly was to cut Maheu out of the loop and seize control of the multi-billion-dollar empire.

Bob Maheu and Ed Morgan told me that Hughes, in his old age, had developed a paralyzing fear of flying. They didn't believe he would ever have consented to fly to the Bahamas. The memo to the police was written by a doctor who had examined Hughes just a couple of months before he disappeared. Hughes was so weak and emaciated, the memo made clear, that he would have been unfit to get out of bed, let alone fly to the Bahamas. Maheu feared that Hughes may have died and that the men around him were keeping it secret so they could run his empire and reap his billions.

To complete the conspiracy scenario, Maheu admitted under my questioning that before Hughes became a complete hermit, he occasionally hired actors to double for him. He would slip unnoticed out the back door of a hotel while the double and the Hughes entourage went out the front door. The doubles were especially handy when Hughes was dodging a subpoena or claiming to be where he was not. His aides also kept a computerized file of everything the boss said or did, so I speculated it would be easy to marry that file with a skilled look-alike and create a new Howard Hughes if the old one became intractable or died.

I followed Hughes's movements for the next six years, never certain whether I was on the trail of the real Hughes. For it became increasingly clear that there were two Howard Hugheses. One Hughes would meet on rare occasions with public figures who uniformly described him as charming, loquacious, and well-groomed, if a bit thin. He usually greeted them with a warm handshake. The other Hughes was described by witnesses as an emaciated old man who lived in his own filth, stored his urine in bottles, and refused to let others touch him.

At one critical point in 1970, Hughes sent word through his underlings that Maheu was fired. Maheu refused to believe the order had come from Hughes himself. Then Hughes, sounding cordial, got on the phone with Nevada Governor Paul Laxalt and confirmed that Maheu indeed was no longer authorized to run the Las Vegas casino operations. Maheu retaliated by suing Hughes for breach of contract; his motive, in part, was to force the real Howard Hughes into the open.

Maheu had proof of his close business relationship with Hughes: a stack of handwritten memos from the eccentric billionaire. Although those memos were put under court seal during the lawsuit, Maheu shared copies with me. Another man with copies of the intriguing memos was Hank Greenspun, who kept them locked in his personal safe at the *Las Vegas Sun*. The memos were such hot property that at one point Richard Nixon's White House Plumbers plotted to break into Greenspun's safe. Watergate burglar James McCord told the grand jury about plans to crack the safe, steal the memos, hustle them to the closest airport, and fly them to Central America. The plane was to be provided by none other than Hughes himself, according to McCord.

The word I got from inside the White House was that Nixon blamed his narrow defeat in the 1960 presidential election on bad publicity over his dealings with Hughes and that he feared what the memos might reveal about the money Hughes had given him and his brother Donald. It was the same fear of what might be in Larry O'Brien's desk at the Watergate office complex, insiders told me, that precipitated the Watergate burglary.

In 1972, I learned that Hughes had hastily changed penthouses, from the Britannia Beach Hotel in Nassau to the Intercontinental Hotel in Managua, Nicaragua. It was an unfortunate choice for a man with an earthquake phobia. The earth began to shake beneath Managua in December 1972, driving Hughes into the street with everybody else. Still on the run from the IRS, he moved to London, then the Bahamas again, then British Columbia, and finally Acapulco. I followed his globe-trotting with fascination, looking for signs that the real Hughes was dead and had been replaced by a double. He had lost his passport in the earthquake and reportedly refused

MISSING MONEY

HOWARD HUGHES BECAME THE MOST HIGH-PROFILE opponent of nuclear bomb testing in the Nevada desert near Las Vegas. The tests represented a threat not only to Hughes's personal safety but to the profits of his casinos. "How can we expect to realize our full potential as a resort if we are scaring people away with bomb-tests and earth-quakes?" he wrote in a memo to Robert Maheu.

His first option, as always, was to try to buy what he wanted. In 1968, Hughes anointed Vice President Hubert Humphrey as his man in Washington on the nuclear issue. "There is one man who can accomplish our objective through [Lyndon] Johnson—and that man is H.H.H.," Hughes wrote.

Hughes instructed Maheu, "Why don't we get word to him on a basis of secrecy that is *really, really, reliable* that we will give him immediately *full unlimited* support for his campaign to enter the White House if he will take this one on for us?" Maheu got word to Humphrey that Hughes had a hefty campaign donation in mind, but Humphrey was skittish and referred the offer to his campaign finance staff.

On July 29, 1968, Maheu met Humphrey in front of the Century Plaza Hotel in Los Angeles. Maheu had $50,000 in cash in his attaché case, but the handoff would be awkward. Humphrey was surrounded by Secret Service agents and well-wishers. The best Maheu could do was leave the case in Humphrey's limousine after he was invited into the car for a chat with the vice president. Neither of them mentioned the money while in the car, but Maheu managed to get in a plug for stopping the nuclear testing.

The contribution never turned up in Humphrey's campaign finance records. I considered Humphrey a close friend and had unreserved respect for him. When I asked him about the money, he admitted receiving the satchel, acknowledged he was aware it was a contribution from Hughes, but swore he left it with aides to count and chronicle. As with the $100,000 Hughes funneled to Richard Nixon through Bebe Rebozo, what happened to this cash remains an enduring mystery.

In 1969 I had reported that President Nixon was so worried about offending Hughes on the testing issue that he sent his most trusted personal friend Bebe Rebozo to Nevada to smooth Hughes's feathers. But judging by the memos, Hughes had a fear of the testing that could not be assuaged by a visit from Rebozo or anyone else.

If the Atomic Energy Commission wasn't willing to come to terms with him, the memos show Hughes was ready to put his considerable empire behind a ban-the-bomb crusade. "I am going to dedicate the rest of my life and every cent I have if necessary to wipe this nuclear test program right out of this country and its possessions."

Hughes's resolve disappeared when he left Las Vegas and the tests were no longer a threat to him personally.

to sit for a new picture, but the lack of a passport didn't seem to interfere with his wanderings.

I sought someone who had seen Hughes in person. Then I read in the newspaper that Nevada's new governor, Mike O'Callaghan, and Phil Hannafin, chairman of the Nevada Gaming Commission, had been granted an audience with Hughes in London on a casino regulatory matter in March 1973. Casino owners are directly accountable to the Gaming Commission, which requires them to appear in person for license hearings. Hughes would not come to Nevada, but he agreed to meet with the two men in London. The accounts in the press said they had been sworn to secrecy.

I hoped that O'Callaghan would still feel beholden to me for my performance in the televised debate with Paul Laxalt in 1970, which news accounts claimed had won the election for O'Callaghan. The new governor had told me that he owed his victory to me. It was payback time. I placed a call to him. "Governor, I'm trying to find out the truth about Howard Hughes."

"I can't talk about it," O'Callaghan said quickly. "I made a solemn promise to Hughes that I would not discuss it."

I pushed my luck. "Governor, who elected you?" There was a long silence.

"You did, you SOB," he grumbled.

"I'm concerned that they may be using a double instead of the real Howard Hughes," I said. "Tell me about the Howard Hughes you met." O'Callaghan described a thin, dignified gentleman with a white Vandyke beard. The governor asked Hannafin to confirm the description. Although neither man had ever met Hughes before, both swore to me that it was the real Hughes. They had asked him detailed questions about his casino operations, and he had answered as only the owner could.

Extracting the details of a second Hughes sighting took more finesse. Before Hughes left Nicaragua, President Anastasio Somoza had demanded a face-to-face meeting. Hughes invited him for a visit aboard his Gulfstream executive jet parked on the tarmac at Managua's airport. U.S. Ambassador to Nicaragua Turner Shelton tagged along. Hughes had established a tenuous relationship with Somoza, the pot-bellied dictator who controlled every profitable industry in that tiny nation.

Somoza and Shelton had pledged, as O'Callaghan had, that after their meeting with Hughes their lips would be sealed. But I got my hands on Shelton's confidential report to his superiors at the State Department. "Hughes walked to the door [of the plane] and shook hands firmly," Shelton wrote. This seemed significant. Could this be the same man who wouldn't let his own wife, whom he loved, into their bedroom for fear of germs?

There were no curling fingernails or long, matted hair. Shelton described Hughes as "about six feet, three inches tall, very thin, weighing from 140–150 pounds, graying hair and neatly trimmed Van Dyke-type beard." Shelton thought the man he had met looked very much like an artist's sketch he had seen of Hughes. The only hint of eccentricity was the attire Hughes chose for his meeting with a head of state. He wore beat-up bedroom slippers and an old bathrobe. The whole outfit, Shelton suggested, "would have gone at a bargain basement for about 80 cents."

Hughes had complained that he was hard of hearing and said he had experimented with forty or fifty different hearing aides. On that day, he was wearing an older device that he said he had repaired with a screwdriver, and he was able to carry on a normal conversation with Somoza and Shelton.

Not at all reticent to talk, Hughes seemed to enjoy this rare visit with outsiders. "Don't rush off," he told his guests. "This plane isn't going anywhere until I tell it to." Then he led them in a wide-ranging discussion on aviation. At one point he explained that he had become a recluse to rid himself of the demands other people placed on his time. Shelton said Hughes admitted his retreat from the world may have been "a mistake."

In the spring of 1976, the other Howard Hughes emerged as proof at last that he was still alive. The skipper of the boat that had spirited Hughes out of the Bahamas in 1972 told me that the man he had transported had hair down to his shoulders, a stringy beard, and yellowed, curling toenails about two inches long. The mysterious passenger was carried onto the boat in a wheelchair. This was just a month before Somoza and Shelton met a well-groomed, ambulatory, and talkative Hughes on his airplane in Managua.

Next, I uncovered the details of another Hughes sighting that had occurred after he left Managua in December 1972. The IRS had learned that Hughes was fleeing Nicaragua and might be headed for Miami International Airport. U.S. Customs officials were alerted that the IRS had a subpoena to serve on Hughes, so both agencies staked out the Miami airport and waited.

But Hughes landed in Ft. Lauderdale instead at about midnight on December 23, 1972. A top Florida IRS official rushed some agents to the airport with orders to insist on a face-to-face meeting with the phantom. They found Hughes's jet sitting in a hangar and one of his aides, Charles Waldron, waiting for them. Waldron boarded the plane and returned with a message from Hughes. The IRS agents were supposed to call his lawyer Chester Davis in New York. Davis asked for a little time. A few minutes later, he called back triumphantly and informed the IRS agents that their assignment had been canceled. Unwilling to take their orders from Hughes's lawyer, the agents called their own superiors. Sure enough, the instructions had come from IRS Commissioner Johnnie Walters that they were not to insist on a confrontation with Hughes.

The IRS may have been ordered to back off, but the Customs agent on duty in Ft. Lauderdale, Harold Sawyer, was not about to be intimidated. He insisted on seeing whoever was on that plane before they would be allowed to stay in the country. The standoff continued until about 2 A.M. when a man with a nasal voice and a Texas accent could be heard in the plane protesting, "No, no." Finally, Sawyer was allowed to board the darkened plane. He carried with him a message from the IRS about Hughes's back taxes.

Sawyer told me Hughes was concealed behind a blanket draped across the aisle of the airplane. The agent clicked on his flashlight and illuminated the form of a man slouched in one of the seats with a black hat pulled down hard over his ears. His face was gaunt and he had a full beard. Sawyer asked if the man was Howard Hughes. "Yes," came the mumbled reply. Sawyer handed Hughes a card with the message from the IRS. With the aid of glasses, Hughes read the message. Did he understand it, Sawyer wanted to know. "Yes."

Three months later, the Howard Hughes seen by Governor O'Callaghan was reportedly a dapper and alert businessman.

I decided to try a different angle after Hughes turned up in Acapulco. I asked my friend Treasury Secretary William Simon if he had any connections in Mexico City who could help me in my quest to find out whether the real Howard Hughes was dead or alive. Simon was interested in anything I might discover about Hughes because of the ongoing tax case, so he called his friend, the attorney general of Mexico, Pedro Ojeda Paullada, and asked him to receive me in Mexico City.

Ojeda Paullada was cordial. "How can I help you?" he asked.

"By sending your federal agents to the Princess Hotel in Acapulco to confront Howard Hughes."

"I can't do that," he shook his head. "We have the same laws as you do. We can't invade a man's privacy."

"Could you do it if he had violated your laws?" I asked. "Wouldn't it be a violation if someone had forged Hughes's signature on his entry papers?"

I had piqued his curiosity. I flew back to Washington and, at his request, obtained handwriting and signature samples and rushed them to Mexico City. Within a few days Ojeda Paullada called back. "We have checked the handwriting on Mr. Hughes's entry form and it is a forgery."

"Can you confront him now?" I asked.

GLOMAR EXPLORER

WHEN THE NIXON ADMINISTRATION NEEDED SOMEONE to build a top-secret deep-sea salvage vessel to pull a Soviet submarine from the bottom of the Pacific Ocean, Howard Hughes with his notorious penchant for secrecy was the ideal person for the job. I broke the story of Hughes's Glomar Explorer in 1975 and suffered the wrath of my peers for doing so.

Reporters at all the big newspapers in the country were after the story of the salvage ship that had tried to pull the Soviet sub up from seventeen thousand feet below the surface. The submarine had exploded and sunk in 1968, taking seventy Soviet seamen and officers to their deaths 750 miles northwest of Oahu, Hawaii. The Soviets searched in vain for their lost sub. When the U.S. Navy finally located it, the CIA decided to spend whatever it would take to pull up the sub and its purported secrets. Hughes's Summa Corporation was hired on the sly to build the salvage vessel at an eventual cost of nearly $400 million.

CIA Director William Colby had successfully talked every other reporter on the story out of printing it on the basis of national security. Colby was a reasonable man who had worked closely with me on other stories. I liked him, but something about his argument this time smacked of boondoggle and cover-up. The Glomar Explorer had pulled the sub up about eight thousand feet and then dropped two-thirds of it when the hull broke apart. The piece that was salvaged contained nothing more revealing than seventy dead bodies. The piece that went back down may have carried nuclear warheads and outmoded Soviet code books, but the sub was eighteen years old and none of its technology was a secret anymore.

When Les Whitten was first tipped off to the story, his source told him the Soviet sub had gone down in the Atlantic instead of the Pacific. Les called Jim Angleton, head of counterespionage at the CIA, and asked, "Did we try to salvage a Russian submarine that went down in the Atlantic Ocean?" Angleton's response was accurate if not exactly candid. "That's absolutely untrue," he told Les.

Les called his friend at the *New York Times,* Seymour Hersh, who said he had checked the rumor also and found nothing to it. In fact, Hersh had already written the story but his editors had bowed to pressure from Colby and were sitting on it.

Les put the story on the back burner until another of my reporters, Jack Cloherty, asked him if he had heard the rumors about the Russian sub that had gone down in the Pacific. As soon as Les heard "Pacific," he knew he had been hoodwinked. Les raced to me with the details of the Glomar Explorer. He was ready to print the story, but I was nervous about the national security problem.

Les was so convinced of the public's right to know about the Glomar Explorer that he decided to hoodwink me.

He called a source of his in the Defense Department, a man whose name I did not know but whose information, through Les, I had come to trust. Les told his source, "I'm about to put Jack Anderson on the phone. No matter what he asks you, just say, 'I don't know all the details, but you can be sure the Russians know about it.' " The source was baffled but said he was game.

Then Les hustled back into my office and made his pitch. If the Russians already knew about the Glomar Explorer, then didn't the American people have the right to know, too? I agreed. Les said his trusted Defense Department source was on the phone to tell me that the Russians did indeed know. I picked up the phone to speak to the anonymous source. "Tell me, do the Russians know all about the Glomar Explorer?" I asked.

"I don't know all the details, Jack, but you can be sure the Russians know about it," replied the source who had never before heard the name Glomar Explorer.

My column had a four-day distribution time between the final edit and the designated publication date. I knew the scoop would not hold that long, so I decided to break the story on my radio broadcast, without giving Colby enough notice to alert the rest of the press. He had promised them he would alert them if anyone was planning to break the embargo. As I typed my radio copy, Les put in a call to Colby. "Jack is going through a terrible decision-making process now," Les said. "We will call you back when he decides."

Colby called as I was putting the final touches on the radio copy. He made his appeal. "Look," I replied. "I have a record of killing stories that genuinely affect the security of the country. But are you trying to tell me that the Soviets don't know what's in their own submarine?" Then I told him I would think about his argument and let him know. I turned back to writing my copy and instructed Joe Spear to call Colby's office one minute before our radio broadcast and tell them we had decided to break the story.

Joe made the call to the amiable CIA public relations man on duty that day, Angus Thurmer. "Angus, we're breaking the Glomar story."

"When?" Thurmer asked, with resignation.

"In 58 seconds."

Thurmer cursed and hung up.

The *New York Times* story came out the next day and other papers quickly followed suit. While they all printed the juicy story, they also piled on me for being the first. I was disappointed to see the reemergence of the pre-Watergate practice of cozy intimacy between press and government. It was a dubious ethic that allowed a camaraderie of secrets to be shared by the press peerage, but kept from the public.

"Mañana," he told me. Tomorrow. Everything there seemed to be better done tomorrow.

A couple of days later, April 5, 1976, he called back. "Mr. Hughes has left Mexico. He is on his way to Texas."

By the time Hughes's plane landed in Texas, he was dead. I rushed over to Bill Simon's office to ask if he had any legal right to intervene. "We can send someone to identify the corpse," Simon told me. Hughes's symptoms were those of a neglected pauper—kidney failure, bed sores, dehydration. His body had wasted away to ninety pounds. His attendants had been loyal and obedient to a fault, not taking him to a hospital when he refused to go, not forcing him to eat when he wouldn't, giving him the drugs he demanded. The only real decision they made without his approval was to fly the dying man back to the United States.

Simon's men took fingerprints and dental molds and sent them to the FBI. Sure enough, it was Howard Hughes.

I hopped another plane to Mexico and sat down with Ojeda Paullada. He told me his officers had shown up at the hotel after Hughes's departure and spotted one of his aides in the lobby. The aide acknowledged that a few men from the Hughes entourage were still upstairs. "I'd like to talk to them," the police captain said.

Hughes's aide picked up a hotel phone and called the suite. "There's a Mexican federal agent here. He wants to talk to us, so wash your hands and come on down."

"Wash your hands?" the police captain repeated the strange instructions, which he correctly identified as a warning code. "I think I'll go up and see for myself," he said. What he found was Hughes's aides shredding documents. He stopped the shredding, confiscated the documents, and delivered them to the attorney general.

"Good," I said when the attorney general told me the story. "Let's see the documents."

"I can't. You're a reporter."

"But the only reason you got them was because of me," I protested.

"Yes, but we have rules."

I thought fast. "If the United States government requested those documents, would you turn them over?

"Yes, of course."

I caught the next plane back to Washington and hurried to Bill Simon's office. He requested the documents and then copied them for me. Included in the cache were detailed logs of Hughes's every bodily function, the food he ate, the orders he issued, the visitors he turned away, and the ones he admitted. I turned quickly in the logs to the date that I knew Hughes had met Anastasio Somoza. There I found the answer to the great mystery: There was only one Howard Hughes.

On March 11, 1972, Hughes's barber Mell Stewart, who was on call twenty-four hours a day, was summoned at 11 P.M. "Mel [*sic*] in to trim hair, beard, and toenails," the log said. The transformation took four hours to complete. I found similar entries before other Hughes sightings. Apparently Hughes would grudgingly submit to grooming when he had to show his face, but for prolonged spells he refused to let the barber near him for fear of germs.

Some of the documents I saw dated back to the 1950s and revealed that Hughes had battled the demon microbes for two decades. In 1958, for example, he issued meticulous instructions about how messengers from his headquarters were supposed to approach him in his Los Angeles bungalow. They were forbidden to touch the door handle or even knock. Instead they had to stand at a window until an aide inside the room noticed them. The two men were then to face each other through the glass, with neither being so foolish as to touch the glass, while the messenger said, "Call the office."

The aide on the inside was then supposed to print the message from headquarters on a yellow tablet in letters "one half the width of the tablet in height," take the message to within a safe distance of Hughes, squat down with forehead facing the floor, extend his arms holding the paper, and wait for Hughes to read. At no time was the messenger allowed to open his mouth to utter a sentence in Hughes's presence lest some germs escape.

Hughes's four-page, single-spaced, typed memo on instructions for delivering messages included two pages about how the contents of that instructional memo itself should be delivered by phone to the two attendants most affected by it: "The man delivering the message must make absolutely certain that each of them is alone, that they have had their breakfast, that they have gone to the toilet, that they are alone in a room that is quiet and private where there is no TV on, where there are no children or other activities to distract them, that they have a pad and pencil, good lighting, a soft chair, are comfortable and are at a phone where they cannot be distracted but can give careful attention and write down each word, punctuation mark and paragraph exactly and precisely as dictated."

The two aides were supposed to take down the memo as they heard it and then repeat it back while the messenger followed on his copy: "He should request them to state, when they read it back, each period and make them state that the next word starts with a capital and be certain that he follows with his finger each punctuation mark, each period, each capital, each sentence, and each paragraph on his own memorandum so that he knows positively and without doubt that they have an absolute true and accurate record of this instruction in every minute detail."

When he was alert, Hughes spent his days and nights watching favorite old movies. There were, however, moments of lucidity that recalled the young and vital Hughes I had once met. In mid-1973, while in London, Hughes announced to his startled aides that despite his fragile health, poor eyesight, and lapsed pilot's license, he was ready to fly again. At the time, he didn't even own any street clothes.

The aides purchased an outfit to Hughes's specifications. On June 9, 1973, Hughes watched a screening of the movie *Strategic Air Command.* Thus mentally conditioned, he slept for ten hours. The next morning barber Mell Stewart arrived at 8:10 A.M. and worked until noon to make Hughes presentable. He slipped out of the hotel about 2 P.M. for an afternoon of flying with a British jet pilot. It was Hughes's last fling. Not long afterward he fell in the bathroom and broke his hip. Doctors and aides tried to persuade him to exercise and get back on his feet, but he remained in bed and consigned himself forever to the gloom of his luxury penthouses.

Hughes kept an erratic schedule, sometimes staying awake for two or three days and then sleeping for thirty hours straight. He demanded that his chair and utensils be insulated with tissues to protect him from germs. He was finicky about food, staying on the same simple diet for weeks and taking hours to complete a meager meal. The routine was punctuated by painful and often prolonged trips to the bathroom. The logs recorded Hughes's every bowel movement and marked time by his enemas. One staff memo, for instance, called Hughes's attention to a statement he had made "several enemas ago."

A large metal box contained Hughes's darkest secrets—the medications reluctantly provided by his doctors, including some unnamed and apparently illegal drugs. Those were referred to as "the items" or "bombers." One memo advised Hughes that his doctors had said it wasn't wise for the staff to be too well versed in the various drugs he was addicted to. "With doctors, it is privileged information and they cannot be forced to testify unless it is a criminal case."

Hughes constantly sought but seldom followed medical advice. Doctors repeatedly warned him about drugs; nevertheless, his last conscious act was a pathetic attempt to inject a hypodermic needle into his shriveled arm.

PART 5

GOOD OL' BOYS

1977 – 1980

WHEN RICHARD NIXON ENTERED THE WHITE HOUSE, I expected the rocky road that we traveled. When Gerald Ford took his place for two years, I expected the caretaker presidency that we got. Then Jimmy Carter breathed hope into a Watergate-weary nation. But I have never been more saddened than I was when Carter left me stuck in the muck.

I voted for Jimmy Carter and settled down contentedly for four years of boredom, at least from an investigative reporter's perspective. When the nation prospers and the president performs with honor, there is little muck to be raked. It was a dearth that I would have welcomed. I was not alone among my colleagues in the press who were eager for respite from the Watergate wars. Contrary to popular belief, we are all Americans first and muckrakers second. As much as any other citizen, we yearn for peace of mind about the ship of state. We want the president to save our money, safeguard our planet, and keep us out of war. Carter had all the makings of that kind of president.

Throughout his term, Carter believed that his heart was pure. But I saw in him an excessive need to prove that purity to himself and to others by wearing his piety on his sleeve. Typical of his born-again diplomacy was an incident that occurred during a summit meeting with Soviet leader Leonid Brezhnev. The wily Brezhnev was an atheist, but he knew how to play his Jimmy Carter card. Carter opened the meeting with a typical Sunday school sermonette about world peace. Brezhnev's response, incredibly, included a pious line about God, in whom he did not believe. My source at the meeting was standing next to a prominent Soviet official, who turned to him, smiled conspiratorially, raised his eyebrows, and whispered, "You know, the man upstairs." While the room rippled with knowing cynicism, Carter enthusiastically jotted down Brezhnev's quote as though the president had made a convert.

At times during the Carter years, I yearned for an authentic southern politician, a good ol' boy who made no pretense about stretching the truth and molding the facts. My experience in Washington had long since taught me that it is hard for an ambitious person to engage in politics and continue to tell the truth. The devout Carter had opened his presidency with a pledge that he would never lie to the American people. Then I watched as he found as many ways to spin the facts as those predecessors he had sworn not to emulate. In fairness, he was not more deceitful than the others, only more pious and less competent.

In an interview with me, Carter admitted his need for solitude, but it was more intense than a normal desire for privacy. He was an introvert in an extrovert's job, just like Richard Nixon. Both of them emotionally barricaded themselves into the Oval Office and surrounded themselves with young and inexperienced staffers who didn't ruffle the presidential feathers.

Granted, Carter had learned something from Nixon. He had watched Nixon try to mimic Camelot with lavish state dinners, gaudy White House staff uniforms, and other echoes of royalty. In a complete turnabout, Carter wore cozy sweaters, revived the "Fireside Chat," and walked home from his inaugural. Carter was even clever enough to understand that his sweet little mother Miss Lillian on her porch in Plains, Georgia, and his crackpot brother, Billy, back home running the family peanut farm, enhanced the president's image as a man of the people. What he hadn't counted on was that his offbeat relatives and friends would become more newsworthy than the president himself.

I came to understand that no two presidents were more alike than Jimmy Carter and Richard Nixon—burdened with insecurities, eager for acceptance, disdainful of critics, trusting of no one, preferring their own company to that of anyone else. Nixon had the advantage in that he knew how to run a nation, albeit without desirable scruples.

My words will sound harsh to those who have let the cleansing waves of time wash over the record of Jimmy Carter. Many remember only that he was a nice guy who tried hard but didn't succeed. He pardoned Vietnam War draft dodgers and tried to make the United States the human rights sheriff for the Third World. He brought Egyptian President Anwar Sadat and Israeli Prime Minister Menachem Begin together at Camp David to sign a peace treaty. He spouted Bob Dylan philosophy and mourned with the nation when Beatle John Lennon was murdered. He wore faded jeans and played softball.

But there the fond memories of Carter end. Inflation soared to 13 percent in 1979 because of Carter's lack of leadership on the economic front. His foreign policy was a roller-coaster ride, in part due to the radically different views of his advisors who dragged him from one strategy to another. The Soviets despised him for his sermonizing, and German leader Willy Brandt likened Carter to a "faith healer, conducting foreign policy from the pulpit." Arab oil-producing countries formed a cartel, raised their prices, and created an energy crisis that Carter tried to solve by wearing sweaters and turning down the thermostat.

Carter's Waterloo came on November 4, 1979, when four hundred Moslem militants stormed the U.S. Embassy in Tehran, Iran, and took the entire American diplomatic team hostage. The militants were followers of Ayatollah Ruhollah Khomeini who, ten months earlier, had chased the Shah of Iran out of the country and enthroned himself as head of the new radical Moslem government. For Carter's support of the Shah, Khomeini cursed the United States as the "Great Satan." The militants holding the American hostages demanded the return of the Shah, whom Carter had allowed to come to New York for medical treatment.

Carter froze like a deer caught in Khomeini's headlights. The leader of the free world made himself a hostage in the White House, mulling over various possible strategies, including a rescue attempt that was botched. It was a demoralizing time for Americans who had already seen their faith in the presidency severely tested and their prestige as a superpower eroded.

On the one-year anniversary of the hostage-taking, with our diplomats still imprisoned in Iran, Americans elected Ronald Reagan president. Minutes after Reagan's inauguration on January 20, 1981, the hostages were released. The 444-day ordeal was over for the hostages, and the four-year ordeal was over for Jimmy Carter.

CHAPTER 19

JIMMY CARTER ONCE PRIVATELY PRAISED ME as a credit to my profession. I have only one witness who can verify the remark, but she is the most truthful person I have ever known. The occasion was a White House Christmas reception to which Libby and I were invited. As we shook the hands of the first family, the president grinned broadly at Libby and in his soothing southern tones told her Jack Anderson was a conscientious reporter who "always checks his facts."

That was before I started checking certain facts about Carter himself. By the time his term in the White House ended in a washout, his brother Billy had assaulted me with barnyard epithets; his mother, the beloved Miss Lillian, had sent me hate mail; and the president himself had decided that, "Jack Anderson is the one columnist in this nation who habitually lies."

During the 1980 election when Carter's first term was in shambles, I asked one of his Cabinet members if he intended to support the president's reelection. "Of course," said the man, who for obvious reasons must remain anonymous. I reminded him of how badly Carter had botched the job thus far.

"He's a good person," the Cabinet member responded with resignation. "But he has one fault."

"What's that?"

"He can't govern."

Indeed, during the four years when Carter should have been on the bridge, he was down in the engine room tinkering with the water pump. History may record that Carter was at least a brilliant tinkerer who knew more about the water pump than most, but I suspect that was a facade. My sources told me how he carefully cultivated the aura of the man for all seasons. He would research the policy issues before him and pick a few obscure details to memorize. Then, in a press conference, he would slip his memorized minutiae into his answers, giving the impression by casual patter that he had total knowledge of his subject. In truth, he was not badly informed, but he was no better informed than the average president.

Nine months into Carter's presidency, I was granted an audience in the Oval Office for a lengthy interview for *Parade* magazine. When I told Carter that I, like him, was an occasional Sunday school teacher and held deep religious beliefs, he seemed to relax and enjoy our talk. The apparent contrast between him and Richard Nixon was remarkable and refreshing. Carter spoke at length and with affection about his Norman Rockwell–like upbringing, his marriage to his childhood sweetheart Rosalynn, his charmed military and political careers. Although I am not a fundamentalist, when he talked of being "born again," I felt that it was an authentic experience that had transformed his life.

Carter did not strike me as brilliant, but I had encountered few public figures with a more crisp or articulate manner of speech. Without awkwardness, he told me of how he prayed privately over his duties several times each day, of how he and Rosalynn read the Bible together each night and were at that time using a Spanish translation to lend variety to their study.

As a Christian, I was inclined to be comforted by the type of lifestyle this president espoused, but even an agnostic or atheist would have warmed to his sincerity, his candor, and his apparent commitment to do right by the American people. Later, I would reread his words and see in them a telltale, shallow piety that put a thin veneer over all-too-mortal weaknesses.

Out of curiosity, I took the transcript of my interview with Carter to a psychologist, Dr. Ted Saretsky, and asked him to put the president's words on the couch. Saretsky said the words were those of a "thoughtful, highly principled man." Carter "seems to view himself as a person with serious responsibilities who must teach, enlighten and motivate others if they are to attain spiritual and worldly excellence." When he falls short of his expectations, he suffers from "temporary periods of despair and disillusionment," the doctor told me.

After hearing Carter describe his expectations for those around him, Saretsky concluded, "there is a possibility that President Carter might be judgmental and quite rigid at times, be impatient and self-righteous regarding differences of opinion, and too intent on persuading and influencing others rather than listening to another point of view."

Then the doctor told me something I would come to understand more fully in the ensuing four years: "President Carter's remarkable loyalty in the face of mounting evidence and negative public opinion could reflect a tendency to deny fault in close associates whom he respects and cares for."

I saw it with Bert Lance, Carter's best friend from Georgia who ran a

A DRESSING DOWN

PRESIDENT CARTER'S MOTHER, THE IRREPRESSIBLE "Miz Lillian," once became so hot under the collar about my treatment of her boys, Jimmy and Billy, that she fired off a letter to me. Her scolding words jumped off the page like an index finger shaken at a naughty child. The occasion was a column I had written that implied Miss Lillian was furious with Billy Carter for neglecting the family peanut farm while he went gallivanting around the world.

Her handwritten note to me dated December 4, 1978, began with an apparently festering resentment about a visit to Plains the prior year by my intrepid reporter Hal Bernton. He was "dirty-ragged," according to the first mother, and was "asked to get out of town."

Hal had been working in Florida in 1977, infiltrating migrant workers' camps to expose shabby conditions. On his way back to Washington, he passed through Plains in dirty blue jeans, posing as a vagabond laborer. I had asked him to get a job at the Carter peanut warehouse and give me a worker's-eye-view of the new president.

There were no openings on the Carter farm so Hal hung around for a few days, went to church with the Carters, and even sat in the pew next to Miss Lillian. Contrary to her recollection of events, he was not asked to leave town, and reported that, in fact, the people of Plains were quite hospitable. Miss Lillian, however, would not likely be the one to invite him back.

Her letter generously conceded my right to report on the president, but she was livid with me for implying that she had criticized Billy's business acumen. "[E]ither *you* or your informant *lied*," she wrote.

Miss Lillian had her own ideas about who my source might be. She didn't name her suspect, but she said, "his word is not taken by anyone around Plains."

---

fast and loose banking business back home until Carter brought him to Washington to be the budget director. Lance did not fare so well once a special counsel got around to investigating his banking practices.

Lance's bank, the National Bank of Georgia, had a history of giving easy loans to the Carter family's peanut business—an arrangement that was finally examined by a federal grand jury and found to be legal, if not smart. I followed the stories about Lance and began to witness for myself Carter's unswerving loyalty to friends and his willingness to put that loyalty above the welfare of the nation.

The comfortably old-shoe Lance conducted his banking business in a disorganized manner. Yet Carter insisted on putting him in charge of the federal budget. I remembered an early interview with Carter during which he told me, "[Lance] was the first person that I thought about when I was finally sure that I would be elected president. I wanted him in a major and very complicated department that had profound influence on the rest of the government."

In the middle of the brouhaha over Lance, Carter did something that puzzled me. He flew to Riyadh, Saudi Arabia, met with King Khalid, and promised the king that he would pressure Congress to approve the sale of F-15 fighter jets to the Saudis. It was a transaction that was bitterly opposed by Israel and by powerful Jewish interests in the United States whom Carter should have been trying to appease.

I didn't know it then, but Bert Lance had just sold a controlling interest in his struggling bank, along with the Carter peanut farm's outstanding loans, to a Saudi businessman who turned out to be not your run-of-the-mill Arab financier. The buyer was a young man named Ghaith R. Pharaon whose father was King Khalid's adviser on American affairs. It took me and my staff until 1980, in the middle of Carter's reelection campaign, to piece together the odiferous sequence of events.

In 1977, the Carter farm was the biggest debtor to Lance's bank and was operating $410,000 in the red. On December 20, 1977, Lance's lawyer in Washington, Robert Altman, announced that Ghaith Pharaon was buying into Lance's bank. There was no explanation as to why an up-and-coming Arab businessman would reach into Georgia to acquire a down-and-out little bank.

Two weeks later, Carter had his meeting with King Khalid and promised to pitch for the sale of the F-15s. The next day, the president of the Bank of Credit and Commerce International (BCCI), Agha Hasan Abedi, who was reportedly the middleman in the negotiations between Lance and Pharaon, loaned Lance $3.5 million, solely on the basis of an oral promise to repay. The day after that, Pharaon paid Lance $2.4 million for a controlling interest in the National Bank of Georgia. The president's peanut farm was now in hock to a Saudi-owned bank.

A little more than a month later, on February 14, 1978, the Carter administration announced its decision to sell the F-15s to Saudi Arabia. Then, on May 1, the Carter peanut business got a break. The National Bank of Georgia renegotiated the Carters' outstanding $830,000 debt under more favorable repayment terms that saved the family $60,000 in the first year alone (the loans were ultimately repaid in full). The final link in the chain of events came two weeks later when the Senate, after a vigorous lobbying effort by the Carter administration, approved the sale of the jets to Saudi Arabia.

When I began to put these pieces together, I called Ghaith Pharaon. I fully expected him to be guarded and to deny that his purchase of the bank had anything to do with Saudi-U.S. relations. Fortunately he was young and more naive than I anticipated, so I worked my way gently around to the subject of his father, the American link with the Saudi king. "I guess you talked it over with your father before you made this investment," I said, as offhandedly as I could.

"Of course," Pharaon said. "He advised me to do it."

When I published the story, there was little splash, but I was not surprised. My fellow reporters were eager to see Carter succeed, and the press seemed to have set a standard with him that a smoking gun was necessary in order to indict. I didn't have that smoking gun, only a suspicious series of events that, I thought, spoke for themselves. As for Carter, he claimed there could have been no connection between the jet sale and the peanut loans because his family farm was in a blind trust during his presidency and he thus knew nothing of its operation.

Blind trust was a fine watchword for Jimmy Carter. He surrounded himself with people who were not always worthy of his trust. To the outside world, the good ol' boys from Georgia put on a show of amiable camaraderie. But I soon realized they were never the relaxed, convivial, cornpone folks they pretended to be. They were intense, coiled, hard-driving, inexperienced, insecure, and always looking for a way to aggrandize themselves.

The mix of greed and good ol' boys was never more evident than in the tangled case of Robert Vesco, the fugitive American financier hiding out in the Caribbean and Central America to avoid the long arm of the U.S. Justice Department.

Even before Jimmy Carter was elected president, Vesco saw in the Carter crowd a certain stupidity that he thought he could turn to his advantage. He didn't even have to initiate the friendship. It wasn't long before Georgians came looking for him. R. L. Herring of Albany, Georgia, a swindler in the southern style, read in the newspaper about Vesco's problems and figured that for a price he could help. Wanted in the United States for stealing millions of dollars from an investment company he had run, Vesco had fled to Costa Rica after being caught trying to buy his way out of the fix with a $200,000 contribution to the Nixon campaign in 1972. The money had been delivered in $100 bills to Nixon's chief fund-raiser Maurice Stans, and was later used to help finance the Watergate burglars.

On the day that the money was delivered by Vesco's aide, Nixon's Attorney General John Mitchell arranged a meeting between the aide and Securities and Exchange Commission Chairman Bill Casey to talk about Vesco's troubles with the SEC. There were more meetings, but Vesco never got his money's worth out of the Nixon administration. He was obliged to skip the country and eventually make Costa Rica his home.

I came to know Vesco as an accomplished manipulator who got what he wanted by suborning others to do his bidding. The Georgia wheeler-dealer

HIGH TIMES

JIMMY CARTER'S MISPLACED FAITH IN THOSE around him some-
times left him looking rather naive. He was embarrassed enough when his drug
advisor, Dr. Peter Bourne, was caught writing a narcotics prescription for a fic-
titious White House aide. But I regrettably had to embarrass the president further by revealing in my column that Bourne did something worse.

In December 1977, at a Washington party hosted by the National Organization for the Reform of Marijuana Laws, Bourne indiscreetly lit up a joint. That
would not have been so unforgivable in a day and age when many people tried
pot and most of them inhaled. But Bourne made the additional mistake of
snorting cocaine at that party, where he was observed by someone whom I knew
well and whose word I trusted. Bourne said my charges were wrong, but on the
day I broadcast the story during my regular spot on ABC's *Good Morning America,* Bourne resigned, ostensibly because of the narcotics prescription.

On his way out the door, Bourne took a parting shot at the White House
staff. He said there was a "high incidence" of pot smoking and occasional
cocaine use by members of the White House staff. And, speaking of the drug
party in December, he said, "about half the White House staff was there that
night looking, well, looking as though they belonged."

At the time, possession of cocaine or marijuana was a misdemeanor in
Washington, punishable by one year in jail. It was not a popular law, but Carter
ordered that his aides obey it or be fired. "Whether you agree with the law or
whether or not others obey the law is totally irrelevant. You will obey or you will
seek employment elsewhere," the president said. Yet my sources told me that
the casual drug use continued. With the contraband in their pockets and the
president preaching over their shoulders, the biggest fear among the young
aides at the White House was the threat of a drug scandal.

R. L. Herring was willing to be suborned for a price, so he flew to Costa Rica
and made an offer. If Vesco would make a generous campaign donation to
presidential candidate Jimmy Carter, Herring had the connections to see that
Vesco's legal problems would disappear during the Carter presidency. Herring
also suggested that the future president would be beholden to Vesco if the millionaire could help out Bert Lance and his struggling bank.

It was all a bluff. Herring was a two-bit operator with only a spitting-
distance connection to Carter. But that distance was about to get shorter.

Vesco was suspicious by nature. He declined the honor of bailing out
Lance's bank, but said that if Carter was successful in the upcoming election,
Herring should get back to him because they might be able to cut a deal. Her-

ring called back on the day after the election and two weeks later he was back in Costa Rica for the handshake. Under the terms of their deal, Herring and any other Georgians he could recruit from the Carter team would get a cut of Vesco's business empire for pleading his case with the president. Vesco also agreed to use his considerable influence with Latin American heads of state, a few of whom were in his pocket, to arrange a favorable renegotiation of the Panama Canal Treaty, which was high on Carter's list of priorities.

Herring hustled back to Albany and scanned the local power brokers for someone close to Carter. He settled on Spencer Lee IV, a boyhood chum of Carter's chief political advisor Hamilton Jordan. Herring explained the scheme to Lee and gave him a retainer of $10,000. Lee went to work quickly, arranging for a letter from Costa Rican President Daniel Oduber to Carter, with Lee as the mailman. In the letter, Oduber promised to be helpful on the Panama Canal negotiations, and added that it was important for Carter to settle the Vesco case.

In January 1977, while Carter planned his inaugural festivities, R. L. Herring and Spencer Lee flew to Costa Rica to carve out their share of the Vesco empire in trade for getting the ear of the new president. They were no match for Vesco, who sold them on an elaborate shell game of dummy corporations and undervalued stock. In the end they were supposed to get $20 million in stock in a company that was, in fact, mired in litigation and bankruptcy problems. The Georgians went home, none the richer and none the wiser.

More than a year later, when the $20 million hadn't materialized, Herring came to me. Faced with a potential blockbuster of a story, I considered his reputation and spent months double-checking everything he told me, traveling to Costa Rica to see Vesco, publishing my findings, and then, in the end, being compromised by Herring.

The Georgians' first move after cutting their deal with Vesco, I learned, was to call on someone close to the president—Charles Kirbo, Jimmy Carter's personal lawyer and perhaps his most trusted advisor. Later, when the house of cards collapsed around the Georgians, they claimed that they'd shared with the venerable and upstanding Kirbo the details of the Vesco portfolio, but that he had declined to join them in the investment. Kirbo would later claim he had no recollection of the meeting, even though the appointment appeared in his office log. Kirbo was only the first who would conveniently forget the brush with the notorious Robert Vesco.

Spencer Lee hustled off to Washington for the inaugural parties while Vesco waited at home for news. Vesco would later tell me that Lee phoned him from one of the inaugural parties, which Lee claimed was fairly crawling with important Carter people. Lee informed Vesco that Hamilton Jordan was with him. "Here's Ham," Lee said, and another voice came on the line.

Vesco acknowledged to me that for all he knew Lee could have put anybody on the phone. This "Ham" asked Vesco if he knew where Costa Rican President Oduber was staying while in Washington for the inauguration because Oduber had an appointment with Carter and "Ham" wanted to reschedule it. It was a bizarre call that left Vesco quizzical.

A few weeks later, Lee and Herring were back in Washington to press Vesco's case with the new president's men. They split up, with Herring going to the State Department to explain what Vesco could do for them on the Panama Canal negotiations and Lee setting out for the White House, ostensibly to collar Hamilton Jordan. Lee later claimed that he never got to the White House because he was waylaid by another Georgia boy, Carter aide Richard Harden.

Spencer Lee, Richard Harden, and Hamilton Jordan had grown up together. One of their friends told me they were "as close as three raccoons in a hollow log," which is apparently about as close as friends get in southern parlance. Lee claimed that as soon as he explained his arrangement with Vesco, Harden told him it wouldn't be smart to drag Hamilton Jordan into it. A week later, according to Harden, he told President Carter about the conversation. But neither of them bothered to tell the Justice Department about this apparent attempt by Lee and Herring to get Vesco off the hook. Instead, Carter inexplicably penned a personal note to Attorney General Griffin Bell, who was overseeing the Vesco investigation: "Please see Spencer Lee from Albany when he requests an appointment." Carter later claimed he didn't remember meeting with Harden or writing the note to Bell, who said he never saw the note, although investigators later found it in his files. Lee never took advantage of the note to get a meeting with the attorney general.

My research turned up so many lost memos, denied meetings, and unconfirmed phone calls that I told Herring I needed more proof before I could publish a story accusing presidential aides and friends of consorting with Robert Vesco. Given Herring's background, I kept a cautious watch over his shoulder. Herring produced written evidence that the Georgians had approached Hamilton Jordan and Charles Kirbo. He showed me his copies of letters from Spencer Lee to the two Carter confidants. The wording of those letters implied that both Kirbo and Jordan were at least aware of the deal.

My heart beat a little faster when I read the letters. "Dear Hamilton," the first began. "Regarding our conversation, it looks as if the PRL [Vesco's corporate flagship Property Resources Limited of which the Georgians had been promised a share] matter will take eight to 12 months to complete. The time frame is well within our agreement with Mr. Herring and the Costa Rican gentleman. I forgot to mention to you when we talked that the necessary arrangements have been made to protect our interests in Nas-

THE ARTFUL DODGER

OVER THE YEARS, I GOT CLOSER to the fugitive financier Robert Vesco than some of my colleagues thought was proper for a newsman, but it would have pleased the consummate advocate Drew Pearson, and it allowed me to stay on top of an important story.

The first time I met Vesco, I wanted him as a guest on my TV show *Truth*. The format involved putting controversial characters on a polygraph machine and letting the world see the uncensored results on the test. Vesco agreed, but only if I would play messenger for him. He wanted me to deliver an offer to Stanley Sporkin, enforcement chief for the Securities and Exchange Commission, which was after him. Vesco wanted immunity from prosecution on his stock-fraud cases in trade for telling all about his attempts to buy the favor of the Carter administration. I passed the offer on to Sporkin, who, as I expected, turned it down flat.

Two years later, in 1980, I played intermediary between Vesco and my friend Utah Senator Orrin Hatch. The Senate Judiciary Committee was investigating Vesco and I thought a face-to-face meeting between the fugitive and the senator would make for some interesting news. Hatch and I traveled to Nassau with Hatch's investigator Thomas Parry and we spent several hours questioning Vesco. He was the usual artful dodger, as I had warned Hatch he would be, but at my suggestion Vesco took a lie detector test in front of Hatch and passed with flying colors.

Later the *Washington Post* made much ado of the scene in Nassau—Hatch and I, both Mormons, sitting at poolside with the notorious international fugitive, sipping piña coladas minus the rum. The *Post* accused me of playing "matchmaker" between Hatch and Vesco, and "midwife" for the struggling Senate investigation. I presume I was supposed to be insulted by the reference, but I saw no ethical breach in arranging the meeting or sitting in as a witness to it.

sau." The Georgians had set up a corporation in Nassau to launder the proceeds from the stock sale.

The letter from Lee to Kirbo began, "Dear Charlie: Enclosed is a copy of how the Costa Rica gentleman wishes to have his matter resolved. I had a long talk with him and I feel that the plan we discussed will be successful and fruitful. It is very hard for me to contact Hamilton because of his busy schedule, but he told me last week that he would condone any decision that I had made along the lines that we had previously discussed. I will proceed as planned and see you in a few days."

Predictably, when I questioned them, Lee denied ever writing the letters and both Kirbo and Jordan denied ever receiving them. At this point I needed the word of someone who had no stake in the deal. I found that person in Gerolyn Hobbs, the secretary who had worked for Herring when he was scheming with Vesco. She had quit and moved to the Northeast. I sent Les Whitten to find her and he tracked her down. She struck Les as a shy, guileless housewife who was innocently oblivious to the ramifications of the negotiations she had witnessed. Les spent three days with her, going over the letters word by word. He also spoke to her friends and neighbors, who vouched for her integrity. I told Les to get her account in writing, and Hobbs willingly signed an affidavit swearing that she had typed and mailed the letters. The one to Kirbo included a list of terms Vesco had dictated to Hobbs over the phone. She also recalled placing calls to Hamilton Jordan at the White House and answering calls from him at Herring's office. Les was convinced Hobbs was telling the truth.

I made a final call to Attorney General Griffin Bell and double-checked something Vesco had confided—that the Justice Department had dropped its efforts to extradite Vesco from Costa Rica. Bell insisted the decision was made because all available means of bringing Vesco back had been exhausted. There had not been any pressure from the White House to leave Vesco alone, Bell said. Significantly, Vesco had told me earlier that he had demanded an end to the extradition hassle before he would deal with the Carter cronies.

Knowing the risks, I wrote my first column on Vesco's attempted fix and sent it to my publisher, United Feature Syndicate, with a publication date of Monday, September 11, 1978. Before it saw the light of day, Carter and his cronies went to work. I was at church Sunday morning when Les answered the phone at the office. It was the former Democratic Party Chairman Robert Strauss, who had a new calling as Carter's troubleshooter. He said Hamilton Jordan had gotten his hands on an advance copy of the column, I don't know how, and had hustled back to Washington from Camp David. Strauss said Jordan was closeted with legendary Washington superlawyer Edward Bennett Williams deciding what to do. The mention of Williams was Strauss's way of saying that if we didn't retract, there was a lawsuit in the offing.

Les told Strauss that I was in church and couldn't be reached. "Well," Strauss responded, "his soul might belong to the church but his ass is going to belong to Ham Jordan."

Les responded gamely that "Hamilton Jordan's ass might belong to the people."

Several derrieres were offered up that Sunday. Vesco said Edward Bennett Williams called him in Costa Rica and caught him at the swimming pool. Williams told Vesco that he had Jordan and Strauss beside him and that from the tone of my upcoming column, it was obvious Vesco had been talking to me. Then, Vesco claimed, Williams told him that his case had been discussed the previous Saturday by Williams, Jordan, Strauss, and Griffin Bell, and they had decided that they would take care of Vesco's problems. According to Vesco's version of the phone call, Williams then advised him to stop talking to Jack Anderson. "Kiss my ass," Vesco responded, and hung up.

By the time I got home from church that Sunday, the denial machine was already in motion at the White House. I had expected that, but what I hadn't expected was the call from Terrence Adamson at the Justice Department. He also had seen my column in advance. (United Feature Syndicate had no idea so many nonpaying customers were mysteriously privy to my words before they were published.) Adamson said the reference in the column to Griffin Bell, and the fact that the extradition efforts against Vesco had been dropped, were not completely true. The attorney general himself had twice given me incomplete information when I asked him if he was still trying to arrest Vesco. Adamson claimed the extradition from Costa Rica had been abandoned, but that it had been replaced by another tactic, to try to lure Vesco out of Costa Rica so he could be arrested in some other country since Costa Rica had refused to give him up. I don't know why Bell had failed to tell me that. I immediately called the syndicate with a correction, but it was late Sunday afternoon and there was little hope that the word could be distributed to the hundreds of newspapers that were already sending the column into print for Monday morning editions.

Before the day was out I had one more phone call, this one from Carter's press secretary Jody Powell, as amiable a wool merchant as ever peddled stories out of the West Wing of the White House. "You have a story coming out Monday," he said. "We're going to deny it."

"That's your privilege."

"We would like you to withdraw the column," he added, throwing in an appeal to my patriotism.

"I can't do that."

"In that case," Powell went on, "I'm going to call a few reporters over and brief them on this."

"All right," I said. "Why don't we do this together. You present your side and I'll present my side. Maybe you can convince me." Powell turned down my offer and then refused to let me attend his gathering as a member of the press corps. I don't normally bother with press conferences, but for that one I would have made an exception. I learned from the next day's press coverage that Powell had trotted out Hamilton Jordan as the lamb who had been shorn of his good name.

In the days that followed, I published more columns, which got a rise out of the Securities and Exchange Commission. They didn't seem concerned that someone might have tried to fix the Vesco case with the White House. They were more annoyed that Vesco had sold stock to the Georgia fixers in violation of an order that froze his assets while he was under indictment. So a federal judge began summoning the characters in my story.

On the night before the secretary Gerolyn Hobbs was to testify, Les got a call from her. She sobbed into the phone. "It was all a mistake. It was all a mistake." Les tried to calm her down, and then asked her if she was recanting her story. "It was all a mistake," she repeated. The next day in court, under oath, she tearfully stuck to her story, that she had typed and mailed the embarrassing letters to Hamilton Jordan and Charles Kirbo. She remembered distinctly, she said. "I was impressed by the names. They were important people." Yet Jordan and Kirbo had publicly denied receiving the letters.

After that, I couldn't shake the feeling that there was something wrong with the letters. Herring was in jail by then, awaiting trial on a fraud charge unrelated to the Vesco deal. I had testified at his bond hearing, hoping to get him bailed out into my charge so I could pump him for more information, but I had been unsuccessful. So I was communicating with him by phone calls and letters, which made it difficult to judge the truth of what he was telling me.

Finally, I got a call in late September from an old friend, private investigator Dick Bast, who was working for Herring's attorney. Herring's wife, Cindy, had confessed something to Bast and asked him to relay the confession to me. The copies of the two letters that she and R. L. Herring had given me were reconstructions, she said. She had typed them herself while Herring dictated them from memory because he had lost his copies of the real letters when his luggage was lost on an airline flight. I had pressed so hard for proof, she said, that the two of them had decided to trump up new letters rather than tell me that they had lost their copies of the originals.

Her confession was devastating. I had to decide within minutes whether this new version of events was true, or whether Herring had been lying all along and there never were any letters. If I didn't announce the new information myself the next day, Jody Powell was sure to get word and beat me to it. In the end, it was a gut feeling about the veracity of Gerolyn Hobbs and her testimony under oath that convinced me that the original letters had existed at one time. Whether they were ever received or taken seriously I did not know. But I had evidence that Vesco was trying to make inroads into the Carter White House. As far as I was concerned, the story was not dead.

When it became obvious to the Carter people that I wasn't going to back away from the story, and when the FBI began looking into my findings, Charles Kirbo began his own investigation. He called Cindy Herring, R. L.'s wife, and asked if he could pay her a visit. He chartered a plane to Albany for the meeting. Cindy prepared in her own way for the session by having private detective Dick Bast outfit her with a hidden tape recorder. Bast had worked closely with me on the Vesco story, so I was guaranteed access to the tapes. The conversation began with Kirbo trying to reassure Mrs. Herring that he was "just an ordinary south Georgia cracker" who felt sorry for the pickle she was in. When they talked about the testimony that she would need to give federal investigators, Kirbo stepped over the line. "I think it's a mistake to be too open with the FBI. . . ." he advised her. It was a dangerous attempt by the president's own lawyer to meddle with a federal investigation by telling a witness to be less than candid. I printed the remarks in my column, and Kirbo denied making them, until he learned that Cindy Herring had been wired for their conversation. Then he changed his story to say that there had been nothing improper in his advice to her.

INTO THIS NEST OF WEASEL WORDS AND outright lies stepped a man who restored my faith in the system. He was Ralph E. Ulmer, the ordinary American picked to be the foreman of the federal grand jury assigned to investigate my allegations. I had little hope of getting much justice out of the grand jury. Prosecutors work for the president and the confidentiality of the system is ideal for a president who wants to keep embarrassing secrets hidden. But nobody bothered to tell Ulmer that he was supposed to roll over.

When the grand jury began its investigation, I quietly checked on the foreman. He was deeply concerned about the integrity of his grand jury. He kept meticulous notes and often stayed up past midnight reviewing those notes. He was getting fed up with the holes in the prosecutors' case and beginning to smell a whitewash. I decided to help him out by filling in a few of those holes. My lawyer Warren Woods sent a letter to grand jury prosecutor Thomas Henderson offering my services as a witness. Henderson had no choice but to accept. I am usually on the wrong side of the closed doors, but on December 15, 1978, I took the stand behind those doors and told the grand jury what I knew.

By the look of surprise on their faces, and by the furious manner in which they were taking notes, I gathered that the grand jury had not heard from the prosecutors most of what I was telling them. I talked for two hours, and when I finished, the silence was broken by a spontaneous round of applause from the jurors. Appalled, the prosecutor raised his hands in a frantic effort to silence them. Then he hustled me out the door with an explanation that he had been planning to introduce the points I had raised, all in due time.

By testifying in person and leaving myself open to questions from the jurors, I one-upped Jimmy Carter, who invoked the dignity of his office to avoid testifying in person. Instead, he gave a taped deposition in which the prosecutor lobbed some softball questions.

Several months into the tepid investigation, Ulmer had had enough. In a letter to the presiding judge, he tendered his resignation as "a protest against the President's reluctance to take the steps called for by the involvement of his own aides." Ulmer charged the administration with "duplicity," foot-dragging, and "harassment." "The cover-up activities are being orchestrated within the Department of Justice under the concept that the Administration must be protected at all costs."

The judge refused to accept Ulmer's resignation, so he stayed on. But the experience became only more frustrating as the case dragged into its second year. Ulmer complained that prosecutors often refused to get information the jurors asked for, telling the jurors instead to get it themselves. Ulmer had to fight prosecutors for the right to hear the incriminating tape of Kirbo telling Cindy Herring "not to be too open with the FBI." Ulmer even began to suspect that the prosecution was trying to sabotage the jury by giving them conflicting times for their meetings so they would not have a quorum. Finally it became clear to Ulmer that the prosecution had no intention of indicting anyone, no matter what the jurors wanted.

In the end, when the prosecution handed the jurors a "bill of ignoramus"—a decision not to indict—Ulmer was so distrustful of the federal prosecutors that he marked a big red "X" across a blank part of the paperwork before signing it. He feared someone would go back later and fill in the blank.

When Ulmer was off the hook as a grand juror and free to talk about the experience, he and I shared our frustration at the outcome of the case. Had that sort of rebellion happened behind the closed doors of the Watergate grand jury, it would have made front-page headlines. But the media gave Carter a pass. He may not have seen it that way. In fact I'm sure he felt badly persecuted. The press had vilified his banker Bert Lance, and his lawyer Charles Kirbo, and his political advisor Hamilton Jordan, and had insulted a host of old Georgia boys. Next would be his brother Billy.

GOOD COP—BAD COP

THE WHITE KNIGHT OF THE CARTER administration was Interior Secretary Cecil Andrus, an amiable sort of man with a disarming frankness that made him a favorite of the media. His confirmation process was smooth sailing and there seemed to be little to fault in him. Then my office took a call from a TV reporter in Salt Lake City who had run into a dead end when tracking down a decade-old rumor about Andrus. The rumor was that while running for governor of Idaho in 1970, Andrus had accepted a hefty campaign contribution from a Mafia-connected sports cartel called Emprise.

I had a new reporter on my staff, Dale Van Atta, who would one day become my partner. He was eager to nail down the Andrus story, so I sent him to Idaho where he spent several weeks crisscrossing the state. He confirmed that Andrus had indeed been investigated in the 1970s for a possible improper campaign contribution. The allegations were never substantiated and no charges resulted. But the bigger news was that a report about the investigation was not included in the investigative file that the White House presented to the Senate for Andrus's confirmation hearing as Interior secretary.

Dale and I made an appointment to confront Andrus with questions about the omitted file before we published anything. I had honed the good-cop/bad-cop interview technique with Les Whitten, but had failed to coach Dale on the finer points of being the bad cop. On the way to Andrus's office I quickly told him to take an aggressive stance and said I would come across as the nice guy.

We were ushered into Andrus's magnificent office filled with Western memorabilia and dominated by a huge fireplace where a cozy fire burned. Dale began interrogating Andrus, while I gently interrupted occasionally to soften the tone of the questioning and chide Dale for his bulldog style. Dale began shooting me confused looks. His questions trailed off and we left with Andrus's denials ringing in our ears. Outside the office, Dale told me that my criticism inside had gotten him thinking that maybe he didn't have a strong story after all. I had played the role of good cop so well that I had talked Dale out of his story. Immediately, I talked him back into it. He did more research to counter Andrus's denials of connections to the cartel and we ran three columns in February 1980.

Andrus was livid. He was on the phone to me demanding a retraction when Dale wandered into my office. Andrus was threatening to put the FBI on the case just to prove his innocence. Having little faith that the FBI would vigorously investigate Andrus at peril of offending the president, I took a gamble. The statute of limitations had run out on any possible offense Andrus may have committed, I said to the simmering Interior secretary. I would accept the conclusions of the FBI if he would, I said. That meant waiving the statute of limitations and taking his punishment like a man if the FBI investigation found him guilty of impropriety. He was silent.

I hung up the phone and turned to Dale. "Where did you get that statute of limitations stuff?" Dale asked.

"I don't know. It just sounded good," I replied. Andrus never bothered to call the FBI, and we never heard from him again.

CHAPTER 20

WHEN I FIRST HEARD OF BILLY Carter's dalliance with Libyan leader Mu'ammar Gadhafi in 1978, I detected the fingerprints of fugitive financier Robert Vesco all over it. Vesco had once explained to me how he manipulated people. He would give them a Cadillac but keep the keys, he boasted. That's how he had dealt with the Georgia boys who had tried to pull strings for him inside the Carter administration. He promised them fabulous wealth through a convoluted stock sale that hinged on his final approval.

When Mu'ammar Gadhafi gave Billy Carter a Cadillac without the keys, it dawned on me that someone had taught Gadhafi the Vesco method. I assumed rightly, as Vesco later admitted to me, that he was advising Gadhafi on how to win friends and influence people in the Carter administration.

Lubricated by beer, shamed by his failure at managing the family business, and jealous of his big brother's fame, Billy Carter was ripe for the picking. There was a time when Billy had been a perverse asset to his brother. During the 1976 campaign, he had provided the contrast Jimmy Carter needed to prove that he had risen above his rural southern roots. There was Billy, sitting in a tattered armchair in his ramshackle gas station swilling beer and telling "nigger" jokes. And there was Jimmy, the governor of Georgia, the soft-spoken, humanitarian, distinguished veteran of the nuclear navy.

They were as different as brothers tend to be, but they were still brothers, and that was enough for Gadhafi whose own culture taught him that family is the only tie that truly binds. Gadhafi figured if he could suborn the vulnerable Billy, he could get what he wanted from Jimmy. What he wanted was for Carter to lift the freeze on eight C-130 airplanes that Libya had paid for but the U.S. government had impounded because of Gadhafi's support of terrorists.

NIXON JR.

MU'AMMAR GADHAFI'S COURTSHIP OF THE PRESIDENT'S bro-
ther was one of the lessons that Gadhafi learned at the knee of Robert Vesco.
Soon after he went into hiding, Vesco tried to exploit family ties as the weak
link in the Nixon administration. This time the kinsman was Donald A. Nixon Jr.,
the son of the president's brother Donald. In 1971, Donald Jr. was living in a
hippie commune in the California mountains. His mere presence there was an
embarrassment to the president, who frequently vilified the pot-smoking, draft-
dodging, bra-burning hippie movement.

I found out that President Nixon had put his trusted aide John Ehrlichman to
work on the problem. Ehrlichman dispatched Anthony Ulasewicz, a private detective on the White House payroll, to find young Don and talk some sense into him.
The burly private eye persuaded Don to cut his hair and come home, where Ehrlichman gave him a two-hour lecture on the virtues of clean living and work.

Don found work, all right. He turned up as an aide to Robert Vesco, who
was on the lam. Don was given an office in Geneva, but the work didn't suit his
free spirit. I saw a letter he wrote to an old neighbor in California, John Meier,
who was also no stranger to the sibling game. Meier was a former aide to
Howard Hughes when young Don's father, the president's brother, was consorting with the billionaire, much to the president's consternation.

Don Jr. wrote to Meier, complaining that he didn't get along with Vesco. "I
got myself into this by letting my parents and the great god in the White House
pull the wool over my eyelids," he wrote. "I'll know where I fit in this organization
in the next couple of weeks, that is, if I don't happen to kill Vesco first. . . ."

My sources told me that Vesco was anxious to avoid embarrassing the
president through his nephew. After all, the connection was supposed to ingra-
tiate Vesco with the administration. He issued instructions that young Don
wasn't to get preferential treatment and was to steer clear of the Vesco subsidiaries that were being investigated by the Securities and Exchange Commission. The president's nephew was supposed to be just another worker bee in
the vast Vesco empire.

But the temptation to get close to the president through his kin was too
much and soon Don was reassigned to the Bahamas as a personal aide to
Vesco himself. The connection never paid off for him because Nixon was
drummed out of office by Watergate. During the Ford administration, Vesco
complained that he had been promised a pardon, but that it was denied because
of the furor over Ford's pardon of Richard Nixon. By the time Carter entered
office, Vesco had soured on relatives and decided to focus on friends, leaving
it to Mu'ammar Gadhafi to get what he could out of the president's kin.

Nixon's nephew stayed close to Vesco, and both of them were arrested in

Cuba on May 31, 1995. Vesco was by then wanted on drug-smuggling charges that connected him with Colombia's Medellin cocaine cartel. Don Jr. claimed he had just happened to be in the wrong place at the wrong time. He said he was using Vesco's Cuban connections and Vesco's house to produce a drug called trioxidal. He had gone to Cuba to do clinical trials there because he couldn't get any attention from U.S. drug companies. He claims the drug helped his wife beat cancer.

Nixon was released and allowed to go home to the United States. Vesco was later convicted in Cuba of "economic crimes against the state," and was imprisoned in 1996.

The word went out to Billy that he would be welcomed as a distinguished visitor in Libya. That invitation traveled a circuitous route. An Atlanta realtor, Mario Leanza, while on a trip to his ancestral homeland of Sicily, met Michele Papa, the president of the Sicilian-Arab association. Papa told Leanza that there would be a substantial finder's fee if he could bring Billy Carter to Libya. Back home, Leanza arranged to have himself introduced to Billy by mutual acquaintances, and then showed up for the scheduled meeting at Billy's gas station with the Libyan ambassador to Italy in tow. Never one to pass up a freebie, Billy accepted the ambassador's invitation to Libya and made the trip in September 1978 accompanied by some local Georgia politicians. The only restriction the Libyans had placed on the party was that Billy not invite any Jews.

I learned from the classified cable traffic between U.S. diplomats in Libya and the State Department that his visit caused a minor panic. William Eagleton, the U.S. chargé d'affaires in Libya, cabled Washington: "Head of foreign liaison bureau of General People's Congress, Ahmed Shahati, told me this morning that a delegation from Georgia would be visiting Libya Sept. 27–Oct.1. He said it would be composed of 'the brother of President Carter who runs the gas station' and two senators (presumably state senators). He suggested that the embassy join in welcoming them at the airport. . . . Please provide us any additional information re this event."

The State Department cabled back, reflecting the confusion in the administration: "Despite inquiries, department unable to identify other people traveling with Billy Carter or purpose of their visit to Libya. Chargé requested to take opportunity of invitation to alert them to sensitive nature of U.S.-Libyan relations and to acquaint them with U.S. positions on issues affecting bilateral relations."

Eagleton met Billy's plane in Tripoli as he would have met any well-known American visiting at that time. An Iranian cleric, Iman Musa Al-Sadr, had recently vanished in Libya, and Gadhafi was thought to be capable of making any foreigner disappear if it suited his whimsical purposes. The American diplomats wanted Gadhafi to realize that they knew Billy Carter was in town and they were keeping an eye on him.

Billy's host, Gadhafi himself, was not in town. He was in Syria for an Arab summit and had left it to functionaries to show Billy a good time. After a briefing by the U.S. embassy staff on the volatility of U.S.-Libyan relations, Billy promised to be a good boy, and, in public at least, he kept that promise, carefully avoiding comment on foreign policy issues. His exemplary public conduct possibly could be attributed to the Moslem ban on alcohol which likely kept him sober for the duration of the visit.

Although nothing happened in public to embarrass President Carter, I suspected that the little matter of the aborted C-130s sale had slipped into the private dialogue between Billy and his hosts. Intelligence sources later confirmed for me that the topic had indeed come up. Billy and his entourage were told, without elaboration, that if the planes were released, the Georgia economy would improve. The Libyans also hinted that there would be a commission in it for the person who secured the delivery of the planes.

It wasn't long before Billy had the opportunity to return Libya's hospitality. In January 1979, a Libyan delegation came to Georgia to begin a five-week tour of the United States with Billy pointing out the sights. As tour guides go, he was unconventional and uninhibited. While waiting on the tarmac for their plane to arrive, for example, he unzipped his fly and urinated on the ground.

"The Libyans are the best friends I got in the world right now," he proclaimed during the visit. When he was called upon to wax political, Billy said, "There's a hell of a lot more Arabians than there is Jews." After the delegation departed, Billy checked himself into an alcohol rehabilitation center for a month while the Justice Department pursued an investigation of his ties to the Libyans, specifically his failure to register as a foreign agent.

GADHAFI MUST HAVE BEEN FEELING SOCIAL during that period because shortly after Billy returned from his trip to Libya, a Libyan government official showed up in my office with an invitation for me. I was to be luckier than Billy, however, because I was to get an audience with Gadhafi himself. I had written an article for *Parade* magazine naming the most reckless leaders in the world and Gadhafi's name topped the list. He wanted the chance to correct my misimpression, so he sent an emissary. I've always felt it was my obligation to hear all sides of a story, though in the case of a radical ruler like Gadhafi, I had my doubts that the same rules of equal time should apply.

"Come to Libya and see for yourself," the diplomat said. "We'll pay your expenses." The Libyans had given Billy Carter $50,000 for his "expenses," so I knew they would be generous with the per diem. I declined the all-expenses-paid trip, saying I would take care of my own bills. I did not mention to Gadhafi's man that I was more interested in following the Billy Carter story than I was in getting to know Mu'ammar Gadhafi on one of his good days.

The State Department advised me not to go, but I understood that the code of the desert required Gadhafi to protect his invited guests. When I arrived in Libya in March 1979, I was greeted at the airport by two clutches of people—representatives from Libya's foreign ministry and a delegation from the U.S. Embassy. The latter had been alerted by the State Department that I was coming, contrary to their counsel. Once again, they weren't taking any chances on losing American visitors following the disappearance of the Moslem cleric who had been critical of Gadhafi. They were aware that my columns dealing with Gadhafi had been less than flattering. "We wanted them to see us here welcoming you," the Americans told me. "We will be here to see you off."

I accepted an invitation to have dinner later with the American chargé d'affaires, Eagleton, and let the Libyans escort me to the hotel they had reserved. It was a dive and they apologized. Apparently all the better hotels were full of important Arabs in Tripoli for a summit.

That night at dinner, I pumped Eagleton for information on Billy Carter's visit. As we were about to part I told him, "I'd like to wander around Tripoli. Is it safe?"

"No one will bother you," he assured me. Libya's draconian laws dictated swift punishment for anyone who crossed Gadhafi. I relaxed in the dubious security of knowing that if anyone was going to harm me, it would have to be a hit man sent by my host.

The next day, Gadhafi's car came for me and drove me to the presidential residence—an almost palatial building, not huge but elegant. But, to my surprise, the car came within about one hundred yards of the place and then veered left onto a dirt field, at the center of which was a sheik's tent of multiple peaks and valleys. I got out of the car and followed my escort into the tent. All sides were festooned with rugs of spectacularly vivid design. The ground was covered with rich carpets, and bright-colored cushions were strewn around the circumference. In the center stood a spindly folding card table and four director's-style canvas chairs.

The escort exited and Mu'ammar Gadhafi entered. He motioned for me to sit in one chair as he settled in. An interpreter planted himself in one of the remaining chairs and cleared his throat. But he never got to do any interpreting.

"Is this here all the time?" I gestured around the garish tent, hoping to appear appreciative of the surroundings.

"Yes, it's here all the time. I think better here, yes. It helps me to think better than when I am surrounded by walls. I see the sky directly."

Even as Gadhafi painted himself as a man of the desert, I felt sure that somewhere in the palace was a plush office with a great wooden desk and an overstuffed chair where he did his real thinking.

Gadhafi spoke to me in clear English but kept the interpreter by his side—a man whose only function was to interrupt and argue when Gadhafi said something the interpreter didn't agree with. I marveled at this little touch of personal freedom in the kingdom of a despot.

He seemed young to have ruled for ten years. In his face I saw an arresting dichotomy. In relaxation, it was strikingly handsome. In agitation, it was a study in latent ferocity, with a magnificent Bedouin scowl that caused my thoughts to stray to the missing Iman Musa Al-Sadr. Gadhafi's face seemed to be divided against itself, the lower half disarming, almost lost in thought, with a wisp of a smile playing across his lips; the upper half fierce, with a trace of distrust in the eyes. Charles Dickens described the same eyes on the horseback messenger who opens A Tale of Two Cities: "He had eyes ... being of surface black, with no depth in the colour or form, and much too near together—as if they were afraid of being found out in something, singly, if they kept too far apart."

He talked, grandly I thought, about lifting the downtrodden, the laughed-at, the pushed-around. He waxed philosophical about the structure of his government. Caught up in his undeniable charisma, I didn't realize until I got back to the hotel and read my notes that very little of what he had said made sense. In the black and white transcript, it was the same self-indulgent blather that all potentates use to justify their excesses.

I tried twice to steer the discussion to Billy Carter. The first time Gadhafi acted as if he had not heard the name. The second time, he said, "We think that through this exchange visit that the American people understood us better and when we found that the American people is not hostile. It is amicable to the struggling peoples."

When I turned directly to the subject of the C-130s, Gadhafi became animated. "The U.S. is behaving as a thief," he scowled. "They didn't give us planes, they didn't give us even our money back." I commiserated with him, hoping to give him the impression that he had found a soul mate in whom he could confide. But it didn't work.

As I stood to leave, I thanked him and said, "I hope you come to Washington and when you do I hope you will remember me and let me give you some tea or coffee." He chuckled, remembering that I had declined his offer of both because my church proscribes them for members. I left without any expectation that I would ever host Mu'ammar Gadhafi across my coffee table.

Although Gadhafi had little to say to me about Billy Carter, it is safe to speculate that Billy was still very much on his mind. After drying out, Billy went to Rome and met with the Libyan foreign minister, who promised to "loan" him $500,000 against a business deal. Carter was to be given an allotment of 100,000 barrels of Libyan oil a day and he was to find an American oil company to buy it. His commission as the middleman could have added up to more than $20 million dollars a year. Billy eventually got $220,000 in installments on his "loan" from Libya, even though he never brokered a drop of oil.

The president had other pressing problems. On November 4, 1979, an Iranian mob, retaliating against the United States for offering sanctuary to the ousted Shah of Iran, stormed the U.S. Embassy in Tehran and took the entire staff hostage in a siege that would last fourteen months. Although Carter remained in office those fourteen months, his presidency, for all practical purposes, ended that day.

My reporter Dale Van Atta got his hands on a confidential memo that had been written by Bruce Laingen, the U.S. chargé d'affaires in Tehran, who became a hostage. Laingen had warned his bosses at the State Department that sanctuary for the Shah could touch off an attack against the embassy, but Washington wasn't listening. In a thousand-word analysis of the Iranian psyche, Laingen correctly predicted the subsequent events and warned that it was impossible to negotiate with the Iranians. Now Laingen was suffering from Washington's stupidity.

Two weeks into the standoff, Carter was desperate to make contact in any way with Iran's religious despot, the Ayatollah Khomeini. While in seclusion at Camp David, Carter called his National Security Advisor Zbigniew Brzezinski to pass along a suggestion from the first lady. Perhaps Billy could persuade Gadhafi to reason with Khomeini. The first lady wanted the first brother, a gas-station owner and failed peanut farmer, to persuade one lunatic head of state to beg another lunatic head of state to spare the lives of American career diplomats. I wasn't impressed by Carter's handling of foreign policy.

Brzezinski didn't have much hope that Mu'ammar Gadhafi could influence the Ayatollah. After all, the missing Iman, who had vanished in Libya, was a devotee of the Ayatollah, so Libyan-Iranian relations were not exactly cozy. Still, Brzezinski feared that the erratic Gadhafi might throw his support behind the Ayatollah in the hostage matter, just to be a stinker. The United States wanted the Iranians to be isolated, so it was important that Gadhafi not back Iran. When duty called, Billy delivered. He introduced Brzezinski to Ali el-Houdari, the equivalent of a Libyan ambassador to the United States.

Brzezinski and el-Houdari had a friendly meeting, followed quickly by a message from Gadhafi hinting that he would cooperate in the hostage negotiations. Then, four days later, Libyans attacked the U.S. embassy in Tripoli and set it on fire. President Carter summoned el-Houdari to the Oval Office for a ticklish conversation. He thanked the Libyans for their offer to help with the hostage crisis and then dressed down el-Houdari for the sacking of the embassy. Things were not going well for anyone except Billy, who collected a check for $20,000 from Houdari as the first install-ment of his $500,000 loan.

Incredibly, though our embassy in Iran had been sacked and the Amer-ican personnel taken hostage, the phone was still working and the Iranian militants were using it to tantalize the State Department with negotiations that went nowhere. That phone link between the captors and the United States became the symbol of all that was wrong at both ends of the line. Anonymous Iranian militants and faceless American bureaucrats, neither of whom had the power to change the situation, had daily, dreary discussions. Hardened intransigence was met with methodical pettifogging.

A CIA source gave me the phone number, so I dialed it. The disem-bodied voice on the other end of the line belonged to one of the captors who knew who I was. He told me the hostages would not be released until the Shah was returned to face justice in Iran.

But the Shah was no longer in American hands. He was in Panama, I said. It didn't matter. The militants wanted the Shah back and were con-vinced the United States had the power to deliver him. What if we didn't?

"I think he will come back," the voice said. It was irrational and typically Persian.

I asked to speak to one of the hostages. "No, you cannot speak with them." Still I argued. "You cannot speak with the hostages," he insisted. "It's not possible."

Finally I asked who was in charge. Was it the Ayatollah Khomeini?

"Ayatollah Khomeini gives orders to all people of Iran, not especially to us," he responded, cryptically.

"You will do, then, what the Ayatollah requests?" I said.

"Yeah," he responded, thus offering the biggest revelation of the con-versation.

SEX AND LIES

THE CASE OF A CONGRESSMAN WHO made sexual advances to teen-age boys presented my staff with a dilemma: Should we expose a basically nice guy for what may have been a one-time lapse? The answer turned out to be "yes" because of what we judged to be the seriousness of the lapse.

The congressman was a champion of decent causes and a nice guy. I'll call him Rep. X here, assuming time has healed his wounds. Les Whitten had prime contacts in the Washington, D.C., police department and they tipped him off to disturbing news about Rep. X—that he had courted a sixteen-year-old boy with such vehemence that the boy had run to the police. In a subsequent sting operation, the boy introduced Rep. X to an undercover police officer who looked young enough to pass for a teen. Rep. X began wooing the officer with promises of an apartment, a car, and up to $100 for weekly assignations.

The police source who told Les about the story didn't think it should be buried just because Rep. X had connections, but the cop was also skittish about handing over the proof to a reporter. "Don't worry," Les said, already hatching a plot for the handoff. Les instructed the cop to stand in front of a particular government office building and wait for a specified car to drive up. "There will be an old lady in the car," Les said. "Just hand her the material."

Then Les called his eighty-year-old mother. "How would you like to go to a movie tonight?" After the movie Les made his pitch. "Mom, the First Amendment is at stake." By the time Les had finished explaining the story and the heroic role he needed his mother to play, she was brimming with excitement over the mission. Mother and son drove to the rendezvous point and the cop sidled up to the passenger window for the handoff. Any hope that he might have had of making a quick drop was dashed when Mrs. Whitten grabbed his hand, shook it vigorously, and refused to let go while she gushed about Les's nobility and the cop's courage. He finally broke out of her grasp and Les drove away with the dynamite file.

A scrupulously honest reporter, Les now could tell Rep. X, if asked, that he hadn't gotten the file from the police. I don't know if he would have gone so far as to say he had gotten it from his mother. Fortunately, he didn't have to decide. When Les confronted Rep. X, the congressman was too busy clutching at the last vestiges of his brilliant political career to worry about where we had gotten the tip.

Les brought along another of my reporters, Jack "Mitch" Mitchell, to play bad cop to Les's good cop in the encounter with Rep. X. His face aged thirty years in ten seconds when Les spread out the documents on the desk. "You can't do this to me," he sputtered. "I'm going to be the next senator from [my state]."

"Forget the Senate. If you throw yourself on the mercy of the court you may be able to save your House seat," Mitch snarled. Les tried to look sympathetic. "We'll put in the story that you're getting psychological counseling for this problem," Les said.

"I've got to call my lawyer," replied the miserable Rep. X.

"Congressman," said Les. "Do you really want me to print that the first thing you said after we laid out all this evidence was 'I've got to call my lawyer?' "

Rep. X jumped up and trotted down the hall, with Mitch and Les running behind him, to the room where the House news teletype machines were clattering loudly. Under cover of the noise, thinking Les might be secretly taping the conversation, Rep. X whined. "At least five percent of Congress is like this," he said, implying that the Congress was infested with sexual deviants. "I'll name the rest of them if you keep me out of this."

A congresswoman passed by out of earshot. "Why don't you write about her?" he said, describing in explicit language her sexual relationships with other women. Then Rep. X named another member of Congress. "He's fooling around with the pages."

Finally, Mitch said to Les, "I think we ought to give this guy a break. Let him talk to his lawyer." Les agreed and they came back to my office to report what had happened. When Rep. X later calmed down, he fell on his sword—admitting the attempted liaison with the cop, but claiming that it was a one-time occurrence caused by the pressure of his job.

The resulting column was as gentle as I thought it should be under the circumstances. Rep. X tried an end run by releasing a statement before we could get into print, but Les leaked our story to the wire services so we could beat Rep. X to the punch.

The attention I had given the "Billygate" story opened up another mystery in the falling-dominoes fashion that characterizes the news business. A reporter who distinguishes him or herself on one story often finds other informers falling into line. As a result of my reporting on Billy, and my meeting with Gadhafi, a call came into the office in the summer of 1980 while President Carter was fighting a losing campaign against the rising star of Ronald Reagan. The caller, who got Dale Van Atta on the phone, claimed to have more interesting information about Billy Carter that he hoped would throw another shovel of dirt on the president. Billy's tiresome and increasingly ineffectual antics were beginning to look less like news and more like a family matter. The caller claimed that Billy was consorting with two Americans—ex-CIA and Special Forces men Edwin Wilson and Frank Terpil—who were now making a living training assassins and brokering weapons deals for Mu'ammar Gadhafi.

Dale had heard some talk in the intelligence community about the two renegades and was intrigued by the tip. The Billy connection turned out to be marginal. The president's brother apparently told Justice Department investigators that he had discussed an arms deal with Terpil while visiting Libya, but Billy later denied having said that. Then he admitted he had autographed a photo of himself and Terpil, "to my friend Frank," but Billy claimed it was just a courtesy and that the two men were not friends at all.

The bigger story was in the documents the tipster had seen—the federal investigative file on the mercenaries Wilson and Terpil who had both skipped the country to avoid prosecution on arms charges. The source had been handed the eighty-page report and left alone with it for a couple of hours. In the absence of a copy machine, he had used the time to read the text into a microcassette recorder. Dale did some fast talking and persuaded the tipster to give him the tape for half a day so he could transcribe it. The tape was a gold mine of names and bizarre plots by Wilson, Terpil, and other American soldiers of fortune. Their job was to assassinate, blow up, and generally obliterate anyone and anything that got in Gadhafi's way, using the skills they had learned from the CIA and Green Berets.

We published a series of columns exposing Wilson and Terpil as the recruiters and ringleaders of Gadhafi's band of American mercenaries. We knew the columns were being read in Libya because of the overnight response we would get from the Libyan government each time we revealed another piece of the story. Dale tried in vain to get comments from Wilson and Terpil, and, though we had their phone numbers at hideouts in Libya and elsewhere, they would not take his calls, at least not until Wilson's own life hung in the balance. He was drawn out of the woodwork by our column alleging that the CIA itself had tried to lure Wilson back to work for them with an assignment to assassinate his new employer, Gadhafi.

Dale's home phone rang at four o'clock one morning in October 1981, a full year after we had first started writing about the mercenaries. "You almost got me killed," the voice on the other end of the line growled. It was Ed Wilson and he had spent the day under interrogation by Gadhafi's goons because our column said he had been approached by the CIA about killing Gadhafi. We had written that one possible weapon in Wilson's arsenal was a poison dart disguised as a black fly. Wilson had gone home from the interrogation and found his apartment in Tripoli speckled with dead flies—exterminated by Gadhafi's men, just in case.

Dale shook the grogginess out of his head. He didn't believe for a moment that we had wronged Wilson. He pulled out the traditional reporter's defense against accusations of unfairness and inaccuracy. "I tried to call you for nine months and you never returned my phone calls."

Wilson pondered this for a moment. "We've got to work together now," he said. Dale wasn't quite sure for what purpose we were supposed to team up with Wilson and his boss Gadhafi. Presumably Wilson figured if he gave us enough juicy tips about other people, we would leave him alone. Dale deftly let Wilson know that the lines of communication would remain open, and Wilson invited us to send a representative to meet him in Libya.

I already knew through intelligence sources that Wilson had a hit list with Dale's name on it, so I was not about to send him to Libya. Instead I called my friend, private investigator Dick Bast. He was game and ended up spending several hours interviewing Wilson on tape. That netted a few columns about CIA plots to wreak havoc around the world, but none of them were as interesting as the Wilson story itself.

Several years later Dale got one of those "it's-a-small-world" lessons when he walked into a gun shop in Virginia to buy a plastic Glock pistol. He had been looking into complaints about the Glock, which, because of its plastic parts, was easy to slip through metal detectors. Dale, a collector of many things, thought that the plastic Glock might someday become a collector's item and he wanted to buy one before the manufacturer was forced to adapt it. The salesman took his order and told him to come back after the required waiting period.

Dale returned a few days later to find a different salesman behind the desk. The man's name, John Henry Harper, should have rung a bell with Dale but it didn't. We had written in a column that Harper was a former CIA explosives expert whom Wilson and Terpil had hired to teach Gadhafi how to hide C-4 plastique explosive material in ashtrays and coat hangers.

Harper pulled the Glock out of its case and pointed it at Dale. "My name is John Harper. You wrote about me and Ed Wilson several years ago. I don't know whether to use this on you or sell it to you."

"Well, I suggest you sell it to me," Dale offered. Harper thought for a moment, then took Dale's money and passed him the Glock.

SHOOT THE MESSENGER

T HE GLOCK PISTOL DALE VAN ATTA bought from one of Edwin Wilson's men continued to accumulate a lively history. Neither a sportsman nor a felon, Dale had little use for the gun. Once he brought it out to shoot up the picture tube of an old TV, Elvis-style, at a staff barbecue. But other than that, it gathered dust until I found a use for it in 1989.

While producing a TV documentary on terrorism that year, I picked up disturbing evidence of how easy it would be to smuggle a weapon into the U.S. Capitol. I wanted to prove, on camera, that it could be done, so I borrowed Dale's plastic gun. Then I made an appointment to meet Senator Bob Dole in his office in the Capitol and talk to him on camera about security.

I took the gun apart, put the plastic pieces in my briefcase, and carried three bullets in my coat pocket. Then, with the camera crew taping me, I sailed through the Capitol metal detector and into the men's room where I reassembled the Glock. In Dole's office, as he was telling me how secure the building was, I produced the gun and handed him the bullets. He smiled sportingly, but his face was ashen.

It made a good piece of TV drama and starkly showed how easy it would be to assassinate a U.S. senator. But no one seemed grateful for the warning—not the Senate, the Capitol security police, the Washington, D.C., police, or even my fellow members of the press. Both police forces threatened to arrest me for bringing a gun into the Capitol and for possessing a weapon in pistol-packing Washington where guns are illegal. The Standing Committee of Correspondents, which controls access to the Senate and House press galleries, threatened to take away my Congressional press pass until they found out that I had never bothered to get one. I never thought an American citizen should have to carry a pass to enter the halls of Congress.

Senator Dole and Senate Majority Leader George Mitchell threatened to have Capitol police frisk all reporters in the future if the Standing Committee of Correspondents couldn't guarantee that such an incident wouldn't happen again. Nobody mentioned tightening security on anyone other than reporters. When the dust cleared, the only change in Capitol security was a little note posted at each metal detector warning guards to watch out for Jack Anderson and his associates.

CHAPTER 21

IN THE PREDAWN STILLNESS OF VALENTINE'S Day 1977, the tiny Colombian village of Macarena was sacked by pro-Communist guerrillas. In the hail of gunfire, three villagers were killed. The others were rounded up in the center of the village, among them a conspicuously white-skinned man who spoke Spanish with an American accent. He was Peace Corps worker Richard Starr, and he looked to the guerrillas like the biggest prize in the village. Surely the rich gringos would pay much money to get him back.

They ordered Starr to pack his duffel bag and put on his hiking boots; he was going for a long walk. For three rugged years, Starr was a hostage of the roving guerrillas while his mother, Charlotte Jensen of Edmonds, Washington, pounded on doors in the nation's capital, pleading her son's case to deaf ears. She sold her car and spent every dollar she could raise to finance her one-woman campaign—back and forth to Washington, to and from Colombia. She even promised to sell her body to science and give the money to the rebels if they would just return her son.

Starr lived those three years under the shelter of a tarp strung between trees. This mild-mannered botanist, with the wide-eyed innocent look of Radar O'Reilly, was out of place in a guerrilla camp. He looked as if he should have been tending tulips in his flower garden. He fought back boredom and hid his fear behind those wide, questioning eyes. He tried to keep up his botanical work, collecting samples of local plants. His only entertainment was provided by two parrots that became his pets. He named them Aleksandr Solzhenitsyn and Andrey Sakharov after two Soviet dissidents, but the irony was lost on his illiterate captors.

Finally, in desperation, Mrs. Jensen came to me in the fall of 1979 and begged for help. She wanted to convince her son's captors that she had no ransom money, and the Peace Corps wasn't allowed to pay for his freedom, nor was any other branch of the U.S. government. My column was widely read in Latin America and Mrs. Jensen hoped that through the column she could convince the rebels that a ransom was out of the question.

Not long after I published her story, the rebels got word to me through intermediaries that they were willing to talk. I sent my reporter Jack "Mitch" Mitchell to Mexico City to make contact in September 1979. For the rest of the year, we continued to negotiate with a Colombian middleman, but we were stonewalled. Then, suddenly, during the last week of January 1980, the negotiator notified Mitch that the rebels were tired of talking and tired of taking care of Richard Starr. They wanted $250,000 in cash or he would die. Feeling ill, I realized that his life was now in my hands.

I ran down the shortlist of wealthy people I knew, picked up the phone, and dialed one. "How much is a human life worth?" I asked this businessman.

"This is going to cost me money, isn't it?" he responded.

"About $250,000." Then I told him the story of Richard Starr. "I want to make a hero out of you," I offered.

"I don't want to be a hero," he said. "Everyone in the United States would be asking me for money." He agreed to give me the money, but only on the condition that I never reveal his name.

A banker friend helped arrange for us to collect the money in cash. It was no small feat. Mitch had to visit three separate banks and give a password each time to get the cash. Meanwhile, fearing Mitch would be arrested as a possible drug dealer or money launderer, I negotiated with the State Department and the U.S. Customs Service to let him through Customs with $250,000 cash in his suitcase. The government was more than willing to cooperate, if for no other reason than to get the persistent Mrs. Jensen off their backs.

Mitch flew to Bogotá February 2, 1980, with a translator, John Longan, and a suitcase filled with cash. They holed up in a hotel to negotiate terms with representatives of the guerrillas. After five days of predawn rendezvous and whispered conversations over pay phones, Mitch was told to fly in a single-engine plane to the city of Neiva north of Bogotá and register in a hotel near the city square. A bagman appeared at the hotel, took the satchel of money, and promised that Starr would arrive in a few days.

Mitch sweated out the next four days in the dingy hotel. Had he been duped? Would I take the money out of his meager salary for the rest of his life? Then one evening, as Mitch was fighting back waves of nausea, a scraggly group of men approached him outside the hotel. With them was Richard Starr and one of his parrots. "How is my mother?" he wanted to know. Had he been holding a teddy bear instead of a parrot, he could have passed for Radar wandering off the set of *M*A*S*H.*

In a Lear jet provided by the Peace Corps, Starr, Mitch, and the parrot flew to Panama where an entire wing of a U.S. military hospital had been reserved for them. The local press corps was convinced by the security and secrecy that the Shah of Iran must have arrived for medical treatment.

Later, the three flew to Andrews Air Force Base outside Washington where my staff and I showed up to meet the freed hostage. We were overshadowed by a bevy of politicians who rushed forward to greet the returning Richard Starr and take credit for his rescue.

The real credit belonged to a dauntless mother and an anonymous benefactor whom Starr never met. I spread the word in my column that we were collecting money to repay the millionaire, but not much trickled in. My friend experienced a financial slump a few years later and called me, almost embarrassed, to ask if there would be any more money forthcoming. I apologized profusely and told him I wasn't optimistic. He urged me not to worry about it, and never mentioned it again.

I FEARED THAT MY INTERVENTION IN that case might encourage other kidnappers to regard me as a ransom raiser of last resort, but I have never received another request to come up with ransom money. I have intervened, short of putting up cold cash, in a few other dramatic rescues. Perhaps the most memorable was the case of Thach Minh Loi.

In the summer of 1979, I got a call from Tim Anderson, a St. George, Utah, lawyer who had helped me with research into polygamist cults in southern Utah. Tim told me about a Vietnamese woman, Chuong Ellis, who had married a U.S. Navy man during the Vietnam War and settled in Veyo, Utah. She had come to Tim in a panic about her brother Thach Minh Loi, a thirty-one-year-old former South Vietnamese army officer who had escaped Vietnam in a boat with his pregnant wife, Vui, and daughter, Tao. Storms battered their boat and sea pirates robbed them of all their possessions, including gold fillings from their teeth. Half dead, they were picked up at sea and sent to a refugee camp in Malaysia.

Chuong Ellis heard of their fate and immediately began petitioning the U.S. Immigration and Naturalization Service (INS) to let her brother's desperate family immigrate to America. While she wrote letters and filed forms, Thach kept his family alive by catching rats and snakes for food. Money that should have gone for provisions in the refugee camp was pocketed instead by opportunists masquerading as humanitarians.

Chuong wrote frequently to her brother about her progress on his immigration application, but the letters that filtered back from Malaysia made it clear that her news was not getting through to him. Finally, he wrote a last despondent letter. Feeling abandoned and without hope, Thach Minh Loi said he had only one option left. Rather than watch his family slowly die, he would kill them and then take his own life. He wanted his sister to understand, should news of their fate reach her.

Unbeknownst to Thach, Chuong's work had already paid off and she had won approval for the family to come to America. But, by the time she received Thach's letter, the bureaucracy had ground to a halt. A notice had been sent to the U.S. embassy in Kuala Lumpur to allow the Thach family to leave, but the word had not been passed to the refugee camp. The Ellises importuned the State Department and the INS. No response.

Chuong appealed to Tim Anderson for help, and he called me. I can't help everyone, I thought, but I can help this one. I called the State Department's coordinator for refugee affairs. One of his underlings told me they couldn't lift a finger for an individual case. "We have thousands dying in Southeast Asia. The ten people on our staff can only deal with over-reaching policy questions. We can't do anything for individuals." I promised her that both she and her boss would be named in my column if this family perished because of red tape.

I called more refugee agencies, each time telling them, "I just want to let you know, if this man kills himself and his family, your name is going to be in the story." Finally I found a sympathetic ear in the deputy commissioner of the INS, Mario Noto. With his help, and the aid of the United Nations High Commissioner on Refugees, and the U.S. Catholic Conference, volunteers combed the refugee camp and, within three days, found the Thach family. They were still alive—even as Thach Minh Loi was agonizing over how to kill them. In a few weeks they were on the way to Utah.

I couldn't break away from Washington, so Tim Anderson rented a van and met them at the airport in Las Vegas, along with Chuong Ellis. The family of four, which by then included little Minh Chow born in Malaysia, straggled off the plane, fatigued and ill. Their Asian stoicism melted at the sight of the waiting sister. Tears streamed down their thin faces. Tim told me that on the two-hour ride to Veyo there was only a reverent silence in the van as the realization sunk in that their long ordeal was over.

Tim steered the van through the hot and hardscrabble little town and pulled up in front of the Thach's new home, a trailer that only the poorest of American families would have considered a refuge. There was silence as Thach Minh Loi climbed out of the van and stood surveying the trailer.

Suddenly, the small man straightened up, thrust his fists to the sky, jumped with joy, and with all his lung power shouted at the nearby mountains, "America!"

ANOTHER TIME, ALL IT TOOK WAS some quick talking to help someone in trouble overseas. It was 1988, and the victim was forty-six-year-old Darrell Alexander, a Los Angeles bird dealer who had landed in jail in Ghana for allegedly trying to export protected African gray parrots. A jail term in Ghana was akin to a death sentence. The prisons were deplorable and the country had no money to pay for the care of prisoners. A month before Alexander was jailed, another American had died of malaria in the same prison. An autopsy showed that he had virtually no body fat at the time of his death.

I heard about Alexander from his wife, Florence, who had called my office and talked to my reporter Daryl Gibson. Mrs. Alexander said her husband had jumped through all the proper hoops in Ghana, paying fees to the proper authorities and filing the paperwork necessary to export hundreds of parrots. Daryl listened to the story and she checked the appropriate wildlife protection treaties. It was indeed illegal to trade African gray parrots internationally, and Alexander should have known that. He may have been paying "fees," Daryl decided, or he may have been paying bribes. But she concluded that guilty or innocent Alexander didn't deserve to starve to death in a foreign prison for bird trafficking. I agreed and published his story.

The reaction was predictable—from bird lovers telling me that Alexander was getting what he deserved, to the State Department reminding all Americans that when they break foreign laws there isn't much the diplomatic corps can do for them. I was more interested in the reaction from Ghana. Word came back to me that Alexander was hauled into an interrogation room and told in strident tones that "this capitalist Jack Anderson is writing untrue material."

Ghana's ambassador to the United States, Eric Otoo, called and invited me to visit his office to see if we could work out a deal. I knew next to nothing about Ghana, but I was sure that at least Otoo must be an influential man, or his small country would not have given him its most important diplomatic posting. Sitting in the fading splendor of an old embassy building on 16th Street in Washington, I listened to Otoo explain the importance of protecting Ghana's natural resources.

I decided to bluff. "Your country has a loan outstanding at the World Bank, doesn't it?" I asked, knowing absolutely nothing about Ghana's finances.

THE AMERICAN DREAM

IN AN AGE OF CYNICISM, I can personally testify that America still has a compassionate heart. In 1984, my readers helped buy a house for a good Samaritan in Arkansas.

I learned about Joann Jones through my Mormon church connections. She was a struggling, middle-aged mother in Paris, Arkansas, supporting three children in the face of daunting odds. She had owned a small restaurant, but lost it when she was overwhelmed by the medical bills of her son, who suffered from a rare disease. Her home had burned down and she had no homeowners insurance because she had had no money to pay the premiums. With all her worldly possessions in ashes, Joann found a cheap, secondhand trailer and rejoiced that her family was still together.

Then one day, as a cold front sent temperatures below zero in western Arkansas, Joann stopped at a country store to use a pay phone. Across the road in a frozen field, she noticed four Mexican men huddled under a tree, shivering in shirtsleeves and sharing a single blanket. Joann put down the phone and crossed the street as the Samaritan in Jesus' story did to help the man left for dead by highway robbers.

The Mexicans didn't speak English and Joann didn't speak Spanish, but it was easy enough for Joann to understand that the men had no money, no food, and no warm clothing. Their simple wish was to go back home to Mexico. Though impoverished herself, Joann brought them home and took blankets off her beds for them. Then she remembered that she had heard the Mormon congregation in Fort Smith was holding a service that night.

Joann carefully counted out enough money to buy gas for the sixty-five-mile round-trip to Fort Smith, where she arrived with the forlorn four and presented them to two dozen Mormons assembled there. The church members gathered warm clothing and collected enough cash for four bus tickets to Dallas. Then they called Spanish-speaking church members there and arranged for them to meet the bus and get the four men back across the border.

When I heard Joann's story, I called her at the diner where she worked. She didn't want to talk about her good deed. "Charity should be given in secret. Anyway, it was no big deal. Anyone would have done the same thing." No, I thought, most people wouldn't help a stranger in need. But I was proved wrong by my own readers.

In a column I wrote telling Joann's story, I took a leap of faith and suggested that the story would have an even happier ending if a few people could chip in and buy Joann a house. Then I sat back and held my breath. Incredibly the cash poured in, much of it from people who seemed to be in circumstances as dire as Joann's. A woman in Pacific Grove, California, wrote, "I have a small savings account and am a senior citizen on social security. I feel if Mrs. Jones can do all she did, I can at least do this much.'' In the envelope was a check for $1,000. An elderly couple living on Social Security in New Jersey sent one dollar each. A widow living on a pension sent six dollars. A man who said he had already given all he thought he could afford to charity wrote, ''After reading your column, I have been moved to give a little more. Thank God for people like Joann Jones.''

Joann was still bewildered by the events when she moved into a modest rural bungalow on thirty acres of backwoods land in Arkansas, thanks to the generosity of people just like herself.

"Uh, yes," Otoo stuttered.

I pressed my luck. "In fact, there is more than one loan, isn't there?"

"Yes," he said quietly. "There are several."

"I have it on good authority that the people at the World Bank are not too pleased with what they have heard about the treatment of Darrell Alexander," I lied.

Otoo sat back and absorbed the information. "I don't think it is the intention of Ghana to see this man die in prison," he said, and promised to intervene. In turn, I promised to write a nice column about Ghana and birds.

Alexander's case went immediately into overdrive. A Ghanaian tribunal ruled that he had been duped by a local exporter who forged the permits for the parrots, but then the kangaroo court convicted him anyway of smuggling and bribery. After serving a few more weeks in prison, Alexander was taken, shoeless, and placed on the porch of "The Castle," the official residence of Ghana's colorful military ruler, Flight Lieutenant Jerry Rawlings. Rawlings, who for unclear reasons wore a pilot's jump suit as his official dress, came out on the porch, said, "We're sorry for the inconvenience," and turned Alexander loose.

When Alexander got home he called my office and thanked Daryl for our intervention. He described how he had been tortured with an electric cattle prod while standing in a bucket of water. Daryl stuck her head in my office. "I know we promised the ambassador that we would do a nice story about Ghana when Darrell Alexander was released. But they tortured him with a cattle prod. What should we do?"

"A cattle prod?" I thought for a moment. "All bets are off. Write about what happened to him."

The followup story brought an angry call from Ambassador Otoo. "That's not true," he blustered defensively. "We don't have any cattle prods in Ghana. The tsetse fly killed off all of our cattle years ago."

CHAPTER 22

WHEN JIMMY CARTER CAME TO WASHINGTON in 1977, he admitted that he didn't even know the names of all the Middle Eastern countries and their leaders, let alone the complex crosswinds swirling in the area. That didn't stop him from taking personal charge of U.S. policy there. He plunged into presidential paperwork on the Middle East like a student might cram for a final exam. He burned the midnight oil and stewed over trivia that his predecessors had left to State Department professionals. Carter emerged from his homework with enough information to write a college thesis, but without a full understanding of the human undercurrents of the Middle East.

He embraced the dangerous and unstable Shah of Iran, Mohammad Reza Pahlavi, who had oppressed and alienated his own people to keep them cowed. There were few Iranians who could not name a friend or relative who had been brutalized by the Shah, yet Carter praised him in language he usually reserved for the Almighty. In spite of the best advice of his own experts, Carter allowed the Shah to come to the United States after he was driven out by radical mullahs in January 1979. That launched a hate-America campaign that climaxed with the takeover of the U.S. embassy in Tehran in November 1979.

The New Year dawned without cheer in 1980, and the frustrations kept piling up. Americans were demoralized by the paralysis in the Middle East. There was crippling inflation; the exodus of ten thousand unwanted Cubans—many of them criminals and mental patients—to the United States in the Mariel boat-lift; the boycott of the Moscow Olympics because of the Soviet invasion of Afghanistan; the botched "Abscam" sting to catch congressmen accepting bribes; even the murder of rock icon John Lennon in front of his New York apartment building.

Then, out of the West, galloped Ronald Reagan, who promised to clean up the mess John Wayne–style. On April 22, 1980, Carter tried his own version of a John Wayne script but it failed miserably. He sent commandos to rescue the embassy hostages, but they never reached Tehran. At a staging area called "Desert One" in Iran's Great Salt Desert, the mission was aborted when three of the eight helicopters were grounded by mechanical problems. It was bad enough for Carter to have to surrender to faulty equipment, but the worst was yet to come. When the troops tried to leave the staging area, a navy helicopter crashed into a C-130 transport plane, killing eight American soldiers.

Carter had played to the classic American love of action heroes. When he failed, many Americans felt he had done something more stupid than heroic. Four months later, I undertook the agonizing task of informing the American public that Carter was about to do something stupid again. Before it was over, I would again experience the peer rejection I had encountered over the Robert Vesco affair.

IT BEGAN IN EARLY AUGUST WITH a long memo from my reporter Dale Van Atta who had been exhaustively checking an almost unbelievable news tip—Carter was planning a second hostage rescue attempt, this one a much bigger military action, almost on the scale of an invasion. D-Day was to be some time in mid-October, conveniently close to the November 4 presidential election.

Dale had at least a dozen trusted sources on the story. He was dealing with the two most sensitive through go-betweens. A member of the Joint Chiefs of Staff and a National Security Council official were so nervous about the planned raid, and so dubious about its chance for success, that they leaked information to trusted intermediaries who were passing it on to Dale. The word from inside the Joint Chiefs was that the military already had egg on its face from the first botched attempt, yet Carter was preparing to micromanage a second attempt. He was likely to make the same mistakes and send the troops into another no-win situation that would further demoralize the already miserable military.

Dale was neutral about Carter as a president and had no political motivation driving his research. But I had long since moved past ambivalence and was convinced that if Carter was reelected, it would be disastrous for the nation. I hadn't yet decided whether I would vote for Reagan or for the independent challenger John Anderson, but I knew I had to do what I could in my legitimate sphere of influence to avoid four more years of Jimmy Carter.

The dilemma was the one I had faced since my days with Drew Pearson—should I remain true to the journalistic code of objectivity or should I exercise the unique license of advocacy that my status as a columnist give me? I thought of Drew's pitched political battles and his maneuvering behind the scenes, which rivaled the manipulations of the best lobbyists. Then I thought of my fellow journalists, many of whom have never accepted my role, or Drew's role, as lone men riding the edge of the herd. No matter what I did, they would find fault with it. My bigger concern was for my readers, who sometimes misunderstood my mission. They had been conditioned to demand objectivity from news reporters. Some readers, judging by my mail, wanted me to be a purist also. I didn't fault their confusion. After all, I was a unique bird—not just an opinion writer, not just a reporter, but a hybrid who uncovered the facts and then opined about what I had uncovered.

My inner debate ended with a call to Reagan's pollster Richard Wirthlin. I knew the Reagan campaign was expecting an October surprise out of the Carter camp, so I told Wirthlin a little of what I had learned. In return, he told me something that ended my debate with myself. He said he had researched the popularity ratings of presidents since the days of John F. Kennedy. Every time there had been a foreign crisis, Americans rallied around their president. Even if he was at fault, the president would enjoy a brief but substantial jump in his approval ratings. American public opinion would go through a circle-the-wagons phase.

Kennedy ran up some of his highest approval ratings right after the Bay of Pigs fiasco. The same was true of Lyndon Johnson after the Gulf of Tonkin incident. Carter's own popularity rating bumped up eight points when the hostages were first taken; he even experienced a slight boost as a result of the first failed rescue mission. Reagan's people were convinced Reagan would lose the election to Carter if the embattled president pulled an October military surprise in Iran. The bump in Carter's popularity would carry him through the election whether the raid was a disaster or a success.

In retrospect, I wonder whether this was the obsessive speculation of people who were too immersed in their political games to trust the good sense of the American voters. But at the time, I, too, feared that Carter's surprise would win him the election, and I was sure from what the military experts were urgently whispering that the surprise would go badly for the hostages and the soldiers.

I asked Dale to draft a series of columns summing up everything he could confirm by my strictest standards of double-checking. Then the two of us headed to New York City to cover the Democratic Convention. Our plan was to drop our bombshell during the week after the convention when

ADVENTURES WITH LILLY

THE BRIGHT LIGHT IN THE HUMDRUM 1980 Democratic convention in New York was a get-together with Lilly Fallah Lawrence, the daughter of the Shah's chief oil engineer Reza Fallah. She had settled with her husband, "Bunty," in an elegant Manhattan apartment overlooking Central Park. On the night of my arrival in New York, she treated me to dinner and delicious gossip about the goings-on in Iran.

Brought up in the court life of the Shah, Lilly had come to hate what he stood for and had become an excellent source on the excesses of the Shah and the cruelty of his secret police force SAVAK.

Lilly's flair for the dramatic at first caused me to question whether she was exaggerating her news tips. She would occasionally make excuses in Tehran about having to fly to London or Athens or Johannesburg to shop, when her sole reason for the visit was to call me from an untapped phone. I smiled indulgently each time she called to tell me, with characteristic alarm in her voice, that the Iranian secret police squad, SAVAK, was after her with instructions to throw acid in her face. Then came the day I learned to take her at her word.

Lilly called from a phone booth in Manhattan. She said a man was trailing her and by the look of him she was sure he was a SAVAK agent. He was right outside the phone booth, she said. "What should I do?"

I chuckled to myself. "Open the door and ask him what he wants," I suggested, fully expecting that the poor man simply wanted to use the phone.

Then I listened with amazement as the brave Lilly swung back the door and, with all the regal righteous indignation she could muster, demanded to know where the man had come from. "Tehran," he mumbled, before beating a hasty retreat down the street.

I later heard that the Shah was so incensed about Lilly's revelations to me that on one of his official visits to the United States he canceled an appearance on an ABC network show because I was a commentator for *Good Morning America.*

the only news would be the aftermath of a predictably dull Carter nomination.

Dale spent Monday of the convention holed up in his hotel room polishing the text for the October surprise columns, while, for ABC's *Good Morning America* and the Mutual Radio Network, I reported from Madison Square Garden on the political happenings. There are few news events less inspiring than a political convention to renominate a sitting president. The speechifying and banner-waving take on an artificial quality that make the observer wonder why the party bothered to convene to do the obvious. This convention was no exception.

Dale dropped off his first draft in my hotel room that night. He had cautiously summed up the troop movements and documents that proved Carter was up to something, quoting carefully from his sources about the folly of Carter's planning. He included the caveat that there were contingency plans and fall-back options and that Carter could yet call off the assault at any one of a number of check points.

I felt it was too cautiously worded and feared the story would be lost in the myriad of speculative press about solutions to the hostage stalemate. So I added an explosive insert about Carter's desperate election strategy. Dale argued against it, preferring to keep politics out of the story, but I was sure it was integral to the president's thinking. I sent the column to our distribution syndicate with a publication date one week away, on August 18. I knew the more than nine hundred subscriber newspapers would start getting it by mail and over the wire from the syndicate within a few days, so I added at the top of the column a stern warning to the editors not to jump the gun.

Dale drafted four more columns to run consecutively. They detailed what we knew about the invasion strategy, the possible Soviet reaction, and the reason October was the best time for an invasion—because of weather conditions and spy satellite placement. Each of the columns noted again Carter's need for a big boost in public confidence going into November.

The convention behind me, I returned to my office on Friday to greet some unexpected guests—Howard Simons, the managing editor of the *Washington Post*, and his Pentagon reporter, George Wilson. The October surprise columns were too explosive, they said, and the *Post* wasn't inclined to run them. Simons was polite and tried to assess the credibility of our sources. Wilson reacted petulantly, which was to be expected from a rival reporter who had been scooped on his own beat. He said he had checked with his own sources and they had told him the story wasn't true. In one day and a few phone calls, he claimed to have covered all the ground Dale had spent months combing. It was not the first time that a reporter cast doubt on one of our stories because he was not able to get the story himself. I offered to show Simons our stash of classified documents as evidence that we had access to information not available to the *Post*. But he left me with little hope that the column would appear in my flagship newspaper.

We parted company cordially, but I was boiling inside. Ben Bradlee, the editor of the *Post*, had gone through the entire Watergate scandal allegedly without knowing who his own reporters' "Deep Throat" was. Now my own credibility was being sacrificed to the remarkable premise that news is not news until the *Post* can confirm it. I thought back to the first rescue attempt, when Hamilton Jordan had withheld information from his own White House staff two days before the mission, telling them no military action was planned.

I called my syndicate and asked them what it would take to sell the column to the *Post's* rival, the *Washington Star*. We always gave our subscriber papers exclusivity in their market, but I was angry enough to endanger my contract with the *Post* to get the story published in Washington. Fortunately, cooler heads at the syndicate talked me out of it. The contract was ironclad and we couldn't sell a single column to the competition, even if the *Post* had chosen not to run it. It would have been a rash move in light of my long and cordial relationship with the *Post*.

On Saturday, the *Modesto Bee* in California broke the embargo and ran the story two days early. We were in for a bumpy ride. Other newspapers began calling my office demanding more details and sources. United Press International published a story that quoted anonymous sources in Congress saying a rescue mission was indeed planned for October with political impetus driving it. The White House issued a statement saying, "The suggestion that this or any other administration would start a war for political benefit is grotesque and totally irresponsible. The allegation made by Jack Anderson is absolutely false."

On Sunday the *Post* ran a story explaining why it had chosen not to run the column and stating that if my information was true, it "would be one of the most damning revelations about any president in history." The *Post* story quoted liberally from the column, allowing them to have it both ways—to run the juicy information so the paper didn't get scooped, and at the same time abdicate responsibility for the information.

A few other papers took that route, including the *Cincinnati Enquirer* whose own columnist John Caldwell summed up the "dance" these newspapers were doing: "The White House statement got top play, while the five-part series was boiled down to only a few paragraphs.... These papers seem to be saying that the denial was a story, but the story itself was not a story."

There were dire predictions passed along the journalists' grapevine that my subscriber newspapers would run from me in droves. In fact, I lost eighteen papers and gained twenty-nine new ones during August 1980. Surprisingly, few editorial writers and even fewer readers who wrote to me accused me of breaching national security by revealing the invasion plan. (In 1983 I found out about the planned U.S. invasion of Grenada two days before D-Day and kept that secret in the interest of national security and the lives of U.S. troops.) The notion of a second military action into Iran was so universally abhorred that I did not offend many people by exposing it. What angered them was my assigning political motives to a desperate president during a losing campaign for reelection.

I LOOKED BACK WITH WRY HUMOR on my earlier fears that the story would be ignored. Instead, I got the ultimate sign that the story was high in the public consciousness—an invitation to appear on the *Donahue* show on September 11. I felt somewhat like Jimmy Carter's mother, Miss Lillian, had when she received a similar invitation. She had responded, "Phil, I don't wear an IUD, I'm not a homosexual, and I don't smoke pot. Just what am I going to talk about?" Washington was not normally Donahue's bailiwick, but he was quick tongued and well read. I invited Dale to come along and advised him to brace himself for some tough questions.

In the hotel room in Chicago, I set out our strategy, just as I had with Brit Hume before we walked into the glaring lights of the ITT–Dita Beard Senate hearing. Dale was to be the voice of reason, the young reporter who had simply gotten the facts and didn't understand why people wouldn't believe the truth. I would take the tough, strident approach with Donahue, defending our right to criticize the president when he was about to step over the line.

From the opening salvo, Donahue's questions indicated that he was most annoyed that I would presume to know the president's motives. I reminded Donahue that after the aborted April raid, columnist Joseph Kraft had written, "At every turn of the Iranian crisis, in big things and in small, in matters of life and death, in military, diplomatic and economic affairs, Carter's actions have at all times been ruled by a single, dominant consideration. That consideration is domestic political advantage."

Donahue protested that there was a difference between Kraft saying that after the aborted raid, and me "presuming to tell America what's motivating the president regarding possible future actions." I failed to see the distinction and told him so. Donahue then chided me for "presuming to be an analyst and accepting the words of various people who fear that President Carter is doing this for political advantage." I reminded him that this was exactly my job—to accept the word of reliable sources and analyze their information. My sources were not just anybody, they were the people who were helping to plan the raid. "We don't make these things up," I told Donahue. "And when we say that the military planners are worried about this, and are fearful that the president's judgment has been distorted, this is something the American people are entitled to know about. They do fear this, but these are military people, and he's their commander in chief, and they cannot call press conferences. They're forbidden from doing that. They would be sent to jail, actually, if they talked about top secret documents in a public meeting."

When Donahue turned to the audience of two hundred for their questions, I found myself as I had hundreds of times before, explaining the role of the press—to lay out the facts as we find them and then let readers draw their own conclusions. One woman chided me for presuming to tell others what to believe. "I say that it's appalling that we have to pick exactly what he says as being honest truth," she said.

"Well," I replied, "I would just say that you're entitled to believe whomever you wish, and I certainly think that you ought to consider the White House statements. If you want to believe them, certainly you're welcome to do that. I have nothing to cite but my record."

Later Donahue asked me, "Isn't there something messianic about your motives, though? You want to stop [the invasion]. You know, who appointed you to make decisions like that?"

"Well, it's in the Constitution, Phil," I said, bringing a ripple of approving laughter from the audience.

After the show, Dale and I sat down for a quiet lunch away from prying ears and assessed the crucible we had been through during the past month. An image came to mind of General McAuliffe and me on the day we walked over the battlefield at Bastogne. I told Dale the story of this man who had impressed me more than any other character I had encountered in more than thirty years of muckraking. Perhaps I needed that memory to help dispel the gloom of that day.

IN LATE SEPTEMBER, DALE SEWED UP another piece of evidence. The National Security Agency at Fort Meade, Maryland, America's electronic spying headquarters, intercepted secret Soviet intelligence cables saying that the Soviets had long expected U.S. military action in Iran in the month of October. Beginning in January 1980, the Red Army had shifted half of its troops in Afghanistan to the Iranian border. Twenty-three divisions were lined up and ready to move into Iran. The Soviet cables warning Warsaw Pact allies repeatedly used the phrase "October Coup." The electronic wizards at NSA were convinced the cables were genuine instead of a bluff because some of them were sent in codes that the Soviets were not aware the NSA had cracked.

Two days before I printed that news, CIA Director Stansfield Turner asked me to kill the column, saying it might jeopardize national security. "They don't know we intercept their cables," Turner told me.

I didn't buy that. "They know damn well we intercept their cables," I said.

"Yes, but they don't know which ones."

Turner's arguments didn't ring true to me, coinciding as they did with Carter's political interests, and I decided to publish the information. The next day the White House issued a blanket denial, claiming my column was false. I noted in a follow-up column that the president couldn't have it both ways. If the column was false, then why did his CIA director appeal to me in a panic not to publish it for the sake of national security?

Throughout October, Dale continued to hear reports from his sources that the invasion plan was still active. We chose not to publish any more details, fearing we might expose too much and endanger the operation should the president be determined to go ahead. It was too close to D-Day this time to write about it.

October passed without incident and on November 4 Carter lost reelection. The Iranian hostage takers waited until Ronald Reagan's inauguration day to release the Americans after 444 days of captivity. The captors made sure Carter couldn't take credit for solving his worst crisis.

I had to wait nearly a year to find out what had happened to Carter's October surprise. It was the Soviet cables that had spooked him away from his folly at the last minute. Dale obtained a copy of the secret Joint Chiefs of Staff report summarizing the events of 1980. It included the details of the Soviet buildup that the White House denied had occurred. Carter had taken the precaution of asking the Defense Intelligence Agency to assess what Moscow would do if U.S. troops invaded Iran. The DIA concluded that Soviet troops would intervene on the side of Iran.

The truth is usually slow to catch up with political fabrications. Not until 1983 was our story confirmed in the public print. Carter's National Security Advisor Zbigniew Brzezinski published his memoirs, which revealed that on the day after the first aborted raid, "I convened a meeting in my office, on the instructions of the President, to plan another rescue mission." Yet at the time I published my columns, the White House flatly denied that a second mission was ever contemplated.

In 1987, former intelligence officer John Barron published his book *Breaking the Ring*, about the John Walker family spy ring. In the book he said the Walkers delivered the Pentagon's secret codes to the Soviet Union, so they could decipher Pentagon correspondence about the planned October invasion: "Humiliated and seemingly impotent, the Carter administration laid plans to redeem itself in the eyes of the electorate by mounting a much larger attack on Iran. During the summer preparations proceeded in unprecedented secrecy. By September the United States had deployed a strike force consisting of five thousand assault troops and ten thousand reserves who could be landed quickly in Iran if needed."

When the Soviets, with equal secrecy, moved in their twenty-three divisions, Carter saw the specter of World War III, wrote Barron, concluding, "Prudently, Carter canceled the raid."

According to sources on the Carter wavelength, the defeated president blamed his loss on the October surprise that misfired, then backfired. His tight little circle of assistants continued to protect the Carter presidency, even after they had been shown the door. Carter's former press aide, Jody Powell, rushed out a response to Barron's book. "That is flat wrong," Powell said. "After the first rescue operation attempt, obviously we did immediately begin to consider contingency plans for another, but never in the whole period after that did the question of setting in motion really arise, because, frankly, there was no way to do it."

Powell continued his disinformation campaign against me for years after Carter left office, calling my documents "forgeries" and my sources "liars." He became a syndicated columnist in his own right and used his ink to paint the Carter minions not as bumbling authors of their own tragedy but as blameless victims of plots most foul. He poisoned my reputation with some important newspaper editors and did significant damage to me professionally. Yet, I don't regret publishing the October surprise columns, nor have I ever doubted that the story was true. But I do agree with the *Washington Post*, that it was "one of the most damning revelations about any president in history."

I have learned to take rejection in stride, knowing that investigative reporting is high-risk journalism. We survive only because of the thin protective shield of the Constitution and a wavering public sentiment that we are of some vague use to society.

It is no accident that for decades the *Washington Post* ran my column on the comics pages—a decision made long before my time by an editor who wanted to insult Drew Pearson. My tongue-wagging critics still thought the spot was fitting. But I was not ashamed to be alongside the comics with their roots in a rich heritage of editorial cartooning that predates the tongue waggers. Neither Drew Pearson nor I ever wanted to be anywhere else. The *Post* and I have been family, albeit with me the prodigal. We had our squabbles, but I'm still proud to have called it home for many years.

When differences arise between a columnist and a newspaper, the smart columnist would rather lose the argument than lose the paper. Such a case involved the kidnapping of CIA Beirut Station Chief William Buckley by the pro-Iranian extremist group Islamic Jihad. Buckley was the first American taken hostage in a string of terrorist acts by Lebanese disciples of the Aya-

FAILING THE BREAKFAST TEST

WHEN I CHOSE THE ROLE OF outrider, I had to expect that my reporting would sometimes be deemed unfit for reader consumption. Such was the case in 1988 when Washington was preparing for the arrival of Soviet leader Mikhail Gorbachev. My partner Dale Van Atta learned that the CIA was disappointed Gorbachev would be staying at the Soviet Embassy compound—not because it was a block from my office, but because the tight embassy security would make it tough to collect a stool sample from Gorbachev's toilet. A team of CIA doctors was assigned to monitor Gorbachev's health and there was only so much they could learn from studying the changing hues of the birthmark on his forehead. In 1959 the CIA had scored a coup by trapping Nikita Khrushchev's excrement, postflush. But we learned that Gorbachev would not be passing any state secrets, at least none that the CIA could catch, so I printed the disappointing news. The delicate sensibilities of the *Washington Post* editors decided the column did not pass the "breakfast test." In other words, it was not suitable to be read at the kitchen table. I understood the decision not to run it.

I was more disappointed when a few newspapers failed to run my 1989 column identifying senators whose drinking problems might be affecting their work. My decision to tackle the subject was not made lightly. Talk of tippling was all over the streets during the bitter battle over the nomination of Senator John Tower for secretary of defense in the Bush administration. Tower had a reputation as a heavy drinker, but it had not been publicized until his Cabinet nomination. I felt the drinking problems of certain other senators should be public knowledge as well, but some editors did not agree.

Reporters who have covered these internecine squabbles over the years inevitably want me to tell them how many newspapers chose not to run any given controversial column. I honestly answer that I don't keep track. Unless an editor calls me to complain about a particular column, I am blissfully ignorant of the censor's pen.

---

tollah Khomeini. My partner Dale Van Atta's intelligence sources told him in late 1985 that Buckley had been tortured to death that spring after surviving a year of savage interrogation in Lebanon. He had been disguised as a wounded soldier of the Iranian revolutionary guard, Pasdaran, and flown to Damascus in a Syrian helicopter. Intelligence reports indicated he had been loaded on an Iran Air 727 and flown to Tehran. The brutal torture continued in the basement of the Iranian foreign ministry; several times Buckley was hospitalized. The last time, he suffered three heart attacks and died.

Islamic Jihad bragged about having "executed" Buckley in retaliation for an Israeli air raid on the headquarters of the Palestinian Liberation Organization in Tunis. They even circulated a grisly Polaroid photo of Buckley in a coffin. But the official story coming out of the White House and the CIA then was that Buckley was still alive and that the negotiations for his release were ongoing.

We wrote a column announcing Buckley's death and sent it out for publication on December 12, 1985. When the column was printed in the *Washington Post*, their reporter covering the Buckley story, the capable Watergate veteran Bob Woodward, told his editors it wasn't true. Clearly Woodward had excellent sources, but if they were telling him that Buckley was still alive, then they were either dreaming, or they were lying while they scrambled to do damage control for the secrets that Buckley had divulged under torture. We later learned that Buckley's revelations filled four hundred pages recorded by his captors. The transcript became hot property for the Iranians. Palestinian terrorist George Habash tried several times to buy it or trade weapons for it.

The *Post* at first refused to run our follow-up columns on Buckley. Each time, when we would call the editors and argue the veracity of our sources, the editors would side with Woodward. Finally, we cut a deal with the *Post* that whenever we mentioned Buckley in a column, it would be written in such a way that they could take out that reference and the rest of the information would still stand up. That worked until we wrote a column summarizing the number of American hostages killed by Iranian agents, with details on each case. When the *Post* took out the reference to Buckley, the numbers didn't add up, and readers called to complain about my math.

The *Post* finally capitulated, in a roundabout way. On November 25, 1986, as the Iran-Contra scandal was unfolding nearly a year after we had reported Buckley's fate, Woodward wrote a front-page story announcing Buckley's death by torture. The story made no mention of the fact that we had been reporting that information for a year.

In my profession, getting credit for being first—the almighty "scoop"—is often more rewarding than the pay scale. Such small victories go unnoticed by the readers, but they loom large in the memories of reporters. I have had to learn to live without the recognition of my peers.

Journalists are like a barrel full of crabs, all trying to crawl out. When one gets a little bit too high, the rest of them drag him back down. My own critics, when they fail at assailing my facts, usually turn to my prose which they think is too lowbrow for newspaper readers. In reply, I say I don't write for college professors.

I've been pilloried by *60 Minutes*, had my portfolio turned inside out by the *Wall Street Journal*, and been skewered through by the *Los Angeles Times*.

Time said I was "a college dropout with no intellectual pretensions." *Newsweek* announced that my socks droop and said I came across as "a pitiless, self-appointed judge of human propriety." I've been called reckless, arrogant, irresponsible, tasteless, portly, rumpled, holier-than-thou, and obsessed with secrets. I have read my obituary more than once in stories written by those who would relish my professional demise. My human imperfections have been writ large in the headlines of newspapers that confess their own mistakes in a small box called "corrections."

In the years soon after Drew Pearson's death, when I was hitting my stride and had won the Pulitzer prize, I got a call from someone in the Gridiron Club, Washington's prestigious fraternity of journalists. In those days, all of the top columnists were members, except for me. The caller, using tentative language, inquired if I would accept membership in the club should it be offered. He wasn't offering, just testing the waters. There was some fear among the club's leadership that I would loudly and publicly spit on an invitation, thus embarrassing the Washington press corps. I am not a joiner, but I would not insult my colleagues by rejecting their invitation. I said I would accept it in the spirit it was offered. That offer never came.

PART 6

MORNING IN AMERICA

1 9 8 1 – 1 9 8 8

THERE IS A FUNDAMENTAL CONFLICT BETWEEN the press and the politician that is built into the American system. The ferreters of facts have always been pitted against the mobilizers of opinion. This has created an alienation that must ever be the rule between muckrakers and presidents.

Not until the election of Ronald Reagan have I beheld a president who could communicate over the heads of us clamoring reporters directly with the people. He generated a tide of affection and optimism that could not be turned back by mere headlines. There was an all-American quality about him. It was reflected in his amiable, open face, which compelled trust and confidence. It was also his easiness of manner, his engaging sincerity, the way his whole personality smiled every time his face lit up in a grin.

He had a gift, too, for expressing himself movingly and for reducing great issues to simple moral principles. On the surface there was nothing suave or subtle about him—none of those sophisticated mannerisms that Americans are inclined to distrust.

On occasions when I met with him after dealing him a blow in the column, he would greet me with an exaggerated wince, and then a broad and welcoming smile. For Reagan, nothing was personal. He could float placidly above the squalls that mere reporters stirred up—secure that he had the edge in public opinion polls.

His fixation with polls influenced our relationship. Early in his first term, Reagan asked his pollster Richard Wirthlin to survey Americans to determine who were the most trusted journalists. I was pleased to learn later from Wirthlin that I was neck and neck with the father of credibility, Walter Cronkite. Reagan used that survey to decide which journalists he should take time for. Thus, I had relatively easy access to the White House during those years.

I was accused by my peers, in print, of being soft on Reagan during his two terms in the White House. Even some members of my staff grumbled that I was not hard enough on Reagan. I confess, I liked him. The Reagan I knew was not, as his critics claimed, an actor playing the role of president, dependent on cue cards for his lines. He was a captain of the ship of state who confidently set the course but let others do the scut work. Unlike Jimmy Carter before him, Reagan stayed on the bridge and left the engine below for subordinates to operate.

His conservative ideals were firmly his own, and his optimism about America was contagious. When that optimism occasionally blinded him to the hardscrabble life of the average American, I raised what Cain I could in behalf of the people.

Reagan ordered impressive tax cuts and a reduction in the federal workforce of nearly five million workers. But his idea of downsizing government meant cutting social welfare programs while pouring money into the military. The tax cuts were popular and stimulated the economy. But the government had to borrow billions of dollars to keep up with his military goals. Welfare cuts emptied the nation's mental hospitals of the poor, and the streets of urban America began teaming with homeless former mental patients, drug addicts, and Vietnam veterans suffering from posttraumatic stress disorders.

With the help of Congress, Reagan deregulated the savings and loan industry, opening the door for mortgage lenders to gamble their customers' savings on risky investments that had nothing to do with housing. The result was a collapse of the federally insured savings and loan system and a $500 billion taxpayer bailout.

Reagan's inauguration brought the release of American embassy hostages in Iran, but that was the last good news from the Middle East. A rising, restive generation was drawing inspiration from Iran's Ayatollah Khomeini, whose shadow was spreading along the curve of the crescent that spans two continents. He was an agitating force that swept across the walled enclaves of the Islamic world. Yet Reagan preferred to deal with a minor irritation; he focused his attention instead on Libya's flaky dictator, Mu'ammar Gadhafi. In 1986, when terrorists bombed a West German disco frequented by U.S. servicemen, Reagan ordered a retaliatory air strike against Libya. The strike showed Reagan's style—shoot now, ask questions later—but did little to solve the problems of the region.

The president's frontier mentality didn't serve him well elsewhere in the Middle East. Reagan sent U.S. peacekeeping troops to Lebanon in 1982. Their mission escalated from peace to war, but Reagan refused to pull them out. He changed his mind in October 1983 when a fanatical Moslem drove a truckload of explosives into the marine compound in Beirut, killing 239 Americans.

Lebanese Moslems under Khomeini's spell continued to pluck American citizens from the streets of Iran and Lebanon, holding them hostage. Mindful of Jimmy Carter's failures, Reagan chose to deal with Iran through back channels. In 1986 he authorized the secret sale of American weapons to Iran, with the expectation that American hostages would be freed in exchange for the weapons. Some hostages were released, but others were quickly taken to replace them.

That was the "Iran" that would become part of the "Iran-Contra" scandal. The "Contra" portion bubbled up in Central America where Reagan was eager to help a rebel group overthrow the Marxist government of Nicaragua. Congress had passed a law to prevent the president from sending military aid to the Contra rebels, but that didn't deter some of Reagan's subordinates who believed fervently in the anti-Communist cause in Central America. Marine Colonel Oliver North, the White House aide in charge of Reagan's Nicaraguan agenda, grabbed the $12 million in profits from the secret sale of arms to Iran. Since the money was already off the books, he decided it could be slipped under the table to the Contras. Heads rolled when his sleight of hand was revealed, and Reagan began to look like a chief who had lost control of his Indians.

Yet a forgiving populace saw in Reagan a father figure who might have made some mistakes but whose intentions were good. Indeed, history may give him high grades. He explained to me that his military spending was intended to lure the Soviet Union into following suit. His strategy was to cause the economic collapse of the Soviet system. History will be obliged to report that his strategy succeeded and that he ended the forty-five-year Cold War without firing a shot.

CHAPTER 23

DURING THE POSTWAR DECADES, I WAS swept up in the anti-Israel jihads and anti-Western spasms that periodically blew up typhoonlike in the Middle East. Out of the brawls and ruckuses, the radical insurgencies and transitory runnings-amok, there emerged a perennial gadfly who mouthed the Arab cause—the Palestine Liberation Organization chief and cat-of-nine-lives, Yasir Arafat.

He was the objective of my visit to the Holy Land in 1982. I landed at Tel Aviv airport on July 28, exhausted from a sleepless flight. But lethargy disappeared when I set foot again on Middle East soil. I was energized by the excitement that awaited me in Israel, across shell-shocked Lebanon, and in the Beirut bunker of the PLO leader.

Israeli troops had invaded Lebanon on June 6. As the pretext, Israel declared its determination to clear a safety zone to protect its borders from crossover PLO terrorist attacks. But as the battle unfolded, the real goal became clear—to push all the way to Beirut and rout the troublesome Arafat from the city where he had taken sanctuary since 1971. Arafat had fled to Beirut when no one else would have him. The Lebanese, caught up in their own civil strife between Christians and Moslems, lacked the will to stop him at their doorstep. The Moslems hoped that if they hosted the infamous pariah and tolerated the political baggage he brought with him, he might tip Lebanon's delicate Moslem-Christian scale in their favor. He ended up being the terrorist who came to dinner and declined to depart.

My first stop was the ranch of Israel's portly Defense Minister Ariel Sharon who was directing the war against Lebanon from his ranch house. Charges and countercharges were swirling around this truculent Israeli George Patton. He had purchased cluster bombs from the United States—on strict condition that they be used only on military targets and only if Israel should be attacked by two or more Arab states. Now he stood accused of using them to rain shrapnel over Lebanon—showers of death upon military and civilian targets alike, including a hospital. The day before I arrived, President Reagan had angrily banned the sale of any more cluster bombs to Israel.

I was met at the airport by Dale Van Atta and Barbara Newman, who had arrived a day ahead of me. Barbara was my television producer who would be filming a documentary. The tension between these two hardshell investigators, though they had been working together only a day, was apparent. Dale, contemptuous of TV, had come to gather news for the column. Barbara wanted to protect the best moments for her documentary.

I was soon to discover that a secret, international romance had aggravated the tension. The woman in this romantic drama was none other than Barbara. I'm usually oblivious to such undercurrents, but Dale had deduced that our Barbara had been carrying on a transoceanic affair with Bashir Gemayel, charismatic leader of the Maronite Christian Phalangists in Lebanon. I didn't get suspicious until I caught her, dressed seductively in the midst of khaki-clad war correspondents, on her way to arrange an interview with Gemayel. When I questioned her, she confessed that Gemayel's bedroom was a regular stop on her visits to the Middle East.

Dale was worried that this entanglement might affect our work in Lebanon—especially our access to Arafat, since Gemayel and Arafat were mortal enemies. There was another problem. Both Barbara and her coproducer Dan Enright were Jewish, increasing the danger of our incursion into Beirut. The risk was greater for them, of course, than for us.

Dan had been the producer of *Twenty-One*, a television quiz show that set new records and gripped millions of viewers in the late 1950s. The show, with Dan at the controls, was shot down in flames by a congressional committee that found that the questions had been rigged. Dan was to be portrayed later in the movie, *Quiz Show*, as a cold-eyed cynic who manipulated the contestants in order to heighten the drama and increase the ratings. The Dan Enright I knew was nothing like that. Yes, he had rigged the questions; that's what all the big quiz shows did for dramatic impact in those days. The networks knew it; the sponsors knew it. But Dan took the rap for all quiz shows without protest, without pointing fingers. I knew him to be a decent man. But above all else, I remember his quiet courage. On the Lebanese battleground, he would dash out in front of me in areas that hadn't been cleared of mines and snipers.

WE DROPPED MY BAGS AT THE hotel and headed straight for Ariel Sharon's sprawling ranch house, which was built around a water tower in Beersheba. I was distracted because a screw had slipped out of the frames of my eyeglasses. Dale mended them with a straight pin. Thus patched together, I entered Sharon's living room. In the background, a bodyguard clicked the shutters of our cameras to assure himself that they contained only film. We settled on an overstuffed couch, and his wife poured soft drinks. Theirs was a happy marriage, she told me. "We never argue. He is home so little that I am just good all the time he's here."

Perhaps because fatigue was catching up with me, I also sensed a weariness in Sharon. "Are you tired?" I asked as an opener. "Why should I be tired?" he boomed back at me. "I have them surrounded." At that moment he did, in fact, have Arafat and the PLO in West Beirut semisurrounded on three sides. I turned to the question of the cluster bombs, the six-foot-long canisters that scatter hundreds of golf-ball-sized bomblets over their targets. "Who ordered their use?" I asked.

"I did," Sharon replied bluntly, without hesitation. He said he regretted the necessity, but he made it clear that limited war was as illogical as half pregnancy. He claimed that the targets had always been tanks and artillery but that errors were unavoidable. He showed me reconnaissance photos of Beirut; I could pick out the PLO tanks and artillery strategically located near embassies, apartment buildings, and other sensitive sites. I recognized a PLO ammunition dump sitting between a church and a cemetery. It is against the nature of warfare to abide by Marquis of Queensberry rules, Sharon said.

I asked if he had a message that he'd like me to deliver to Arafat. Sharon cordially repeated his earlier boast: "Tell him we have him surrounded on three sides. We have nothing to worry about." We left Sharon's ranch with at least one solid scoop—his candid owning up to the cluster bombs.

In the morning, we headed for the Lebanese border. Hundreds of Israelis were bunched around the border checkpoint, staring into the Arab world with curiosity and confidence. They expected the invasion of this latest Arab land to end in a routine rout of the PLO. Despite a surfeit of oil wealth and arms purchases, the Arab world was still inherently fearful, weak and helpless—afraid of Iran's Ayatollah Khomeini, dependent on the West for protection against Soviet ambition, and powerless before Israel. Arabs were still looking for a man on a white stallion, who would raise their banner and end their frustrations and yearnings—a hero of deeds who would avenge common shames, expel foreigners, and mastermind a modern Moslem technology. They craved to unite all the miniature Arab states into one powerful Arab nation—in spirit if not sovereignty—no longer the pawn of outsiders but standing independent of all the great powers, making them bid against each other for the friendship of the Arab heartland.

As we drove toward the fighting front, I decided that the embattled

Arafat in his Beirut bunker was not that Arab hero incarnate. The closer we got to the fighting, the more obvious it became that he was better at talking. He had more manpower than the Israelis sent against him, yet his ragtag force was no match for the Israelis. Arafat also had more firepower. Yet I saw evidence that the Israelis captured more weaponry than they brought with them.

We stopped to catch our breath in Tyre, and I strolled the streets of the ancient city. Perhaps because I was wearing a suit and surrounded by an entourage, the locals decided I must be an official with the occupying Israeli army. A toothless old woman stopped me and insisted that I fix her roof, which had been blown away by Israeli shelling. A shopkeeper railed at me because the Israeli army would not patronize him as the Palestinians always had done. I was greeted by Tyre's mayor, who complained bitterly about what the PLO had done to his city. But when we turned on the camera to record his comments, he had only nice things to say. "People are afraid of the PLO," the mayor's aide whispered to me sheepishly.

A short drive into the nearby hills took us to a makeshift POW camp where, behind a triple layer of barbed wire, the Israelis were warehousing Palestinians captured during the invasion. I had permission from Sharon to interview the prisoners, but the word hadn't yet reached the camp. Barbara Newman rushed off to find a phone and call Sharon's office while I chatted with the guards. I became increasingly impatient with the delay; we had been held up so long that we might be unable to reach Beirut before nightfall. Then we'd have to return to Israel for the night because it was decidedly unsafe to loiter in the war zone. And cars were banned from the roads after dark; anything that moved was a fair target.

In frustration, I grabbed my microphone and told the cameraman to start filming. I launched into an angry diatribe about how the Israelis were keeping us out of their POW camp for reasons unknown. With just the right touch of melodrama, I implied that they must have something to hide. The guards listened with growing apprehension, which was broken when Barbara returned with official confirmation from Sharon that we could go in.

The first prisoners we reached were not Palestinians, but poor Africans who had been service workers doing menial chores for the Palestinians in Beirut. Barbara told them they could approach me and ask questions while the cameras rolled. They misunderstood the instructions, hastily formed into rank-and-file order, and began marching around me in a circle. It was a snapshot of pathetic people caught up in someone else's war doing their best to please their captors. I asked if any of them had worked for the PLO. It took a few minutes for them to understand the question, then they erupted with a chorus of "No, no, no." They loved the Israelis and had no complaints about conditions in the camp. I noted that they slept in the open on thin ground cloths.

I moved to the section of the camp where Palestinian prisoners were fenced in. The guards on the Israeli side and POW leaders on the Palestinian side alike discouraged prisoners from talking to me through the fence. There was no more time to argue; we beat the sinking sun back to Israel and spent the night in the guest house of a charming kibbutz near the Mediterranean.

THE NEXT MORNING, WE CROSSED THE border again and stopped for nothing until we reached the Israeli-controlled sector of Beirut. Once we were installed in the Hotel Alexandre, the hangout of the foreign press corps, I contacted Arafat's office and asked to see him. While we waited for a reply, an Israeli journalist recognized me in the hotel lobby and began asking some ticklish political questions, with his tape recorder rolling. I didn't want to offend my Israeli hosts, nor did I want to anger Arafat before meeting him. "Why are the Israelis winning the military war but losing the public relations war?" the reporter asked me. I had learned in Washington how to say nothing but make it sound like something. "The Israelis are great soldiers," I replied solemnly.

Dale and I huddled for a realistic talk about the dangers of going into West Beirut uninvited. We decided that only the two of us should take the risk, but Dan Enright insisted on coming along. He would take his chances, he said. We didn't even consider taking Barbara.

It did nothing for our qualms when a Lebanese taxi driver demanded $200 to drive us three blocks across the green line into West Beirut. He hit this shell-pocked no-man's-land at reckless speed. Dale leaned out the window with his camera to immortalize the moment. "Put down your camera!" screamed the driver as he tried to avoid the shell holes without losing momentum. "The snipers will think it's a gun!"

On the Palestinian side, the driver followed directions to Arafat's headquarters. There, a young aide said he was aware of my request for a meeting with Arafat and would try to arrange it. While we were engaged with Arafat's aide, I later learned, one of Arafat's armed guards nudged our taxi driver with a rifle and demanded gasoline. The driver quickly agreed and watched in dismay as the Palestinian nearly drained the tank.

We started to do an on-camera standup in front of the building when we heard a commotion. I turned to see Arafat coming around the corner surrounded by a clutch of admirers. On closer examination, I realized they were all PLO press people who followed him around to give the impression that their chairman drew a crowd wherever he went. We approached Arafat,

A GIFT FROM ARAFAT

AN UNFLAPPABLE COLLECTOR OF SOUVENIRS ON our travels, Dale Van Atta asked Yasir Arafat on a street corner in West Beirut if we could take home a cluster bomb. The bemused Arafat gave him a thirteen-inch-long, bell-shaped Rockeye bomblet. When fully loaded, it had a "shaped charge" designed to penetrate twelve inches of tank armor, leaving the main charge intact to explode inside the vehicle. I don't remember Arafat's exact words, but Dale and I felt certain that the stockpile of bombs sitting on the street corner for show had been defused.

Before we left Israel, Israeli military officers gave the bomb a cursory check and pronounced it safe. Dale stored it for several months on a shelf in his garage. Then one day, a friend at the Pentagon urged Dale to call the 57th Ordnance Detachment at Fort Belvoir, Virginia, and let the experts examine the bomb. Two men arrived at the Van Atta house, took one look at the bomb, and told Dale he and his family were lucky to be alive. They gingerly carried the fully armed bomb away and detonated it on a firing range.

In a second meeting with Arafat in 1989, Dale, only half-jokingly, asked him why he had not mentioned that the bomb was live. Arafat chuckled and said, "Next question."

and I introduced myself. His mouth opened in that famous full-lipped smile, and he said he was pleased to finally meet "the famous Zionist reporter, Jack Anderson." I wasn't sure whether I had been flattered or insulted.

He launched into his sidewalk act for my cameras, kissing his followers and pulling up the pant leg of one bystander to reveal a wound inflicted by a cluster bomb. Leaning against the wall of his headquarters, next to a barricade of sandbags, were half a dozen cluster bomb canisters. The markings revealed they had been bought from the U.S. Navy. Arafat made sure we saw the canisters.

He then led us on a quick tour of the destruction that the Israelis had wrought, ending up at a hospital with unwanted air-conditioning caused by Israeli bombs. An anguished man approached Arafat and launched into an animated discussion. Arafat explained afterward that the man was the hospital administrator despairing over Israeli air attacks on his hospital. As Arafat paused to soothe a patient, I dropped back and spoke to our taxi driver who was tagging along.

"Did you understand what the hospital administrator was saying?" I asked.

The driver nodded affirmatively, and said, "He begged Arafat to move the anti-aircraft guns away from the hospital, because they were attracting Israeli attacks."

Arafat sped off in a Mercedes, and we returned on foot to his head-quarters. We were ushered into his basement "war room" to wait for him; then after a short delay, we were summoned into his inner sanctum. The electric supply had been cut off by the Israelis, so Arafat sat behind a desk illuminated by candlelight. A portrait of him was dimly visible on the wall behind his desk. It was all highly dramatic, except that the air was too hot to breathe and the room too dark for my cameras to record. Arafat barked an order, and somewhere a backup generator surged to life and the lights and air-conditioning came on simultaneously. The spell was broken and we got down to business.

Arafat appeared as the personification of the landless Palestinians he represented—the deprived and the dispossessed who, by accident of geography, had become the oil sheiks' poor relations. He had turned his ugliness—stunted and ungainly as he was—into a political asset. He carefully cultivated the careless image of an unshaved, disheveled Arab ruffian. I marveled at his ability to keep his chin stubble at the perpetual length of someone who hadn't shaved in five days.

He was also an unsurpassed operator at the subterranean level of Arab politics, ever managing to be heard above the chorus of obstreperous voices that rose out of the Middle East. On the level of personal charisma, he could twang the chords of Arab emotion. He also knew his way around the labyrinth of fanatical groups that infest the Arab netherworld. But he was a talker who looked like a fighter.

Arafat spoke in English. The Israelis were hitting his people with every-thing they had, he claimed, including gas, white phosphorous, and napalm. "I'm sorry to say they are trying to make this war as an experimental field for the Israeli-American weapons. I am sorry to say this, but I have to ask the whole public opinion in America, in the whole world, would they accept this barbarian, savage war? I have to ask them that."

An aide entered the room and looked at me, then whispered something in Arafat's ear. Arafat also looked my way, and I felt a sudden chill in the air. Perhaps they had just picked up word of my column, published the previous day, favorably appraising the Lebanese Christian leader Gemayel, or maybe my praise of Israeli soldiers given that morning to the Israeli radio reporter had already made the airwaves. It was better, I thought, that we were not spending the night as Arafat's guests in West Beirut.

He continued to speak cordially, but his answers were carefully crafted not to reveal much. He told me he would leave Lebanon if the Lebanese asked him to (a promise he would fulfill a month later). I delivered the message that Ariel Sharon had sent: "Tell him we have him surrounded on three sides. We have nothing to worry about."

"Now, what do you say back to him?" I asked.

"You see, he is threatening me by this. I am not threatening anybody. But this is a part of our strengths in our case." Arafat recalled Masada, the mountain in Israel where, in A.D. 73, 960 Jewish patriots killed themselves rather than be taken captive by the Romans. "They used to speak too much about their Masada. And I am not worried for myself. If he is ready to start a big Masada in Beirut, we are waiting for him."

As I got up to leave, Arafat unexpectedly came around from behind the desk and gave me a bear hug. I recognized this as a gesture of Mideast hospitality and returned the squeeze briefly before I disengaged myself.

Outside Arafat's bunker, I learned for the first time that his men had drained our gas tank. I was obliged to return inside and delicately request enough gas for the taxi to deliver us to our hotel. They poured a couple quarts of gas into our tank, and the driver gunned the taxi back across the green line. Twenty minutes later, the Israelis bombed the route we had taken.

We reached the Hotel Alexandre about dusk. Dale and I climbed up on the roof to join other journalists watching the nightly Israeli bombing raids over the city. Between bomb blasts, a sniper began firing at our rooftop terrace. The veteran war correspondents ducked for cover, but Dale and I stood, half out of ignorance of what was happening and half out of fascination with the spectacle of war.

That night I had dinner with Christian leader Bashir Gemayel. He could have been cast by Hollywood for the role—a darkly handsome man, firm-jawed and big-shouldered, with a caring face, sensitive eyes, and a contagious smile. He spoke in a lilting voice, blaming the PLO for bringing devastation to his beloved Beirut. "Lebanon is not their country. Beirut is not their city," Gemayel said. The Palestinians are "indifferent to its destruction, unless the buildings happen to fall on their heads." Three weeks later Gemayel was elected president of Lebanon, and three weeks after that he was assassinated by a bomb blast at his party's headquarters. Back in Washington, alone in her small home, Barbara Newman wept bitterly.

Also home again, Dale and I debated fiercely over the stand our column should take on the Arab-Israeli conflict. Catastrophe and war and death have been commonplace in the Holy Land, a piece of earth abused by man and nature. Though sympathetic to the Israeli cause, Dale thought the Palestinians had been grievously wronged. I agreed that the Palestinians were a tragic people, but I left Lebanon feeling that the PLO had contributed to their own tragedy. Supporting the PLO, I felt, would be an abrogation of America's historic commitment to champion democracy around the world.

Dale feared that the Israelis would go from victory to victory until their pride clouded their judgment. "Arrogance is dangerous," he said. "When you're so sure of the moral high ground, it leads to tragic mistakes." I had to concede his point in mid-September when the headlines blared the tragedy Dale had predicted. Lebanese Christian militiamen entered Palestinian refugee camps outside Beirut and massacred the unarmed inhabitants. Even friends of Israel were appalled by the brutality. Israel at first denied culpability but Sharon eventually resigned after an Israeli tribunal determined that he was indirectly responsible for the attacks. I realized then that only politics can repeal reality and that reporters should never be blinded by politics from reporting reality.

Ronald Reagan battled the demons of that region throughout his tenure as president, even as Carter had done before him. But there were distinct differences in their approaches. Carter got bogged down in the Middle East. Reagan kept extricating himself from one Middle East mess only to step into another, trying carefully to avoid any painful solutions by quick moves and distractions.

"Let terrorists be aware," declared the newly installed President Reagan, "that when the rules of international behavior are violated, our policy will be one of swift and effective retribution." In his first term, 262 Americans were killed in terrorist operations instigated by Iran; yet there was no retaliation, no retribution against Iran. Reagan preferred to make a villain out of an easier target, Mu'ammar Gadhafi—while opening back channels to negotiate with the intractable Ayatollah Khomeini.

IN OCTOBER 1981, I WAS THE first to reveal that Gadhafi had put Reagan's name at the top of his private hit list. I reported that the National Security Agency had intercepted a conversation between Gadhafi and Ethiopian strongman Mengistu Haile Mariam shortly after the U.S. Navy shot down two Libyan jets. Gadhafi was so incensed that he told his fellow dictator that Reagan had to die, along with Defense Secretary Caspar Weinberger and Secretary of State Alexander Haig.

But the story took on a Hollywood quality as it circulated, and again I was the first reporter to point it out. Nearly two months after I exposed Gadhafi's plot, the press was pulsing with reports that Gadhafi had actually dispatched a hit squad packing missiles, grenade launchers, and bazookas. Reagan himself stoked the rumors with relish, as if his role as the hunted was a Hollywood script. Then a source slipped me a copy of the pictures and biographies of the alleged assassins—hush-hush stuff that had been dispatched throughout the country to FBI and immigration offices. Federal agents everywhere were studying the pictures and watching for these desperadoes.

I examined the mug shots and checked out the accompanying political vitae. Something didn't ring right. Then it hit me; some of the listed assassins would have more cause to knock off Gadhafi than Reagan. Two of them were members of the Lebanese Shiite Moslem sect called Amal, which had been engaged in a blood feud with Gadhafi since their leader, the Iman Musa Al-Sadr, disappeared in Libya in 1978 after antagonizing Gadhafi. I made my suspicions public, and the FBI scrambled to explain them away. They said the two names had ended up on the hit-squad list by "computer error." But the computers, I suggested, had human operators. That was the last we heard of Gadhafi's hit squad.

About the same time, I wrote that the CIA was now spinning a web of disinformation around Gadhafi, spreading tales that he was connected to the slave trade in Mauritania and mismanaging precious Libyan petro-dollars in international bank accounts. The CIA even considered arranging the disappearance of another Moslem cleric in Libya to stir up outrage against Gadhafi in the Moslem world.

That's when it struck me that Reagan was setting up Gadhafi as an enemy he could handle. Reagan focused the spotlight on the hawkish Gadhafi with the classic Bedouin scowl, calling him the "mad dog of the Middle East." Not as remorseless a protagonist as Khomeini, or as wily as Saddam Hussein, or as tenacious as Yasir Arafat, Gadhafi was more a lap dog than a mad dog. He strutted on a small stage as one who carried the double burden of leading the Arab race to a glorious destiny and of shaping up that race's miserable contemporary specimens for the journey. He complained that Allah had given him poor, frivolous clay to work with. In other words, he was the oddball dictator of a stretch of underpopulated desert, a goofball who had spent too much time brooding among the dunes.

From where I sat, Khomeini looked like the real mad dog, and Iran had a kennel full of them. As early as May 1983, I accused Khomeini of training terrorists to battle the "Great Satan," whom he identified as Uncle Sam. I reported that U.S. intelligence intercepts had picked up advance warnings, which were ignored, that pro-Khomeini factions in Lebanon would bomb the U.S. embassy in Beirut. The best evidence of the reliability of this intelligence was that it happened; the embassy was bombed on April 18. Then in October 1983, a suicide truck crammed with explosives plowed into the U.S. Marine barracks in Beirut and killed 239 Americans; I saw the hand of Khomeini again. With Dale doing the reporting, I ended up writing eighty-four columns on state-sponsored terrorism and Reagan's secret negotiations with the worst offender, Iran.

THE SERIES BEGAN SIMPLY ENOUGH WITH an anonymous phone call to the office, and it unraveled a year later into what became known as the Iran-Contra scandal. An unpaid intern in our office took the phone call from a mystery woman in early December 1985, and left a note for Dale that began, "For what it's worth..." The woman claimed that ex-CIA official Thomas Clines and retired General Richard Secord were in Tel Aviv negotiating for the release of American hostages held by Khomeini's sympathizers in Lebanon. Dale didn't have much confidence in the tip, but he made one phone call to a friend of Secord's who confirmed that the general was indeed up to his brass in hostage negotiations—trading weapons for hostages. The man in charge of the operation, Dale was told, was a marine lieutenant colonel on the National Security Council named Oliver North. Dale and I were incredulous.

Dale had scarcely started the investigation when he received an urgent phone call from Noel Koch, the deputy assistant secretary of defense for international affairs. "I understand you know about the Secord mission," Koch said. "I would like to persuade you not to run the story. You may get somebody killed." As he talked, he dropped the key words, "hostage negotiations" and "arms deal." We knew then that the anonymous tip was golden.

Within a few days Dale was able to put some flesh on the bare bones of the story. But his sources on the National Security Council and inside the White House pleaded with him not to print it. He came to me with the dilemma. Dealing with the treacherous Khomeini appeared stupid to us, and the public had a right to know about it. But the lives of the hostages were at stake. We chose to compromise. We would not write anything specific about the arms-for-hostages mission, but we would hammer the White House with column after column about the folly of dealing with the Iranians.

Our first volley caused explosions in the back rooms of Washington. We reported on December 13, 1985, that hostage William Buckley had been tortured to death by his pro-Iranian captors. Karna Small Stringer, press spokeswoman for the National Security Council, called Dale in an uproar. She literally screamed that we had put all the other hostages at risk. If we wrote any more similar columns, she said, President Reagan was ready to castigate us publicly as irresponsible, even traitorous. We responded with five columns in a row on Iranian-sponsored terrorism. The terrorists themselves punctuated our series on December 27 with simultaneous attacks on the Rome and Vienna airports. Five dead Americans lay in their wake.

Reagan used the attacks masterfully to turn up the heat on Gadhafi whom he blamed for the outrages. Gadhafi was involved, all right, but he had two partners—Syria and Iran. Reagan delicately avoided mentioning these formidable culprits and directed his ire against the vulnerable Gadhafi. We knew that the terrorists had been trained in Iran and that their leader, Abu Nidal, punched a clock on Khomeini's payroll.

During the next two months, Dale and I both chafed at our self-imposed censorship and wondered whether our duty was to expose the madness or hope it might somehow result in the return of the hostages. In January 1986, Dale went to a conference organized by Noel Koch on low-intensity warfare and heard a speech by Secretary of State George Shultz. The sincerity of Shultz's diatribe on terrorism brought Dale up short. Either Shultz had a great poker face or the secretary of state knew nothing about the dealings with Iran. Maybe the notoriously hands-off Reagan didn't know the whole story either. Maybe this was just a rogue operation being run by Oliver North. At the conference, Dale was approached by Bruce Laingen, the former chargé d'affaires who had been robbed of 444 days of his life as a hostage during the Iranian takeover of the U.S. embassy in Tehran. Through CIA contacts, I had managed to get the private number of the phone in the room where Laingen was held. We had developed a telephone acquaintance during those tense times. Laingen told Dale he'd been following our stories on Iranian-sponsored terrorism. He quietly urged Dale to keep the focus on Iran, the administration notwithstanding.

President Reagan learned that we were sitting on the arms-for-hostages story and invited Dale to the Oval Office on February 24, 1986. The president received Dale in the middle of an international crisis. Philippine President Ferdinand Marcos was barricaded in his palace, trying to decide whether he should leave his country and turn it over to his duly elected successor Corazon Aquino. Minutes before Dale's appointment, Reagan had taken a phone call from Marcos asking whether the president wanted him to resign. Dale fully expected the interview to be canceled, but he was ushered past a bevy of national security types into the presidential sanctum.

Dale was chagrined to see that Reagan's spokesman Larry Speakes planned to hang around during the interview. Dale felt sure Speakes wasn't in the loop of the sensitive Iran operation, and his presence forced both Dale and Reagan to talk around the subject. Dale began with some obligatory small talk about the Philippines and then moved on to the main course, Iran.

Reagan confirmed with a nod of his head that hostage William Buckley was dead, an admission the CIA was still unwilling to make. Then, after Dale indicated he knew about the arms-for-hostages operation and said he would not print anything about the negotiations until after the hostages were released, Reagan spelled out the reason he was dealing with terrorists:

"We have to remember that we had a pretty solid relationship with Iran during the time of the Shah. We have to realize also that that was a very key ally in that particular area in preventing the Soviets from reaching their age-old goal of the warm water ports, and so forth. And now with the takeover by the present ruler [Khomeini], we have to believe that there must be elements present in Iran that—when nature takes its inevitable course [meaning, when Khomeini dies]—they want to return to different relationships. . . . We have to oppose what they are doing. We at the same time must recognize we do not want to make enemies of those who today could be our friends."

Dale left knowing that the president had foolishly bought the premise that the people he was toying with in Iran were capable of being converted into America's allies. We later learned that Reagan went straight to National Security Advisor Admiral John Poindexter and told him about the conversation. Poindexter was alarmed that Reagan had let too much slip about the operation and feared we would not honor the agreement to keep the conversation off the record.

We continued to write about the folly of trusting Iran and the error of scapegoating Libya until Reagan went beyond rhetoric to action. On April 5, a bomb exploded in a West Berlin discotheque frequented by American servicemen. One soldier was killed. Reagan used the incident as an excuse to retaliate on April 14 with a bombing raid on Libya. "No one can kill Americans and brag about it," Reagan said in triumph. But Gadhafi had the last word. Immediately after the air raid, he bought American hostage Peter Kilburn and two British captives from their pro-Iranian captors for $1 million. A Libyan army officer flew to Beirut to pick up the captives. Then he shot them to death and left their bodies along a road near Beirut.

Dale and I agreed that Reagan's game of Arabian Nights was whirling out of control. The time had come to tell, in part, what we knew. On April 28 we announced in the column that Reagan had begun "a hush-hush, barely perceptible tilt toward Iran." Two days later we reported that Israel was selling American-made arms to Iran with the tacit approval of the CIA and that the administration was considering a direct pipeline of weapons to Iran without going through Israel. The White House flatly denied the stories, and two of Dale's three major sources in the administration clammed up. We were flooded with calls from other reporters. All of them told us they couldn't confirm our stories. Meanwhile, the arms shipments to Iran had already begun.

On June 29 we went one step further and wrote that "secret negotiations

POPULARITY CONTESTS

R ONALD REAGAN HAD AN ATTACHMENT TO public opinion polls that must have come from the days when he worried about box office numbers. After Reagan left office I learned that he and his minions had watched the numbers like stockbrokers looking for the best times to buy and sell.

Reagan and his wife, Nancy, were pilloried for sometimes consulting their astrologer before they made decisions. But the more disturbing story was the president's use of polls to weight the pros and cons of major foreign policy decisions. If General Custer had known Reagan's pollster Richard Wirthlin, Custer could have read the numbers and skipped the Little Big Horn.

During the pivotal year of 1986, when the administration was gambling in the Middle East, the National Security Council paid for polls that helped shape foreign policy. For example, even before Reagan ordered the bombing of Libya, he knew he had popular support behind him. The polls told him so. In January, Wirthlin's pollsters had asked in a confidential poll whether respondents would support a military strike against a country that supported terrorism. Forty-nine percent said yes. A second poll conducted two months later for the National Security Council by a Washington think tank showed that 66 percent were by then ready for military action. But the pollsters, after reading the public mood, advised that the attack should appear to be carried out reluctantly, and only because nothing else would work.

A month later, knowing that the numbers were in his favor, and possibly the stars, too, Reagan ordered the attack on Libya. The after-action poll recorded a 75 percent approval rating. The president had successfully convinced the public that Mu'ammar Gadhafi needed to be spanked.

Other pollsters were busy at the same time tracking sentiment about Iran for Oliver North, but he ignored the results, possibly assuming he knew better. A poll commissioned by the National Security Council in March 1986 told North and company that 78 percent of Americans favored military action against Iran. On the issue of the hostages, 47 percent thought the president should negotiate quietly without making major concessions. In November 1986 as the arms-for-hostages trade was rebounding in the headlines, another poll showed that 76 percent of Americans thought it had been wrong to send arms to Iran.

There was some solace for Reagan in the final poll. The Teflon president had managed to put the blame on me and the rest of the media. Sixty-seven percent of the respondents thought that the news stories about the arms deal hurt the hostages and 82 percent felt that we reporters had jeopardized national security.

over arms supply and release of American hostages have involved members of the National Security Council and a former official of the CIA." We had planned to name names, including Oliver North's, but others on the National Security Council pulled out all the stops. They said if North was publicly linked to the operation, he or his family might be harmed. There was precedent, they claimed. Terrorists who would stop at nothing had already poisoned North's dog, or so the lieutenant colonel said. We learned months later from North's neighbors that the dog had died of old age.

No other reporter was able to verify our work, and the stories were dismissed as speculative. On August 11 we threw in the towel with a column saying we had reported all we could without endangering the lives of the hostages. Don Oberdorfer of the *Washington Post* called to say he was on his way over to the National Security Council for a background briefing. He wanted to know if there was any way to break through the wall of denials on the story. "Find Oliver North and ask him what Richard Secord has been up to," Dale said. North refused to talk to Oberdorfer, so the reporter asked North's boss, Howard Teicher, if there was any truth to our stories. Absolutely not, said Teicher, who had just returned from Tehran, where he had participated in the negotiations.

FOR THE UMPTEENTH TIME IN MY career, I had been stymied by the journalistic fraternity. Other reporters could not substantiate our stories, so they dismissed them. This time the president himself had confirmed the details, and still the news had the impact of yesterday's horoscope. Dale turned his attention to investigating legendary Washington power broker Roy Cohn who was dying of AIDS and using his influence to get himself moved to the top of a waiting list for experimental treatment at the National Institutes of Health. That was a story we didn't have to shout about. It was picked up immediately by the journalistic pack. Jonathan Alter, media critic for *Newsweek*, interviewed Dale about the Cohn exposé and said it had to be the best work we had done all year. "No," said Dale, "the best thing we did this year was to expose the secret Iran deals." Alter let the comment pass.

On November 3, a pro-Syrian magazine in Beirut, *Al Shiraa*, finally published a story that the whole world would believe. The United States had been selling arms to Iran in hopes of getting hostages in return. Three weeks later the Iran story got its hyphen and became Iran-Contra when Attorney General Edwin Meese announced that North had taken some of the ill-gotten gain from the arms sales and bypassed the budget process by giving it to the struggling Contra civil rebellion in Nicaragua—a cause that Con-

TERRY ANDERSON'S HELL

THOUGH I TRAVELED THE MIDDLE EAST in safety, I never forgot my colleagues in the press who were among the hostages taken to please the Ayatollah Khomeini. In 1989 I sent Dale Van Atta back to Beirut to follow the path of one hostage, Associated Press correspondent Terry Anderson. We were preparing a TV documentary on terrorism and I wanted to make sure the viewers saw the faces that were by then in danger of becoming statistics.

Dale talked his Syrian escorts into driving him to the underground parking garage where sources had told him Terry Anderson had once been held. The eerie garage was deserted as Dale wandered through with the skittish footsteps of the Syrians behind him. The bodyguards would only let him stay ten minutes.

The walls were covered with elaborately painted Shiite graffiti, apparently the work of bored captors. On one wall was a horrific caricature of Ronald Reagan as a vampire. The Star of David was branded on his forehead and the flags of U.S. allies sprouted from his scalp. The stench of human excrement clung to Dale's nose.

On the first level underground, where the captors prayed, a wall was painted as if it was a mosque. The hostages were kept three floors below that in darkness and chains.

Dale's own fear of being taken hostage was crowded out by despair for a fellow journalist, inhumanely held by irrational strangers.

gress had forbidden the administration to bankroll. The Contra connection was an extraordinary piece of the story that Dale and I had heard nothing about until we read it in the papers.

It was all over but for the recriminations. More than $30 million in weaponry had been sold to a terrorist government in a caper that smacked of Maxwell Smart. For its part of the deal, Iran had released three American hostages and kidnapped three more. Reagan had trusted the so-called moderates in Iran and tragically had swapped hostages for hostages. Unlike the classic Greek tragedies, this was not a case of great and powerful men betrayed by hubris. These were ambitious little men with a sophomoric plan who were betrayed by their own mediocrity.

CHAPTER 24

I WAS AN UNLIKELY PEACEMAKER TO be let loose on the Soviet Union. Yet no less than the president of the United States had asked me to make an approach to the Kremlin to reduce tensions between the two nuclear superpowers.

World peace was not foremost in my mind when I came up with the idea of a Young Astronaut program. Children were growing up around me who were technologically illiterate. They wouldn't be able to operate the complex computers, robots, lasers, and other high-tech tools that would become standard equipment in the twenty-first century. Most U.S. schools simply weren't teaching the basic scientific skills that would be needed in everyday life.

Every generation needs a dream to inspire it and an adventure to ennoble it. Seldom if ever have young people had an incentive to rise above themselves in such a way as the lure of space offers. They are living in a new age of Columbuses and Magellans. Marvels beyond comprehension are waiting to be discovered on the last frontier that stretches beyond the earth. If they could see realistic possibilities of participating in the space adventure, I thought, they might be willing to tackle the tough disciplines that are prerequisite to meeting the challenge of the stars.

This was much on my mind when I called on President Reagan in October 1982. I steered the conversation around to education. We both deplored the poor performance of American students in science and math, and we agreed that our kids needed to be jump-started into the technological age.

"I'll tell you what turns on my grandchildren," I said. "What stimulates them is space. If we could turn science classes into space adventures, we'd get a better response from the kids." I told the president my idea. A Young

Astronaut program, I said, might stir their imaginations, shake them out of the doldrums, and prepare them for the technological challenges ahead.

Reagan seemed impressed. He called in an aide and dictated a note about my idea. Then we moved off the subject, which drifted to the back of my mind until about a year later when my assistant, Opal Ginn, buzzed me to report that the president was calling. "We've decided to go ahead with your idea," he announced. For an agonizing instant, my mind froze. What idea? Reagan saved me. "We're going to start a Young Astronaut program." He said the Education Department, after studying the idea for a year, had no objections.

Later he asked me to be the chairman. I scrambled for a way to extricate myself from this flattering but unwanted responsibility. I was a journalist, not an astronaut or a political climber. I was reluctant to chair a White House–sponsored program after spending so much of my career avoiding entanglements with the people and agencies I covered. Yet this was my idea; I believed in it; that meant I should take responsibility for it. I told the president I would accept the chairmanship if he would give me one of his standout aides, Wendell Butler, to run it. Reagan agreed.

Thereafter, he became enamored with the Young Astronauts. He launched the program at a White House ceremony on October 17, 1984. Then he made personal phone calls to line up corporate sponsors. All I had to do to get into the Oval Office, I learned, was to tell Reagan's handlers that I needed to see the president on Young Astronaut business. He would always let me in—even when my column was battering him over the arms-for-hostages debacle.

He never turned down an invitation to participate in a Young Astronaut function. This resulted in so many appearances that a White House scheduler called me, off the record. He explained that because of the demands on the president, the staff had adopted a rigid rule limiting him to one appearance before any single organization in a year. On rare occasions, he had appeared twice before the same group. "He's already appeared for the Young Astronauts seven times this year," the man whined. "Please don't ask him again, because he'll do it."

Not long after the program was founded, I paid a call on President Reagan and found him in a troubled mood. The Soviet Union was beginning to crack at the seams, and he feared Kremlin leaders might make some desperate, reckless move to avert a collapse. He wanted to reassure the Soviets that the United States would not take advantage of their plight.

I suggested that an initiative be made through the children. Why not invite the Soviets to join us in establishing a space program for young people? I suggested that he write a letter to Soviet leader Konstantin Chernenko, pointing out that the earth was merely an oversized spaceship and that any damage to its parts could endanger its entire human manifest. The letter could then propose establishing ties between America's Young Astronauts and Russia's Young Cosmonauts.

Reagan liked the idea, with one change. "You write the letter," he said. "They don't like me. I called them an Evil Empire." I protested that I had no official standing, that the Soviets, therefore, wouldn't pay much attention to a letter from me. He said the letter could mention the White House connection.

So I wrote Chernenko a letter and entrusted it to a messenger, my daughter Tanya who was leaving for the Soviet Union with a tour group. Her Russian name, I thought, might give her an edge. Tanya didn't quite know how she was going to pull off the personal delivery, but as it turned out, the Soviets arranged that for her. Soviet customs officials, pawing through her luggage at the Moscow airport, came across the letter addressed to the secretary-general of the Communist Party. Tanya explained her mission to the authorities, and they disappeared with the letter for two hours. When they returned, they told Tanya to present herself to Chernenko's office at an appointed hour.

She was greeted by an aide who said Chernenko would have received her personally, except that he was ill. The aide promised to hand-deliver the letter to the Soviet leader. He didn't mention that Chernenko was not receiving visitors personally because he was dying.

Within a few weeks, I got a phone call from the Soviet embassy. A man with a gruff Russian accent got straight to the point. "Chairman Chernenko has read your letter."

"I'm pleased to hear that. What is his response?"

"His response is positive."

After we talked about where to go from there, the Russian paused, then asked, "Did Tanya enjoy her visit to the Soviet Union?"

"She had a marvelous time," I effused. "She was greatly impressed with your country."

There was another pause, then this grave rejoinder, "Too bad she doesn't write the column."

AS RIVAL CHAMPIONS OF THE WORLD'S reigning ideologies, the United States and Soviet Union did not find it easy to reconcile their differences. But they took the next major step in 1985. On the eve of a Geneva summit meeting between Reagan and the new Soviet leader, Mikhail Gorbachev, the president again spoke to me about his concerns. The cracks in the Soviet system were widening, and an economic collapse seemed inevitable. Relations between the two superpowers were delicate. I reminded him of the Young Astronaut initiative and suggested that it might be a good time to arrange exchange visits between Young Astronauts and Young Cosmonauts.

Upon his return from Geneva, Reagan notified me that Gorbachev had agreed to the exchange. This resulted in the first official youth exchange in the history of Soviet-American relations. In October 1986, ten Young Astronauts toured Soviet space facilities. They were the first Americans ever to be admitted to Star City, the Soviet space center, where they were taken aboard a mock-up of the space station Mir and spoke to the cosmonauts who were manning the real craft in orbit.

The following December, I stood at Dulles International airport outside Washington awaiting the return delegation of Young Cosmonauts. I was flanked by State Department officials and congressional representatives standing and fidgeting stiffly. The Soviet delegation clustered tightly and somberly around the ambassador. The rank and demeanor of both groups said that the visit of these children was serious diplomacy.

In between us, half a dozen Young Astronauts hopped from foot to foot, craning their necks, whispering and giggling breathlessly in anticipation of welcoming the young friends who had hosted their visit to Moscow.

The first Russian girl emerged from the Immigration-Customs labyrinth. She swept the crowd with her eyes and then, with a squeal of delight, ran exuberantly into the arms of an American friend. The two of them hugged and bounced with undiplomatic abandon. The effect was electric on the adult welcoming committees from both sides of the Iron Curtain. Smiles blossomed; tension evaporated. Our two clusters merged into one as we shook hands and exchanged warm greetings.

Astronauts say that from space, the earth looks like a sparking blue jewel against a black backdrop, a speck of warmth in the cold reaches of the galaxy. They agree that the farther they get from Earth, the closer they feel to the people they left behind. They recognize how fragile our biosphere is and how much it depends on the cooperation of all its inhabitants. Next to children, I have found no one more eager to let bygones be bygones than American astronauts and Russian cosmonauts. One cosmonaut quietly confided in me that he had carried a photo of the ill-fated *Challenger* space shuttle and its crew with him on one of his trips into space. In honor of that crew, he had pinned the photo on a wall inside the Soviet space station.

FROM WASHINGTON AND MOSCOW, YOUNG ASTRO-
NAUTS International sprouted up and spread like a vine around the globe, reaching eventually into China. In 1991, Wendell Butler and I were attending our international convention in Tokyo when we received a terse message from Beijing asking if we could fly there the next day. Our welcoming committee was late reaching the airport because their car had broken down. They delivered Wendell and me to a hotel and kept us up past midnight asking questions about Young Astronauts. "We will be back tomorrow at nine to continue our discussions," their leader announced.

Nine o'clock passed, and then ten and eleven without any sign of our hosts. At 11:30 A.M., they showed up with no explanation for their tardiness. "We have briefed our minister and he wishes to invite you to lunch." It turned out to be a major affair with the cabinet minister in charge of the Chinese space program and several of his subordinates. We were ushered into a large room, bereft of furnishings except for two large bamboo chairs at the head. I knew enough about how the Chinese do business to recognize a formal setting when I saw one.

The cabinet minister and I were seated in the chairs while the rest of the entourage, outnumbering Wendell by a couple dozen, stood at a discreet distance and waited. The minister asked me a few questions to satisfy himself. Then he stood and grasped my hand. "We will have a Young Astronaut program in China," he proclaimed, compressing into a single sentence what I had expected would take months of Chinese-style, back-and-forth negotiations.

The founding of the Young Astronaut program has been a thrilling experience. I have visited underfunded, understaffed ghetto schools where proud Young Astronauts have shown me wonderful hands-on science projects. I have been stopped on the streets by teachers who tell me the program works wonders for their students. I sat in the Oval Office with George Bush and watched a serious little boy fire questions at astronauts in the space shuttle via a special telephone hookup. His informed questions made the president's light banter with the astronauts seem trivial by comparison.

I have broken into the most elite circle on earth—the small band of space explorers who are blazing trails into the last frontier. They have landed on the moon. Their next stop will be Mars. The sheer size of this giant leap across the universe—the enormity of its demands for technology, the unlimited possibilities it portends for the future—has dwarfed any differences or vanities that may once have divided American astronauts and Russian cosmonauts.

One of my close friends today is cosmonaut Alexander Serebrov, chairman of our sister organization in Russia, who also holds the record for space walks. No other human being has spent as much time as he has outside the space station alone in space. Once he spotted out of the corner of his eye that his tether was jiggling loose. In that split second, he grabbed the line; otherwise he would still be drifting out there in his own space coffin.

On my 1989 visit to Moscow, he invited me to dinner at his home in the cosmonaut housing enclave. As we drove up to his house, Alexander's car bounced through some potholes, reminiscent of the streets of Washington. "They can send us into space, but they can't fix the potholes," he said, echoing a common American complaint. He introduced me to his wife, a petite ballerina. "I am the head of the house," he said firmly, then confessed: "She is the neck. She turns the head."

After dinner, Alexander said he wanted to treat me to an evening of Russian music. He cranked an old windup phonograph and my American ears endured a couple albums of mournful Russian music. Then he brought out his "favorite." He turned the crank, queued the record, and sang the first line in a clipped, coarse baritone: "Pardon me boy, is that the Chattanooga choo choo . . ."

PART 7

TOUGH CHOICES

1 9 8 9 — 1 9 9 7

THE COLD WAR, WHICH BEGAN THE year I came to Washington, ended in 1991 when the Soviet Union collapsed. Communism had failed in large part because the Soviets could no longer afford to keep pace with U.S. military spending. Ronald Reagan had financed his years of the war by borrowing heavily. Americans celebrated, little knowing what price they had paid and would continue to pay for victory.

By the luck of the draw, George Bush was president when this "new world order" was ushered in. He did little to bring it about, but was happy to ride the wave of popularity that came with being leader of the free world during the transition. Bush was criticized by myself and others as a man of no vision. He seemed puzzled that he was even expected to have what he called, "the vision thing." A career bureaucrat, Bush ascended to the presidency on the coattails of the Republican revolution captained by Reagan.

Yet Bush proved to be a surprisingly determined leader, especially in the area of foreign policy. When Panamanian strongman Manuel Noriega refused to step down after a national election, Bush didn't hesitate to send U.S. troops into Panama in 1989 to get Noriega out of the way of democracy.

A year later, when Iraq invaded Kuwait and took control of the oil fields there, Bush again didn't hesitate. With Congress's approval, he dispatched hundreds of thousands of U.S. soldiers to the Persian Gulf to chase the Iraqi troops back home. The Persian Gulf War, with few casualties, was a chance to show off the American military might that taxpayers had spent so much money on during the Cold War.

We acquired two new national heros, General Colin Powell, the chairman of the Joint Chiefs of Staff, and General Norman "Stormin' Norman" Schwarzkopf, head of the U.S. forces in the Gulf War and a man about whom I was privileged to write a biography in 1991. An outpouring of patriotism and national pride obscured the wishy-washy American policy in the Gulf that had given Iraq reason to believe it could get away with an invasion in the first place.

Bush's victories abroad could not overcome his perceived lack of interest in the problems back home. Wallowing in a budget deficit and fearful of declining status as a world economic power, Americans were ready for a big change. In the 1992 election they threw out Bush and elected a baby boomer Democrat, Bill Clinton. My generation was officially retired from the Oval Office.

Then, two years later, voters sent the Democratic majority in the House and Senate packing. Republicans had lost the White House after twelve years, but they took control of Congress and had the president by the tail. Clinton tried gamely to enact the progressive social welfare programs that his constituency expected of him, but he was stymied at every turn by the Republicans and what they called their "Contract with America"—a scorched-earth strategy to shrink the powers and budget of the federal government.

What we got was impasse, brought about in no small measure by Americans themselves who were happy to see their taxes cut but unwilling to give up any of the services to which they had become accustomed.

When I came to Washington, the United States was the world's number one military power, economic power, industrial power, agricultural power, financial power, and technological power. But some terrible enervation of common sense has been dragging down the American nation. Our political leaders have fostered a climate of complacency, refusing to make decisions that might cause us temporary pain, or cost them their offices. I fear the 1990s will be remembered as the decade when that cowardice caught up with us.

CHAPTER 25

I LIKE TO THINK I PLAYED a part in Boris Yeltsin's first visit to the United States. At least I issued the invitation to this up-and-coming member of the Supreme Soviet in July 1989, and he responded with a booming, "I go to America!" Within two months he was indeed in the United States, charming Americans and thawing the chill of the Cold War.

I met Yeltsin on my first visit to the Soviet Union in 1989. For a journalist with more than four decades of experience reporting on the Cold War, the trip was too long coming. Yet in retrospect I could not have picked a more dynamic time, with the dissolution of the Soviet empire in its early stage. My friend Howard Ruff, the publisher of financial books and journals, invited Dale Van Atta and me to accompany a group of his disciples on a tour of Russia. My role was to enjoy the ride but to keep one step ahead of the group, briefing them on the latest intelligence on the Soviet Union.

At the jumping-off point of our tour in Helsinki the night before we flew into Moscow, I confessed to the group, "This will be my first trip, so it will be the blind leading the blind." Then I joked, "You can become an expert in two or three days. If you stay longer, you'll get confused." Truer words were never uttered about the Soviet Union at the close of that decade. In the shifting panorama of rising and falling political fortunes, today's expert was destined to become tomorrow's anachronism.

Mikhail Gorbachev, then sitting precariously in the Kremlin catbird's seat, had been exhaustively profiled by the CIA's wise men. As they portrayed him, Gorbachev was determined to drag his country kicking and screaming into the twentieth century about ninety years behind schedule. He was no lover of freedom, but he stuck a wet finger into the wind and rightly assessed that the current was blowing in the direction of reform. If he was to remain in power, he had to make accommodations.

Gorbachev had risen to the top with the cunning of a Mafia don warily playing the power game on the backs of the common people. During seventy years under communism, the masses had learned to adjust, but the oppressive bureaucracy had slowly strangled their doomed system until it barely functioned. The Russians knew how to survive within the system—just keep your head below the purge line—but they didn't know how to survive without food. Gorbachev realized that his own survival would depend not on the politics he served up, but on the food he put on their tables. So it was to save his own skin that he cracked open the door to the free market. It was to buttress his reputation that he instituted glasnost, which was supposed to give the appearance of democracy, without the power.

Before my trip, I had seen one CIA study that gave Gorbachev two years to spur the Soviet economy. If he failed, his enemies would overthrow him. As it turned out, the CIA was right about the timing, but wrong about who would do the overthrowing. That job went to Gorbachev's former friend, Boris Yeltsin.

Gorbachev had plucked Yeltsin out of the boondocks in 1985 and made him Moscow party chief. Yeltsin's rocket rise could be attributed to his reputation as a reformer. He had become known in his small corner of the Soviet mosaic for putting the people back in the "people's democracy." His new orders were to clean house, but he got carried away. He mingled with the people, stood in the food lines, rode the buses, and argued with the shop clerks—all to see how the Moscow system really worked. Of course, he learned that it was breaking down. He threw out lazy functionaries and added his own voice to the growing clamor.

Gorbachev used Yeltsin as a stalking horse, pitting him against the conservative party ideologues, but Yeltsin's fiery rhetoric inevitably offended even his mentor. In a speech in 1987, Yeltsin's tongue got away from him, and he implied that Gorbachev was moving too slowly. As soon as the words were out, Yeltsin knew he had made a mistake and offered his resignation on the spot. Gorbachev accepted and shipped Yeltsin off to the Construction Ministry to bide his time in anonymity.

Political exile was hard on Yeltsin. With the taste of power still in his mouth, he saw a need for bold moves and strong measures. He was privately contemptuous of his mentor's caution, which he regarded as timidity. Yeltsin was frustrated, a hero in an unheroic post, unhappily hemmed in by the bureaucratic humdrum and the political flummery, a leader looking for his star of destiny. There were rumors of a heart attack or a nervous breakdown.

He could stand it no longer. He put glasnost to the test and declared his candidacy for a seat in the Supreme Soviet. Only a few harmless dissidents had dared to run against the Communist candidates. For appearances sake, they were allowed to go through the democratic motions. But Yeltsin was the first opposition leader, worthy of the name, who challenged a candidate backed by the party and endorsed by Gorbachev. Muscovites had not forgotten their brief exposure to politics, Yeltsin style. So in 1989, just before I arrived in Moscow, they elected him as their people's deputy with 90 percent of the vote.

Though Dale and I were enjoying the sights, we were newsmen first and tour guides second. It would be against our nature to leave Moscow without an interview with Yeltsin. As we saw it, he had the potential to become either the next Soviet premier stirring his people to new heights, or the next Andrey Sakharov preaching to the silent walls in a gulag.

With some difficulty, I got an appointment with Yeltsin, who had been avoiding foreign reporters. But first I sat down with Leonid Kravchenko, the director of the Soviet news agency TASS. Ever since I had taken over the Washington Merry-Go-Round from Drew Pearson, I had been castigated by the Soviet press. But on that day, Kravchenko, the top journalist in the land, candidly chatted with me like an old friend. He told me his reporters had been stringers for the KGB, filing their propaganda for publication and then filing their intelligence reports for the spy agency.

As Kravchenko bared these secrets, I could understand how the Soviet Union of 1989 resembled America of 1776. There was a compulsion to tell the truth just in case the newly granted freedom of speech was short-lived. The democratic reforms were bringing to the surface social, political, ethnic, and economic conflicts that eventually would tear the Soviet Union apart. The televised sessions of the Supreme Soviet were so lively and contentious that the productivity of Soviet workers dropped off 20 percent because they were glued to their TV sets. The streets of Moscow fairly throbbed with the tempo of freedom. I got more straight answers from Muscovites on that short trip than I was accustomed to getting on my own turf in Washington.

Yeltsin mirrored that ebullient openness. At the time I met him, he was fifty-eight years old, cast in the mold of a classic Russian hero—tall, bold, and brusque, with a crown of white hair and a stevedore's grip. He had the theatrical flair, the oratorical artillery, and the messianic urge—combined with the brains and the guile—to lead Russia into a new day.

We were told we had forty-five minutes of his time. His English was poor, so I had brought an interpreter. I had intended to interview Yeltsin, but the reverse happened. He fully expected the Communist hierarchy to pull him down and trample him to death. Foremost in his mind was how

A TICKET OUT

AFTER THE NAMES AND FACES HAVE faded, I will long remember the generosity of my American companions on my Soviet trip in 1989. In Leningrad, one member of our group, David Golding, had found Alexander and Alla Tsveyer, both thirty-seven, who had been trying for eight years to get out of the Soviet Union. The bureaucracy had given them one excuse after another. But the bottom line was, they were Jews.

When our group encountered them, they had finally received permission to immigrate to Israel, but it was a hollow approval since the couple had no money for the airline tickets or the various "departure taxes" that amounted to either bribes or deliberate impediments to those who wanted to leave. Alla said they were willing to sell everything they had, but the possessions of Jews in the Soviet Union, even the new and improved Soviet Union, didn't amount to much. And other Soviets were often reluctant to buy from them for fear of being tainted by association.

On our group's last night in the country, the Americans gathered at a private club in Leningrad for dinner. Our leader, Howard Ruff, presented the case of the Tsveyer family. He said they had stripped their walls of their art. It was nothing of great value, but it was all they had. What were the Americans willing to bid for it?

Everyone had a few rubles to dispose of before leaving the country, and they were eagerly handed over in a lively auction for the Tsveyer's paintings. When the rubles ran out, the Americans opened up their wallets and brought out dollars. Since Alexander and Alla couldn't leave the country with American currency, the money was set aside to be banked for them in the United States. Midway through the auction, a KGB official dropped in to check on the party of Americans. When she figured out what was happening she opened her mouth to protest, but was plied with vodka until she was so drunk she didn't dare report the incident when she sobered up.

At midnight, Howard Ruff rendezvoused with Alexander and Alla and gave them the rubles, enough to get them to Israel. They were moved to tears.

to avoid the fate of all opposition leaders who had challenged the system. Even as we spoke, he said, the KGB was plotting his demise. His name was at the top of their political hit list, he assured me. Maybe I had some advice for him. I suggested that he organize all opposition deputies into a caucus, and then as their leader he could establish a direct relationship with American congressional leaders.

"What is caucus?" Yeltsin blurted in English.

I tried to explain through the interpreter how small groups can band together and form a caucus to promote a minority issue.

For two hours, he pumped me for information. I stressed that he needed to find an issue bigger than perestroika, or reform.

"There is no such issue," Yeltsin replied.

"There is," said Dale. "It's Russian nationalism." Yeltsin's face lit up as Dale suggested that even Russians who resisted reforms were probably tired of bankrolling the rest of the Soviet Union.

"You're right!" Yeltsin said, obviously delighted with the concept of Russians shaking off the other republics that were sucking Mother Russia dry. Yeltsin didn't follow our advice precisely, but he did something else that was unexpected. He abandoned the People's Congress as a route to power and decided instead to run for president of the Russian republic, a position that at the time meant nothing. But, as Yeltsin confided in us, he anticipated that Gorbachev would wind up heading a shell of a government, a confederation of independent Soviet republics. He predicted that Gorbachev would become the Soviet version of the Queen of England—all pomp and no substance.

Yeltsin told me that he and Gorbachev had always maintained a polite relationship but had never been friends. "Our relations were warm, but official," he said, then added a characteristic Russian description of distance: "We never drank together." Those words would come back to me again and again in Yeltsin's spotty political career as he was accused repeatedly of being an imprudent drinker.

As our philosophical discussion wound down, we asked a few personal questions. Had he really suffered a nervous breakdown during his hiatus from power? "I had very bad headaches for two months," was Yeltsin's reply. The headaches stopped, he explained, when he decided to fight back.

Yeltsin kept one hand hidden in his lap during the interview. Dale and I were aware that he was missing a thumb and a forefinger on that hand. The condition was the subject of much speculation in the international press, so Dale pressed him for an explanation, which turned out to be typically Yeltsin. As a curious and irrepressible eleven-year-old, he had tried to take apart a hand grenade, and it had blown up in his fingers. As a grown man, he was now tinkering with a political hand grenade.

Yeltsin was convinced that the KGB was after him, and he seemed genuinely baffled about how to combat its unseen spooks. "You should go to the United States," I said. "Make a trip abroad. Get some overseas exposure. The visibility would make it much more difficult for the KGB to move against you."

Yeltsin nodded, but didn't say yea or nay. Then he walked us to the elevator and at that point, with a big smile, uttered his second English phrase: "I go to America!"

Once outside, we noticed that our interpreter was positively glowing. She kept repeating, "What a wonderful man. What a wonderful man." Until I saw the admiration in her eyes, I had not fully appreciated Yeltsin's charisma. Something overarching in his appeal spanned the chasm that separated the masses from the intellectuals. To this sophisticated young woman at least, Boris Yeltsin had become the bearer of the true flame.

YELTSIN CAME TO AMERICA, AS HE said he would, in September. He was booked for a few speeches and began each of them by saying, "I have come to America because Jack Anderson told me to." This was not the best way to win friends and influence politicians in Washington, where I would win no popularity contests. To hold the KGB at bay, Yeltsin was eager to be seen with President George Bush. But the president, out of deference to Gorbachev, chose not to invite Yeltsin to the White House. I importuned every contact I knew and pulled every string I could to get Yeltsin into the Oval Office. Meanwhile, he barnstormed across America like a homegrown politician, rolling up his sleeves, slapping backs, and shaking hands.

Finally, I arranged a visit that was not a visit at the White House. With some adroit sleight of hand to satisfy the protocol people, I scheduled a White House meeting between Yeltsin and the president's national security advisor, Brent Scowcroft. By a prearranged "coincidence," Bush would drop in, shake hands, and exchange a few friendly words. The only time Scowcroft could see him, it turned out, was the exact time that had been set aside for my own visit with Yeltsin. So my appointment was postponed until the next morning.

The KGB, meanwhile, had already made its move. It had planted some devastating disinformation calculated to turn Yeltsin's triumphant American tour into a debacle. It was splashed on the front page of the Communist Party newspaper, *Pravda*. I was familiar with the KGB's methods and recognized at once who was behind the Yeltsin smear. *Pravda* was so discredited at home that in order to convince its readers a story was true, it would quote from the Western press. So the KGB had first planted the phony story in an Italian newspaper, making Yeltsin out to be the Soviet Spuds MacKenzie, saying that during his travels he had boozed too much, schmoozed too much, and generally behaved like a fraternity boy on spring break.

The morning after the damning KGB story hit *Pravda*, Yeltsin rushed back to Moscow. My rescheduled visit with him was canceled. Instead, he asked members of his staff to stay behind and seek my advice. Over breakfast at the Madison Hotel, they assured me that the story planted by the KGB was false, and I was inclined to believe them. In the ensuing years, I observed from a distance signs of an ambition that overrode his convictions, and a taste for vodka that occasionally blurred his judgment. But it was a sober Yeltsin who pitted his wits against the KGB in those crucial days.

"He wants to know what you think he should do," one of his aides said to me.

"Keep on the offensive," I replied, "I would accuse *Pravda* of concocting the story, accuse them of being a tool of the KGB. I wouldn't utter a single word in defense."

I promised to check out the story and, if I could make the case, to expose the KGB connection. I was able to track down the Italian writer. After a few minutes talking with him, I could easily determine that he hadn't verified the story but had reported what he had been fed by, I suspected, the KGB. So I printed a defense of Yeltsin in my column. Escorts who had been with him twenty-four hours a day gave me a more sober version of events. Yeltsin followed my advice and loudly assailed the KGB when he got home. For the first time under communism, *Pravda* actually printed a retraction.

Yeltsin had passed a big test. Gorbachev had been watching him, hoping for a slipup. When that didn't happen, the KGB had invented a slipup. Since *Pravda* had printed the news, I surmised that Gorbachev had endorsed the smear campaign. But Yeltsin's popularity at home ultimately spoke louder than the KGB's innuendo. He won the presidency in a free election. During his first two years in power, his ministers would call upon me when they came to Washington, explaining that Yeltsin had asked them to consult with me. Then I stopped hearing from him.

THAT WAS A GOLDEN TIME, WHEN the will of the people was finally resounding more loudly than the guns of the oppressors across all of the Eastern Bloc. The dissidents who had been persecuted and imprisoned were now taking their places in the seats of power. I had long admired one voice in particular—that of Polish labor leader Lech Walesa.

Over the years, Walesa and I had corresponded, and I had attempted repeatedly to interview him in Poland. But the Polish government would never grant me a visa. Once the Polish ambassador came personally to my office to apologize for rejecting my application for a visa. He told me the problem was technical, and I should apply again. I did and was rejected again. This time a less agreeable diplomat at the Polish embassy made it quite clear that in Poland I was about as popular as a polecat at a lawn party.

In 1990, I finally got to meet the former electrician, who, a decade earlier, had scrambled over the wall of the Lenin shipyards to rally striking workers and jump-start the destruction of the Iron Curtain. Dale and I traveled to Eastern Europe just as leaders of the new democracies were settling into office. In Gdansk, Poland, I immediately felt an affinity for Walesa. He wore a tie, and on his lapel was a symbol of his faith, a button of the Black Madonna of Czestochowa. But under the table, his feet were clad in comfortable bedroom slippers—my own favorite footwear.

With a straight face, Walesa told us that the long years of Communist oppression had been good for his marriage. "Many people didn't like their flat being bugged, but I liked it because my wife knew it was bugged and she didn't quarrel with me." He was surprisingly good humored for a man who had endured so much.

I knew that the Solidarity movement had nearly cost him his life. The Turkish gunman Mehmet Ali Agca, who had shot Pope John Paul II, testified in court that the Bulgarian secret police also wanted him to shoot Walesa. For two years the Polish security police also plotted to kill Walesa, using an ex-mental patient as the trigger man. The poor fellow foiled the plot himself by showing up on Walesa's doorstep to confess.

Walesa told me that the threats didn't bother him. "The only thing in the world I am afraid of is God and his judgments. That doesn't mean I am going to put my head on the rails and wait for the train to cut it off. I don't expect that angels will lift the train so my head will not be cut off." In view of all Walesa had accomplished to liberate the oppressed, I could think of no one more deserving of divine intervention.

GIVEN MY ADMIRATION FOR WALESA, I hadn't expected that he would be eclipsed by someone else I met on that same trip—Václav Havel, the playwright, who became the reluctant president of Czechoslovakia.

Politics was a profession forced on Havel by circumstances. He was born into a moneyed Czechoslovakian family that was punished for its politics. After the Communists clamped down on the upper class, Havel was not allowed to go to a university or hold down a substantial job. So he settled for odd jobs and worked his way up through a theater company from stagehand to resident playwright. Reflections on the absurdity of communism became the thread running through his work. His greatest accolade was having his plays banned from 1968 until he became president in 1989.

When I arrived in Prague, I was received warmly by U.S. Ambassador Shirley Temple Black. I was prepared to find a lightweight trying to run the U.S. Embassy—a grown-up little tap dancer in curls and crinolines who had been rewarded as America's little sweetheart with a diplomatic post. I could not have been more mistaken. Black had arrived in Czechoslovakia in the fall of 1989. She started off by insisting that her license plate bear her initials, "STB," just to pique the Communist government. STB was the acronym for the dreaded Czech secret police.

Black immediately befriended the dissident Havel, who had spent five years in prison for his outspoken anti-Communist views. By the time Havel was elected to the presidency, Black had established herself as part of his inner circle of confidants and was deft at nudging him in the direction of U.S. interests.

Before my appointment with Havel, his secretary called me and asked if the president needed to dress formally for the interview. Of course not, I assured her. There would be no TV cameras or photographers along with me. "Good, he'll like that," she responded with enthusiasm.

I had heard stories about how he liked to tool around the palace on a small motor scooter, but I wasn't prepared for Havel's idea of dressing down. Dale and I sat in the gray, yet grand presidential palace, Hradcany Castle, that had survived two world wars. A door squeaked open, and a man I took to be the custodian shuffled in. He was wearing a UCLA T-shirt, his hands stuffed in the pockets of faded blue jeans. The man didn't look Czech; rather, he resembled a Dutch cobbler with a round, flushed face and tousled reddish-blond hair. To my surprise, he approached Dale and me. Our interpreter introduced him as Václav Havel.

In a matter of minutes, I felt as if I was in the presence of a 1960s flower child caught in a time warp. His speech was laced with hippie jargon, and he wore an Indian talisman on his wrist to give him energy. In the back window of his presidential limousine was painted a ring of pink hearts, and he regularly signed his name with a heart as the final flourish.

As I listened to Havel talk, his words resonated deep in my own heart. "When you came into our country, you couldn't help but notice the pollution the Communists left us," he said. "Our air is almost unbreathable, our water almost undrinkable. Ah, but there's a worse pollution. You wouldn't notice it because it's an invisible pollution—a pollution of the spirit. Our people saw nothing wrong with lying to the government that lied to them. Our people saw nothing wrong with cheating the government that cheated them. Our people saw nothing wrong with stealing from the government that stole from them."

Havel shrugged sorrowfully. "I'm afraid they've gotten in the habit. Our greatest danger is no longer totalitarianism, not even the mafioso that is springing up in our midst. Our greatest menace is our own bad qualities. What Czechoslovakia needs is a moral resurgence." As he spoke, I thought his remarks could have been addressed just as appropriately to the American people.

Havel became most animated when talking about the protest music of the sixties. He described it as the candle that had kept the hope of freedom burning during the dark days of communism in Czechoslovakia. "The forbidden music brought us together—a very broad spectrum of people who were united by the spirit of resistance. And music, thus, became resistance. It was the little candle in a dark forest that gradually became a torch."

The arrest and trial of a Czech band called Plastic People of the Universe, named after a song by American rocker Frank Zappa, had mobilized Havel and others in 1977 to write "Charter '77," an intellectuals' manifesto calling for freedom from the Communists.

Havel was so taken with Zappa that when the rocker visited Prague in January 1990, Havel impulsively offered to make him a special trade ambassador. I learned the story behind that appointment when I got back home. Just two weeks after Havel offered Zappa the diplomatic job, Secretary of State James Baker arrived in Prague nursing an old grudge that dated back to 1985. His wife, Susan Baker, together with other well-connected Washington wives including Tipper Gore, had formed a parents' group to push for warning labels on music with lyrics too sexual, profane, or violent. Zappa, the purveyor of all three, had breezed into Washington for a Senate hearing about the ratings. He had been grossly undiplomatic, calling Susan Baker and the others "a group of bored Washington housewives"; then he had mimicked Mrs. Baker's southern accent.

When James Baker arrived in Prague, his aides delicately let Havel know that an American should not serve as a trade representative for Czechoslovakia. Not only was Baker still boiling about the insult to his wife, but he thought the appointment would make Havel look like an amateur. Havel dragged his feet on making Zappa's appointment official, giving excuses about red tape. Then he finally made Zappa an unofficial cultural ambassador—a formal title for a Czech musical hero.

At the base of the hill coming down from Hradcany Castle, Dale and I paused at the Lennon Wall, which had become a national graffiti board about the time of Beatle John Lennon's murder in 1980. As fast as the Communist authorities cleaned the wall, new graffiti would appear glorifying freedom. The day we were there, the lyrics from one of Havel's favorite Lennon songs, "Imagine," were scrawled on the wall: "I hope some day you'll join us, and the world will live as one."

I RETURNED TO THE FORMER SOVIET empire in 1994, this time as chairman of Young Astronauts International, which held its annual convention in Ukraine. Our interpreter's sister was married to a nuclear physicist, who invited me to dinner. He had the look of an obscure file clerk, but his mild mien was just the moss on a character of granite. I learned that he was a Soviet hero who had volunteered to help cap the Chernobyl nuclear plant after it blew its top in 1986. No one knew whether the protective clothing was adequate to shield him from the heavy radiation that was erupting from the damaged plant. For his courage, he was rewarded with a 50 percent discount in rent, and for a lifetime of distinguished work, he drew a salary of ten dollars a month. He could not afford to put meat on the table for our dinner, but he treated us to vegetables and a watermelon. The latter cost him half his monthly pay.

This brave man's pitiable financial condition was on my mind the next day when I toured the missile plant where intercontinental ballistic missiles had been produced for the old Soviet Union. It took the personal approval of the Ukrainian president to get me inside. Even with these credentials, I was kept waiting an hour while the plant authorities verified the paperwork. But once I passed all the barriers, the plant managers showed me everything I wanted to see and answered my questions with startling candor.

I asked the head of the plant whether there had been any defections among his scientists based on financial need. "It must be a temptation for some of your top scientists to accept work in such oil-rich countries as Iran and Libya," I said.

"Yes, there is a great temptation. But none of them have done that," he said. "What they have done is to sell their knowledge to those countries. They have even smuggled materials from the plant. It's hard to blame them. They have to survive."

I went away staggered by what I had heard. After World War II, the United States had quickly snapped up German rocket scientists before the Soviets could get their hands on them. Now, when for a few million dollars we could take care of the nuclear scientists in the former Soviet bloc, we let poverty drive them into the irresponsible hands of radical regimes.

"THEY'RE GOING TO GET ME NOW"

THE FIRST AMENDMENT HAS SHELTERED MY work, so no matter what scrape I find myself in, the stakes are rarely life threatening. Thus my own determination pales when stacked up against the work of reporters who labor under oppressive regimes.

Dragisa Kasikovich had the umbrella of the First Amendment over him, too, publishing a Serbian-American newspaper called *Liberty* in Chicago. But it could not protect him from the Yugoslav secret police, who had no regard for the U.S. Constitution. They brutally beat and then stabbed Kasikovich to death on a Chicago street the day after his newspaper reprinted one of my columns in June 1977.

Les Whitten had done the legwork on the column that exposed how the Communist-controlled Serbian Orthodox Church had become a front for the Yugoslav secret police, the UDB. Les had found the chilling story of the takeover of the church in secret FBI files, which also described an ugly attempt to discredit the anti-Communist leader of the church in the United States. The defamation campaign ended with the mother church in Belgrade defrocking the American bishop.

Kasikovich reprinted the column in his paper and added his own strident editor's note. Then he told friends, "They're going to get me now. I'm the next one." It is possible the UDB assumed Kasikovich had been Les's source for the information, but he was not. The day after his paper went to press, he was murdered in an attack made to look like a common street mugging gone awry. The only witness to the murder was killed along with him—the nine-year-old daughter of Kasikovich's fiancée.

This mistake will plague the world with a new nuclear menace even more ominous than the nuclear buildup by the Soviet and American superpowers. Now religious and revolutionary fanatics are gaining the means to blow up the earth. But at least the scientist I met, the hero of Chernobyl, won't go to Iran or Iraq or Libya. I have helped to bring him and his family to America.

CHAPTER 26

I HAVE NEVER LOST A LIBEL suit, although I have been dragged into court often enough. Politicians have sued me as a public relations ploy; once the lawsuits have drawn the desired headlines, they slowly disappear through the legal process like a sausage going through a meat grinder. Individuals have filed nuisance suits against me—tickets in a legal lottery— hoping to hit the jackpot or at least negotiate a settlement in return for ending the extortion. Still others use the libel laws as a deterrent; if I expose them in print, they retaliate with a lawsuit they can't win, and in the process they drain my resources. These suits have cost me dearly in legal fees, so my unblemished record in the courtroom gives me only small comfort. I have learned that one can emerge from a lawsuit with reputation intact but wallet substantially lighter.

Drew Pearson would turn over in his grave if he knew that my lawyer now has the final say-so on every Washington Merry-Go-Round column that goes out with my name where Drew's used to be. America has become so bogged down in litigation that the only safe course is to avoid the quagmire. Drew would never believe—I can hardly believe it myself—that I had to back away from one of the biggest stories of the 1980s because of the potential for a lawsuit.

The circumstances started to come together in 1984 when I assigned Mike Binstein, then a new face in my office, to cover the economic side of the news. The economy, I told him, would become the most important story of the 1990s. Joe Spear collared Mike in the kitchen one morning and further whetted his appetite by dangling the word "Pulitzer" in front of him. "You should be looking at bank failures," Joe said. "If you can get the inside story, you're going to win a Pulitzer." By the end of the day, Mike was at the Federal Deposit Insurance Corporation studying the agency's annual report.

The instability in the commercial banking industry, brought on by the deregulation fever of the Reagan years, was just beginning to be felt.

Mike called a stranger, Al Whitney, the press relations man for FDIC Chairman William Isaac. Mike wanted an interview with Isaac, but Whitney was wary about tangling with a Jack Anderson reporter. "Come on over for breakfast," Whitney said, promising nothing more than something to eat. The breakfast lasted two and a half hours. Mike, who went into the interview knowing barely enough about the banking business to balance his own checkbook, came out a budding financial reporter.

He was particularly fascinated by the commando-raid tactics the FDIC used to take over a bank when it failed. Without the experience to know that his request was outrageous, Mike asked if he could tag along on one of the raids. It wasn't the kind of feature story that fit into my column format, but it was tailor-made for *Parade* magazine. Whitney spoke to Isaac, and they agreed that Mike could be the first reporter ever allowed to witness a federal bank takeover.

On a Thursday morning in May 1984, Mike boarded a plane with a squad of FDIC bank closers. They didn't tell him where they were going until the plane was in the air. Their first stop was Dallas, where the Washington contingent met secretly with Texas bank regulators. No one introduced Mike, who sat quietly at the back of the room taking notes, until Jim Sexton, the top banking regulator in Texas, asked Al Whitney, "Who's that guy with you?" "Oh," said Whitney nonchalantly, "that's a Jack Anderson reporter." Sexton responded with an astonished expletive that he repeated periodically, shaking his head, until the meeting adjourned. Some of the old warhorses in the Texas delegation declared Mike's presence a sacrilege. Whitney had to place a call to Bill Isaac in their presence and hear him vouch for Mike.

The gang piled into rental cars and headed across west Texas for the little town of Snyder. The local bank was about to be taken over by Uncle Sam, and if all went as planned, the bankers and townspeople would be the last ones to know. The secrecy was critical to prevent bankers at a failing institution from shredding incriminating records or pocketing money before the federal commandos arrived. Snyder was such a tiny town that the presence of dozens of briefcase-toting strangers in gray suits would prompt a run on a tottering bank. At the very least, the local bankers would know something was up. So Mike and the FDIC squad booked hotel rooms in Big Springs, about fifty miles away.

The bank raid was set for 5 P.M. Friday. On Thursday night a carload of regulators, plus Mike and his tape recorder, drove into Snyder to scope out the town, pick a staging area, and inform the local constabulary of their plans—

so no one would mistake them for robbers. Then they returned to Big Springs. At 3 P.M. Friday, Mike was sitting by the hotel pool with the FDIC crew, waiting for zero hour, when one of their number rushed in with news. "We've got to go!" he shouted. "Some stupid jerk from the Federal Reserve just walked into the bank!" The bank had borrowed heavily from the Federal Reserve, so as part of the shutdown, a Fed representative was supposed to be on hand to call the loan. He had arrived at the bank two hours ahead of schedule, blowing the secrecy and sending the bankers into a panic.

Mike and the FDIC crew raced to their cars, pulling clothes on over their bathing suits as they ran. The caravan sped across the barren Texas landscape where Mike, a wide-eyed Chicago boy, swore he saw coyotes hanging from the farmers' fence posts. The team arrived to find the bank in chaos but the records intact. They spent most of the night sifting through papers and taking inventory of every paper clip and penny roll.

THIS SINGLE STORY ESTABLISHED MIKE AS an able financial reporter and earned him the confidence of key sources on the financial beat. These sources handed Mike the most sensitive, most secret, most explosive document in finance—the FDIC's secret list of failing banks. I counted seven hundred banks on the list, nearly 5 percent of all the banks in the country. I salivated; I cogitated; I tried to dream up justification for publishing the story. But to publish this hot list would have been irresponsible, because it would have triggered a run on every one of those banks.

Mike continued to bring me inside information on the mushrooming banking crisis. Individual deposits in fifteen thousand commercial banks were guaranteed up to $100,000 by the federal government. These banks were sitting on risky loans totaling hundreds of billions of dollars—potential losses that exceeded their stockholders' equity and loan-loss reserves. They were writing off bad loans by the billions each year, with billions more in hopeless Third World debt hanging over their vaults. About half the bad loans were written off in taxes that the banks were excused from paying, thus sticking the taxpayers with the staggering cost of the banking industry's financial follies.

As if this were not enough to cause a monumental migraine, Mike discovered that the condition of commercial banks was a mere decimal-point fraction compared to the trouble the savings and loan industry was in. The S&L regulators were sitting on a Vesuvius that was about to erupt. Before we would let go of the story, it would become the mother of all boondoggles.

I picked up the first hint from no less than President Reagan's chief of staff, Don Regan, who traveled the eight blocks from the White House to my office in an official limousine, with tiny flags fluttering on the front fenders. He came to confess that the White House had made a grave mistake. The president wanted me to know about it and would cooperate with me in exposing it, Regan said. This horrible error, he revealed, was the appointment of Ed Gray as chairman of the Federal Home Loan Bank Board. The dour-faced Gray was a disaster in the job and was recklessly threatening to drive the thrifts out of business, Regan confided.

I called for Mike and told him what I'd learned. Our mission was to prevent shady and shaky S&Ls from getting their hands in the pockets of the depositors, I instructed Mike. He departed, with fire in his belly, to investigate Gray.

Mike arranged an interview with Gray and found him surrounded by half a dozen staffers with notebooks and tape recorders. Mike was aggressive, Gray was defensive, and the interview ended in a stalemate. But Gray left Mike so troubled and ambivalent that he wrote nothing, preferring instead to wait and watch.

At a party two months later, Mike spotted Gray across the room, waited until the crowd thinned, and then approached him. Mike and Gray were still talking two hours later when the cleaning crew began vacuuming the place, "Let's have dinner," Mike said, sensing that Gray was not the villain in the woodpile. Gray agreed, provided that they choose a restaurant with something bland on the menu. Gray's stomach was so torn up from his battles with the S&L barons that he was living on broth and white bread. Mike received a primer that night on the simmering S&L scandal. From that moment on, he was far ahead of everyone else on the story of the decade.

GRAY TOLD MIKE, AMONG OTHER THINGS, about a man named Charlie Keating—fabulously wealthy and impossibly eccentric with a gold-plated lifestyle that was financed by a California cash cow called Lincoln Savings and Loan. The deregulation of S&Ls had allowed Keating and other owners to invest their customers' savings in high-risk ventures, with the assurance that the federal deposit insurance program would cover any losses.

But one man stood in their way. He was Ed Gray, the real-life counterpart of Jimmy Stewart in the classic movie, *Mr. Smith Goes to Washington*. Gray had taken an oath as the chief regulator of the S&L industry, and he intended to keep it. He could see that S&Ls were becoming an endangered species; many were close to rupturing. He knew this would cause a massive bloodletting, yet he seemed to be the only Washington official who wanted to stanch the hemorrhage. No, Ed Gray was not the villain in this saga. He was the intense, idealistic hero, with ulcers. And White House chief of staff Don Regan, who had baited me to blow the whistle on Gray, would gag on his own whistle.

Charlie Keating had protected his S&L empire by contributing heavily to various members of Congress. The donations weren't offered out of civic virtue; he expected a return on his investment. Many of the members began to tend his cash register on the floors of the Senate and the House. Mike learned from his sources that Keating was working every side of the federal triangle. Keating even offered Gray a job, dangling the promise of several hundred thousand dollars a year in front of a public servant who was already living on credit cards and money borrowed from his mother.

Mike quickly drafted a column, summing up the case against Keating. I had in mind a devastating series, using Keating as the personification of a multibillion-dollar scandal. Half a dozen other funds, all clones of the S&L, were likewise insured by Uncle Sam with only token reserves. Other monster collapses could prove to be the force that would bring down the federal government's strange financial house.

As customary, I passed the draft to my lawyer, David Branson, for his legal scrutiny. He usually reviewed it with a cold, professional eye. But this column touched a sensitive nerve that sent him bouncing off the ceiling. He announced that it was hogwash and pressed Mike for documentation. Mike and I were spooked by Dave's reaction. We thought the story was solid and couldn't understand why he should panic.

Not long afterward, Dave requested a meeting at my place and brought along a senior partner from the head office in New York City. They stunned us with a revelation. Their law firm, Kaye, Scholer, Fierman, Hays & Handler, represented Charlie Keating. All the time Mike and I had been talking with our lawyer about this hot story, we had been talking to Keating's lawyer, too. They now acknowledged the potential conflict; if litigation ensued they could no longer represent us both. They'd have to choose between a pro bono client and a multimillion-dollar client.

Swallowing my anger, I smiled sweetly and said: "Please convey to Mr. Keating my regrets for depriving him of a great law firm." It was their turn to appear stunned. "No, no, no . . ." both lawyers sputtered at the same time. They explained gravely that the law firm was dropping me, not Keating.

I remained angry long enough to tell Mike we'd publish the column anyway. Damn the libel threat! Full speed ahead! But because Branson worked for me pro bono out of a commitment to the First Amendment, that left me in a bind. I couldn't afford such top-notch legal help otherwise, yet I couldn't publish a column in a litigious environment without daily review by a lawyer.

I had learned by sad experience that I could spend a fortune in legal fees to prove that I was right all along. My lawyer's job was to sew up the language of my columns so tightly that no one would want to venture a lawsuit, even a frivolous one. After that first column on Keating, I told Mike we couldn't continue to walk the high wire without a net. With bitter regret, I freed Mike to peddle his S&L stories elsewhere, sensing that I was throwing a big one back into the water. Mike took his growing portfolio on Keating to a regional Washington magazine, *Regardie's*.

The ink on Mike's first story published in that magazine was barely dry before Keating sued the Federal Home Loan Bank Board, charging that Gray's staff was leaking confidential bank board documents to the press. When Mike saw a copy of the lawsuit, he was shocked to learn that he was going to be called to testify and that Branson had signed the complaint as the attorney of record for Keating. Branson's law firm claimed this was no conflict of interest because they had represented me, not Mike, and the key story had appeared in *Regardie's*, not in my column. But Mike had developed the story under my supervision, and in that capacity, he had discussed his investigation with Branson. Mike and I tried to reconstruct every conversation we'd had with Branson on the Keating story when we had thought we were protected by attorney-client privilege. A week later the suit was dropped, but my relationship with Branson was irreparably damaged.

No sooner had Keating dropped one lawsuit than he filed another. This time Branson's firm brought a libel suit for Keating against another magazine, *Arizona Trend*, for publishing an edited version of Mike's article that had first appeared in *Regardie's*. I didn't understand the legal strategy, but I suspected Branson was behind it, and I knew he was a brilliant litigator. That suit eventually cost *Arizona Trend* $150,000.

In 1993, Keating was convicted on seventy-three counts of fraud, conspiracy, and racketeering. He successfully appealed and is currently awaiting a new trial. The bailout of his mismanaged S&L was the most expensive of all the sleazy thrifts, costing taxpayers $2.6 billion. But the fact that Mike was right would not have saved me from crippling lawsuits had I chosen to print his story. The cost of winning lawsuits, never mind the risk of losing them, has become prohibitive. The awful fact is that lawyers have successfully hog-tied the First Amendment.

I tried to stay on the fringes of the S&L story, approaching it from the Congressional angle. It is less risky to write about public figures, particularly politicians who serve in Congress. Mike learned that House Speaker Jim Wright was up to his bushy eyebrows in the S&L scandal. The Speaker was running interference for friends in Texas who were playing games with the thrifts they controlled. From reliable sources, we heard an almost unbelievable story that was so sensitive, we chose not to print it. I will retell it here without details that might injure the innocent.

An expert at pressure politics, Wright brought it to bear upon Gray to remove a certain federal S&L regulator off a certain case. Gray grew another ulcer, but he would not submit to political pressure. Then Wright found the regulator's Achilles' heel—he was a closet homosexual. The powerful and usually proper Speaker of the House called Gray and railed at him, "How could you hire a queer? How could you keep a queer on the payroll?" Gray was astonished at Wright's invective, but still refused to fire the man. I can report that poor Ed Gray paid dearly for his courage, with stomach distress and sleepless nights.

I hated to assail Jim Wright, who could charm the indignation out of the most righteous. I couldn't help liking him. But in my profession, duty must come before personal feelings. And so I pounded Wright repeatedly for coddling the S&L industry. He reminded me of another Texan, Lyndon Johnson, who could also be a man of grand vision but narrow view. Wright's hands were stained green from handling political greenbacks, and I said as much in print—until he decided that the most expedient course for him was to resign. Despite our differences, Wright was a forgiving person who could separate politics from personalities. Not so his press officer, George Mair.

I received a bitter rebuke from Mair in 1988. He was fed up with my columns about his boss. Instead of the usual form of Capitol Hill protest—public silence and discreet backstabbing—Mair accused me in a letter of "a cut-and-paste job stolen from worn-out, inaccurate and long-repudiated gossip." That was a predictable response from a press aide. But it was Mair's testy sign-off that floored me: "The Church of the Latter Day Saints must be particularly proud."

An apology for the slap followed quickly, not from Mair, but from his boss, Speaker Wright: "A couple of days ago, I answered a newsman's question by saying that if ever anyone on my staff should express disparagement of another's religious faith, I'd not wait for the staffer to apologize; I'd apologize. George Mair assures me that he intended no offense to you or Dale [my partner at the time, Dale Van Atta, also a Mormon] and most especially not to the Church of Jesus Christ of Latter-day Saints. While I accept his word respecting his intentions, I do want to express to you and to Dale my profound apology for any impression to the contrary...." I framed the two letters and hung them on my wall as a reminder of the way Washington used to work before the spin doctors were unleashed on the Washington press corps. I admit I miss the old slam-bang attacks. In those days, a critic might step up to Drew Pearson or myself and deliver a punch in the nose. Today, they spin and they sue.

My pursuit of the S&L story cost me a good lawyer, Dave Branson, whose work I had valued over the years. When a member of Dave's firm, Mike Sullivan, changed law firms, he took me along with him as a client. The soft-spoken Sullivan, a ferocious defender of the First Amendment, has

THE HORSE'S ASS

WHENEVER I MAKE ONE OF MY frequent speaking appearances before a special-interest group, I stick to my policy of not knowing who my audience is until just before I arrive. My agent Jim Keppler handles all the details until the last minute. It is one of the ways I have of assuring myself that I don't subconsciously tailor my columns to my speech clientele. No one can argue that I am influenced by my speaking fees.

In one case, a week after I blasted lawyers in my column, I wound up speaking to the Trial Lawyers Association. One of them had taken the offending column, photocopied it, and passed it around to the others with a notation that I was bent on putting lawyers out of business. I warmed the chilly room by waving a copy of the man's tract in front of the crowd and telling them that I had no intention of putting them all out of business because my own son was a trial lawyer.

In a similar case, I spoke to a group of realtors shortly after publishing a column attacking their trade. My hosts had reprinted the column with a screaming banner headline, "Hit the Road, Jack!" to the group's credit, they let me go ahead with my speech, and I shared with them a true story:

On boarding an airplane, I found that my seat partner was a realtor, a big Texan in a Stetson and cowboy boots. I wanted to sleep but he wanted to talk, and he won. Amiable and gregarious, he reached across the seat, grabbed my hand, and introduced himself by name. I told him my name was Anderson.

"Where are you from?" he asked.

"Washington," I said, hoping to avoid revealing any more about myself.

"Are you with the government?" he pressed.

"No. I'm in the news business."

"With the *Washington Post*?"

I was trapped. "No, I write a column."

There was a long pause and he narrowed his eyes. "What's your first name?"

"Jack," I said, somehow sensing that with this man, my name would be mud.

"Oh!" the cowboy said with a booming voice. "You're the horse's ass!"

been my lawyer ever since. I never think of him as a censor, but as one who helps me tell as much of the truth as possible. I appreciate the fact that he has been brilliant in his efforts to keep me out of the courtroom, but I flinch each time he runs his pencil through a sentence. It is a frequent reminder of how times have changed.

C H A P T E R 2 7

AS A CONFESSED MUCKRAKER, I AM expected to cover not only the seamy but also the steamy side of Washington. Frankly, I abhor the bedroom beat, confounding as it does my boyhood visions of heroic figures in marble halls. I still see the Oval Office as the setting for historical drama, not soap opera.

Yet because of my peculiar calling, women scorned constantly come to me with tales of blighted love affairs. The scenarios are remarkably similar. A high muck-a-muck entices the poor lass into an affair, with promises of undying love. In the fullness of time, the VIP's ardor dampens, and there follows those mundanities that apparently attend the paling of covert love even among the nation's immortals.

Mind you, I believe strongly that morality matters and that character counts. Yet I think an office holder should answer to a Higher Power than a muckraker for what he or she does in the privacy of the bedroom. Sources brought me photographic evidence, for example, of John F. Kennedy's close encounters of the first kind. Had the voters of the 1960s known about his womanizing, they would have cared; it would have damaged him politically. But I had no intention of tattling on the president. Three decades later, the front pages carried the serial story of Bill Clinton's sexual misadventures, and the voters responded with a massive ho-hum. They no longer cared about the personal morality of their president as long as he kept the cash jingling in their pockets.

In between Jack Kennedy and Bill Clinton, I was lured into occasional snoopery. I was always a reluctant snoop who thought substance was more important than sex. Take the case of Jennifer Fitzgerald, who was the subject of a windstorm of whispers during George Bush's years in the White House. She followed him like a shadow; wherever he went, she was not far behind.

TOO GOOD TO PASS UP

I HAVE NEVER RELISHED WRITING ABOUT the private sex lives of public personalities, with a few notable exceptions. I'll leave out their names here on the assumption that the intervening years have washed their records clean.

First there was the tale of the libidinous mayor from a midsized western city. He came to Washington in 1970 for a National League of Cities meeting and spent one night wining and dining two female League clerks. After the two women had retired to their hotel room, they were surprised by a knock on the door. It was the mayor, shoeless and wearing a cowboy hat. He walked into the room, made a few incoherent remarks, and then bit one of the women above her left knee. Despite what some may say, I am not a gossip columnist. But I do confess that this story strained the ground rules for the people's right to know.

Also in the "too-good-to-pass-up" category was the story of a senator, a staid conservative who belittled the wife of Atlanta Mayor Andrew Young for her campaign to supply contraceptives to teenagers. I stayed out of that fray until Joe Spear got a tip in 1984 that the senator's own wife was a member of the American College of Orgonomy—a school of psychological thought focused on orgasms. The basic tenet of orgonomy was that orgasms are essential to a healthy psyche, even in children, and the founder of the movement even went so far as to encourage sex between consenting children. Mrs. Senator was a big fund-raiser for the movement and had written articles for the *American Journal of Orgonomy*. When confronted with my news, the senator claimed he knew nothing about orgonomy or his wife's fascination with it.

Normally I would not write about the private hobbies of a senator's wife, no matter how tempting. What qualified this tidbit as more than sheer gossip was one politician's criticism of another politician's wife for her condom campaign. I thanked the news muses for that peg and ran the column. Other news organizations prided themselves on not stooping so low. *Time* magazine was a good example. What they did instead was to report that Jack Anderson had stooped so low, and then used that as an excuse to replay all the steamy details themselves.

There was a perfectly innocent explanation for this. She was, after all, the president's appointment secretary and unofficial gatekeeper. People she turned away didn't always speak kindly of her. That may have been all it took to start the tongue-waggling.

Then she moved a few blocks down to Foggy Bottom where she went on the State Department payroll as deputy chief of protocol. She arrived on a gust of whispers. Because she had a way of getting what she wanted, the whispers never subsided. Word spread that there might be something more than friendship between Fitzgerald and the president. Yet it was all wind and no substance. No one came up with evidence that Fitzgerald was anything more than the president's close friend and loyal employee.

The speculation hung over the Bush-Clinton election campaign, nevertheless, like a dark, threatening cloud. When Clinton's own alleged lover Genifer Flowers surfaced, the unproven scandal and the unspoken rumor became known in the backrooms of Washington as the story of the two Jennifers.

I shied away from this little morality play, because I had a distaste for it and because it could never be documented. At least it was unlikely that witnesses were present in the president's bedroom. Dale Van Atta, however, was tipped off to a tidbit that raised an eyebrow.

He discovered that Jennifer Fitzgerald had bought fur coats on an official trip to Argentina; then she had undervalued them by $2,100 on her Customs declaration. An anonymous tipster called a Customs Department hotline with the report. Fitzgerald was found out and quietly fined. As news items go, this was hardly Jack Anderson material—a bureaucrat fudges or makes a mistake on a customs form and gets caught. Case closed. But I couldn't resist the opportunity to drop Fitzgerald's name in print and sit back to watch the reaction.

Like crows hungry for a june bug, my fellow reporters devoured the news. It got big play in newspapers across the country. Curious readers must surely have wondered why an obscure bureaucrat, who allegedly had tried to shortchange Customs, warranted national coverage.

IF I AM UNCOMFORTABLE WRITING ABOUT heterosexual affairs, I am even more leery of reporting homosexual stories. Yet in 1991 I broke the personal story of Pete Williams, then the highly visible spokesman for the Defense Department. Williams had become a household name and face during the Persian Gulf War when he gave daily, sometimes hourly briefings on the progress of the war.

He was entitled to keep his sex life private. But he caught the attention of Queer Nation, a radical homosexual group that specialized in "outing" gays who would rather remain in the closet. Some other activists agreed that all gays were demeaned as long as some felt they had to keep their sexual preference a secret. Queer Nation mounted 250 crude posters around Washington with Williams's picture under the headline "Absolutely Queer." Dale learned that *The Advocate,* a more staid gay magazine published in Los Angeles, planned to print a story on the Queer Nation's campaign against Williams.

I was inclined to ignore the brewing storm, until Dale learned from a Pentagon source that Williams might resign rather than embarrass his boss and friend, Defense Secretary Dick Cheney. That, I decided, was a story. The military bureaucracy had fired ten thousand officers and enlisted people in the prior decade for nothing more consequential than the discovery that they were gay. There was no similar policy for civilians, which Williams was, despite the fact that civilians held the same security clearances and were privy to the same secrets as uniformed personnel. The Defense Department policy, dating from 1943, was that "homosexuality is incompatible with military service," because "the presence of such members adversely affects the ability of the Military Services to maintain discipline, good order and morale . . . and to prevent breaches of security." But to my way of thinking, gay soldiers were more vulnerable to blackmail, and therefore breaches of security, because the Pentagon forced them to stay in the closet.

I knew other reporters were working the Williams story, but experience had taught me that most of them, probably all of them, would never print it. Dale and I called a staff meeting where debate was hot about whether we should break from the pack. I was persuaded by the double standard and outdated piety of the Defense Department's policy on gays. But it was Williams's agonizing over whether to resign that made it a poignant story. Dale called Williams, who was characteristically facile, declining to discuss his personal life and demurring from any opinion on the Defense Department policy.

We sent out the column, and though source papers published it, the *Washington Post*, as I anticipated, declined. As did a few other newspapers. The debate among reporters raged briefly, and I took a lot of heat. I called Williams to tell him I was sorry for any pain the story may have caused him, but that I still felt my reason for publishing the story was valid; whether he was gay or straight I do not know, but this was not a factor in my decision to publish. He was gracious and said he understood.

His boss Dick Cheney certainly did not. He had brought Williams with him to Washington from their home state of Wyoming, where Williams had been a successful TV newsman and then a press aide to Cheney as congressman. I encountered Cheney and his wife Lynne at a party. Dick Cheney spoke to me, with a disapproving edge to his voice. His wife could barely be civil. But I didn't fault her; Williams was their friend.

My decision had necessarily been impersonal, based on my perception of the facts and my mandate to expose government hypocrisy when I see it. But I am not so foolish as to think there are no human consequences to such decisions, nor am I so arrogant that I think I'm always the best judge of journalistic ethics and propriety. But on most stories in dispute, I am disposed to side against the timid tone-setters of our profession who look for justification to *not* publish.

IN 1967, DREW ASKED MY HELP with a story about what he called a "homosexual ring" operating in the office of California's then-Governor Ronald Reagan. The language was strong for what we uncovered. Two Reagan aides had been caught on audiotape frolicking with six other men in a cabin near Lake Tahoe. It wasn't much of a "ring." Only two of the eight had current ties to the Reagan gubernatorial administration.

Reagan had been critical of President Lyndon Johnson in 1964 for jettisoning an assistant who was involved in a homosexual episode. In 1966, when Reagan heard rumors about two of his own staffers, he had his security chief follow them. The result was the audiotape of the Lake Tahoe party. Yet Reagan didn't get around to firing the two until August of 1967, and then no explanation was given. Later, reporters pressed Reagan's communications director Lynn Nofziger who said bluntly that the two were dropped because of their homosexual activities. It could be argued that the public had a right to read this story, but the harsh language was reserved for politicians Drew opposed.

I cite this story to illustrate my differences with Drew Pearson over journalistic standards. Please understand, I admired Drew's ethics on the grand scale—his foul-weather championship of the rights of the weak, his courageous confrontations with the high and mighty, his discriminating delineation of the elements of social justice.

But there was also a cleavage between us. I tended to lock on journalism as a craft to be learned, a vocation to excel in. Drew, for all the fire and ingenuity he brought to journalism, saw it essentially as a tool for the advancement of higher causes. His columns and broadcasts were to him weapons in a just war, with the truth as their only acknowledged restriction—and truth was often a subjective matter. I would raise misgivings with him about a particular tactic, but I was too much bound to him, too largely in agreement with him, to let these misgivings become a cause of personal division.

I contented myself with making mental lists of abuses to be shunned in the future when I would be on my own: no ideological excursions or propaganda; no Captain Ahab-like pursuit of adversaries; no behind-the-scenes machinations with the political rivals of an adversary; no rehashes of old charges unless justified by a fresh discovery; no bolstering up of a story that couldn't stand on its own. Just the spare, hard exposé.

As Drew himself once advised me, "Just write a good column."

CHAPTER 28

FOR THREE DECADES, I HAVE HAD the privilege of managing an irrepressible and irreverent staff that has always been the best of the next generation of reporters. Our arrangement has been quite satisfying; they have done most of the work, and I have gotten most of the credit. They have come to my shop for the sheer excitement of uncovering what the authorities cover up. Together we have created a working environment that might be called *M*A*S*H* on the Potomac.

Young reporters often arrive at my door schooled in the virtues of the unsplit infinitive and the intact modifier. I'm not so much concerned about their academic credentials as I am about their sense of indignation—something that has sadly fallen out of fashion. I look for the fire in the eyes that says, "I can make a difference." I call them muckrakers, and if they balk at this unseemly moniker, I know they are better suited for a news job where they'll get a wardrobe allowance and a chance to trade witticisms with Henry Kissinger.

When new reporters join my staff, I give them a standard speech. "I'm a muckraker," I begin. "Now you're a muckraker, too. We're Muckrakers, Incorporated. But until you prove yourself, remember, you're just a junior muckraker."

We the muckrakers like to think we man the last line of defense against the tidy specialists who are vandalizing our world—lawyers who endlessly complicate their procedures while justice languishes; politicians who, in the name of getting more for their districts, bankrupt the commonwealth; economists whose rules speed the materialistic change that is obliterating social mores; chemists whose wonders pollute the air and the sea; agri-scientists who would foul the land tomorrow so that it might yield a bigger crop today.

In my own early days as a junior muckraker, I found my sources by combing the corridors of government. I listened patiently to thousands of inconsequential stories awaiting one that would be consequential. When I achieved notoriety and private conversations became impossible, I kept a light burning in my window for informers and listened carefully to their whispered telephone tips. Now and then, I still kept trysts in the dark of night, but most of the legwork was left to my younger associates. They have brought me some of the biggest scoops of my career.

WHEN LES WHITTEN AND JOE SPEAR had adjoining offices, Les was fond of sliding open the door between them to introduce Joe to a source. "This is Mr. X," Les would whisper conspiratorially. "Forget you ever saw his face." Then he would slam the door shut.

Although I pride myself on creating an atmosphere where young muck-rakers can learn the craft, passing the torch gracefully is not a strong tradition in my office. My own introduction to Capitol Hill by Andy Older was a bust. But the record for disastrous orientation sessions goes to Mike Binstein. One of my seasoned reporters, Indy Badhwar, took pity on the newcomer whose most recent job had been as a security guard. On the way to Capitol Hill one morning, Indy waved at Mike to follow him and get a lesson on how the pros work. Mike grabbed a notebook and set out with eager anticipation.

They arrived in the office of Senator Dennis DeConcini, and, while they sat in the waiting room, Indy noticed a letter to DeConcini from FBI Director William Webster lying open on a desk near Mike's elbow. Indy raised his eyebrows and rolled his eyes in the direction of the desktop—an exaggerated signal to Mike to scan the letter if he could. Mike at first looked confused. Then a light went on in his head, and he solemnly nodded back that he could handle the job. Indy was then ushered into DeConcini's private office, leaving Mike with his mission in the outer room. When Mike and Indy finally emerged into the hallway from the interview and got a safe distance away from the office, Indy whispered, "Well? Did you get it?" Mike triumphantly drew back his coat to reveal one of the senator's ashtrays hidden under his arm.

Despite this inauspicious beginning, Mike would eventually come into his own, becoming the first reporter to break the savings-and-loan scandal and taking the reins as managing partner of my enterprises in 1991. But first he had to learn the scut work. One particular reporter on my staff had a habit of slipping over to the bar next door when he was most needed to help get the column out. Mike was summoned one day to fetch him, so he trotted out the door, looked down the block, and stopped in his tracks. I was standing near the entrance of the bar trying to hail a cab.

This left Mike on the horns of a dilemma. He knew I was a Mormon, who didn't indulge in liquor, tobacco, tea, or coffee. On his first day at work, he had even gone so far as to carry his coffee into the office in a plain brown bag, assuming that such vices must be banned from the office. He quickly wised up when he saw the half gallon of Cutty Sark on Opal's desk. But Mike was savvy enough to fear that I would wonder why he was going into a bar at three in the afternoon. He was also noble enough not to explain his errand to me and let the other reporter take the fall—although, truth be told, I was well aware of the other man's midafternoon siestas.

In the thirty paces between Mike and me lay his salvation—a bank of newspaper dispensing boxes. Pretending he didn't see me, Mike walked as slowly as he could to the boxes. He pulled a handful of change from his pocket and began plunking coins in the dispensers at the pace of an old man on a Sunday outing with no place else to go. He must have circled the boxes four times before a cab finally stopped and whisked me away. Mike finally made it back to the office, with the other reporter in tow and an armload of newspapers.

Not only was Joe a superb editor and motivator of young talent; he was also an unregenerated populist—which was reflected in the stories he submitted. One of his reports concerned high-ranking military officers who were surrounded by a royal entourage of servants. Young men who had joined the military to serve their country were instead serving vichyssoise, answering the doors, and chauffeuring the wives of generals and admirals. One afternoon Joe drove onto the grounds of Fort Myer, the army post in northern Virginia where the Joint Chiefs of Staff reside. Unchallenged by the military police, Joe parked his car at the home of the Joint Chiefs chairman and rang the doorbell. A white-jacketed soldier, serving his country as a butler, opened the door. Joe fudged a bit, saying he was with *Parade* magazine, doing a story about the social lives of generals.

The butler was no fool. He disappeared briefly, returned to the door, and cordially invited Joe to step around to the staff office at the back of the house where they could talk. Unbeknownst to Joe, the butler had already called the MPs. The butler's mistake was to choose the staff office for Joe's wait. It was a beehive of activity with house servants, all military men, bustling in and out, shouting orders about fetching this and that for the general and his wife. The walls were hung with every household uniform imaginable, from butlers' jackets to waiters' tuxedos. Sensing that his minutes might be numbered, Joe took furious notes until the MPs arrived to escort him off the post.

CRAYOLA

MY PREFERENCE FOR OFFBEAT SOURCES HAS its hazards. I have learned to scrutinize tipsters carefully for signs of ax-grinding, borderline behavior, and downright lunacy. I found a little bit of everything in the mysterious source "Crayola."

He appeared in our office in the summer of 1973 dressed in a flowered shirt and flared pants. My associate Joe Spear listened with skepticism as the man tried to pawn off a dubious story about how the FBI had callously mishandled an extortion case. Joe said he would have to see some proof and the tipster promised to deliver. But he never had the chance. He and an accomplice were arrested by the FBI, whose agents then unfolded the story to Joe. Crayola had tried and failed to suck me into the vortex of a bizarre extortion scheme.

It began with a letter to the manager of the posh Concord Hotel in New York's Catskill Mountains: Unless the hotel handed over $320,000 in unmarked bills, the hotel's guests would be dosed with LSD. It was signed with a bright crayon, "Crayola." Hotel officials called in the FBI, and the drop for the extortion payment was arranged. Following Crayola's instructions, a hotel employee carrying two bags of money answered a pay phone at the corner of Fifth Avenue and Forty-fourth Street in New York. Crayola, watching her from a high-rise building, directed the woman to another pay phone for directions, then on to other pay phones for further directions, and finally to Grand Central Station.

Inside, Crayola's accomplices had set the scene. They had pasted a "closed" sign on the women's restroom and had discreetly broken out a glass panel at the base of the restroom door while oblivious New York commuters streamed by. The girl with the money bags was instructed by pay phone to slide the bags through the broken panel. They landed inside on a throw rug that was attached to a piece of rope. At the other end of the rope was Crayola's accomplice "Inez." She reeled in the loot from the far recesses of the restroom, losing one of the bags in the process. With the FBI pounding on the locked restroom door, Inez panicked, grabbed the other bag, and hotfooted it up a staircase that led to a restroom on the next floor. She and the bag were long gone by the time the FBI got into the restroom.

When Inez passed the bag on to Crayola, he found it full of useless paper. He sent the FBI an angry letter claiming that the whole extortion attempt was just his sting to see how the FBI would handle it, and the FBI had failed his test. "The Bureau blundered disasterously [*sic*] and irretrievably by substituting fake money for real," he wrote. This was "irrefutable proof of the Bureau's knowing, deliberate and wanton engandering [*sic*] of hundreds of unsuspecting guests at the Concord." Furthermore, Crayola threatened, if the FBI didn't immediately release jailed LSD guru Timothy Leary, Crayola would personally inform Jack Anderson of how incompetent the agents were.

Crayola was carrying out his threat, tailed by the FBI, when he was arrested trying to make a photocopy of his extortion letter for me. Fortunately, I didn't fall for his story of FBI incompetence, but Crayola did get his day in print. I couldn't resist publishing a column about his twisted plot.

My reporters pride themselves on being the fools who rush in where stuffed shirts fear to tread. Their philosophy is that it's easier to apologize later than get permission in advance. Operating on that theory, Dale Van Atta walked into the headquarters of the General Services Administration one summer day in 1982 to find out how close he could get to sensitive plans for the White House before someone stopped him. Clad in corduroy pants, a garish sports coat, and cowboy boots, looking nothing like a staid GSA bureaucrat, Dale helped himself to the White House blueprints—architectural drawings, a guide to the grounds showing ducts, conduits, and manholes, and a detailed map of electrical circuits, sewer lines, drains, and protective fences.

When Dale spread the drawings out on a table to examine them, no one asked what he was doing. In fact, one helpful GSA employee offered to photocopy the material for Dale. We printed enough of the information to let the Secret Service know what we had, but not enough to help a potential terrorist. The Secret Service was appalled and assured me that security would be tightened.

In 1974, Les Whitten heard about a confidential Senate study that claimed some elderly people on fixed incomes were reduced to eating cheap pet food. Thinking it would be unfair to judge the quality of the diet without trying it himself, Les became a pet food gourmet. He prepared a plate of hors d'oeuvres, spreading cat food on crackers and dog food on bread. Then he added seasoning, held his nose, and nibbled away. He washed down dry kibbles with beer and fine wine. The result was a severe case of queasiness. For his pains, he produced one column and drew howls of complaint from the pet food industry.

THE CHARACTERS WHO HAVE POPULATED MY staff have not exactly been screened from the finest journalism schools. I found Mike Binstein, for example, working the midnight shift as a security guard for Mobile Oil in 1982. I had met him earlier when I delivered a speech to journalism students at American University in Washington. Mike was then one of the students. He snaked his way through the crowd that had gathered around me after the speech, thinking he might impress me with an informed question. "So," he said, "are you still doing karate?" His pride at having remembered my hobby was replaced by embarrassment as the inane question hung in the air. I said yes and moved on to the next student.

Mike dropped out of journalism school, not necessarily because of that encounter, but because he wanted to dabble in the real world. He started his own newspaper in Washington—a newspaper that used my column for one issue before canceling it because he thought it was too expensive. When the paper fell victim to Mike's poor bookkeeping skills, he started his own gardening business. That came to an abrupt halt when he killed the lawn of an esteemed client, columnist George Will. Despite Mike's dubious resumé, I saw a spark of the muckraker in him that was borne out by later experience.

I found Jon Lee Anderson in a prison in Colombia in the mid-1970s. Jon, who spoke fluent Spanish, had landed a job at a Colombian newspaper where he became a crusader against the drug cartels. But after someone planted cocaine in his room, he was falsely arrested and thrown in prison. He made the best of the circumstance by becoming the ringleader of his cell block. I did a series of columns on Americans wrongly held in foreign jails, which brought his name to my attention. When Jon was sprung, he dropped by to say thanks and offer his services as a freelance writer. He felt claustrophobic behind a desk, so he was soon trotting around Central America filing stories for me wherever the action was.

Another of my globe-trotters, Peter Grant, was the first reporter to travel with the guerrillas in Afghanistan. With his dark complexion, Peter was able to disguise himself in native clothing and slip into the war-torn country on a bus. At the first checkpoint, an armed soldier boarded the bus to make sure everyone had a right to be there. The guard scanned Peter's outfit right down to its fatal flaw—sparkling new Adidas tennis shoes. "Do you speak English?" the guard demanded in English. "No!" Peter sputtered, also in English. He was hauled off the bus, but managed to bribe his way back on—a sum that turned up on his next expense account. Dan Rather eventually joined the Afghan guerrillas, with more flair and a bigger budget, but Peter got there first and stayed longer. My reporter Bob Sherman traveled with guerrillas on both sides of the Nicaraguan conflict and survived to tell the story.

Hal Bernton, my reporter who offended Miss Lillian Carter by sitting next to her in church, had a knack for stirring up excitement wherever he went. He craved assignments that got him in and out of scrapes. His idea of a good time was to get himself thrown into a prison camp in Mississippi so he could write about deplorable conditions there, or to infiltrate a ring that was smuggling illegal immigrants across the U.S.-Mexico border.

NONE DARE CALL IT MUCKRAKING

ALL OF US DEVELOPED A NEW respect for the chutzpah of green interns after a source at the Justice Department called to report that a Jack Anderson reporter had been caught trying to sneak into a secured area by flashing a bubble gum card for identification. It was our intern Murray Waas.

Murray was a prankster and gifted impressionist. He once called a fellow columnist, Victor Lasky, who had written a favorable article about Richard Nixon, and in a perfect imitation of the president, praised the breathless columnist to the skies.

During the period when I had a daily spot on *Good Morning America*, Murray took a call from a GMA gopher one night just before leaving the office. GMA needed to have a teaser for our news spot scheduled for the next morning. The teaser was to be read by GMA host David Hartman. Without pausing for breath, Murray dictated off the top of his head a teaser—a hair-brained story about how I had uncovered a nest of transvestites on Capitol Hill. The producer smelled a rat and called back that night. Fortunately he got ahold of another staffer who confessed Murray's story was a prank.

Hal was subject to absentminded spells that produced office legends. He was the kind of guy who buttered his bread before toasting it. Once he talked me into letting him use my wife's car for investigative forays to out-of-the-way places. He wound up in San Francisco where he parked on one of the city's steep hills. Hal was lost in one of his daydreams, oblivious to the law of gravity. He neglected to apply the parking brake, and the car started to roll. Snapped back to reality, he stepped in front of the car and held out his hands to stop it. The car, having a weight advantage, ran over him and broke his leg in several places. He not only hobbled around in a cast for weeks but had to endure the gibes of his unsympathetic colleagues.

Jock Hatfield arrived in my chaotic office from California in 1983 with one rumpled suit, enough money for about three meals, and a burning ambition. We didn't know then that cancer was eating his insides, but something else was obvious; he had serious deformities in his hands and arms. None of us had the nerve to inquire why until one day Dale figured it was time to ask the obvious. "What's wrong with your arms?"

"Original equipment," Jock replied. That was it. We learned later that he had been conceived while his parents lived near the site of above-ground nuclear testing in the Nevada desert.

Roaming Washington's sterile corridors of power, Jock was soon diligently and cheerfully exposing the graft and the gaffes that are red meat to a good reporter. His personal courage was limitless. I sent him to Haiti, where he ventured into the hinterland at no small risk to himself and filed stories about the wretched conditions under the Duvalier regime. He planned to return a second time, but when he learned he had inoperable cancer, he chose to spend his remaining weeks doing investigative stories on Capitol Hill. Never revealing the hopelessness of his situation and refusing to play his sources for sympathy, Jock poured all his energy into his chosen craft. He died in 1984 without self-pity or a word of complaint.

The great reporters who worked with me shunned the big-name politicians and the cocktail parties, knowing that the people with the keys to the Xerox machines often prove to be the most valuable sources.

When Mike Binstein started as an intern with me, he kept his night job as a security guard. One morning he heard his name called out with gusto by a familiar voice. It was a former fellow security guard whom Mike hadn't seen for a while. Mike was in a hurry and wanted to shake the guy, but the man persisted. He was working on the Hill now, he said, and he wanted to show Mike his new office at the Congressional Research Service.

"No, I gotta go," Mike begged off, but his friend prevailed. Unbeknownst to Mike, the man had been hired to run the photocopy operations at CRS. This happened to be the crossroads through which sensitive requests for information came. If a member of Congress wanted something, CRS would get it and Mike's friend would copy it. Mike's eye fell immediately on an advance copy of the hush-hush Joint Economic Committee report on the future of the Soviet economy. "Hey, can I have one of those?" he asked his buddy, with a growing interest in renewing their friendship. From then on, Mike's first stop in his daily rounds was to visit his friend.

FOR DECADES, THE KITCHEN WAS THE hub of my office. I don't know how others get by with just a watercooler or a coffeepot. Our kitchen was always a multipurpose room where interns staked out scarce office space on the countertops, and where lunches were made for my guests so I didn't have to publicize a tête-à-tête by dining out. My crusty assistant Opal Ginn would take over the kitchen before my guests arrived, prepare the meal, and then enjoy the spectacle of the power lunch. Opal was not domestic by nature, but she had her standards. When a high-ranking Chinese diplomat came to dine on filet mignon and asked for catsup, Opal refused to give it to him.

Zbigniew Brzezinski's secretary called ahead to say that he liked his salads made with three kinds of lettuce, and his steak served with french fries and wine. Opal toiled that day over homemade fries to go with the steaks while the junior staff held out hopes for leftovers. There were none. Brzezinski and I polished off the whole lunch.

When comedian Dick Gregory came for lunch, Opal set out various juices, knowing he was diet-conscious. But that day Gregory informed her he was living only on air, to purify his soul. It turned out to be polluted air. He chain-smoked cigarettes and explained the biological principle behind the male erection, while I tried to appear nonplussed.

On the day we entertained Marlon Brando from our modest kitchen, the secretarial pool at the office next door put a sign outside their door that pleaded, "Please come in, Mr. Brando!" Despite his reputation for arrogance, I found Brando to be a warm person, who didn't disappoint the ladies next door. When he left our office, he popped into theirs, shook hands all around, and left them breathless.

RECEPTIONIST ROBIN REYNOLDS was territorial about the kitchen. A sack lunch left more than a day in the refrigerator would ignite her, producing verbal fireworks. And she guarded my personal eating implements like Cerberus guarding the gates of hell. One morning an intern walked past Robin's desk, and she loudly notified him that he had dog excrement on his shoes that he had better scrape off ASAP. The next thing she heard was Joe Spear's voice from the kitchen, "Robin, you're not going to believe what this guy is doing with Jack's grapefruit spoon."

Robin's constant litany of complaints about kitchen etiquette was the bane of the staff: "Wash your dishes. Take out the trash. You ate someone else's apple." It was worse than working for your mother. One night Mike Binstein and Indy Badhwar decided it was time Robin got her comeuppance in the kitchen. Mike bought a twenty-pound turkey and slipped into the office in the wee hours of the morning to pop it in the oven. By the time Robin arrived at 8 A.M., the aroma of turkey had permeated the place.

She was incensed, marching from cubicle to cubicle, her heels beating an angry staccato on the floor, as she demanded to know who had deposited a turkey in the oven. Everyone gave her blank stares, so she burst through the door that separated our offices from the real estate law practice downstairs. Robin leaned over the stair railing and shouted down to a cluster of $250-an-hour lawyers and their astonished clients: "Are you guys cooking a turkey?"

As the mysterious turkey slowly roasted, Indy used his exceptional skills at mimicry and phoned Robin, feigning the voice of the night custodian, "Robin, would you please turn down the oven and baste my turkey?"

We had to forgive Robin for her fastidiousness, if only because her first day on the job had been traumatic enough to scar her for the duration of her service. It was the day one of my readers registered his displeasure by mailing me an envelope full of feces, I assume his own.

It was delivered on February 28, 1974, and I remember the date only because it was one of the more hectic in the history of my office. That morning I had published a column about Samuel Joseph Byck, the Philadelphia man who killed himself after trying to hijack a jet airliner in Baltimore the week before. My scoop that day was that Byck had intended to crash-dive the plane into the White House. I knew this because a few hours before Byck attempted the hijacking, he mailed me a tape recording explaining the plan in his own words.

"I will try to get the plane aloft and fly it towards the target area which will be Washington, D.C., the capital of the most powerful, wealthiest nation of the world," he said in a deadpan voice. "By guise, threats, or trickery, I hope to force the pilot to buzz the White House, I mean, sort of dive toward the White House. When the plane is in this position, I will shoot the pilot and then, in the last few minutes, try to steer the plane into the target, which is the White House." Throughout the tape, Byck insisted he was sane, although he admitted he had been diagnosed as manic-depressive. "I go to a psychiatrist every four or five weeks, which, I missed the last visit, by the way."

Byck's plot never got off the ground. He shot his way onto the plane and killed two people before a security guard wounded him. Then Byck turned his gun on himself. Our publication of excerpts from the tape brought a barrage of attention from other media that would have rattled even the most even-tempered receptionist. Robin's first morning was occupied by fielding requests from reporters who wanted to hear the tape. The office was overrun with reporters and photographers, all jostling to meet their deadlines. They were photographing the front door, photographing the hallway, photographing each other. In the middle of the hubbub, the morning mail arrived and poor Robin opened the envelope containing one reader's scatological comment on muckraking. The man's complaint has long since been forgotten, but his method of delivery became office legend.

WE MADE OUR REPUTATIONS IN PRINT journalism, but I have always been drawn to television, as evidenced by a nine-year stint with ABC's *Good Morning America*, followed by a string of my own, short-term TV programs. The staff has rarely shared my enthusiasm for the small screen, but they have been game when I recruited them for various TV shows. They even tolerated my Hollywood phase, when I hired a drama coach to come to the office every Tuesday to teach them the finer points of being talking heads.

Les Whitten learned his drama lessons too well. We were preparing a TV pilot on various investigative exploits of derring-do. Joe Spear had discovered the location of some CIA safe houses in the Virginia countryside, and I had interviewed a Mafia hoodlum with a bag on his head. Les's assignment was to test hair spray to prove it was a fire hazard. Disgruntled over the humble nature of the consumer spot, he nevertheless decided he would be the best darn hair-spray tester in the history of investigative journalism. With the cameras rolling in our kitchen—a spare-no-expense studio improvisation—Les held a lighted cigarette in his hand and sprayed hair-spray over it. A ball of fire blazed in front of him, the camera man bolted, and Les's TV career came to a flaming halt. Though unhurt, he decided he had been burned enough by TV.

Somewhere in my piles of memorabilia is the film of an outtake from one TV pilot showing my reporter Jack Cloherty railing about the injustice of wealthy tax cheats. I had assigned Jack to find some big-name tax dodgers so I could expose them on the air. To my delight, Jack came up with one of the heirs to the Mellon fortune in Pittsburgh. He called the corporate offices numerous times, explained what he was doing, and left messages for the man to return the calls, but to no avail. The time came to film the segment and Jack still hadn't heard the deadbeat's side of the story. Jack went ahead anyway, with melodramatic footage of himself stalking over to a file cabinet, pulling out the Mellon file, and chastising the millionaire for not giving the U.S. Treasury its due. As luck would have it, we didn't have room for that segment in the pilot. Thus we were spared the embarrassment of having to explain the reason the man hadn't paid his taxes, and the reason he hadn't return Jack's phone calls. He was beyond our reach, having died years before.

That particular TV series went belly up, probably to the everlasting gratitude of most of my staffers, who preferred the anonymity of newsprint. They patiently endured several experiments including one of my personal favorites, a show I called *Truth*. Our format was to persuade controversial characters to let us wire them to a lie detector and ask them questions to prove whether they were telling the truth about the hot stories of the day. I soon learned that the number of liars willing to take a polygraph is few.

In desperation I turned to an old friend, Bobby Baker. I had not treated him too unkindly in 1963 when he was accused of influence peddling as a fixer for Lyndon Johnson in the Senate. Bobby eventually went to prison for sixteen hard months, but he remained a gentleman. When Les was facing a prison sentence for "theft" of the BIA Indian documents, Bobby graciously offered to give him tips on how a nice guy survives in a federal penitentiary.

Although Bobby wanted to forget his past, he reluctantly agreed, as a favor to me, to take the polygraph for my show. With the cameras rolling and the machine scribbling, I grilled Bobby about his past and in the end the machine said he was not being completely candid. I swallowed my embarrassment for him and announced, "Well, Bobby, the machine indicates you're not quite telling the truth." From then on it became almost impossible to find guests, and the show mercifully folded.

MY WIFE, LIBBY, IS THE KEEPER of my wallet and for years managed the office finances. Her penury was legendary. I liked the luxury of ordering my reporters to take off for parts unknown to track the promise of a story, but Libby would rein them in when they submitted their expenses. When Indy Badhwar was chasing the ABSCAM sting in the early 1980s, I dispatched him to Florida on the spur of the moment to interview the disenchanted wife of Mel Weinberg, the convicted con artist who was the FBI's chief informant in the sting. Marie Weinberg had agreed to let Indy see her husband's little black book, and I was afraid she would change her mind if he didn't go immediately.

Indy came back from the trip and presented Libby with receipts for a fresh shirt and a toothbrush. "I don't know," she shook her head. "I'll talk to Jack about it." Weeks went by, and Indy still didn't have his money, so he came to me to complain. I picked up the phone and dialed Libby at home. "I don't know about the shirt," I told her, "but the man has a right to brush his teeth." She paid for the shirt and the toothbrush.

On the ABSCAM story as on others, private detective Dick Bast was our eager ally. He was an old friend who took delight in working with us on particularly sticky investigations. I don't think I ever paid Dick a dime for his help, but he traveled around the country gathering information for me, once even going to Libya to pump Mu'ammar Gadhafi's people for information. Dick was a street-smart guy who preferred unconventional approaches to problem solving, which is why he crops up so often in my story files.

One afternoon as I was agonizing with my staff over a now-forgotten libel suit, Dick wandered into the office and listened to the conversation. When he had heard enough talk of legal maneuvering, he offered his solution. "Let's file a Freedom-of-Information request on the judge."

"A what?" I replied, not seeing how a search of government files on the judge in the case would help us. I had no reason to believe the judge was anything but clean.

FBI SCAM

I WAS APPALLED TO SEE THE videotapes of the ABSCAM operation—the FBI sting of congressmen who took money from an FBI man posing as a wealthy Arab sheik with an immigration problem. But the more I saw of the tapes, the more my disgust switched focus from the congressmen to the fast-talking FBI agents.

My reporter Gary Cohn got his hands on the full tapes, and our column was the first place where the illegal and unethical antics of the FBI agents were exposed. What we saw on those tapes was blatant entrapment. We saw FBI agents forcing money on confused congressmen. We saw evidence of illegal FBI bank accounts. But most disturbing, we saw the work of Mel Weinberg, who was paid handsomely by the FBI to use his con artistry and devise a sting to trap congressmen. All of this was done not to expose an existing crime, but to create a crime and embroil men whom the FBI suspected of having a "criminal predisposition."

Indy Badhwar picked up the story and zeroed in on Weinberg, the foppish crook with a taste for three-piece suits and flashy pinky rings. Indy began hearing evidence that Weinberg might have conned the FBI by pocketing some of the bribe money and soliciting expensive gifts from the targets of the sting.

We hammered Weinberg and the FBI in several columns until one day we got a call from the FBI. Director William Webster wanted to see us. I told Indy he could rail on Webster while I played the voice of reason. When we arrived at Webster's outer office, we bumped into a wall of agents, all loaded for bear. They stared at us, we stared back at them. A moment passed. Then, I broke the silence. "Gentlemen, could I have a Pepsi?" Half a dozen of those stiff-suited agents scrambled to get me a soda, and we were ushered into Webster's office.

I let Indy scold Webster for a while, then I held up my hand to stop his diatribe. I told Webster I was sure that the entrapment we suspected was the work of a few hotheads and not representative of the whole bureau. Webster and I traded pleasantries. Then Indy and I left. On the way to the car, a disappointed Indy turned to me. "Jack, you really let me down in there." Once again my own reporter had been baffled by the good-cop, bad-cop approach.

"You just keep doing what you're doing," I said. He did, and after dozens of columns on Weinberg's shenanigans, Indy got the call from the con man's wife, Marie, in January 1982. She had the goods on her husband, and she wanted to show us. Marie Weinberg had enough reason to turn her husband in. She had discovered that he had been cheating on her for years. I ordered Indy to fly immediately to Miami and take my private investigator friend Dick Bast and three photographers along with him.

Somehow, the FBI found out my people were on their way to Florida. Indy and Dick got to Marie first and took her to a hotel room near her home to talk to her. They brought her home at 3 A.M. and learned that four FBI agents had come looking for her at the house at about midnight. Indy and Dick returned to Marie's house at 7 A.M. with the three photographers to take pictures of the booty Weinberg had hidden in the house—gifts Marie claimed he had conned out of the ABSCAM targets. While the photographers were working, the FBI agents showed up again. This time they were met at the door by Bast. "My name is Bast, as in bastard," Dick snarled.

"Well, who *are* you?" the agents demanded, expecting more than just a name.

"I'm an American citizen, who the hell are you?" Bast shot back. They identified themselves as FBI agents and Bast told them to get lost, which they did.

Using Marie's evidence, we strengthened our case against Weinberg in print. Then one afternoon a few weeks later, Indy came into my office looking shaken. Marie Weinberg was dead, he said. She had been strangled with a rope. The coroner declared it suicide. Before she took her own life, she wrote us a nineteen-page narrative of her husband's sins.

"Indy," I said, "you're a reporter. You had to do what you did. Tomorrow the phones are going to start ringing off the hook here. You've got to tell the truth about what happened to that poor woman." While Weinberg tried to paint his dead wife as a lunatic and liar, Indy churned out several columns about how she had been victimized, conned, and finally driven to suicide. Indy's work eventually prompted a congressional investigation into the mishandling of ABSCAM by the Justice Department.

"If we file," Dick explained, "then we're investigating him. And if we're investigating him, he has to recuse himself because obviously he has a conflict of interest." That was the kind of creative thinking Dick brought to our team. Although I valued his advice, in that case I didn't take it.

DALE JOINED THE STAFF IN 1979, SPARKING talk around the office that he was being groomed to take my place. He was a fellow Mormon who came from the *Deseret News* in Salt Lake City and had even dated my daughter Cheri in college.

One of Dale's first coups was the discovery that members of Congress were selectively revising the prepublication transcripts of their public testimony. Following a hunch, Dale showed up at the Government Printing Office one evening and introduced himself to the man whose job it was to make the changes the members wanted. It was late in the day, and with most of the employees gone, the atmosphere was casual, as Dale had hoped it would be. The editor, not blessed with the devious nature necessary to protect Washington's elected elite, obligingly gave Dale copies of the public hearing transcripts with the scribbled changes from members of Congress.

After participating in debate, Congress members would go back to their offices, send for the transcript, and revise it at their leisure. Not only did they correct their grammar, but they were known to reverse their arguments and change their positions.

The story made only a small splash in Washington, where such sleight of hand is considered par for the course, but in Middle America, my readers were outraged by the deception. The printing office barred access for reporters to the marked-up transcripts, and the practice continued until cable TV's gavel-to-gavel coverage of congressional hearings made changing the record a bit awkward.

At a staff meeting in 1979, Joe Spear told the staff that he'd heard rumors of a secret Senate committee report detailing how foreign spies of U.S. allies were allowed to run amok in the United States. The written report was out there somewhere, Joe told the staff, and challenged our reporters to be the first to get it.

Dale was still new to Washington and figured if he could get what every Washington reporter was after, he would be off to a great start. He learned that less than a dozen copies of the report had been distributed, and he found out who had received them. Dale selected one target—a man of high rank and great prestige, who had never leaked a document to a reporter in his life—and zeroed in on him. For two months, Dale badgered the poor fellow relentlessly, appealing to his sense of justice and the public's right to know.

Finally, on a quiet Saturday afternoon this virgin source made the handoff to Dale. It turned out that the man was willing to share only a five-page executive summary. In it, Dale read tantalizing references to international terrorist Carlos the Jackal and how the United States had let him slip away. There was an incredible story about the botched mission of a bomb-carrying dog that was supposed to blow up itself and Chou En-lai. Most compelling was the story of "Operation Condor," a consortium of Latin American spy services that had a reciprocal agreement to assassinate each other's dissidents at home and abroad.

Dale went back to his source. "I've got to have the whole report," he said. It took two more weeks to wear the great man down completely. Then, on another Saturday afternoon, Dale was admitted to his office. The source handed Dale a pair of gloves and a stack of papers. "Here. You have half an hour."

GOSSIP AT 35,000 FEET

BECAUSE WEASEL-WORDING AND OUTRIGHT LIES are the norm in Washington, some of my favorite stories have been the ones where I've been able to expose the weasels for what they were. A call in early 1982 from a ham radio hobbyist in the South gave me one such golden opportunity.

"Would you be interested in transmissions from Air Force One?" the man asked me. I couldn't believe what he was offering—tape recordings of conversations from bigwigs on the president's plane as they talked to other bigwigs on the ground. He had been scanning the radio waves one day and by chance tuned into the transmissions, which, incredibly, where not cloaked from amateur eavesdroppers. The power brokers on the plane were smart enough not to spread national security secrets through the ether from 35,000 feet up, but my source had heard some great gossip, which I was not averse to printing.

During dual international crises in the Falkland Islands and the Middle East, Reagan's Secretary of State Alexander Haig was understandably busy. He decided to manage the Falklands war himself and had to choose between his number two deputy, Walter Stoessel, or his number three man, Lawrence Eagleburger, to be point man in the Middle East. Eagleburger graciously sent a cable to Haig recommending Stoessel for the prestigious assignment. But before the cable could reach Haig, Eagleburger called the White House from Air Force One to recommend himself for the job instead. He talked to one of Haig's aides and this is what my ham radio source taped:

"Uh, listen," Eagleburger began. "I want to make one point. In one of the cables you'll be getting, you will find Mr. Stoessel's name. I have put that in the cable because I'm a nice fellow, but I feel very strongly that if he's going to buy—if [Haig] is going to buy the proposal at all, it would be better if my name were there, because I'm nastier. Do you understand?"

The reception was bad so Eagleburger had to repeat his cryptic message. "I frankly think it ought to be my name, not his, because I will be nastier. You won't understand what I'm talking about until you read the cable. But when you do, would you make the point to the secretary that I would prefer the other name?" Stoessel wasn't aware of the backstabbing until he read it in my column, but he got the last laugh. Haig sent him instead of Eagleburger to the Middle East.

The tapes from the ham radio operator allowed me to say "I told you so" on another hot issue—the precarious position of the quixotic Secretary of State Haig. In November 1981 I had prepared a column based on tips from White House sources who told me Haig was a big disappointment on the Cabinet. My statement, that Haig had "one foot on a banana peel," set off alarms one weekend at the White House. The column had not yet been published, but

Reagan's spokesman David Gergen got his hands on an advance copy and called to assure me that Haig was in good graces with the president. The next time my phone rang, it was Reagan himself calling from Camp David to say he was completely satisfied with Haig.

They caught me in a good mood, and I agreed to rewrite the column to include claims by Haig that someone on the Reagan staff was out to smear him. Despite Reagan's personal reassurances, I still suspected that Haig had few friends in the White House. My suspicions were confirmed when I heard the tapes of Air Force One transmissions from the day Reagan was shot, March 30, 1981. Flustered White House aides traded air-to-ground comments about Haig's flaky behavior during the crisis when he overstepped the constitutional order of succession and claimed he was in charge. I reported their words and added my own: "Haig still has one foot on a banana peel."

"Can I at least use a typewriter to copy information," pleaded Dale, who types faster than he writes. The source agreed and left the room. Half an hour later he was back to collect the secrets, but Dale wasn't about to give them up. "Just let me xerox a few pages," Dale said. After some more agonizing, the source agreed. "Put paper clips on the pages you want and I'll copy them." So Dale began paper-clipping page one, two, three, four, and so on. After the source had shuttled the first seventy pages to the copier room, he drew the line. The copier was out of paper, and he didn't know how to reload it. Dale offered to do it, but the man stood firm. He wasn't about to escort Jack Anderson's man into the photocopy center.

Dale knew he had pushed as far as he could. He took the first seventy pages of the report and found in them enough material for ten columns about foreign spies and their nefarious operations in the United States and elsewhere, all condoned by the U.S. government.

Dale was my choice to cover the Persian Gulf War. After his arrival on the battlefront, he telephoned me to report that the correspondents couldn't go anywhere without a military escort. This was inhibiting, he said, to a reporter who was supposed to be on the prowl for unauthorized stories. "You're an enterprising newsman," I replied. "I have confidence you'll find a way." He did. He roamed the battle area, and even inspected the supersecret war room, without anyone watching over his shoulder. I learned later how he managed this; he finagled credentials as a chaplain on a mission of mercy to administer to the spiritual needs of one of my reporters whose husband was at the front.

Dale has an affable, nonthreatening manner that gets him into the darnedest places. He has interviewed notorious terrorists in their hideouts. He even persuaded a Syrian military escort to take him to a parking garage in Beirut where CIA sources had told him terrorists were holding American hostages. He found no hostages, but they had left behind evidence that he'd just missed them.

Dale also holds the record for traveling the longest distance to find a story for the column. The National Science Foundation takes a few journalists to the South Pole every year. The competition is stiff and the application process lengthy. Usually the coveted slots go to distinguished science writers. Dale's companions were science reporters from the *New York Times, Time* magazine, and *National Geographic*—all of whom wondered what Dale was up to. I wondered, too, but I was confident he would come back with something worthwhile. As he was running to catch the ski-equipped C-130 before it took off from the ice to carry the journalists home, Dale was grabbed by a stranger. "I understand you're the one with Jack Anderson. Here, you'll find these interesting," the man said, as he stuffed a fat envelope into Dale's coat. "A friend of mine sent them from Washington." Then the man was gone. On the plane, Dale had time to examine the package. It contained a series of secret documents about Soviet antisubmarine warfare. We've all dealt with sources through intermediaries, or "cutouts," but Dale figured this particular cutout must have broken a distance record. Someone in Washington, still unknown to Dale, heard he was going to the South Pole and mailed documents to a friend there to place in Dale's hands. But the information turned out to be too sensitive to use, and for reasons of national security, we never printed it.

The story Dale could print from that trip, however, came to him after he had sat through a briefing on ozone depletion while at the South Pole's Amundsen-Scott Station. He had decided to wander off on his own when a man in greasy overalls approached him. "Are you the guy with Jack Anderson? I've been waiting months to show you something. I have a big scandal." Dale donned the forty pounds of clothing necessary to go outside and followed the mysterious workman through a manhole in the ground. They made their way along what looked like a huge sewer pipe until they came to a small underground lake of steaming human sewage. Dale didn't see the significance of this find. "They have to put the sewage somewhere," he reasoned. But the plumber was undeterred.

"When they built this pipe, they put it under the station," the plumber explained. He pointed up and Dale saw the problem—ice from the ground above was slowly melting and dripping into the lake. Amundsen-Scott Station, the headquarters of scientists dedicated to preserving the pristine environment of the South Pole, was sliding into its own sewage. The plumber threw his arms out wide. "You see. The South Pole station is sinking." Dale looked around himself and smiled. "Okay, Jack, now I *am* a muckraker!"

EPILOGUE

THE CONSTITUTION MENTIONS ONLY ONE PROFESSION by name. It happens to be my chosen profession. Freedom of the press was included for an important reason—because our founding fathers understood that government, by its nature, tends to oppress those it has power over. The drafters of the Constitution understood the need to keep government under the control of the people, so they appointed a watchdog, and it is our responsibility to be that watchdog. Sometimes we've been good, sometimes bad. Sometimes we bark, sometimes we whine. Like all watchdogs, we're imperfect, but it's our job, and the job is essential.

Aleksandr Solzhenitsyn has written: "For every country to have a great writer is like having another government. That is why no regime has ever loved great writers, only minor ones." We in America do not have—nor need we rely on—a literary and moral giant comparable to that Russian immortal. In our Lilliputian way, we have evolved an entire institution—a free press—to undertake the mission that in a tyranny falls to the lonely genius or hero.

What is this mission? To give the people an alternative to the official version of things, a rival account of reality, a measure for judging the efficacy of rulers and whether the truth is in them, an unauthorized stimulus to action or resistance.

Long before Americans could vote directly for their presidents, before the vote was given to the poor or women or blacks, before our present political parties existed, the role of the village editor and dissenting pamphleteer—as monitor, arbiter, critic, and rival of the politician—was embedded as a fundamental of the American system. It was of this role that Thomas Jefferson spoke when he declared that if he had to choose between a government without newspapers or newspapers without a government, he would take his morning paper.

From its primitive state, when any wanderer—if he was cantankerous enough—might set up his press and begin to assail his townsmen, the media as an institution has evolved through alternating chapters of disgrace and honor, of prostitution and martyrdom, of somnolence and vigilance. Theodore White has described its function: "The power of the press in America is a primordial one. It sets the agenda of public discussion; and this sweeping political power is unrestrained by any law. It determines what people will talk about and think about."

That mission thrills me as much today as it did when I started. I was just twelve years old with a Boy Scout merit badge in journalism as my credentials. A friend of mine riding his bicycle across a narrow bridge tried to share the bridge with a car and was knocked into the creek below. Though he wasn't badly hurt, I was flushed with moral outrage. Between backbreaking shifts of work in the best fields, I wrote a story for the local weekly assailing the bridge builders. This brought a letter from the county commissioner thanking me for calling the problem to his attention. The bridge was widened. That was the day I decided to be a newspaperman, and I've been writing about dangerous bridges ever since.

At midcentury, when I was let loose on the nation's capital, Drew Pearson's muckrakers were at the vortex of the Washington maelstrom. What comes back to me with greatest pungency is the atmosphere of combat, of shooting and being shot at, of exposing villainies and being despised for it. The Pearson gang, as the only investigative reporters in town, were outcasts from our own profession. The politicians who inhabited the towers of power regarded us as outright pariahs. Not even the public we strove to inform appreciated our contribution to the democratic process.

Drew died a pariah before Watergate suddenly transformed his heirs into folk heroes. But investigative reporting, though now considered a romantic profession, is still not a roundly respected one. As a confessed muckraker who specializes in the butchery of sacred cows, I must expect—though of course I do not like—to be widely reviled, especially by the highest authorities of the state. I am aware that my profession survives only because of the thin protective shield of the Constitution and an inconstant public sentiment that investigative reporting may be of some vague use to society.

EVERY PRESIDENT SINCE HARRY TRUMAN MOVED into the White House has tried at one time or another either to furtively suppress my reports or to publicly discredit me. I have always regarded myself as a maverick, yes, but as part of the system, not as an alienated critic.

I still find the view of the Capitol dome inspiring in the morning light. That dome is the symbol of man's most intensive effort to subject the function of governing to the will of the governed—a cathedral to the memory of the nation's founders, a breast to nourish the hopes of those who follow.

In the full sun, the rays reflect off the dome a look of pure whiteness. Beneath Capitol Hill, the sunlight on the surrounding granite and sandstone compounds of government project the same illusion of whiteness. But the enamel on the Capitol dome is gray, and with my small spotlight, I have exposed vast patches of gray morality throughout the government—abuses of power, transgressions of the law by those whom we entrusted to uphold the law.

This has forced me to conclude, to paraphrase Winston Churchill, that the United States has the worst possible government—except for all the others.

INDEX